MARK TWAIN'S AMERICA

Books by Bernard DeVoto

MARK TWAIN'S
America

by

BERNARD DeVOTO

illustrated

GREENWOOD PRESS, PUBLISHERS
WESTPORT, CONNECTICUT

Library of Congress Cataloging-in-Publication Data

De Voto, Bernard Augustine, 1897-1955.
  Mark Twain's America.

  Reprinted from the 1967 ed. published by Houghton
Mifflin. Boston under title: Mark Twain's America,
and Mark Twain at work.
  Bibliography: p.
  1. Clemens, Samuel Langhorne, 1835-1910.
2. Clemens, Samuel Langhorne, 1835-1910—Contemporary
United States.   3. Authors, American—19th century—
Biography.   I. Title.
[PS1331.D4   1978]   818'.4'09   78-4109
ISBN 0-313-20368-7

Reprinted with the permission of Houghton Mifflin Company

Reprinted in 1978 by Greenwood Press
An imprint of Greenwood Publishing Group, Inc.
88 Post Road West, Westport, Connecticut 06881

Library of Congress Catalog Card Number 78-4109
ISBN 0-313-20368-7

Printed in the United States of America

The paper used in this book complies with the
Permanent Paper Standard issued by the National
Information Standards Organization (Z39.48-1984).

10 9 8 7 6 5 4 3

MARK TWAIN'S
America

with illustrations by
M. J. GALLAGHER

ACKNOWLEDGMENTS

I AM indebted to *Harper's Magazine, The American Mercury, The Bookman,* and *The Harvard Graduates' Magazine* for permission to reprint here parts of chapters which first appeared in their pages.

Copyrighted material in the text is used by permission of: Harper and Brothers (all copyrighted material from Mark Twain's works, including the "Autobiography" and the "Letters", as well as from Mr. Paine's "Mark Twain: a Biography").

Houghton, Mifflin and Company (material from the "Letters of Richard Watson Gilder").

E. P. Dutton and Company (material from "The Ordeal of Mark Twain").

Boni and Liveright (material from "Our America").

Messrs. Harper and Brothers have been extraordinarily kind to me over the whole period during which this book was being composed. I desire to express my thanks for their constant and freely given information, much of it no doubt a laborious annoyance to them, and especially for their willingness to inform me about comparative sales and other business secrets. In particular, I am indebted to the kindness and patience of Mr. Lee F. Hartman and Mr. Eugene Saxton.

My thanks are due to the officers and employes of many libraries, especially the Harvard College Library, the Library of the American Antiquarian Society, the Bancroft Library, and the Library of the State Historical Society of Missouri.

The kindness of scores of collectors should also be acknowledged.

To acknowledge the help of all who have contributed information, the means of information, actual research, or profitable suggestions would be impossible. For assistance which I regard as finally important, I am indebted to Robert F. Almy, Thomas

Beer, Donald Born, Ernest Boyd, Walter B. Briggs, James A. DeLacey, Clifton J. Furness, J. Lesser Goldman, R. H. Gordon, Robert Hillyer, Mildred Howells, Garrett Mattingly, Frederick Merk, Albert Bigelow Paine, Budd Pollak, Constance Rourke, Lyle Saxon, Arthur M. Schlesinger, Henry Alden Shaw, Edwin Willys Taylor.

The enormous labor of checking dates, sources, and quotations has been performed by Miss Mary Ellen Whelpley, my assistant on *The Harvard Graduates' Magazine*. She has also done much research on behalf of this book, prepared its manuscript two separate times, reduced the chaotic bibliography to order, written the index, and read the proofs. No way exists of adequately expressing my appreciation of her care, patience, and enthusiasm.

FOREWORD TO ROBERT S. FORSYTHE

My dear Forsythe:

I caution you to expect some difficulty in classifying this book. The depressing statistics at the year's end which measure the depravity of man by the consumption of wood pulp will probably file it among biography, and yet I do not carry Samuel Clemens past the year of his greatest embarrassment and at no time is my interest in him biographical. Even if Mr. Paine had not succeeded so admirably, I should not have tried to represent on paper the most engaging personality in American letters. Nor have I adventured far into literary criticism: that department of beautiful thinking is too insulated from reality for my taste. Mr. Arthur Schlesinger has suggested that I am writing the social history of Mark Twain, but history aspires to a comprehensiveness I have not attempted. For purposes of dedication I have called the book an essay in the correction of ideas — need I confess that I am not naïve enough to suppose ideas, among the literary, susceptible to correction? Perhaps the act of classification must take this form: herein is the kind of book I have wanted to write about Mark Twain.

Nearly every one, you will say, has written about Mark Twain; can this particular book be needed? Oh, I assure, it is cried aloud for. Some years ago, when I was beginning it, Mr. Paine, the literary executor, informed me that nothing more need ever be written about Mark Twain. The canon was established, and whatever biography or criticism had to say could be found in the six pounds of letterpress that composed Mr. Paine's official Life. He may be forgiven a certain exasperation. He had denied me access to the unpublished material and I was engaged in a species of blackmail. Mr. Paine's desire was to have no traffic with an upstart, but, denied that material, I had composed a series of questions which his Biography omitted to answer, and was forcing his hand by threatening to publish the best ascertainable rumors if he would not answer them. He answered my questions — his kindness is here acknowledged — but a permissible testiness made him remind me that further books about Mark Twain were unnecessary. Time has convinced him that he was wrong. Clara Clemens has decided that her father's love letters have a public value, and now Mr. Paine himself has prepared yet another book about Mark Twain. Perhaps this revision of his opinion will suggest that my effort is legitimate.

Before I explain its legitimacy, a word about Mr. Paine's attitude and that of the Mark Twain Estate. No one can question their right to establish a boundary beyond which investigation must not go. Property is property and so, in a way, is propriety — though perhaps love letters are not — and literary reticence is, these days, refreshing. Still, they are known to be angry because the past fifteen years have produced various misrepresentations of their property. Anger must content them, however, along with misrepresentation, until they are willing to exhibit the literary estate. In Samuel Clemens, the private citizen, the public has no interest that Mr. Paine is bound to respect. But Mark Twain, the literary artist, is in some degree a public possession, and the public is not bound to suppose that Mr. Paine has declared all the truth about him unto eternity. I for one doubt the validity of Mr. Paine's literary ideas. I am afraid that he must encounter the skepticism of people who share my opinion until much material now buried in bank vaults has been made public. Until that time no conclusions about Mark Twain will be worth much, and I caution the reader to accept mine, along with all others, as tentative only. Also I suggest to the heirs of Mark Twain that they will not be committing sacrilege if they make available, to research if not to publication, that vast heap of unpublished manuscript and those letters which it was discreet to withhold from Mr. Paine's collection.

Shall I specify? To write with an authority lacking to these pages, one should be able to report on, say, the rejected portions

of "Huckleberry Finn", the corollaries of "1601", the debates
on God's providence and Satan and the depravity of man, the
long letters which Howells did not dare to keep in his desk and
yet could not quite bring himself to destroy (they were returned
to the Estate when Mr. Paine was writing his Biography), the
fragmentary volumes about the matured Huck and Tom, and a
good many of the extravaganzas. Until some one can report
on these, all criticism of Mark Twain must be insecure. Mr.
Paine, though a formidably good biographer, is something less
than infallible as a critic; no one else has seen these manuscripts;
yet, obviously, they must some day be accounted for. Public
benevolence constrains me to offer the Estate my services.

Even though these manuscripts are withheld, there is still
need of such a book as this. Since 1869 Mark Twain has been
more widely read than any other American. He is one of the
two or three of our writers to whom not even envy can deny the
adjective great. Work of his has passed into our common speech;
towns and characters and ways of thinking that he created have
enlarged our consciousness and enriched our heritage for all
time. Yet the criticism of literature in America is so frail, so
capricious, so immature a force, that discussion has moved away
from what a great man wrote, to what he was or was not, what
he should have been, what America has failed to be, and what
the reformation of society might achieve if the world were
amenable to pretty thoughts. I may claim a startling originality
in that I have nowhere so distrusted humor as to call Mark
Twain a buffoon. But it is a greater originality, in this generation,
that I have based my book solidly on the books of Mark Twain.
For the chapters that follow, I have no interest beyond his books.
My effort has been to perceive where and how they issue from
American life. How much money he made from them — a
young faith in the worthlessness of all books that make money
is the basis of much written about him before now — has for my
present purpose no more interest than the color of their bindings.
What he might or should have written has, for me, no importance whatever. I am completely uninterested in what psychology, politics, economics, or evangelism may reveal about him.

I believe, merely, that some of his books have a kind of greatness to which American literature nowhere else attains, and that
much in them is interesting and amusing. My intent has been
to restore discussion of Mark Twain to these values — to what he
wrote. I do not cajole myself into believing that I have succeeded: literary opinion is a function of wishfulness. But perhaps I have made it possible for heretics to enjoy with intellectual self-respect books which the lay popes of our thinking
command them to despise on moral grounds. If, in addition, I
have suggested that it is possible to laugh at humor without
apology, I shall be content. The color-blind are unqualified
critics of painting, but because the solemn have been granted
authority about humor I have had, very tiresomely, to insist
that laughter is not shameful.

As you know, my book is the result of Mr. Ernest Boyd's
suggestion that my acquaintance with frontier society might
be serviceable in the explanation of Mark Twain. My claim to
some measure of authority in these pages derives from the fact
that I have lived in a frontier community and known frontiersmen, as none of the literary folk who now exhibit ideas about
frontier life have done, and that for many years my interests
have led me to study the frontier, a study that has never commended itself to those exhibitors. This qualification has persuaded me to devote more space to some aspects of the frontier than my immediate object required. If you find certain
discussions conducted at tiresome length, reflect that this particular job will probably not be done again in this generation. It
has therefore seemed wise to put as much evidence as possible at
the disposal of those who are asked to accept conclusions based
upon it. These matters — I mean such things as negro witchcraft and the idiom of frontier humor — have proved to be of
absolute importance for the object of this book. At the sacrifice
of your patience, I have taken this way of calling them to the
attention of literary discussion in America. Surely any addition
to the data of that amusement is an act of piety.

Finally, my dear Forsythe, you will observe that I have arrived at no simple, unified formula for the explanation of Mark

Twain, and that I have refused to answer a good many questions on the ground that a factual answer is impossible and I dislike theoretical ones. I do not believe in simplicities about art, artists, or the subjects of criticism. I have no theory about Mark Twain. It is harder to conform one's book to ascertainable fact than to theorize, and harder to ascertain facts than to ignore them. In literature, beautiful simplicities usually result from the easier method, and, in literature, the armchair assertion that something must be true is the begetter of unity. One who is not content with assertion must usually be prepared to do without the unity also. I have examined everything I could find that seemed related to Mark Twain's books. My conclusions, with as much of the evidence for them as my publishers will print, follow in these pages. You and whoever else may take up my book are reminded that the proper time to read a preface is after reading the work it introduces, and that it is then usually superfluous. But the literary have fallen out of the habit of reading Mark Twain's books, on the ground that they are humorous or popular or repressed, and so the literary may find the first preface to them informative. My hope is that they will hereafter understand the desirability of reading his books before passing judgment on them.

Faithfully yours,

BERNARD DeVOTO

CAMBRIDGE, MASSACHUSETTS
May 1, 1932

NOTE

AN expression of my indebtedness to various firms and persons will be found in the customary place. I desire, however, to acknowledge more conspicuously the assistance of four men whose services to me have gone far beyond those which any one is entitled to expect, even in the coöperative enterprise of social history. Let this page express my gratitude:

To the Reverend C. J. Armstrong of Hannibal: whose discovery of the files of Orion Clemens's newspapers has enabled me to write authoritatively about matters of fundamental importance which have hitherto been beyond even the guesses of theorists; whose intimate knowledge of Mark Twain's boyhood, of his friends and relatives, and of the geography of Hannibal has been graciously put at my disposal over a period of three years; who has indefatigably tracked down information I have asked for; and who has read in manuscript, to verify my facts, all of this book that deals with the midwestern frontier.

To Robert S. Forsythe of Grand Forks: who has supervised this labor from its beginning; whose encyclopedic knowledge of American literature and history has saved me innumerable hours of research and innumerable errors; who has checked the manuscript with critical attention to detail; and whose judgment has been my principal reliance in the almost preposterous undertaking of correcting literary ideas by matching them against fact.

To Lawrence J. Henderson of Cambridge: at whose summer place on Lake Seymour the last phase of the enterprise began; who led me to the *Traité de Sociologie Générale*; who has long assisted me in the cultivation of literary skepticism; and who, by exercising an informed skepticism, has enabled me to rid my manuscript of considerable emotion.

To Franklin J. Meine of Chicago: whose exhaustive knowledge of frontier humor was made available to me too late to save me two years of fumbling search but not too late to clarify the field so laboriously reached; who has answered a thousand and one questions, most of which must have seemed to him puerile; who has found or verified or suggested many of the facts that I consider important in this book; who has put at my disposal not only his bibliographies and collections of biographical material but also his library and the facilities of his old-book business; who first showed me "The Dandy Frightening the Squatter" and "Frogs Shot without Powder"; and who edited for my series of reprints, *Americana Deserta*, a volume of selections from our mutual field to which I refer much that follows in these pages.

CONTENTS

MARK TWAIN'S
America

1835: THE NEW JERUSALEM

HALLEY's comet blazed in the night sky. In England, Thomas Taylor, the Platonist, died slowly. Once he raised his head and inquired whether the comet had appeared. Friends told him that it had come. The philosopher nodded. "Then," he said, "I shall die. I was born with it and I shall die with it."

But in America, troubadours smeared with burnt cork sang:

> With every day, I've heard people say,
> There's something new starts in a marvelous way:
> Cork legs, and steam arms, no doubt hath their charms,
> But the tale that I sing of with wonderment swarms!
> It's the *tail* of the fiery comet!
> This gay roving spark of a comet!
> Once near it, you'll never get from it;
> You're booked for a tenant *en*tail!
> O! This wonderful, wonderful comet!
> *Whisht!* went the comet's long tail!

A tenant entail in New Jerusalem seemed presaged by this flaming courier in space. Throughout America, sects whose long desire for perfection had lately found amazing encouragement beheld the new marvel and were content. It presaged the dreadful day of God, but it presaged also the perfection of mankind and of society.

Others found in the comet no token of dread. In West Tennessee there was little apprehension. Colonel David Crockett was the yaller flower of the forest. He was all brimstone but the head and ears and they were *aqua fortis*. West Tennessee understood that the President, Old Hickory, had commissioned Colonel Crockett to climb the Alleghenies and wring off the comet's tail.

On the eighth of January twenty years before, militiamen under Andrew Jackson had established a precedent that would endure long enough to reassure Mr. Bryan, by wounding or killing nearly two thousand of His Majesty's infantry, almost without retaliation. Ogreish redcoats had been lampooned in broadsides and boys had chanted doggerel about General Pakenham, who was among the killed, and the eagle had been everywhere displayed with beak and talons poised for destruction. A song that was to last to our times attributed Old Hickory's triumph to the hunters of Kentucky, whom it described as half horse and half alligator. Andrew Jackson had required but thirteen years to march from New Orleans to the White House, where he had inaugurated a society of whose perfection he was a symbol. Now, after seven years of perfection, the United States were clearly the New Jerusalem of prophecy, and Mr. Woodbury had been able to announce the clearing of the public debt. Therefore a decree issued from the White House constituting January 8, 1835, Jackson Day. It would not be seemly for the President to attend the commemoration, and besides, the intent was to add stature to Mr. Van Buren, the heir apparent. But Old Hickory might send a toast to remind the populace of his latest triumph. "The Payment of the Public Debt," his toast ran: "Let us commemorate it as an event which gives us increased power as a nation and reflects luster on our Federal Union, of whose justice, fidelity, and wisdom it is a glorious illustration."

Toasts multiplied. Colonel Benton, whom Harriet Martineau would presently describe as a fantastic Senator from Missouri, offered "President Jackson. May the evening of his days be as tranquil and as happy for himself as their meridian has been resplendent, glorious, and beneficent for the country." The fantastic Senator then believed himself destined for the White House when Mr. Van Buren should leave it, but he never got there and his son-in-law, General Fremont, fared as disastrously. . . . . The toasts went on. Mr. Dickerson alluded to New Orleans. The eighth of January, 1815, he thought, was "an important era in the history of America — second only to the Fourth of July, 1776," an impression that has its value still. Mr. Woodbury called the President "Venerable in years — illustrious in deed", and the collarless Colonel Johnson sang the refrain of New Orleans, where "He prevented booty and he protected beauty." Italics made the whimsy plain in to-morrow's newsprint and added force to Mr. Wright's, "The Citizen Soldier. The *strength* and *security* of free governments. Washington, Lafayette, and Jackson personified the character."

The banquet table was but one focus of a glory that overspread the nation and the toasts merely recognized the accomplishment of a millennium. Mr. Van Buren would succeed to the greatness prepared for him and the common man had at last inherited America. That meant, solely, that society was made perfect.

A week later Miss Martineau was in Washington. When she was received at the White House she found herself surrounded by Congressmen whose names began with J., K., or L. The common man insisted upon equality, to which the alphabet was a safe index. She made a note of Old Hickory's kindness to children and his belief that after March 4, when he should have a majority of two, the Congress would be much more worthy of the perfected country. She was an Englishwoman of thirty-three, whose love affair had not been happy, who had been born with-

out the ability to taste or smell, and who by now was so deaf that
a vast ear trumpet gaped at the chins of her auditors. By virtue
of needlework, determination, and a fierce literary intelligence,
she had made herself a person of consequence in England who
could now tour America in behalf of adventure, feminism, and
abolition. Since Hallam, Malthus, Sydney Smith and Bulwer
were her intimates, it is worth recording that, unlike most British
travelers, whose disdain was already a reverend tradition, she
found the American intelligence not inferior to that she had
left.

She had already made herself disliked in the South and, in
New England, had prepared the way for mischief least dreadful
in the millennial trances of Bronson Alcott. She brought to the
imperium of the common man in Washington an observation
far subtler than has been generally employed by British lecturers. Davy Crockett, a common man from the canebrakes, was
beyond her understanding, but she found Mr. Clay less im-
petuous than she had expected. Mr. Webster was droll, entertaining and intelligent, and as for Mr. Calhoun, "I never saw
any one who so completely gave me the idea of possession." He
was possessed by his doctrines of nullification and his mind had
"long lost all power of communication with any other." Colonel
Johnson, who was to be Van Buren's Vice President, amazed her
by his wild countenance and his disdain of cravats. At a dinner
with the seven justices of the Supreme Court and the seven
greatest lawyers of the time — of whom Mr. Webster fell to
her share — she met Justice Story. He was an amazing man
and she would have liked to "bring him face to face with a person
who entertains the common English idea of how an American
looks and behaves." But in all Washington the person who most
charmed her was a "tall, majestic, bright-eyed old man" who
wondered if England was not ready for Disestablishment. He
captivated her by his reverence for women and for "the awe
of purity which they excite in the minds of the pure." He had
"a steady conviction of their intellectual equality with men and
a deep sense of their social injuries." Miss Martineau, the first
practical feminist, therefore quite understood the distinction

of John Marshall, the Chief Justice. Six months later he was dead in Philadelphia.

The common man occupied the society of Washington, but he was less strident than his wife. Ladies, whose purity excited awe in the minds of the pure, stood at the very doors of the Senate and Supreme Court and astonished Miss Martineau by exercising their democratic right to send in the doorkeeper with their albums for the signatures of the great. They could interrupt Mr. Webster or Mr. Calhoun or Mr. Clay in debate, or harass Mr. Marshall on the bench. These had the devices of invention at their command and could rhyme autographs extempore, but to the poor President, who was terribly persecuted, it was a real burden. He had no poetical resource but Watts's hymns.

On the thirtieth of January the common man alleged a flaw in New Jerusalem. Both houses of Congress assembled for the funeral of Warren Davis of South Carolina. On the way out of the Capitol, when the President was walking between Mr. Woodbury and Mr. Dickerson, one David Lawrence approached him. Carefully stepping to one side, for the protection of Mr. Woodbury and the crowd behind him, Mr. Lawrence aimed two pistols at Old Hickory. Both missed fire and the President rushed upon the assassin, raising his cane, but Mr. Woodbury and Lieutenant Gedney of the navy were before him. Jackson's strength was not equal to his anger and he had to be taken home, trembling, certain that Senator Poindexter or some agent of Nicholas Biddle had plotted his destruction. No such malevolence existed. David Lawrence was a common man, an English house painter who had been thrown out of work by the perfecting of society. With democratic simplicity, he desired to avenge that injury on Old Hickory. He had, too, another injury. For, it appeared, David Lawrence was the rightful heir to the British Crown and Jackson had kept him from his inheritance. And, further, angels conversed with David Lawrence.

Angels conversed with many Americans, as winter yielded to an early spring. At Harvard Village, Massachusetts, forty thousand of them hovered above a Shaker meeting, not far from

the hillside where Bronson Alcott, with converts made through
the agency of Harriet Martineau, would soon found a perfect
society on barley and the shoulders of Mrs. Alcott. In upstate
New York, from February on, William Miller was at last an-
nouncing the fruit of a long meditation, the ascertained date of
the world's end and the establishment of a perfect society. He
was an old soldier who had fought at Plattsburg and had been,
in the days of his folly, a deist who mocked Christian piety and
thought all religions superstition. Mathematics and the logic of
words had converted him to prophecy, and he had at last sun-
dered the veils that hid the true meaning of the Scriptures. The
veils destroyed, it appeared that judgment would begin sometime during 1843 or 1844; after further calculus the dread day
was assigned to October, 1843. Eight years allowed scant time
for the necessary conversions, and while Jackson stormed against
his assassins and Massachuetts Whigs named Mr. Webster to
oppose Van Buren, William Miller went out from Troy on a
mission that would display the folly and the ending of all campaigns. Meanwhile the heavens announced the judgment.
Halley's comet swerved nearer and there were spiritual lights
in the midnight sky, and cataracts of mobile stars, and solar
haloes braided around the symbols of the dreadful God. William
Miller preached, and his presses printed, a text that revealed
the meaning of these things, for Luke had written "great earth-
quakes shall be in divers places, and famines and pestilences; and
fearful sights and great signs shall there be from heaven."

The text had meaning for many more sects than William
Miller's, sects that had their own revelations and found the
celestial fireworks and the earthly cholera as significant as he.
They, too, talked with angels; but few of them were to endure
as long as Miller's — or as Joseph Smith's.

Smith had conversed with angels since boyhood. He was now
at Kirtland, in Ohio, where he reared a temple to the dreadful
God, and speculated in real estate, and prepared to found a bank.
In March the dreadful God informed him that Adam, dying,
had become "Michael the Prince, the Archangel"; and defined
for him the privileges of the Melchisedek Priesthood, more ac-

curately called The Holy Priesthood after the Order of the Son of God. Only the true church could hold this priesthood, and, in these days of degeneration looking toward the end, only Mormons belonged to the true church. The privileges included the right to receive the mysteries of the kingdom of heaven and to have the heavens opened on behalf of the priesthood. This consecration Joseph conferred on his brethren. In October, with Oliver Cowdery, he received from heaven the principles of celestial astronomy as understood by Father Abraham, which may have interpreted solar haloes and the flight of stars.

But no prophet foresaw the outcome of Smith's church in Missouri, the State that had sent the fantastic Benton to the Senate. In Jackson County, the common man had driven the Mormons out into the wilderness. It was too bad, for Jackson County, on the authority of God himself, was the authentic site of the Garden of Eden and the New Jerusalem to which the Church must turn when the dreadful God should come down there and institute a perfect society. It was also the frontier, whence Mormon proselyters went out to convert the Lamanites who had slaughtered the early Church and still had a lamentable custom of scalping its successors. But Governor Dunklin's message to the legislature mentioned lawlessness by the true Church and said that "conviction for any violence committed against a Mormon cannot be had in Jackson County." So the Mormons were driven out, in the first of a series of expulsions, eastward toward a town they would call Nauvoo, on the Mississippi. But they had touched the frontier at Independence and had talked with fur traders, such as Lucien Fontenelle, to whom a valley in distant Mexico was familiar, a valley beyond the Rocky or Chepywan Mountains, fertile and solitary and blessed with a river like Jordan flowing into a Dead Sea.

Angels conversed with Spiritualists and Perfectionists on the high places of New York and Massachusetts — the hills that have given America most of its religions. Above Onondaga Lake the heavens had been filled with spirits announcing the death of this world in holy wrath and the birth of a perfect society. Lucina Umphreville's baptismal name was strikingly inappropriate to her doctrines, but these were corrected by the vision of a clergyman who beheld the congress of the sexes in heaven, as Joseph Smith did later. Lucina joined herself in spiritual marriage to Jarvis Rider. The union was dissolved and Lucina's second spiritual husband had word of one John H. Noyes, of New Haven. Noyes foresaw the end of the world and the beginning of a perfect society. He had himself been made perfect beyond the power to sin and anticipated a similar grace for every one. The Saints at Brimfield greeted him with holy love and Maria Brown and Mary Lincoln saluted him with the kiss of the new brotherhood. But Noyes fled from them, finding perfection ambiguous, and their doctrines grew toward the ancestral practice of bundling, made over for holy ends. This was in February. Mary and Maria, for the sake of chaste perfection, offered themselves for bundling with the spiritual husband of Lucina Umphreville. The sacrifice was acceptable and then, in March, Mary asked God for judgment, and, with Sister Flavilla, was led naked to a mountain top by night through mire and brambles for the proof of perfection. Then she wrote Noyes that the Everlasting Father had married her to Himself in a covenant stronger than death. Satan might rage and attempt to deceive but his time was short. Mary's letter was headed "Eternity."

Satan fared badly everywhere in America in 1835, for eternity was either already here or hastening hither with the speed of light. The stars drew near, and the dreadful day, and the thousand years of perfection, and a society without a flaw.

From Washington Miss Martineau went South, to the domain of the Nullifiers. "Elnathan Elmwood" had preceded her by two years and had reported a pointed dislike of abolitionists. But Miss Martineau, though an abolitionist, was a female and was, to boot, a lady. In the South, a lady's opinions could not be more important than a drawing-room charade, an accompaniment to sillabubs and cobbler. No one affronted Miss Martineau. As she traveled, in Augusta, Georgia, American fiction made its first vigorous experiment in realism, when Augustus Baldwin

Longstreet published pseudonymously the "Georgia Scenes" which he had contributed to the Augusta *Sentinel*. He had been educated among the Yankees but was orthodox on the question of nullification; and he too, unaware, was headed toward the state of the fantastic Benton. But ladies were exempt from realism, though females were not; therefore "Georgia Scenes" omits comment on the ladies of the day. For that one must go to the works of Miss Martineau.

She struck westward, overland, for New Orleans. Spring sent the rivers flooding into the fields and set the mocking birds throbbing in woods where flowers made a tropical Easter. She was almost an invalid, not having experimented with the mesmerism that would heal her, but she bore the stagecoaches and the squatter cookery with fortitude not devoid of pleasure. In the South there were no perfect societies. But as the stages crawled down roads hub deep in April mire, she beheld an energy as vigorous as the lust for perfection. America was moving westward. The planters were leaving the exhausted seaboard for new lands which they might disastrously mismanage. The humble were leaving for — for squatters' rights, for deliverance from the contempt of gentry and slaves, for adventure, for the setting sun. It was not possible to make out just why they were leaving, but the migration was under way. Their horses and their oxen and their store were moving down the miry roads. One passed them and shouts came from the trudgers, and songs that would one day be nostalgic in American ears. Off to Alabama, to Mississippi, to Arkansas, to Texas; to Missouri, Illinois, Iowa. Westward. The American folk wandering was already old. Its great days were just around the turn of spring — and an April restlessness, a stirring in the blood, a wind from beyond the oak openings, spoke of the prairies, the great desert, and the western sea.

If the prairies did not contain a perfect society, at least the advertisements of land agents promised New Jerusalem there without need of grace or intervention of the angels. In the letters of emigrants it was measurably near achievement. Illinois, where the upriver migration of suckers gave a nickname to

the migrants from the East, was not yet the second Eden of
the Mormons, but it was, demonstrably, Utopia. From the
South and from the East desirous inheritors were rushing by the
thousand to Illinois. In the yeasty summer of 1835 squatters
there made their first riot against the laws of real estate, which
had not been expunged from Utopia. In Pope County there was
another riot, this one against an organized outlawry, and Regulators rode masked and booted on errands not susceptible to
too accurate explanation. Williamson County, later to germinate
Herrin, was invoked for aid against Pope and Massac. In Chicago, which could not ever become such a metropolis as Vandalia
or Alton or Galena, there was a market place where whole
towns were sold at auction for the shearing of eastern lambs.
Utopia was marked out with glistening stakes, avenues and
public squares, steamboat landings and the brotherhood of man.
Rivers ran westward, flood water, mire, and the microörganisms
of democracy.

So Miss Martineau, two thousand miles away, heard tales of
Illinois and saw the piney-woods people driving their oxen
toward the Sangamon. She herself went on through forests big
with April to New Orleans, where on the sixth of May she
boarded the *Henry Clay*. She was now immersed in the unimaginable romance of the Mississippi and was headed for St.
Louis, the domain of the fantastic Senator Benton.

Down the Ohio went another party toward this same Utopia.
There was choice, for travelers on the Ohio, between Missouri
and Illinois, but such choice as could not trouble an aristocrat,
a slaveholder, and a landed proprietor. John Marshall Clemens,
whose namesake had charmed Miss Martineau and was about
to die, could not possibly choose the Utopia of poor whites
and abolitionists. The family of John Clemens had always been
gentry, though of late come upon hard times. The line went
back as purely as any other of the South's dubious genealogies.
Noble blood warmed it and one ancestor had pronounced the
doom of kings. The blood had mixed, in this generation, with
the blood of earls. Jane Lampton Clemens, a Kentuckian as her
husband was a Virginian, was a Lambton and therefore kin to the

earls of Durham, and a cousin of hers was the rightful heir, the American claimant. The Clemenses had traveled to Louisville in a barouche, which exhibited their difference from the plebs, and a slave girl went with them. Of Utopias, they must perforce select Missouri.

This was not the first migration of the Clemenses or the Lambtons. True to the genius of America, both families had moved westward from the seaboard. Kentucky had received the Lambtons and had mixed in Jane's heritage the blood of Montgomerys and Caseys, log-cabin pioneers who had lived on bear steaks and warred against the Indians. The breed had made a world, a civilization, and a peace. The ancestors of John Marshall Clemens, Virginians, had also answered the tug of migration, the passionate lodestone of the West. He himself had removed from Adair County to Kentucky, where he studied law and married Jane Lampton. Then he had removed from Kentucky to Tennessee, and, after three changes of estate on that frontier, was now once more joined to the rhythm and flowing with the tide.

They were quality, the Clemenses, and they traveled with their slave. Quality had suffered reverses so that John Marshall Clemens, at his last habitation in Tennessee, had practiced no law but had become a tradesman and kept store. But he had made sure the future of his line, he had set fast the stake of his succession. He had bought a hundred thousand acres of land in Fentress County. Land, the everlasting rock of aristocracy. He was a patroon, an earl, and his children's children should be secured a birthright. His family's honor made secure, he could negligently answer a cousin's call to Senator Benton's Utopia.

So, when Jane Clemens's brother-in-law, John Quarles, wrote that millions were to be made in Monroe County, Missouri, it was natural for John Marshall Clemens to turn from his secured estate. John Quarles was living in Florida, in Monroe County, a hamlet on the Salt River. In Utopia there is no present: there is only the future. History says nothing of Florida, Missouri. The river guides of 1835 make the Salt River navigable, but that was the vision — the fact awaited appropriation from Congress — toward the Gilded Age. John Quarles's millions must delay till the bars were dredged out and the channel deepened. The guides say nothing of Florida, which was at the forks of the river, eighty-five miles above its juncture with the Mississippi. Ten years later it had its first mention in literature when Hoss Allen swam it without clothes, but statistics are lacking and one has only a great man's memory that, in 1835, a hundred people lived there. In Utopia there is only the future: Florida had St. Louis for its hope and Acts of Congress could outface destiny.

John Marshall Clemens and his wife joined the rhythm of America in that April flow. In a barouche, with their four children and their slave, they advanced westward upon Utopia. At Louisville they boarded a steamboat for St. Louis, as thousands of Americans had done before them in 1835. They came to St. Louis and left it behind them to the southeast, and were finally at Florida, Monroe County, on Salt River.

Somewhere on that April pilgrimage, Jane Lampton Clemens had conceived her fifth child.

The *Henry Clay* had made ninety-six trips without an accident, which, on the lower Mississippi, neighbored with miracle. Nevertheless, her friends were appalled when it transpired that Miss Martineau had come on board without a life preserver. Nature shone through civilization in their word that "there are always companies of gamblers in these boats who, being awake and dressed during the hours of darkness, are able to seize the boats on the first alarm of an accident in the night, and are apt to leave the rest of the passengers behind."

But the *Henry Clay* completed her ninety-seventh trip without accident. Otherwise, she gave Miss Martineau full measure of experience. A wreck drifted downstream, its burst cylinders a memento of what might have happened to the *Henry Clay*. Only one passenger died of cholera, but on a boat that hailed them, the dying made an orderly row along the boiler deck, and at Memphis the river front was raging with the plague. From the guards, sportsmen shot at imagined bears on shore or real ones swimming in the river. They were God's Englishmen, these sportsmen, and persistently delayed the boat in the assurance that schedules were a function of British convenience. One of the river's peripatetic Sauls preached the wrath to come, spraying his congregation with tobacco juice. An old woman on tour inquired Miss Martineau's religion. It proved to be the Unitarian. She had better, the hag advised her, have done with that, for it wouldn't go down with us. Her morality was again scrutinized when a thunderstorm failed to adjourn her whist. When there were signs in the heavens, she was informed, whist was a blasphemy.

The *Henry Clay* ran close to shores whose forests sometimes opened on white mansions with porticoes half buried in rhododendron and azalea. Black gangs syncopated the hymns which the river-Saul had sung; hounds keened through the forests while mounted gentlemen followed them toward the kill; ladies did needlework on the porticoes or paced through formal gardens in frail brocades or, in slave cabins, competently presided at childbirth. There was no pretense that this society was perfect; the deep South, though given to illusions, had not invented that one. But it was at least kind, and sometimes gracious. It had its ritual, a little adolescent, a little preposterous in its code of verbal honor, but still a ritual. Gentlemen might go uncertainly among the pitfalls of grammar and might not understand why their debts increased year by year as the unfertilized earth slackened; but they were punctilious at cards and censored one another's speech, if not its conjugations, with the duelling pistol. Ladies were superior to their sex's rebellion in the North, which they held to be a mischief of frumps, and counted ignorance a bulwark to gentility; but they enforced a pleasing amenity of intercourse. Life on the plantations was scored to a slow tempo; it was a languor sweet with tropical flowers, incapable of disturbance, warmed with the security of impregnable power.

But the white marble of its surface was streaked with jet. Miss Martineau was just two months too early to witness an unloveliness. In the first week of July, 1835, Madison County,

Mississippi, flamed into terror. The Shacklefords (Jane Clemens's fifth child was to employ their name) and the Mabrys and the Claibornes called their fellows together in a Committee of Public Safety. In one week they hanged from available sycamores Joshua Cotton, Ruel Blake, Lee Smith, Albe Dean, Angus Donovan, William Saunders, and two more white men whose names were not set down, and more Negroes than any one bothered to list. The terrors of Madison were communicated to neighboring counties, where no census of lynchings was made, and to Vicksburg, where on the sixth of July an unofficial militia invaded the water front and found six gamblers whose acquaintance in Madison County required erasure with the rope.

The monster that had shown itself and was thus slain was the oldest of terrors, the slaves' rebellion. The languor of the plantations where gentlemen fought amiably over the significance of words and ladies embroidered a ceremony of flirtation, overlay a century-old dread of insurrection. Of the three or four uprisings actually conceived, none ever had a slight chance of success. The certainty of ultimate failure, however, was little comfort to a planter miles distant from his neighbors, surrounded by blacks who, though they would eventually be hunted down, might easily slit his throat and rape his daughters before the alarm went out. Such an insurrection had actually been planned in Madison County, and the Fourth of July had actually been named as the day of holocaust. Whether all who were lynched with Cotton and Blake were joined with them in the plot cannot now be discovered. If any were not, then they merely paid the price of a reputation for being abolitionists in the deep South in 1835.

The conspirators were not pretentious rogues. Four of them were "steam doctors", who boiled malarial tremors out of poor whites and slaves, and whose previous villainies had gone no farther than nigger-stealing and petty theft. They were, however, ancillary to greatness. For the abortive uprising in Madison County was part of a plan that was designed to engulf the whole South in anarchy. The lynched were "strikers" in the clan of John A. Murrell. And John A. Murrell, who had been secured just a year before, had bent his energies toward a revolution among the slaves, dated to break out everywhere on Christmas Day, 1835.

The significance of Murrell is that, though the most renowned, he was only one of the Turpins spawned innumerably along the river. American lawlessness towered everywhere on the border and reached its zenith on the Mississippi. Islands and bayous held confederacies of outlaws, whose living came from the piracy of barges and the murder of wayfarers. Before 1840 there were few places on the border where solitary travel was safe; until about that time, too, no barge could tie up by night anywhere from Cincinnati to New Orleans without taking thought of pillage. The "butcher-knife boys", the offscourings, lived by outlawry; and along a thousand miles they were known to one another. Peace officers and revenue agents were usually selected from this class, for the economy of the system.

Murrell brought to his trade an intelligence altogether superior to the ordinary river rat's. Pathologists may explain the cold ferocity with which he shot down a man for the sake of ten dollars in dubious banknotes and then disembowelled the corpse so that it would sink in the river. He might well have been a fantastic senator, but he turned his talents instead to outlawry. He was a general practitioner of crime, robbing, murdering, pirating barges, circulating counterfeit bills — but his specialty was nigger-stealing. He would induce a slave to run off, promising to sell him, to steal him again, and then to convey him to free soil as a reward. The slave would be hidden in the deep woods or the swamps, taken southward by night, sold, stolen again, and resold and stolen so long as the traffic could be carried on securely. Then, when pursuit began or the slave protested the direction of travel, there was another murder in the swamps and another corpse with gashed abdomen settling to the mud.

The traffic moved southwest and westward, down the Mississippi and up its lower tributaries. Along this highway, too, went the trade in stolen horses and the goods pirated from broad-

horns. Murrell organized a confederacy of thieves. When he
was caught, the names of nearly five hundred clansmen were
obtained; there is no reason to believe that this number made
even a half of those who had taken dreadful oaths, imitated
from Masonry, to obey Murrell. The clan was distributed all
along the rivers and across the deep South, perhaps the most
dangerous and certainly the most widespread criminal organization in America. It robbed and murdered with complete impu-
nity, for the peace officers had mostly taken its oaths or could be
waylaid if they hadn't. Its profits were enormous and it was
strong enough to plan an uprising of the slaves.

Looking toward this climax, Murrell could expect to "have
the pleasure and honor of seeing and knowing that by my management I have glutted the earth with more human gore, and
destroyed more property than any other robber who has ever
lived in America or the known world." His desire was not
emancipation, though he perceived that the idealists of abolition and their inflammatory press might do him service. Simply,
he hoped to turn the slaves loose on their masters, so that the
Murrell clan might be free to loot the banks and stores. To that
end his strikers stored up ammunition and preached whisky and
white mistresses to disaffected slaves. But the torches were never
lighted, save for the anticlimax in Madison County after Murrell's arrest. A young man named Virgil A. Stewart presented
himself for admission to the clan, received the signs and secrets,
and presently was discovered to be an agent of righteousness. For
a generation there were Virgil A. Stewarts along the Mississippi,
boys born when the great land pirate was arrested, or steamboats whose saloons bore chromos celebrating the destroyer of
banditti.

Stewart made an end to the clan. But the name of John A.
Murrell lingered after him. It lived in the balladry of the
countryside and in the legends of the river. By winter hearths
and on the boiler decks of steamboats and in the gossip of crossroads stores men spoke it, relating the terrors it had caused,
which lost little as the years grew. It made a quickening of breath
on lonely roads by night, an unrest where swamps stank or black

water ran under moss that drooped above hidden bayous. It meant a knife going home between a traveler's ribs, and the rush of yelling men coming down upon a tied-up barge, and a corpse sinking to the mud with a hole gaping where its bowels had been.

The name, too, attached to legends of lost or buried treasure. For the clan had taken much gold and clearly must have hidden it somewhere, sunk in swamps in a bee line with a blasted cottonwood or buried under an oak where some outlaw had been gibbetted. One such depository was the haunted house by the old tree on Cardiff Hill, back of the widow's. To Tom Sawyer and Huckleberry Finn the loneliness of the place suggested treasure, but Injun Joe preceded them and took from its resting place an iron-bound box. He carried it to the cave and died there, after hiding the treasure under a cross burned with candle flame on the limestone, an amulet which happily kept his ghost from guarding his desire. There at last Huck and Tom found the box and an old saying was recalled that "Murrell's gang used to be around here one summer."

America was on the move that spring and summer of 1835. It was late May when Miss Martineau, passing by Madison County, came to St. Louis. She was just a month too late to see the beginning of a journey of greater consequence than any other made that year. (Except one that, towards September, took young Charles Darwin to the Galapagos.) The Reverend Samuel Parker, M.A., had come down the Ohio from New England, at the command of the American Board of Commissioners for Foreign Missions. At St. Louis he was joined by a physician, Doctor Marcus Whitman, who was to be his companion. On April seventh, the *St. Charles* bore them up the Missouri toward Liberty, whence they were to journey to the Rocky or Chepywan Mountains and Indian tribes whose darkness required the bringing of a light. The Missouri collected its tax. A boy of six was drowned. The *St. Charles* struck a snag. Her successor, the *Siam*, grounded on a sandbar, was pried loose only to ground on another and another, and at last broke her main shaft under heavy steam. The doctor and the clergyman had to finish their journey to Liberty overland. Passing the Mormons newly driven out of Jackson County, they had no way of foreseeing that after eleven years these wretched men would take the road they were themselves preparing. They went on to Liberty, on the far fringe of what was called civilization, and waited there three weeks for the assembly of a fur-trade caravan that was to take them west.

Parker and Whitman were simple folk. They could not appreciate Lucien Fontenelle, the leader of the caravan. They could not know that, in his way, he was a great man. It was a frontier greatness; the partisan of a fur brigade must be a master of the mountaineering craft that was more hazardous and more expert than any other ever practiced in America. Only four others of the trade ever attained his eminence; of these, Jedediah Smith was dead and the missionaries were to come this summer under the protection of Tom Fitzpatrick and Jim Bridger, and were to see Kit Carson plain. Fontenelle had taken the place in the trade to which his attainments entitled him, but the melancholy of the peaks was on him. Not much later it would deepen; and at far camp-fires trappers would relate how Lucien Fontenelle had gone mad and killed himself.

If the missionaries could not understand the partisan, they actively blundered with his trappers. These were the privates of the trade, skilled, case-hardened, vindictive, reckless of life and abstemious of speech. When the caravan continued its march through the first Sabbath, the men of God stayed behind for worship and rode hard the next day to catch up with it. Such niceness offended the mountain men, who nevertheless offered peace with a cup of the raw alcohol that was called whisky in the trade. The men of God refused the libation, whereupon the trappers plotted their death. That this was not an idle threat was apparent when, at Bellevue, they murdered and scalped one Garrio, a half-breed whom they disliked. But at Bellevue, also, cholera broke out in the brigade, and the three who died would have had many more companions if Whitman's medicine and Parker's nursing had not saved them. The mountain men now

gave up their animosity, bewildered by the piety of the missionaries but no longer resentful of it.

The pathway up the wide and shallow valley of the Platte
was already old in the trade. The caravan that took the mission-
ries along this avenue merely repeated the monotony of a hundred predecessors, but to Parker and Whitman all was strange.
They met bands of Sioux, who bartered for tobacco and listened courteously to Parker's tales of the white Father who
had been tortured to save their souls. In the buffalo country they
made trouble for their guides by incautious hunting. The un-
coiling trail now produced a whole village of Ogallalas, who
were bound for their summer hunt and desired the caravan to
halt till they could reach the herd. Fontenelle granted his
men a "day of indulgence", with full ration of alcohol. The missionaries were again appalled by debauchery and one trapper
shot a companion. Then the Ogallalas reverently commended
the hunt to their gods, with dog and buffalo dances. Parker recorded that he "was not much amused to see how well they could
imitate brute beasts, while ignorant of God and salvation." So
he took aside a handful of panoplied bucks and initiated them in
Christian medicine by singing "Watchman, tell us of the night."

On up the dwindling Platte they went, then overland
through waste places to the post at the mouth of the Laramie.
Here Fontenelle turned over his command to Tom Fitzpatrick.
This was "The Broken Hand" or "White Head", the greatest
of all the partisans. His hair had turned white when he lay
hidden for two days with yelling Blackfeet scouring the mountainside to take his scalp. He had made Kit Carson eminent and
would later do much for the reputation of Captain Fremont.
Under him, the caravan moved on through dreadful desert. At
last, where a brief oasis widened on the banks of Green River,
it reached the rendezvous of the fur trade.

Here at Green River, America was incandescent and an era
reached its end. No one could have known that the doctor and
the parson were symbols of a beginning, a new order, but they
were. The rendezvous of 1835 was the culminating splendor
of the fur trade, which thereafter declined with the growing

scarcity of fur, corrupt and ruinous competition, a shift in fashion that made silk hats acceptable, and the fierce invasion of emigrants whose inconspicuous spearhead was Samuel Parker. But at Green River there was no foreshadowing of this tragedy. An arc drawn northward, westward and southward for a thousand miles would hardly have circumscribed the wilderness of peaks, canyons and deserts from which the trappers came to rendezvous. In twenty years they had made this country their own and had created, for survival there, the illimitable craft of the mountain men. The "Voyages" of Richard Hakluyt are many volumes brimful of Elizabethan mariners who sailed into the unknown and charted its hazards. No smaller work could contain the venturings of these American land-mariners to whom this wilderness was a city square, and the dangers they had passed needed no condescension from Captain Drake. All this was ending now and missionaries were charting the way for lesser men who would bring their plows and move in safety down known trails.

Westward they came from Brown's Hole and the slopes of the main Rockies. Northward from Taos and the three Parks. Eastward from Ogden's Hole and the Great Salt Lake and Beer Spring on the Bear and Fort Hall. Southward from Pierre's Hole and Jackson's Hole, from Salmon and Frazer and Snake rivers, from the three forks of the Yellowstone, from Colter's Hell, from the Wind River Mountains and the Three Tetons and the bad lands that Captain Fremont was to suppose he was discovering. Canadian Frenchmen, Mexican Spaniards, Scotch, Irish, Cockneys, Yankees, Kentuckians, Virginians, Missourians. Nor may any one guess how many foreign offices had agents among these illiterate men, with an eye to the coasts of Oregon and California. Probably from this rendezvous reports went secretly to London, Paris, and St. Petersburg; and for three years no one had been able to explain Captain Bonneville, of the United States army, who came for fur but seldom tried to trap it, though he tirelessly made maps of the country he passed through. There were also three villages of Indians, together with delegations from most of the mountain tribes.

The end of an era was glorious. For a year these men had
been buried deep in canyons. For a year they had had no touch
with other white men, only the privations of the desert and the
hazard of lonely and savage death. Now the pack trains were in
from the States and the brotherhood was gathered together,
those of it who had survived the year. There were wages and
squaws and liquor. In a week they would be among the peaks
again but — waugh! — here was ecstasy.

The crescendo rose through drinking and quarreling to
fighting and bloodshed. Kit Carson, resenting the taunts of one
Shunar, a Canuck, tilted at him formally and extinguished him
with a shot that was not quite fatal. Lesser battles freckled the
riverside while the mountain men pledged one another and
competed for the purchase of squaws. The tribes rode their mock
battles for pay; the trappers sang Injun and joined themselves
to scalp dances, counting their coups and rehearsing their murders. Stupefaction ensued and the extremes of carousal in the
wilderness. But happily there were nobler occupations of the
men of God. Whitman operated on Jim Bridger, extracting from
his shoulder an arrowhead that had lodged there three years
before. Then the Flathead chiefs arrived. It was a rumor of
their desire to learn of the white man's God and His black book
that, reaching the Board of Missions in the East, had started
these two upon their journey.

The Flatheads and the Nez Percés proposed, merely, a
stronger magic. They were hemmed around by tribes more successful than they on the warpath. Their young men were valiant
but their scalps too often hung from poles around which the
Blackfeet danced. The palefaces had done well against the
Blackfeet. The spirit they prayed to and the Hawkins rifles
he vouchsafed them in inexhaustible quantities might restore the
Flathead tribe to wealth and reputation. The chiefs recalled the
muscular Christianity of Jed Smith, who had once wintered with
them. His medicine had been powerful. . . . But to the missionaries this eagerness for light was proof of God's providence.
They conferred with the chiefs. The mission field proved wider
than they had thought, the need more urgent. So Marcus Whit-

man would go back to the States and come again next year with
assistants. Parker went on with Jim Bridger's men into the deep
canyons; then commended himself to his God and, with only a
few Indians, struck overland through wilderness for the scene
of his mission.

And, with the Broken Hand, Marcus Whitman turned
eastward toward the States. That winter he gathered a larger
mission. Also, he found a wife; and she and another woman
joined the caravan that took the trail the following spring. The
caravan possessed, too, wagons and a light cart that were to go
farther into transalpine America than wheels had ever gone
before. Somewhere in the Bad Lands of Wyoming the trappers
met them, charging down with a frenzy of rifle shots and Injun
yells to welcome the first white woman who ever traveled the
road to Oregon. The demonstration was a tribute to muliebrity,
and — it fixed a seal to the passing of a civilization.

For the wife of Marcus Whitman, and his two caravans, had
opened the road. The march was swift. The Western filtrate
had now no boundary to its passage but the Pacific sea. After
eight short years, Jim Bridger abandoned the fur trade to sell
supplies to trains of white-tops bound for Oregon and California,
and with Old Gabe's renunciation, the mountains became a
tamed spectacle. The trains were already common along the
trails that Parker and Whitman had passed and the emigrants
were using Parker's book for compass. Whitman's mission had
grown into a settlement, where he was to be a guardian to the
emigrants who followed him, to have a part in the troubles that
were almost a war with England, to create a myth still taught in
our schools, and to be murdered at last by the Indians whose
souls he had saved for the pale God. He had founded the first
permanent settlement beyond the border. That accomplished,
the rest followed necessarily. The trains yoked up for Oregon
and the China trade, for California and sea otters, for fertile
land, for Manifest Destiny. That was all latent in the mission of
Samuel Parker and Marcus Whitman. And with it — the gold
at Sutter's mill, the Biblical wanderings of the Mormons, and
the silver on the Mountain of the Sun that was to take westward

in this farthest American migration an unnoticed item, Jane Clemens's fifth child.

Mr. Van Buren was nominated at Baltimore about the time Miss Martineau reached St. Louis. The year unfolded without sense or order. The Carlists seemed victorious in Spain and the Court abolished the Inquisition, but three great railroads were opened in eastern America. Louis Philippe's life was endangered by an infernal machine, wherefore the liberties of the French press must be curtailed, but in America all that was noteworthy was the venom of abolitionists, whose meetings had to be mobbed in Utica and Boston. Signs in the heavens foretelling the wrath to come were now buttressed by disastrous fires, hurricanes, and tidal waves — portents of cumulative significance to Millerites and Mormons. Santa Anna returned victorious to Mexico City. He would shortly move upon the Texans, a few of whom were prematurely declaring themselves free. England celebrated the tercentenary of Coverdale's Bible, but a less sacred literature was read in America, where Sam Slick the Clockmaker made his appearance in the *Nova Scotian.*

The Americans are not a solemn race. In September, Mr. Richard Adams Locke relieved the New York *Sun* of apprehension about its future. This penny newspaper had lived insecurely but now, over a period of some days, Mr. Locke related the discoveries made by Sir John Herschel by means of a gigantic new telescope. Sir John, it appeared, had focused his instrument on the moon and had been able to observe the domestic manners of the Lunarians. The countryside thus revealed was very strange, but the inhabitants were stranger still. Strangest of all were certain private amusements which Mr. Locke delicately avoided by means of asterisks. Public delight quadrupled the *Sun's* circulation. The nation boundlessly applauded the hoax. Edgar Allan Poe felt sure that the idea had been lifted from one of his tales.

November presented the beginning of the New York and Erie Railroad, which was to be of import to Jim Fisk, then in swaddlings, and Jay Gould, as yet unborn. Next, a tempest scattered wrecks along the shore of Lake Erie, driving waves farther up Buffalo's water front than waves had ever gone before. Tampico forecast the headlines of a century by imprisoning eleven American freebooters, who were shot within the month. The signs in the heavens grew more dreadful. For three nights the skies of all America blazed with an aurora surpassing any other recorded. The newspapers celebrated it, while children screamed and literary folk filled their journals with poetry; and Mormons, Millerites, and other millenialists knew that the end was at hand. The aurora ceased on the twentieth, and three days later snow fell throughout the north, beginning the "winter of '35", as yet without parallel in our history. It made a frigid world, especially on the frontier, and tales that grew out of it remain current in the press.

And on the thirtieth of November, the population of Florida, Monroe County, Missouri, was increased by one per cent. Two months prematurely, Jane Lampton Clemens was delivered of her fifth child, a boy whose frailty gave little promise that he could survive this winter on the frontier. He was named Samuel, after his grandfather, and Langhorne after his grandfather's benefactor. His cries were feeble on the icebound frontier, in a nation about to perfect society, where the common man had asserted domination, and signs in the heavens announced the cleansing wrath to come.

II

IDYL: ST. PETERSBURG

ANNOTATION is essential. The Missouri in which the infant's eyes opened was frontier, and that it was frontier is the whole truth about the books of Mark Twain. But the word "frontier" has passed into the custody of ideologues, whose notions have marvelously distorted it. Florida, Missouri, where Samuel Clemens was born, and Hannibal, Missouri, where he grew up, were "frontier." Both villages were "border." Necessarily Samuel Clemens was a leaf that took its color from the sun: the sun of Florida and Hannibal shone on Western rural slaveholding communities near the fringe of settlement during years when a boundless vigor was making America something it had not been, something not reducible to formula. Theories cluster. Opinions about that western fringe, those years, that vigor, and that America make an abundance of systems, canons for the orthodox whose distressing quality is that they cannot all be true. Conflict produces a residue, a literary notion: that it was all pretty detestable. The notion and the industry that has begotten it make laborious an effort to arrive at two drowsy hamlets beyond the river, whose life was umbilical to a great man's mind.

A literary theory is a form of metaphysical autobiography. It permits its contriver to reconstruct facts in harmony with his prepossessions. It is also a kind of speculation, secure from overthrow since the past is irrevocable, and a convenient bludgeon with which its contriver may assault whatever he dislikes. It is a purely subjective creation, amusing enough to the inventor and capable of entertaining the leisure of other minds. But when a set of notions arranged in the form of a literary system is submitted as objective truth, as a description of something, it must accept sterner criteria. In America such systems have passed judgment on society. Literary notions, and literary biography which is a specialized form of them, have offered themselves as a description of America. They thus invade a field less conformable to sentiment and must submit to examination. Of the requirements they must meet, two are important here. The theorist must show that what he alleges as fact has some correspondence in reality and he must be capable of distinguishing between facts and his emotions about them.

Literary opinion fails to approve the frontier. On evidence not submitted, the frontier folk are held to be Puritans given to a rigid suppression of emotion and particularly sexual emotion, and given also to deplorable license in emotion which produced camp meetings, lynchings, and sexual debauch. Also, the Puritans were disciples of Rousseau, who had moved west with an idea of sucking at nature's breast doctrines of primitive perfection and finding in the wilderness an age of innocence conducted by the noble savage. A Calvinist thus becomes an infidel philosopher and the relations of his fathers with the Iroquois were fraternal. The perceptible incompatibilities, however, cause no embarrassment, for it is also to be charged against frontiersmen that they offered no encouragement whatever to artists, neglecting to praise "Moby Dick" and "Leaves of Grass" a generation before they were written. They were extroverted, they suppressed individuality, they obeyed the dreadful compulsions of the herd, they were barren of art, they scourged their souls with Old Testament terrors. Above all, they were universally a repressed people who feared joy and pleasure, living out their lives in gloom. And further, the land they lived in was repellent.

For a moment, the land. Urban America, developing a generation of urban theorists, has found its sentiments condemning rural America. One wonders why an environment held to be commendable for Thoreau is thought unfortunate for Mark Twain.

Hannibal was a town. A gentry lived there; it was a port on the Mississippi; houses, even mansions, had displaced such shacks as covered the population of Florida; and, one day, a railroad would join it to St. Joseph. But though a metropolis beside Florida, it was not sufficiently important to appear on John Banvard's panorama. Mr. Banvard was a New Yorker who believed himself kin to the prisoner of Chillon, and who grew to manhood with an ambition of striking simplicity. He aspired to paint the largest picture in the world. Clearly, the largest river in the world was a subject appropriate to the desire; therefore, after an interlude on the Wabash, ingenuously displaying the beaux arts to the communists, he made an apprentice voyage down the Mississippi. By 1846 he was painting his masterpiece on three miles of canvas. He exhibited it in the East, where Longfellow desired a national epic superior to all others as Banvard's panorama was to all other paintings, the largest in the world, and Nat Willis conceded that America at last had an artist commensurate with the grandeur of its scenery. The panorama moved to England, where Charles Dickens commended its size. Banvard's painting had a nice realism in detail, but, on the scale of one to four hundred, it was unable to discover Hannibal.

The river was one side of the village; the other three were countryside, prairie, and forest. The actual border had withdrawn almost to the boundaries of Missouri, so that nowhere within those limits was a family endangered by starvation. There was no menace of attack by the noble savage, who entered Hannibal merely as a herb doctor, a beggar, or a horse thief, and then was usually one of the half-breeds whom a sexually puritanical race had begotten. The frontier, as a line of hazard, was extinct. But as a condition of simplicity, isolation, and noncompetitive society it existed in Hannibal till after Samuel Clemens had gone elsewhere.

The loveliness of prairie and forest suffuses American literature, to make our most authentic theme. It was not hidden from boys. Wilderness, tamed past actual menace, nurtured the memories of Samuel Clemens, out of which came five-sevenths of his books and those of men who were boys when he was. He and they had only to lope past the town pump and on beyond the shot-tower to step into enchantment. One could call one's sling shot Long Rifle there, beyond Cardiff Hill, rehearsing the still young deeds of Boone or those of Davy Crockett, just then finding print. Bears and wolves had withdrawn westward but a doe or her fawn was not beyond conjecture. One would remember the strut of turkeys and the drumming of grouse. Spring and fall brought the migratory hordes, — geese, brant, ducks, cranes. No one yet wasted powder on wild pigeons, since they could be knocked from trees with clubs, their eyes dazzled by light-wood fires. Samuel Clemens remembered flocks of them that hid the sun.

The forest sheltered the outlawry of Robin Hood. One might pass from that to make romance of Murrell, and Lafitte, and Captain Kidd, whose heroisms were popular in paper-backed literature. But enchantment was not solely the freedom to be Uncas or Friar Tuck or the Red Handed — though some one may yet find forest boyhood in America's buccaneering businesses in the last decades of the century. There was a deeper enchantment. The rural nation had isolation at arm's length; if transcendentalism had not crossed the sea, it must have developed here independently. American pantheism added solitude to German metaphysics, necessarily. Frontier mothers taught their sons astronomy so that the planets made a map in the minds of boys as surely as spark plugs ignite carburetted gasoline in the minds of their great-grandchildren in the 1930's. One was a botanist and a mineralogist at ten, in outward expression of the enforced communion with the earth. One was bound intimately with the progress of the year. It is all difficult to recover, now, the autumn fulness when one scuffed through fallen leaves after the nut harvest and the yarbs that would cure toothache or dyspepsia — summer dawns when one lay listening to Jackson's Island coming awake — the tracks of mink or foxes in snow that hid the underbrush — under a faint moon, ice on the river that creaked but would not break till the year turned and sap rose in the maples toward the tree-sweetenin' for next year's coffee. Difficult to recover and easy to forget, when a theory reads the machine age and the reek of slums into a society that knew solitude and was not frightened by it.

Always a mile would take one into that quiet. Always, too, one was in touch with the crafts and handicrafts the wilderness had generated. If in Hannibal one wore clothes made from store cloth, that meant that one's family was affluent; there were neighbors who wove their own. No one rived the beams for his ceiling, or quarter-sawed oak for his chairs; no one cared to be the wright of his own cartwheels or the cooper of his own barrels — but a hundred miles to the west one might find a householder doing all these things. A soap barrel stood in the dooryard, waiting the leach of ashes which few to-day would be able to select; and if Hannibal no longer butchered its own beef, its outlanders had not degenerated. But these are routine crafts, items in the hundred skills the householder possessed as a matter of course, and hardly touched the forest. There, meanwhile, one read the signs as Boone and Girty had done, as Fontenelle and Bridger were doing some weeks' journey to the west. There was now no premium of survival on this skill, as there had been when young men in Hannibal were boys. It was reduced to a pride or pageantry, part of the enchantment. But, a vestige, it still lived, and the elders who drowsed along the water front were alive to tell about it because they had learned it in their time. The motion of a bough, the tone of a bird's cry that meant surprise, the direction of the wind and of growing moss, the not accidental posture of a stick, the sunbath of a turtle or a water moccasin, the flight of birds before a storm, the indelible markings of a man's voice or his unconscious tics, or a slave's or even a dog's — all this one grew from babyhood to read as a chapter in the frontier's Bible. One would fill pages with such lore when one came to tell about the suspicion of murder in Arkansas or Dawson's Landing, or about the flight of a slave.

Charles Godfrey Leland managed to observe most of America that was incandescent and a good part of Europe in a long lifetime. He was an initiate of strange secret cults; he knew empirically many things which celebrated people won fame for guessing about; and his competence was in all things amazing but principally so in the accuracy of his judgment. In Florence he met another American man of letters, whose books he liked but whose finest works, he said, were invariably bound in silk or muslin and were called "The Three Daughters, or the Misses Clemens." The author of these works he found keenly American, a sharer in a literary quality which Leland knew was confined to the western shore of the Atlantic. "Mark Twain," Leland wrote in 1893, "has the peculiar Indian-like or American faculty of observing innumerable little things which no European would ever think of. There is, I think, a great deal of 'hard old Injun' in him." Mr. Leland confused the Indian's craft with that of his conqueror, which to be sure it created. The Indian in Mark was the Indian essential to a race which, for good or ill but to the despair of theorists, had occupied a continent that was all frontier.

The frontiersmen neglected to behave according to the theories. Notably, he forgot to be joyless. At the moment there is no relevance in his religion, an emotional exuberance. Calvinism forbade amusements; therefore the obedient tossed a badger into a barrel with a terrier, or dug a pit for twenty terriers and a bear. Local strains of cocks and race horses were probably not the outgrowth of an interest in biology, though the tenet that forbade a Calvinist to throw a card held also for the laying of bets. Competition flourished. Shooting matches, an ancient sport, became less common as marksmanship ceased to have a value for survival, but all bucolic contests abounded. Nothing is so clearly of hell, in Calvinism, as the theater; yet the tributaries of the great river, so far as there was draft, were the itinerary of countless show boats. One heard a whistle bellowing in hoarse thirds above the bend; one shouted and raced for the landing, where a tug nursed the *Snow Queen* or the *Fanny Ellsler* inshore and a uniformed band mounted the texas for a concert. She had been preceded some weeks by another floating hippodrome and brought rumor of still another to come within a fortnight. Whatever orthodoxy said about pleasure, these could hardly have played to empty benches. Still less, the strolling players.

In the Forties, the itinerant actor was already a stock figure in literature. There is, furthermore, no limit to his wanderings. The paper backs present him indifferently in Virginia and Arkansas, and at least one company got far enough west to suffer attrition from Indians. Libraries are filled with the masterpieces acted for the approval of Calvinists before smoky oil lamps in the lofts above crossroads stores. They are melodrama of the type that it has recently been held literary to revive. Heroines, for the most part, have been stolen at birth from noble cradles and are threatened by Englishmen, though Mexicans become villainous with the sharpening of the Texan crisis. The framework of Charles Warner's half of "The Gilded Age" might have been lifted from any of them. One nourished one's glimpses of this alien enchantment; they would blossom for a while, then ripen into the Royal Nonesuch and his adventures in Arkansas — where Sol Smith and a score of others had preceded him.

From 1835 on the melodramas were amplified by the discovery that the stage Negro was laughable. The Main Street of Hannibal, familiar with the displays of circuses and menageries, had now, periodically, the glory of another kind of parade. An actor was more than ever magnificent in black-face, violet swallowtails, and saffron linen, swinging up the street behind a coon band that played the compositions of Dan Rice or Stephen Foster. That night the footlights would smoke before a semicircle of starched bosoms that, in time, managed to create myths. The discovery that Sambo was funny was, in the main, a Northern one; for the writers of Southern humor preferred the poor white. This observation may account for the atrocity of negro dialect, or coon talk, that fastened itself on literature. Mrs. Stowe merely lifted it from Christy's Minstrels, making it more abominable as perhaps a saintly woman must. Christy in turn had got it from Northern broadsides and newspapers, where Poe also had observed it; much later it worked back into the South, Nelson Page presenting it with a spurious nicety that passed as realism. Samuel Clemens and George W. Cable and Joel Chandler Harris, meanwhile, had written negro speech, but the convention ignored them, and of late, transferred to Harlem and the Caribbean, has again been accepted as realism.

Christy's eye was better than his ear. He, and his imitators, saw what was a common sight to even such a casual steamboat passenger as Miss Martineau, — the slave dances. Roustabouts, between jobs, patted Juba and jumped Jim Crow; they skinned the Yaller Cat, cut the Pigeon's Wing, raised the hatch, turned Juba into a Jubal Jew, and manipulated the Long Dog scratch — flowing from codified steps to impromptu ones that might become traditional. Christy reproduced these dances to music fashioned by Rice or Foster or the anonymous Shuberts of the first tin-pan alley. He added improvements of his own, a formality called the cakewalk, unrecognizable in the institution whose name it usurped, and the walk-around, a species of indoor parade. To the dances, which flowed on from him to the vaudeville stage, where they lived unchanged till the recent revival of Christy's sources, he added songs of many kinds. Some were merely the saccharine balladry of the day, others were ingenious burlesques of the operas then current in New Orleans and the East. And still others, contrived by Foster or men who perceived what Foster had done, precipitated an American art. The jubilee, or spiritual, had numerous begetters. It is worth remembering that one of these was the contrivance of white men smeared with burnt cork, who sang slave songs as interludes between the buck-and-wing and conversation with Mr. Bones.

But first one must scrutinize another attribute of the frontiersman.

Incurably musical, Americans working westward carried with them fiddles and a folk art. While the frontier was still a boundary of exploration, the wayfarer expected to find a fiddle or a banjo hanging beside the rifle in the shanty when he sought hospitality. The Calvinist could tune his instrument as handily as he could make hinges for his door; when it was smashed, he could make another, one which would be no Guarnarius, truly, but served its end. He would make a graduated series for his children, whose education included a rule-of-thumb harmony as universal as the astronomy that permitted them to tell time by the seven stars. Hamlin Garland's childhood near Dutcher's Cooly was tinged with the balladry of the Scotch border, sung to fiddles; there was a more native music at Vandemark's Folly, where Herbert Quick grew up; and indeed catgut strings were an article of commerce in the fur trade, that there might be music near the Three Tetons in the country of the Blackfeet.

A corn-shucking or a roof-raising would bring out the fiddlers from a day's riding. Contests among them were as common and as enjoyable as camp meetings. They were conduits for the music of the frontier. Antiquarians of our generation have threshed this lowly art, with a surprising yield. The songs the frontiersmen sang ranged over a field hardly to be surveyed. The native genius for adaptability was nowhere more resplendent than in this music, making improbable transformations in easy stride. The march time of a walk-around, intended for display in black-face, became a war tune and in time a sacred anthem, the inheritors of the lost cause having consecrated "Dixie." One of Watts's hymns was corrupted to the Log Cabin campaign. Mormon soldiers going out to crush the army of Albert Sidney Johnston adapted to their need "De Camptown Races", which Foster had composed for the minstrel stage. His "Susanna", of the same species, became a celebration of the trail to Oregon and the gold in Alta California. The folk seized upon fires, shipwrecks, and jail deliveries as promptly as their descendants make use of transatlantic flights. The resulting ballads worked westward with the migration and have sometimes been fossilized in their perfect state. More often they have incorporated immemorably old French songs that reached the Mississippi with Canadian voyageurs from the north, the *volkslieder* that crossed from Germany with the emigrants of the Thirties, famine-redolent hoedowns from Ireland, and Spanish love songs that came northward from Taos or lingered on among the chivalry of New Orleans. A Montana cowboy, singing for amusement and the reassurance of his steers, might voice the melancholy of Oregon caravans, and through it, the anti-Catholic sentiments of Massachusetts, the desire of Count Zinzendorf to wash in the Lamb's blood, or the impeccable passions of opera under the Directory. And all of them would have been Americanized almost beyond identification.

Notably, the songs that made the American passage with seventeenth-century Englishmen, sometimes called Puritans. These journeyed westward with the frontier, and sometimes they lingered on, so that Nebraska and Idaho as well as the poor-white mountains have discovered Lord Lovel riding away on a journey that would keep him from his true love forever. In Missouri, young Sam Clemens might hear about the cherry tree that bowed down for the Virgin, though Twelfth Night was not a Calvinist feast day, or about the cuckoo, a bird not discoverable in the woods beyond Cardiff Hill.[1] Illiterate villagers across the width of the Great Valley sang about one Barbry Ellen, a heroine unknown to the native saga. She might be displayed in the native idiom:

> She looked to the east and she looked to the west
> And she seen the corpse a-comin'
> Set you down upon this road
> Till I git one kiss upon him.

The grammar of "Barbara Allen" had been a little alien to the conjugation. All along the Mississippi and Ohio, all through the

---

[1] This is a guess. That young Clemens must have heard these ballads throughout his childhood is a conclusion necessitated by available facts. But there is no evidence in his works or memoirs that he ever did. One recognizes the ballad formulas in the chivalry of Tom Sawyer—that is all.

backwoods, joyless extroverts were singing about the Gypsy Laddie, the Wife of Usher's Well, the Farmer's Curst Wife, and hundreds of other personages of an alien balladry, and were adapting tunes and words to their own experience. Milk-white steeds are perhaps a ridiculous conception for Hannibal, where steeds were only plugs. But very certainly they were mentioned there in songs now of interest to collectors, along with such other ridiculous formulas as snow-white breasts (snow-balls with ripe strawberries stuck butt-ended onto 'em, Sut Lovingood made them), thorns and briars, red gold and yellow gold, castles by the sea, lords and ladies and magicians, nightingales, and whipped apple trees. The frontiersman could record

> Out of her breast grew a red, red rose
> And out of his'n there grew a briar

with no awareness that he was committing an adaptation or grievously offending against a theory.

Children listened to this wide, rich music. So did the childlike race of slaves. Melody is not the genius of the jubilees, whose airs have been traced through all this complexity. Simply, the Negro took a melody where he found it, but mainly from minstrel ballads or camp-meeting hymns, and then transmuted it. Rhythms beyond the attainment of whites and a genius for intricate harmonization were his portion from Africa. These he welded with the music he heard and the most poignant American art resulted. There was, except for the tales, no other expression out of slavery. A Biblical mythology, a Biblical immediacy, overlay the ghouls and spirits of Africa, and with this alphabet the Negro spelled the longing, the labor, and the terror of his estate.

Here a certain emphasis is necessary. The undertaking has been to discern what went into the crucible in which the author of "Huckleberry Finn" was shaped. Slavery, in its least repellent form, was part of Hannibal, of St. Petersburg, and Dawson's Landing. The boy Samuel Clemens entered wholly into the slave's world. It was a much more developed, much more various world than is ingenuously believed. Abysses of horror it contained were to have their share in the soul of Samuel Clemens, but his shaping soul was to bear other impresses of that world. Fundamental among these was the singing of the slaves.

By day, sometimes, one could hear a Negro in the fields or in the kitchen, crooning something that sounded like a jig and made merry with Joshua or Zekiel. That was gay, but when night crept out from the forest, the singing created something at once awful and sublime. Here the fables of Sunday-school were given a tremendous reality. The Son of Nun shouted and the walls came tumblin' down; bands of angels filled a sky swept with radiance from a chariot of fire; Daniel walked into a furnace but the Lord delivered him and the blood came trinkling down. Moses smote upon the waters, the sea divided, and then ol' Pharaoh's army done got drowned. Meanwhile King Jedus came a-ridin' crost Jurdan to feed his lams. . . . Ecstasy lifted the songs above the fables till a race spoke, out of its suffering, a poetry unequalled on this continent. Go down, Moses, tell ol' Pharaoh to let my people go! The chariot swung lower, oh, yes, Lord! — green trees abendin', poor sinner stands atremblin', the trumpet sounds within my soul, I ain't got long to stay here. And nobody knows the trouble I see, nobody knows but Jedus. I know moonlight, I know starlight — I lie in the grave an' stretch out my arms — I lay dis body down. A motherless child, that's what I feel like; Oh, yes, Lord, a long way from home. But I'm goin' to tell him the road was rocky, I'm goin' to tell God all of my troubles when I git home. The trumpet sounds within my soul! Swing low, sweet chariot. I want to cross over where all is peace. . . . A humble race, simpler than most, more joyful, more bawdy, finding expression for a labor and a sorrow not now to be comprehended.

The child listened and the trumpet sounded in his soul. . . . Mrs. Charles Warner's brilliant playing yielded at last to the moonlight and she left the piano, pinching out the candles so that the room might have only the silver from without. Hannibal had been buried under years extraordinarily crowded and Hannibal meant nothing, anyway, to these careful, pleasant folk in Hartford. But the moon was full. And after a while Samuel Clemens stood up and one could see the shadow on his hair. His eyes were closed and he began to sing, song after song, all jubilees, slowly, with an infinite sadness. One had an awed notion that Samuel Clemens was not here in Hartford, that Hartford had ceased to exist. Still he sang and, in the moonlight, his face was strained. "He put his two hands up to his head," Katy Leary said, "just as though all the sorrow of them negroes was upon him," and he began to sing, "Nobody knows the trouble I see." Nobody . . . nobody, surely, in Hartford. He ended the "Glory Hallelujah" with a great shout. But for the moment, in Hartford, Samuel Clemens was a motherless child, a long way from home. . . . He was always singing them. His children would find him at the piano in the Hartford house, singing about King Jesus on his white horse, or the wheel in a wheel, or about Moses or Joshua, the Son of Nun. What made George Cable's smug piety tolerable, on that four months' tour, was Cable's memory of the jubilees. They would sing them in cramped hotel rooms, in railway compartments, in deserted streets late at night — alone, or to Major Pond, who would secretly instruct the cab driver to take the longest way home, so that he could listen to a poetry that had welled up in lost and nameless singers, in Hannibal, before the war. . . . Susy had died, and the world grew a more fitting habitation for the damned human race. He was in Lucerne, desperately trying to crowd work over the thought of her. Some of the Fisk singers came there and he saw the well-known chords overcome the apathy of Swiss and Germans who sat behind their beer mugs prepared to be bored. Hannibal could come home to Lucerne, and he wrote Joe Twichell that in the jubilees America had produced the perfectest flower of the ages, and he wished it were a foreign product, so that she would worship it and lavish money on it and go perfectly crazy over it. "Away back in the beginning — to my mind — their music made all other vocal music cheap; and that early notion is emphasized now. It is utterly beautiful, to me; and it moves me more than any other music can."

It was Hannibal that throbbed in these songs, with their imperfect healing for a man who was aging and had lost his child. He had written "All say 'How hard it is that we have to die' — a strange complaint to come from the mouths of people who have had to live" — and this maxim of Pudd'nhead Wilson's has required, in our day, the machinery of an exquisite and immaterial analysis according to the Vienna school. But the explanations of Freud and Jung hardly appear necessary for the singer of "I lie in de grave an' stretch out my arms — I lay dis body down."

The air of this region is fatal to the Muses. — Duvallon, "Vue de la Colonie Espagnole du Mississippi" (1803).

On the frontier: *lachrymoso* by Mr. Waldo Frank.

Pioneer and Puritan met on a base of psychological and temperamental unity. They merged and became one. The Puritan's nature fitted him superbly to be a Pioneer. The pioneer existence made permanent the Puritan's nature. . . . We have seen a genius like Mark Twain stifled beneath the brutal burden of the pioneering West. . . . Puritanism in its historic form had controlled the direction of pioneering. . . . When you study these long, rigid rows of dessicated men and women, you feel that you are in the presence of some form of life that has hardened but not grown. . . . Their jaws are rigid. Their eyes are as lead, they have so long denied the beauties of the world. Their complexions are like greasy ash. On the brow of the young man is the bland complacency of a feeble mind, and the shoulders of the girl twitch with the energy she dares not utter. . . . Their veins have hardened. Their blood has soured. . . . A drooping generation, godless yet stomachless: without any joy beyond the dogged cultivation of self-pain. Insanity is common. Neurosis is birthright. Life, downed by precept, has become a hidden thing that gnaws and festers. . . . No aspiration beyond the immediate object. No loveliness in women beyond the bare business of their sex. A people stripped indeed for material possession. A people stripped, in consequence, even of the capacity to enjoy it. Men who cultivate alone the soil [*sic*] soon lose the sun that makes it fecund. . . . A starved sick world. Rocky and stubborn and full of weeds. A world in which old passions lie stiff upon the ground and rot, and poison the water and blot the air.[2]

[2] I may seem to misrepresent Mr. Frank, since several of these quotations (all taken from "Our America") are devoted not to frontier America but to

On the frontier, variation by Mr. Van Wyck Brooks.

A desert of human sand! — the barrenest spot in all Christendom, surely, for the seed of genius to fall in. . . . Essentially, America was not happy: it was a dark jumble of decayed faiths, of unconfessed class distinctions, of inarticulate misery . . . it was a nation that had no folk-music, no folk-art, no folk-poetry, or next to none, to express it, to console it. It was a horde-life, a herd-life, an epoch without sun or stars, the twilight of a human spirit that had nothing upon which to feed but the living waters of Camden and the dried manna of Concord.[3]

On the frontier, variation by Mr. Lewis Mumford.

Woman was the chief enemy of the pioneer: she courageously rose to the burdens of the new life and demanded her place side by side in the legislature; but in the end she had her revenge, in temperance clubs, in anti-vice societies, or in the general tarnation tidiness of Tom Sawyer's aunt . . . the epic of the covered wagon, leaving behind it deserted villages, bleak cities, depleted soils, and the sick and exhausted souls that engraved their epitaphs in Mr. Master's "Spoon River Anthology." Against the genuine heroism and derring-do that accompanied this movement, and against the real gains that it achieved here and there in the spread of social well being, must be set off the crudities of the pioneer's sexual life, his bestial swilling and drinking and bullying and his barbarities in dealing with the original inhabitants.

its modern inheritors. But it is Mr. Frank's charmingly simple thesis that everything unlovely in contemporary America proceeds from something detestable in frontier America. He specifically asserts these sentiments about the frontier, but I have sometimes selected the sequelæ as more compactly phrased. A certain lyric quality in the prose of "Our America" dictates its selection rather than that of Mr. Frank's later books—in which the same thesis is maintained, but at a certain sacrifice in intelligibility.

[3] While this book remains in galley proof, announcement has just been made that a revised edition of Mr. Brooks's "Ordeal of Mark Twain" is to be issued. Mr. Brooks's publishers at first refused me permission to quote from his book on the specific ground that some of the opinions I desired to quote from it were to be reversed in the second edition. As the reader will see, I consider Mr. Brooks's ideas, as expressed in the first edition, wholly wrong. Because they have dominated all discussion of Mark Twain since their appearance, I have no choice but to examine them herein. The fact that Mr. Brooks has altered some of them twelve years after they founded a school of American criticism is significant and, I think, revelatory. The reader must bear in mind that all my quotations from "The Ordeal of Mark Twain" are taken from the first edition.

Incompatibility is perceptible, but a residue remains: it was all pretty detestable.

A critical theory is a notion which may be converted to the assault of what one dislikes, and to submit a sentiment to the correction of fact is unquestionably an irrelevance. Thus to inquire what a theorist means by "Pioneer", "Puritan", or "frontier", or to request evidence of suppression of emotion, fear of sex, the non-existence of folk art, anæsthesia to loveliness, or any other villainy charged against the Puritan-Pioneer, would be to commit rudeness.

There is no desire, here, to defend the frontiersman by writing an apologia on his behalf. He was, God knows, not a genteel person. He neglected to praise "Moby Dick" and "Leaves of Grass" a generation before they were written, as has been mentioned, and a good many of his characteristics were deplorable. In the more literary suburbs of New York City to-day he would be unlikely to hold up his end of the conversation and he would certainly eat with a knife. Nevertheless, whatever may be thus deplored, the frontiersman was not in any particular what the theorists make him out. Let the assertion be repeated. The frontier was in no particular whatever such a place as theories like those quoted make it out to have been. Not one item in the lines quoted from Messrs. Frank, Brooks, and Mumford, who are merely the most prominent theorists, can be substantiated.

This preface is concerned with the frontier only in so far as the frontier may have begotten the books of Samuel Clemens. It has, therefore, no time to examine palpably absurd generalizations. But the Puritan is nowhere discoverable on the frontier, if the Puritan is a man who hates loveliness, fears passion, represses his instincts, and abstains from joy. The religion of the frontier was — the religion of the time. Evangelism is evangelism, whether one find it in Lancaster, in Kings County, or along Salt River. Evangelism racked the frontier with visions of hell and the major symptoms of hysteria — at certain periods, among certain classes. But to suppose that Peter Cartwright, a Savonarola of the frontier, succeeded in destroying dancing and jewelry and fornication throughout interior America, is to behold the

Reverend Billy Sunday making a Thaïs of a night-club hostess. The camp meeting was truly a harrowing experience to a fair one fifth of those who attended it. It was also, like the Sunday services which the frontier attended unanimously, a social diversion, a commercial bazaar, and a focus of dynamic joy. Mr. Thomas Beer has recorded Mark Twain's remarks about campmeeting babies and the phenomenon alluded to is a commonplace.

For the sexual customs of the frontier, like all its customs, were freer than those of the seaboard. The notion of Puritanical abhorrence of sex is critical cliché and has no correspondence in fact. Its conflict with other clichés of the theory, the size of pioneer families (which were frequently large) and the ruthlessness with which a pioneer wore out a succession of wives (as sometimes happened), is obvious. The clichés must have been born of miracle, for the frontiersman was not often a hypocrite and made little effort to disguise himself. To him, universally, a virgin was a woman who had not married — for Charlotte McGinnity's achievement in retaining her virginity till she was fifteen was a damned good record for his vicinity. He suffered few inhibitions of this nature. Marriages clustered in the three months succeeding every camp meeting, and if young people were to suppress their instincts, the dances, hoedowns, roof raisings, fanning bees, bobsled rides, barbecues, fiddling matches, and a hundred other kinds of parties were a singularly paradoxical way of restraining them.

Behold the sex-abhorring Puritan-Pioneer suppressing his instincts and abstaining from joy while he describes a girl whom he is courting; "She shows among women like a sunflower among dog fennel, or a hollihock in a patch of smartweed. Such a bosom! Just think of two snow balls with a strawberry stuck butt-ended into both of them. She takes exactly fifteen inches of garter clear of the knot, stands sixteen and a half hands high and weighs one hundred and twenty-six in her petticoat before breakfast. She could crawl through a whisky-barrel with both heads stove out, while you could lock the top hoop of a churn, or a big dog collar, round the hugging place. . . . Her ankles were as round and not much bigger than the wrist of a rifle, and when she was dancing, or making up a bed, or getting over a fence — oh, durn such women!"[4]

Simplicity is not precisely simple-mindedness. Mr. Carl Sandburg has lately revived a few of the tunes played for dances at such frolics as one that was to follow the wedding of Sicily Burns. Imitators follow him, and it is possible to recover "Money Musk" and "Rocky Mountain" and "Ol' Dan Tucker" and "Weevily Wheat." Hundreds of others may be found in the glee-books, "singers", and "minstrelsies" that peddlers were solicitous to offer among those who abstained from joy. Other thousands have perished. But where are "Sister Phoebe", "Forked Deer", "The Frog with a Fiddle" — where are the thousand others to which a joyless race measured out its dances? They will be found, no doubt, but there is need for another kind of research. The joyless frolic itself should be restored. A barn or a threshing floor, the schoolhouse — church, perhaps — with the slab benches shoved back; or merely an expanse of clay under the stars, well trodden down and watered, and trodden again. There was a platform for fiddlers and perhaps another for the personage who called the turns. There were sauce-

---

[4] Sut Lovingood, in "Blown up with Soda", describing Sicily Burns. I have translitterated Sut's dialect, for the protection of the reader. This passage from the newspaper humor more extensively studied in Chapter IV is one item from a continuity. No absurdity in the ideologues' picture of the frontier is more childlike than Mr. Brooks's belief that the pioneer had no sex life or Mr. Mumford's assumption that what he had must have been crude. Plain absurdities should not require rebuttal; but if one has not experienced frontier society and distrusts the conclusions of common sense, a brief examination of the realistic literature of the frontier will suffice to make clear that the relations of men and women remained the relations of men and women even beyond the Mississippi in 1845. Perhaps "Sut Lovingood's Yarns" or Cobb's "Mississippi Scenes" is in itself enough. If not, a somewhat longer education should include the following, selected arbitrarily from hundreds of examples: "Going to Bed before a Young Lady" and "Dick Harlan's Tennessee Frolic" in "A Quarter Race in Kentucky"; "Billy Warrick's Courtship and Wedding" and "Life and Manners in Arkansas" in "The Big Bear of Arkansaw"; "A Tight Race Considerin' " and "Love in a Garden" in "Odd Leaves from the Life of a Louisiana Swamp Doctor"; "Nettle Bottom Ball", "Yaller Pledges", and "Settlement Fun" in "Streaks of Squatter Life" and "A Fair Offender" in "The Widow Rugby's Husband."

pans of punch and an eight-gallon keg of whisky for the bestial drinking alluded to. The farm-wife's hearth, or stove if civilization had progressed that far, blazed for frontier cookery to feed the guests from twenty miles around. And, asking forgiveness, gentlemen, frontier cookery was not a matter solely of grease-bread and fried pork.

All day they had labored, the "men who cultivated alone the soil" and their women who had no loveliness. They jolted twenty miles on horseback for a frolic. They were not, of course, dancing along Murray Hill. A beau's calfskin vest with the hair left on would offend the fastidious. Unaccustomed shoes might so irk a frankly nubile wench that, to sustain competition, she must take them off and dance barefoot. The cosmetics she had employed were no more sophisticated than thick cream, flour, and the juice of strawberries. Her bustle, though adequate, was probably extemporized from a cushion or even more forthright material. Her stockings, when she had any, were her own handiwork. ["Het Goins, stop tumblin' that bed an' tie your sock." "Thankee, marm, it's a longer stockin' than you've got — *look at it*". . . . . "Come here, Suse Thompson, and let me pin your dress behind. Your back looks adzactly like a blaze in a white oak." "My *back* ain't nuffin' to you, Mister Smarty."] Their amenities composed a pattern — civilization constructed a code which possessed no refinement and no inhibition.

A personage stood on a platform, or a log or a chair, and uttered calls. Jigs and reels were native to the frontier and to them were added the manifold inventions of the slaves. There appeared also gavottes that had traveled from Paris and boleros from Madrid, by way of Montreal, New Orleans, and St. Louis, and round dances that had the common man turning in waltzes and polkas inconceivable to the repressed. Whisky and the punch in the milkpan had to be replenished. Breast of partridge, pigeon pie, conserve of wild crab apple, honey cake, and intricate confections of nuts and fruit in jellied homemade wines sustained them. The elders withdrew to the benches, where it is unlikely they occupied themselves with infant damnation. The marriageable danced on, withdrawing into darkness for what was neither a suppression of emotion nor the crudities of the pioneer's sexual life. There was meanwhile a boisterousness of buck-and-wing solo, of fighting, or extemporized drama imitated from the strolling players. Then, when the seven stars had gone down, the common man rode homeward, his girl astride behind him, or slept on the host's floor in rows, with a line drawn chastely between the sexes. . . . Simplicity, one insists, is not simple-mindedness; nor is it, quite, the bile of repression. Here is merely the common man, diverting himself with the means at his command. And doing so universally, invariably, with a persistence that would not seem to be native to Puritans. The earlier experiments of Mark Twain include a party in which a young man creates merriment by tumbling among girls when he is wearing only a nightshirt, and he is seen at another party where inhibited girls strangely laugh at young Sam Clemens dancing naked in the moonlight.

Three sides of the village were prairie and forest, where boys found an enchantment that was to become the very tissue of certain books. The village itself was the abode of the common man and, while it remained St. Petersburg, had the graces of leisure, and humanity, and sun. The actual frontier had withdrawn westward and northward: here remained an ease in its wake. Life was without pressure. There were no castes, except the three constant ones, — the respectable, the squatters, and the slaves. Neither wealth nor poverty really existed, for the earth was opulent to all and disproportionately enriched no one. The village was a little world, where an observant boy laid the basis for five sevenths of his books, but a somewhat simplified one. It was a steamboat landing, a street or two, and roads leading into the countryside. Its traffic was outward bound in hemp, tobacco, flour, pork, and lard; and, from without, products of the factories that had not yet reached Hannibal. There was coal at hand, but no one mined it; there was limestone, but kilns and quarries were important only to boys who played among them. A drowsy sunlight — and little more. There were courts and judges. There were stores and warehouses. There were

"groceries" — thus, and as "doggeries", the frontier distinguished its saloons — and if the name of a stream in "Tom Sawyer" is evidence, a stillhouse. There were Sunday-schools and
meetinghouses, where slab benches and puncheon floors were
still thought adequate. These fostered the embryo societies of
women which were to become important in America and the uniformed parades that seduced boys into propriety. A newspaper
— there was always at least one — printed the literature of
Europe and the East, made a lyceum for the exhibition of local
talents, and cannonaded opponents with the lyric fervor that
has distinguished politics in America.

Joe Harper had been nearly to Coonville and Becky
Thatcher was a globe trotter, having traveled the full distance
from her home in Herculaneum. Rumor of distances but little
disturbed the village — except by one medium at which we
shall arrive in a moment — and the man who had visited St.
Louis had led a full and rich life. The fantastic Senator Benton,
like Hoss Allen, came to commemorate the Fourth of July
and brought with him mention of unbelievable places and activities as little credible as the romances of Walter Scott and
Emerson Bennett which the village admired with an unpreju-
diced catholicity. . . . A drowsy sunshine — a village simple
and not of the world, provincial, ignorant, and obscure. But, be
very sure, not therefore repellent or contemptible. That the
villagers were not too enlightened is apparent; that they were
therefore fools or savages or Puritans is a judgment that lacks
a probably desirable logic. At least, they created St. Petersburg,
a lovely idyll that has neither peer nor competitor in American
literature.

The boy went among them, certainly, and was well content.
The village came to have an impelling loveliness in his mind.
It was hardly separable into parts. In Hartford, in New York, in
London and Florence and Vienna, he was always harking back
to it, nostalgic for a known beauty. "I can call back the solemn
twilight and mystery of the deep woods, the earthy smells, the
faint odors of the wild flowers, the sheen of rain-washed foliage
. . . the far-off hammering of woodpeckers and the muffled

drumming of wood pheasants in the remoteness of the forests
. . . the oaks purple, the hickories marked with gold, the maples
and the sumachs luminous with crimson fires. . . . I can remember the howling of the wind and the quaking of the house on
stormy nights, and how snug and cozy one felt under the
blankets, listening; and how the powdery snow used to sift in,
around the sashes, and lie in little ridges on the floor. . . . Fried
chicken, roast pig; wild and tame turkeys, ducks and geese;
venison just killed; squirrels, rabbits, pheasants, partridges,
prairie chickens; biscuits, hot batter cakes, hot 'wheat bread',
hot rolls, hot corn pone; fresh corn boiled on the ear, succo-
tash, butter beans, string beans, tomatoes, peas, sweet potatoes;
buttermilk, sweet milk, 'clabber'; watermelons, muskmelons,
cantaloupes — all fresh from the garden; apple pie, peach pie,
pumpkin pie, apple dumplings, peach cobbler. . . . It was
a heavenly place for a boy."

And on the fourth side, where the roads ran down — the
Mississippi. Cosmopolis. For on the fourth side St. Petersburg
opened on the world. Here the energy of America boiled violently, and here passed, daily, all that St. Petersburg was not.
The village slumbered in its sun till smoke was black above
the bluffs and some one cried "Steamboat a-comin'!" Then it
woke and went to the wharves to touch the infinite. This was
pageantry. For the rivers were the conduits of the national adventure and the Mississippi was fable itself given life. The
boats themselves were objects of romance, but the greater romance was the bales and casks they carried, the trade route of
Marco Polo spun out to touch a waterside village of the great
river, and most of all, the men who drove the boats and the
men they carried.

Here passed the world. A boundless vigor was making
America something it had not been. The years were an acceleration. The border pushed farther to the north, the west, and the
southwest. The families whom Miss Martineau had seen swarming toward Texas snatched their land from its extemporized
oppressors, steered it near the Union Jack, and then brought it

safely home. Marcus Whitman's mission at Waiilatpu prospered and trains of white-tops crawled toward it endlessly.
Upriver from St. Petersburg, Joseph Smith was dispatched to
a final meeting with the God he had so often patronized and the
wretched Mormons roved westward to the Dead Sea. Wagons,
too, left for Santa Fe and Taos, where trade was brisk; and of
the white-tops that crawled toward Waiilatpu, some turned
southwestward at the head of Raft River for the kingdom of
Sutter the Swiss. The young Bostonian, Francis Parkman, who
traveled westward for health and adventure, saw them all,
Texans and Mormons, the white-tops loosed for Oregon and
California, the Taos trade — and the dragoons. For British
agents at the mountain camp fires had looked with concern on
the journeyings of Captain Bonneville and Captain Wilkes
and the march of the white-tops, and on Marcus Whitman at
Waiilatpu. The complements of marines on Her Majesty's war
vessels were doubled and James K. Polk was an anxiety over-
seas, for the common man sang about 54° 40'. Mr. Polk began
with the firmness promised his electors but his mood changed,
for the Texans made a wedding gift to their new nation and it
was war. The chorus of 54° 40' was allowed to perish and Oregon came under the flag while troops hurried southwestward.
Texas was secured and with it all California, so that the wretched
Mormons fleeing that damned flag found it blowing over Yarba
Buena and the Bay of St. Francis and found it irrevocably sovereign in the alkali wastes that lay about the Dead Sea. The
continent was now wholly the common man's and the white-
tops made larger swarms moving westward. And Marcus Whitman would soon be dead at Waiilatpu, for the Indians to whom
he preached the pale God looked at the white-tops and understood them.

The common man fled westward. A thirsty land swallowed
him insatiably. There is no comprehending the frenzy of the
American folk-migration. God's gadfly had stung us mad.
"Westward," Mr. Masefield says, "till all are drowned, those
Lemmings go." Their little brains, he thinks, are burned with
the memory of a land westward from death. Poetry has no ac-

ceptance in seminars of history, but this is as adequate to explain the œstrus for an empty land as any reason historians have offered.

But westward they went and the land drank them up. Meanwhile the rivers were their highways and the energy of their passing made an incandescence. And the fourth side of St. Petersburg was the Mississippi, along which the great world passed. Oh, quite all of it. There were the barges, the broadhorns, and the scows — the slow freight of the world moved by creatures of terror and romance. There were rafts of timber and of lumber floating from the forests to build the houses of democracy by the half-million. And the steamboats. Boats of the Cairo line and the Memphis line tied up daily at the wharf. So did boats from the Illinois River, the Red River, the White River, the Missouri, the upper Mississippi, the Ohio, the Monongahela, the Tennessee, the Cumberland, the Arkansas, the Yazoo. The "stately packets of the Orleans trade" seldom ventured this far — for this was the Upper River — or when they did, enroute to the Falls of St. Anthony, stopped only on hail and for the convenience of passengers. But these sufficed.

When Samuel Clemens grew up and went tirelessly about the world, he found no one, he said, whom he had not met before on the river. He spoke the truth. The packets bore the democrat swarming westward, and with him all the life that flooded in his wake. From the four corners of America they came, and the corners of the world. Here passed commerce, the factory system, the machine age — if one craves these tags — traders, drovers, farmers, homesteaders, tinmen, miners, masons, shipwrights, actors, minstrels, mesmerists, phrenologists, bear leaders, circus men, gamblers, prostitutes, and prophets. The sportsmen whom Harriet Martineau had seen were one group of a thousand among God's English who shot their game and went home to write books about it. Frenchmen and Germans and Swedes mingled with them and wrote books. All the world, quite all of it, paused at St. Petersburg while roustabouts hustled bales and cases down the gangplank to a coonjine song, and while Sam Clemens gaped, seeing strange clothes and hearing stranger tongues. He gaped — and the first of his writing that has been recovered recorded the passing of a strange creature from the world outside.

No symbol wholly comprehends the Mississippi. The vast life of a vast nation existed there. And floating downstream came every variant of human experience. . . . For instance, the Pilgrims whom Timothy Flint saw. God's word had reached them in eastern Canada, bidding them sell all that they had and set out for the New Jerusalem. They would find it in the mystical direction along the ways taken by those whom the gadfly had stung — southwestward. They pooled the money their sales had made and started west. They traveled in single file, the prophet at the head, and as they walked they spoke to no one but only chanted "Praise God! Praise God! Repent, fast, pray!" Piety required them, through revelation, to stand like statues when they halted and to torture the impure flesh with starvation and with aberrant exercises. Moreover, God said, the good life consisted in wearing loathsome clothes and in loving filth. They passed southwestward through Vermont and New York, where the native hankering for mad religions commended them. Augmented by converts, fifty true believers in all, they reached the Ohio, floated down it to the Mississippi, and set out on those tolerant waters for New Jerusalem. They were for a time at New Madrid but moved always southward, expecting the lost city. An island appeared to be at least its outpost; so they halted there, redoubled their aberrations, scourged the vile flesh, and praised God. The file of the saved passed along the waterside, the prophet leading, followed in order by his males, their wives, and the starved children. Their clothes were daubed with filth and they gave off a loathsome odor, but they chanted "Praise God! Praise God!" Housewives ran from them, and even the rivermen fell silent, while children who had been playing on the wharves fled terrified. The Pilgrims lost their pooled money to boatmen, who joined them professing righteousness. The New Jerusalem still beckoned, though half of them died from ague and infections generated by filth. They moved southward once more, the city of gold a mist in dazzled eyes, and there were six of them at the mouth of the Arkansas when Flint saw them. Six of them sucking their food from a trough through hollow canes, flogging the vile flesh, and shivering in ague fits while they prepared to move onward toward the city of fine gold.

All the world moved down the Mississippi. And here was Hannibal, at the waterside. It was an idyll and a cosmos. The democrat possessed America and his incandescent energy was making it something it had not been. This was democracy or the New Jerusalem. The dilemma of democracy has been insoluble to more minds than Mark Twain's. Here at least was its lovelier horn, a waterside village drowsing in the sun between the prairies and the chocolate waters of the Mississippi.

One would record the idyll. One would make Hannibal into St. Petersburg with the forests and the river. Then, after a time, there would be something else. St. Petersburg would grow into Hadleyburg and Dawson's Landing, for the dilemma had another horn. And then Nigger Jim and Huckleberry Finn would put out on a fragment of a lumber raft, by night, and the current would take them southward through eternity.

III

DAWSON'S LANDING

THE upriver migration of suckers gave a name to the democrats who swarmed into Illinois. It was shouted at them by the Missourians from the far shore of the river. Pride demanded retaliation and the democrat was fertile in invention. From the eastern bank he shouted back an epithet to describe the Missourians: let them be called Pukes.

The tender-minded recoil from the frontier for many reasons: one abhorrence may be its demonstration that nature is not concerned with loveliness, perfect societies, or New Jerusalem. Westward the Lemmings came and on the frontier they survived, they perished, or they fell into apathy, but all fates were equally indifferent to the frontier, which would not be personified. A wilderness does no coddling and the energy of a race that moved to subdue it must sometimes fail. No loveliness attended such failure. The tide swept on and there was never a possibility that it might be halted. This was a necessity, a determinism, a tiderace of life. It swept on. When it passed there remained the habitations of the fit — or call them, if you like, the Philistines, the puritanical, the pioneers. These, under any name, had moved with the rhythm, though the rhythm may have been deplorable. There remained also the habitations of the unfit. Theory sometimes calls these poets and frustrated artists; it calls them also withered, repellent and loathsome. They had not moved with the rhythm; and the frontier, an impersonal selection, discarded them without rancor and without pity. The idea may be studied in the works of Charles Darwin — who conceived nature as dispassionate.

They were everywhere a thin deposit on society, an interpenetrating influence. The tide passed over the Appalachians; its rejectamenta there were called "mountain whites." It passed through the forests, where the discards remained "pineywoods people." In the canebrakes they were "clay eaters"; along the turbid waters, "river rats." Generically, they were "squatters." The term at first implied admiration, for it signified people who had outdistanced the surveyors and had driven a stake into land that no one had claimed. It passed, with a lessening commendation, to those who upheld the right of pioneers against absentee owners of land patents. Then the tide swept by and, without praise, a squatter was one whom the tide had left to rot amidst refuse on the beach. Literature knows them chiefly under the name of a Missouri county a few miles down river from Hannibal: the Pike County Man.

The image is of men in calico coats, jean pants, and yarn suspenders. They wear no beards except a fringe at the chin; in intent, they are elsewhere clean-shaven. The stubble is matched by matted hair that falls to the shoulders. Their skin is pasty, between the color of jaundice and the pallor of a corpse. This hue results, perhaps, from a habit they have of sucking pellets of clay between the upper lip and the gums, or it may be the stigma of malaria. They chew tobacco, universally and endlessly. Calico coat, jean pants, hickory shirt compose three garments, a third or two thirds more than their females wear. These are frowsy in coveralls of linsey-woolsey. The children of such couplings recline in sun or mire, clad in a briefer garment or none at all. Men, women, children, infants at slackened breasts, are alike drowsy, apathetic, and damned. The energy of the frontier has departed from them.

That this description is lifted from the first chapter of "The Gilded Age" signifies little, for it is repeated in other books of Mark Twain's and was a commonplace in literature before he made use of his observation. It portrays, merely, the type species, the squatter. Into the mentality of this race much exploring has been done and explanations of its unconscious have been hazarded. They are not relevant here. But the presence of these defeated on the frontier is responsible for many misconceptions and it is here suggested that the squatter, the rejected, is the frontiersman that the theories know.

Is the frontier distinguished for squalor, unimaginable lethargy, filth, repellent social relations, a hideousness of wretched life, the degradation of mankind to a larval form that burrowed protectively into the clay? Unquestionably . . . in part. Defeat is defeat. The frontier left its wreckage, those who in one way or another its selection found to be unfit. Hence the pathology of the frontier — and one ventures to point out that it was a pathology. At the basis of much of it was — well, let us commit an impiety. This slothfulness, this utter lethargy, is not a neurosis; it does not flow from Puritanism, repression, or the commercial ruthlessness of America. These people, being rejected, were too poor to buy or make shoes, and their privies were the naked earth. Medical science had not yet studied the etiology of the hookworm disease.

The frontier is the acknowledged source of many insanities. American social ideas have been warped and colored and transformed by it. It has been an unimaginable ferment, a stew of violent yeasts out of which have risen the gigantic fungi of our national delusions. The millennial energy that flooded westward to find or establish New Jerusalem flooded eastward again in wave after wave of messianic delusion. From the frontier eastward passed religious frenzy — whether of holiness, or greenbackery, of anti-rents furor, or populism, or prohibition. The frontiersman has been a rider on a holy quest, dropping his scythe to form the charge under bright banners. He has desired to die for some vision, no matter what. The vision changes, the fire behind it burns steady. New Jerusalem in one form or another, whether its pinnacles glisten in the name of free silver or of a soul unstained by tobacco. A cloudland, a mirage. It is hot-blooded. It is a fever.

The word is fever. . . . Historians have made a pretty graph of the epidemics that spread over the great valley. Cholera and yellow fever and dysentery, "the bloody flux", were a constant along the frontier: they heated the blood and whole populations were racked with them. Yet no historian, however fluent in describing the psychology of land-mania, has thought to explore the mental sequelæ of these fevers. And no historian has yet done research in the life and times of the archvillain of the frontier, *Anopheles.*

The forests were flattened and strange fevers fed upon those who had cut them down. Ploughs broke prairie soil for the first time and fevers rioted in the blood of those who had driven them. The valley was the world's watershed. Its streams ran sluggish between low banks over which the springtime floods spread for the creation of bayous, swamps, and marshes — where gigantic flocks of wildfowl nested, moccasins slid into brown water, and the frontiersman came about his business. For centuries before him the fevers that he now found had been explained as he explained them. There was a *mala aria* — an evil air. Where ground was broken or trees felled, wherever vapors hung above low-lying land, clearly, a miasma was bred. The fevers came, alternations of cold that sank inward and of delirious sweats that sent the mind ballooning among cloud shapes. Medical lore classified them by the appearance of the chill. They might be quotidian or alternative or tertian or quaternian. They lasted about sixty days, two months of frenetic languor while the mind passed among shapeless things in pursuit of visions. Then they subsided and the frontiersman went more vigorously about his work; but microörganisms remained in his blood, pending next year's *Anopheles.* Against chills and fever the frontier exhausted its *materia medica.* Mineralists attacked them with calomel, so vigorously that the frontiersman's teeth fell out. Herbalists griped his bowels with jalap. Empirics bled him. Naturopaths boiled him in steam vapors and put him to bed between iced blankets. Grandmothers dug in woods and gardens for bitter yarbs — sheep saffron, elecampane, rue, pennyroyal, hoarhound, camomile, fenugreek. Squaws gave such plants a ruder name and stewed them to incantations hallowed by centuries of tribal lore; among them, traveling northward from Peru, came the specific for these torments, "Cinchony bark." Black wenches who had spilled chicken's blood on corn meal with appropriate charms anointed the Calvinist pioneer with unguents that had been sanctified by Congo deities.

Quite uselessly. Throughout the duration of the frontier every one who was not biologically immune suffered one or another of these bilious fevers. Malaria was endemic. Few escaped it. Some developed immunity after a year or two, others must expect the old torment annually, with the turn of summer or the approach of autumn. . . . The frontiersman, we have seen, rallied after some sixty days and went about his routine with a clearer head. But the microörganisms slept uneasily in his blood and, mostly, there was a thin sweat on his forehead. A clinical thermometer would have shown about one degree of fever. This was the constant temperature of a population.

The frontiersman has attached himself to one delusion after another. He was a crusader who asked only to attach his fiery loyalty to a vision madder than last year's. And have the delusions of the frontier, its manias of God or government or economics, been a marvel and an embarrassment to more skeptical folk? Well, a population suffered from malaria without cessation, and the mind was always vertiginous, moving with the buoyant catalepsy of dreams among shapes that wavered at the edges perhaps, but were lovelier always than the mudflats of this world.

Malaria fell heaviest, of course, on the squatters. They were underfed and defeated. Nematode worms in the intestines had weakened and brutalized them, giving them the characteristic apathy, languor, surliness, and depravity. Malarial proto-

zoa warmed their blood sporadically and fever contended with
the nematodes, alternating its aberrant energy with that lethargy. The squatter was therefore most given to visions and
could be most easily aroused to crusade. Thus his proneness to
poor-white honor, civil war, rape, lynching, and the mind's
crasser pestilences.

"Squatters" included, then, the unfit of the frontier and the
permanently diseased. They included also the unadjusted. One
must tiresomely insist that the common man, the democrat,
was, whatever his defects, incurably addicted to civilization.
He desired the fetish of liberals, the good life. He desired sta-
bility, order, peace, the fruits of labor. Desiring these, he
formed leagues of regulators, patrollers, and vigilantes, to secure
them. For the spate of America moving westward brought
along with him, the butcher-knife boys. These were the untamable. America has always been fecund in the production of
roughs. A flowering of the genus has been alluded to, — John
A. Murrell. His significance is that he was only a representative.
The frontier was never a soft country, wherever its borderline
halted, and the men who inhabited it were not remarkable for
softness.

The untamable were called butcher-knife boys, flat-footed
boys, huge-pawed boys. They had been among the first seekers of the West. Over the mountains came the long hunters of
Kentucky. From the north Canadian voyageurs brought a folklore and left a legend of murder and light irony. These vanished westward up the rivers; they sought beaver, and Marcus
Whitman found them on the Great Divide. After them came
other hunters, a migratory race, immensely celebrated in fiction. Then the frontier pushed down the streams its first harvests and a new species agreeably spawned itself to move the
freight. Keelboats, broadhorns, barges, flatboats, were rived from
the waterside forests and the freight floated southwestward.
The butcher-knife boys found an admissible destiny as their
crews and the nation's art acquired a new type, the boatman.
This image is a sun-scorched man in a red shirt and a blue capote
with a white fringe — swarthy, powerful, obscene. Shirt and

capote were display: in most weathers the boatmen worked
naked to the waist. They were the lees of America but their
labor was enormous and their gusto greater still. They warred
inimitably upon one another and then allied for the spoliation
of the tender when the boats tied up beside the little towns.
They swaggered down the streets while the citizenry trembled.
They drank what pleased them: they levied on shops and poultry
runs; they marched upon brothels where white whores worn
out in the cities competed for their favors with young black
wenches and mulattoes. Their choruses were terrifying by midnight — only a few of them have been preserved — and then
the boats cast off and floated downstream. There was now need
of vigilance, for the streams swarmed with other roughs who
were not content with manning barges. These were the river
pirates who, from such strongholds as Plumb Point, the Crow's
Nest, Hurricane Island, and Cave-In Rock, descended on the
barges for pillage. Colonel Plug, John A. Murrell, and James
Copeland were "river pirates" who climbed from among anonymous hundreds to permanence in history. Throughout the duration of the flatboat era this species preyed upon the commerce.
Conflict with them was a permanent hazard of the trade and
made attractive the boatman's calling. They fell upon the crews
when they pushed out, stone drunk, or came down upon them
when the boats tied up at night, or sometimes led flotillas against
them in broad day. The shock was brief, with pistols and knives.
Then the pirates pushed the barges shoreward, rifled them of
goods, and sank them with the corpses of the crews. Or they fled
backward while the victorious crews pushed them off with rifles
and brandished knives. The boats moved on. The boatmen tied
up their wounds. A song floated across the chocolate water:

> Hard upon the beech oar
> She moves too slow
> All the way to Shawneetown
> Long while ago.

A jigging tune, the words far decenter than most. Cairo lay
ahead. There would be fillies of whisky, an awed citizenry, and

wenches. The boats drifted on. They would come back upstream, shoved painfully by roughnecks with their shoulders at long poles, or pulled at the end of ropes which the bully-boys lugged through swamp and mire, through rain and sun.

The boatmen were the sublimate of frontier hardness. And America, incurably artistic, demanded a culture hero. Mike Fink, a living man, became the symbol. The legend of Mike Fink is the boatman apotheosized. He was the marksman who could not miss, the bully-boy who could not be felled, unmatchable in drink, invincible with wenches. He was a Salt River roarer, half horse, half alligator. To the admiration of the frontier, he shot the protuberant heel from a nigger's foot or the scalplock from an Indian's head. He fought a thousand combats, whose resonance increases through the years till they are hardly separable from Paul Bunyan's. He was superior to the ethics of timid souls and no court restrained him, though, for a favor, he might ride to one in his keelboat pulled by oxen, while his bully-boys held their oars at the feather. His purer escapades rippled in newsprint across the nation, in his lifetime. The water fronts of three thousand miles cherished the less printable stories of a frontier Casanova. Casanova, together with Paul Bunyan, merges into Thor, and Mike is a demigod of the rivers even before he dies — the boatman immortally violent, heroic, unconquerable.

Twilight overtook the trade. Steamboats made an end of it and with it most of the pirates, who were impotent against swift travel. Mike Fink, the world barren, withdrew beyond the reach of steamboats. There was welcome for heroes in the fur trade, then exploiting the upper reaches of the Missouri, where he was appropriately murdered. His brethren accepted compromise and supplied the victorious steamboats with their roustabouts and deckhands. Economy displaced them from the boats, substituting blacks. Whereupon the breed found a new vocation, equally glamorous, on the rafts, first of timber and then of lumber, that now floated down the Mississippi increasingly. The raftsman inherited the boatman's reputation and his terrorism. It was a similar trade, equally skilled, equally rugged, and equally romantic. The raftsman lived greatly on the waters and came ashore to go among the villages, swilling liquor, wenching, terrorizing the peaceful. They came to Hannibal, as the future would record.

Meanwhile the river pirates did a lessening traffic along the river front, among the small fry of emigrants and bargemen. Necessity made them "land pirates" like Murrell. There was trade enough in the pillage of freight caravans and the raiding of isolated farms, where frontiersmen habitually kept a loaded rifle at the door. The more ambitious dealt in highway robbery, in counterfeit notes, and in the most remunerative villainy, nigger-stealing. Their confederacies made an actual network spread widely over interior America. They were an element in every frontier community, whether furtive where Regulators were active, keeping them to back roads and midnight ventures, or whether arrogantly dominant. Wherever they were, in whatever proportion, they were the untamed. A disruptive element, turbulent and violent, giving a menace to lonely roads and woodlands; hiders-out whose ways were terrifying, a counter current against the frontier's progress.

The breed bloomed nobly when the Fifties brought on the anarchy of Kansas. The untamed flocked there under both guidons, for in Kansas the frontier relaxed its lawfulness for the sake of a holy war. Bushwhackers and Jayhawkers roved in hostile bands. They vented casual malice in maiming horses and poisoning cattle, or flicked themselves to a sharper ecstasy by shooting one another from ambush or slashing opponents to bits with knives. Frontier turbulence came into harvest with these murderers and kidnapers who hutted with their drabs in river bottoms and found the approaching war a gorgeous license. The flower of these prairie De Sades was Charley Hart, whose other and true name was William Clark Quantrill. His biographer was at pains to discover congenital cruelty in Quantrill's boyhood diversion of nailing live snakes to woodshed doors, but the explanation was not needed, since life among the border ruffians would suffice. America has nowhere equalled this guerrilla chieftain; he has no peer among the Jameses, the

Daltons, or other legendary ruffians whom the holy war brought
to be. Most of these in fact rode with him, humble auxiliaries
to greatness. They sought out wounded whom they might set
up in rows for the amusement of shooting at them. Taking prisoners sometimes, they might fill their ears with gunpowder and
set it off. They harassed the countryside of Kansas and Missouri
through a monotony of rapine and murder. They came down on
Lawrence and the story of the raid is not something created by
journalists to illuminate the ferocity of Germans. When the
last women and children had been killed and Quantrill had ridden back toward Missouri, it seemed natural to see a Negro
dragging the body of a dead guerrilla at the end of a rope, while
townsmen who had escaped, and their children, pelted the corpse
with stones. . . . Merely the untamable. These were the unadjusted among the squatters, hiders-out in dubious forests, a
terror but a constant element on the frontier.

The cave near Hannibal contained a copper cylinder which
itself contained one of glass. In the second cylinder was the body
of a young girl preserved in alcohol. The whole was suspended
from one of the fragile bridges that led across curves in the wind-
ings of the cave. Sometimes venturers from Hannibal would
drag the corpse up by the hair from the preserving fluid, and
stare at its face. . . . The boy Sam witnessed the murder of
"poor old Smarr" at noonday in the Main Street. Spectators
carried the victim to a neighboring office, Sam following them,
and laid him out there. His dying agony was enhanced by the
forethought of one who gave the sufferer consolation by laying
a heavy Bible on his chest. The old man gasped his life out against
that weight. And the boy carried the memory with him and in
his nightmares "gasped and struggled for breath under the
crush of that vast book for many a night.". . . When Sam was
ten, he saw a man throw a lump of iron ore at a slave and crush
his skull. In an hour the Negro was dead and Sam had watched
him die. . . . The rush to California eddied through Hannibal.
A quarrel sprang up between two immigrants, while Sam
Clemens was at hand. Bowie knives clashed and one of the

disputants died at Sam's feet. . . . Another youth bound for the gold fields got drunk and announced, loudly, his intention of going to a widow's house and seducing, or raping, her daughters. The boy Sam and a comrade skulked through the shadows while the rough made his way toward the widow's, shouting ribaldries. The widow stood on the porch, displaying a musket. She told the ruffian that he might go away in safety while she counted ten. She began to count. The fool stood there, gaping in the darkness, swaying stuporously on his feet. She paused at "nine" for a long interval. Then she said "ten" and darkness was shattered by the gush of flame. The whole charge struck the ruffian in the chest. "Then the rain and the thunder burst loose and the waiting town swarmed up the hill in the glare of the lightning like an invasion of ants. Those people saw the rest; I had had my share and was satisfied. I went home to dream and was not disappointed.". . . There were also the two brothers who were not fond of their uncle. Sam happened by one day and found one of them kneeling on the uncle's breast while the other methodically tried to fire a bulky Allen's pepperbox at the old man's head. . . . Some boy's necessity kept him out very late one night and he decided, for comfort, to sleep in his father's law office rather than at home. He went in and lay down on the couch but could not sleep. He was "like the rest of the race, not quite sane at night", and a prescience of evil was on him. The room held some awful terror, invisible. He tried to face the wall and close his eyes but he must turn back toward the room and open them. Moonlight from the window moved slowly across the floor. After a while it made visible a white human hand and the boy could not move. The light moved further while the boy agonized, and at last disclosed "the pallid face of a man . . . with the corners of the mouth drawn down and the eyes fixed and glassy in death." The revelation included a bared chest with a wound gaping below the nipple. There had been a casual stabbing in Hannibal and the corpse was disposed for the evening in the office of John Clemens. . . . He was ten years old and was staying for a time at Marion City, a few miles from Hannibal. A visionary there announced himself an abolitionist. Lynching was averted by a minister's assertion that the man was obviously insane. He went on proclaiming abolition and the shedding of blood. One day a slave escaped. A constable apprehended him. The abolitionist killed the constable, helped the slave across the river to freedom, and came back to give himself up. Lynching was again averted by the assurance of hanging. He was tried, condemned, and hanged. "People came from miles around to see the hanging, they brought cakes and cider, also the women and children, and made a picnic of the matter. It was the largest crowd the village had ever seen. The rope that hanged Hardy was eagerly bought up, in inch samples, for everybody wanted a memento of the memorable event." But the hanging of Robert Hardy, the abolitionist, had revealed a vision, the glory of martyrdom. Young men declared themselves abolitionists and composed a band of black avengers of the Spanish Main, with secret passwords, grips, and signs. They paraded to drums at midnight, masked and robed in black, after notifying the villagers to keep within their darkened homes. Mumbo jumbo frightened the villagers, but after weeks of terror a few offered opposition. The leader of these was blown up, with his house and slave. Terror succeeded again. Then the blacksmith, lusting for martyrdom, proclaimed himself the murderer. He had his glory, declaiming from the dock, and ending his evidence with melodrama: "Death to all slave tyrants." He had more oratory for the scaffold and his martyrdom was assured. He commanded his fraternity to avenge him. . . .

Wales McCormick, an apprentice in Mr. Ament's shop, amused himself by making lascivious gestures toward a mulatto girl, in the presence of her mother. The frightened old woman protested but without conviction, for "she quite well understood that by the customs of slaveholding communities, it was Wales's right to make love to that girl if he wanted to." Such mulatto girls peopled the crib-houses of the more pretentious towns and composed a willing concubinage in the villages. At fourteen they had usually served society by initiating their quota of pubescent boys. They were also the mistresses of gentility, so that Tom Driscoll was the highest quality in Dawson's Landing, being the son of Colonel Cecil Burleigh Essex. Tom's true name was Valet de Chambre and though only one thirty-second black, he was a slave. His foster father, Percy Northumberland Driscoll, "was a fairly humane man toward slaves and other animals." Moreover, young Sam Clemens understood from John Marshall Clemens that slavery was a great wrong. The Clemens slaves would have been given their freedom, except that that would have entailed a loss of money.

His father's assertion did not agree with the texts mentioned in pulpits, which held that "slavery was right, righteous, sacred, the peculiar pet of the deity, and a condition which the slave himself ought to be daily and nightly thankful for." Observation confirmed the texts. Sam sometimes saw black folk chained together and lying in the sun, waiting to be shipped south to the auction. He saw one slave murdered in anger. His mother was pleased when the black boy Sandy sang, for that meant that Sandy had forgotten the loss of his eastern home. But, mostly, the slaves were happy, the happiest folk in that contented countryside. Laughter was constant among them, and singing, and horseplay. They were the nearest associates of boys. Black and white children grew up together, without distinction except that when wills crossed blacks must yield. They were herded indiscriminately by black wenches, who kept order among both by threatening the terrors of ghosts, witches, and devils. They investigated all things together, exploring life. They hunted, swam, and fought together and the complaisance of Huck Finn included a willingness to sit down and eat with a nigger. Moreover, slaves were the most agreeable of adults. Between a boy and a white man was the barrier of age, but the slave met the boy as an equal, instructing him and sharing with him what the whites denied him because of his age.

So the days of Sam Clemens were spent among the blacks. Negro girls watched over his infancy. Negro boys shared his childhood. Negroes were a fountain of wisdom and terror and adventure. There was Sandy and the other slave boys who played bear with him. These and others preserved him sometimes from drowning. There was the bedridden old woman who had known Moses and had lost her health in the exodus from Egypt. There was Uncle Dan'l who told the stories that Harris was to put in the mouth of Uncle Remus, and, while the fire died, revealed the awful world of the ghosts. There were the Negroes with whom he roamed the woods, hunting coons and pigeons. There were the roustabouts of the steamboats, the field hands shouting calls over their hoes, and all the leisurely domestic servants of the town. . . . Olivia Langdon, whom he married, was to give him a principle for doing justly with the human race. He ought, she said, to consider every man black until he was proved white.

Sam Clemens grew up among Negroes: the fact is important for Mark Twain. Mark Twain became, in his way, an artist. In his books the Negro is consistently a noble character, and much that is fruitful in his art springs from the slaves.

"I lie in the grave and stretch out my arms." That was the nobler aspect of the only religion that was ever vital to him. But Uncle Dan'l sat in the cabin of a winter night, telling of the ghost who came looking for her golden arm.

The result of Wesleyan exhortation of the American Negro was a living religion. The Negro received the splendors of Methodism and did with them what he could. King Jedus was comin' on his white horse, though mankind sinned exceedingly, and across Jordan a kind old black man waited to take his children home. Heaven was about six miles away and completely recognizable. This was a living creed, with a strange loveliness and a touching faith. It was what the Wesleys, Asbury, and similar evangelists did for the consolation of slaves and for their good order. It gave us the jubilee. But it was a thin veneer above horror.

In the sixteenth century in Europe, the old gods were born again as monsters. Christians extirpated them by killing thousands of men, women, and infants. Seventeenth-century Englishmen in the colonies shared the terror. Witches were as abhorrent as Quakers in New England and were similarly disposed of.

The South discovered only a few witches but the gods do not perish. Their worship in sabbats disappeared, but their power remained. It was exhibited chiefly in the potency of spirits and in the glimpses of the mysterious world afforded by charms and signs. Witches in America, understand, did not often fly to worship a goat but they attended the processes of nature and were especially troublesome in the conduct of farms, birth, and death. Definitely, a kind of progress exists. In order to accept new delusions, the mind must shed some of the old. Through the eighteenth century there was a gradual recession of witchcraft. It lapsed to the lore of gaffers, catching in the weather or in night noises some swift hint of the unseen world.

But English witchcraft had met a congenial religion and the old gods were allowed to live on among their foreign relatives. The slaves had been brought from a continent acceptably dark, where spirits were recognized for what they were and where any god was voodoo, a being who inspired fear. These had sweat darkly, worshiping corpses, blood, and serpents. It was another religion of terror and its creatures were of death. Its rites came to America with the first slaves and were observed secretly by night in the deep woods. Mementoes of dead bodies had their power for the homage of a voodoo and tranced worshipers spilled blood over fragments of corpses for the adoration of serpents. When such communicants met the European gods they were on familiar ground. This Christian devil was a voodoo with a white skin. These English witches were another habitation of the spirits of evil. Two unseen worlds mingled and drew very near.

To this living religion European witchcraft contributed witches, ghosts, and signs. Africa added conjuration or spells, the evil eye, and the ritual of prophylaxis and infection — of sympathetic magic. It was a living religion — no longer dreadful to most whites except after dark, in the woods, and in the vicinity of graveyards, but binding on slaves and through them on children. It comprised the energies of a dreadful unseen, working malignantly for the destruction of peace. Some of its aspects must be examined.

The unseen was horrible with death. A corpse was a dynamo which generated evil. Everything that resembled or belonged to it shared its power. Cerements could work magic, ill or good; so could the earth of graves, the leaves that fell on them, the rats that entered them, and the maggots which competed with the rats. Breath departed from a tired body and at once the corpse was a frightful thing. While its friends still bent over it, demons squatted unseen and the poor corruption was already at work doing the behests of witches. Thus the terror of the dead that woke children screaming when a dog howled or an owl hooted or a beetle set up his ticking in the wall.

The spirit left the corpse and entered a dreary state, less than life, not quite extinction. Such half-creatures flitted endlessly about the world, their passage marked by a small rustling or a tiny beat of wings. Sometimes they were invisible to human eyes, though a hound might bare his teeth and whine, staring at blankness, or a horse snort and tremble and bolt away from what no one had seen. Sometimes they came as they were, black or white, or drifted down empty lanes, taking such shapes as suited their purposes. But for their envy, they would have had pathos. They could not think clearly; they could be hoodwinked and deceived, sent on false chases, deluded by signs and spells. They were afflicted with gloomy compulsions and could be forced to give up their evil works by taking advantage of the laws that bound them. They clung to the living who possessed the sun they had once enjoyed, following us happy ones about with a sad wish to warm themselves at our life. And they were condemned to journeyings and vigils that they could not end. So they waited in the woods and Huck Finn, half pitying, heard "that kind of a sound that a ghost makes when it wants to tell you something that's on its mind and can't make itself understood, and so can't rest easy in its grave and has to go about that way every night grieving."

But they envied warm blood, and so you could not be sure that any shape moving across a dark field, whether dog or cow or rabbit or black cat, might not turn on you and reveal eyes of fire. Lights flitted above swamps or clung to the sides of rotting logs; these were the devices of ghosts to lure you to destruction, for the slaking of their envy. Windows of churches or of lone houses gleamed with candle shine; but do not enter or dank hands will have you by the throat. They called to you across the dark fields; but do not answer, for that is death. They mourned like wind in the tree tops, they sobbed, they screamed; the noises of the night were their anger. They paraded without heads, or left an arm or leg behind, for terror. Night was their kingdom and they would somehow get even with the warm living. They must do you hurt for reprisal. They must reduce you to this chilly gray. They must touch you and their touch was death. You might arm yourself with spells and hang about you fetishes consecrated with unguents correctly made, but at best you ventured into terror and the risk of death when night fell. At any step a ha'nt might reach a hand through your protections and at once you were dead, a corpse sweating evil at the command of other ghosts, to the hurt of those who had been your friends.

Companions and overseers of these ha'nts and allies with them in the manipulation of death, were the accursed living who had sold their fealty to devils for a price. Witches might be male or female, but mostly, for the solace of goats, they preferred to be females. Mostly they were old. In sixteenth-century Europe to be gray, writhen, and friendless was to invite death by torture. In southern countrysides it was to be no less a witch to Negroes and children, and adults saw reason for distrust. That the residue has not vanished is attested by the appearance of goofers and hexes, while this book remains in manuscript, in Louisiana, Arkansas, West Virginia, Maryland, Pennsylvania, and New York.

The witch, then, might be male or might be a beautiful girl, but was usually a hag. Sometimes her breasts were in her armpits and the skin of her neck hung in folds like a collar. She had the ghost's power of metamorphosis. Whatever shape might expedite her malign ends was available to her. Cats, wolves, and bats were obviously attractive, since they trafficked with death, but moles were of darkness, too, and so were night birds and especially those that loved carrion. A buzzard flapping loathsomely above a corpse meant that somewhere a woman's skin was slackly hidden awaiting her satiated return. This gave mankind a weapon, for if you wounded the animal familiar, the witch would show a cognate wound when she resumed her skin and you could then deal with her.

Witches lurked in caves, ruined barns, stumps, hollow logs — in all dark lonely places. Night was their kingdom, when the fellowship of death awoke and corpses, devils, and ghosts were loosed upon the world. They had an ecstatic energy of evil. Their obligation was to harm mankind, toward culmination in murder. But murder was not so easy for them as for ha'nts: their jurisdiction was annoyance, misfortune, and bad health. Falling asleep, you were all but defenseless against them. When a person talked or cried out in his sleep, that was an infallible sign that a witch was after him. She had entered the house through some undefended opening, the fireplace, a gap under the door, a keyhole, a rathole. She would slip a bit in the sleeper's mouth and leap upon him. His breath was shut off, his feet tingled, his hair crawled, he could not cry out. Ghastly pictures of corpses, pursuits, tortures, dreadful deaths filled his mind. The next morning the marks of the witch's whip might be on his back and of her bit in the corners of his mouth. His hair was ragged from her fingers and his eyes were red. He was weary and dispirited — and no wonder. For, while his body seemed to lie uneasy in bed, she had ridden him out over the trees and fields, careening toward the devil and debauchery. He had been a part of repellent labors and a mark was on him that could never be erased.

Witch-riding was a dreadful practice, but merely one of many mischiefs. These hags could afflict you with disease or madness. They could grind your bones with aches sharper than ague. They could transfix you with the evil eye and quite addle you. They could decoy you on glittering quests into the power of ha'nts and so kill you. But mostly they could frustrate your desires, bring your designs to failure, set ill luck on all your affairs, and out of sterile malice pursue you forever with the twin ills of fear and failure. Unnoticed or in the oblique stares of women there was always in operation against you the machinery of the whole world of evil.

Defense against this machinery was precariously possible. The clairvoyance of animals might suffice to give warning of witches, as of ha'nts; the eyes of dogs and horses, of owls and beetles, lacked the veils that obscured human sight, and their skins perceived approaches too subtle for human sense. There were dependable spells, too, by which malign presences could be detected, and revelatory signs. Water, salt, pepper, fetishes of animals' bones, finger-nail parings of corpses, earth from graves, a myriad objects sympathetically associated with the horrors of death sufficed not only for the detection of witches, but also for the neutralization of their power. These magics, and various rituals and incantations, revealed the laws of their estate, a logical system, and permitted the sufferer to control and frustrate them. Witches, like ha'nts, were subject to immutable necessities of their nature and these could be taken advantage of. That they might not cross running water was well known and that they were impotent in the presence of religious and phallic tokens. Moreover, they had deep compulsions and could be betrayed by numbers and untidiness. Strew corn meal by the doorway or the hearth, wherever the witch must cross it, and her vertiginous mania compelled her to pick it up grain by grain, enumerating each one. This held her till the antisepsis of daybreak, and any multiplicity would do as well: she must count the straws of a broom, the needles of an evergreen branch, or the corns of spilt pepper, sitting there helpless to be about her mischief while any item of the crazy sum remained untold. The efficacy of a horseshoe above a door was that it slipped into these manic necessities and obliged a witch to set off at once upon the track the horse had made. Sharp instruments were dangerous to witches. A fork beneath your bed might ward off a night-riding, or pointed stakes strategically disposed might catch the abandoned skin. She might be shot, too, with gold or silver bullets. She might be prevented from reëntering her skin when the night's mischief was over.

She might be trapped in a greased gourd or a milkpan or a bottle over which the proper conjuration had been said.

Few witches were trapped thus, conceivably, but conjurations out of Africa and spells out of England defended all Negroes, all children, and thousands of white adults from the malice of witches and the other evils of the unseen world. And a myriad signs gave hints of what was happening in that world.

To this day you may observe boys joining their little fingers and pulling hard while looking at a dog in the way of nature. By immemorial principles, the tightness thus produced tightens the cur's bowels. It is a slave spell and its frankness is typical. Excremental processes and substances have had magic power throughout time, and a race as religious as the Negro must make use of them. Catamenial items, of great dread among most primitives, were to the Negro deeply potent for love. Dung was mostly remedial, to be used in poultices for toothache, whooping cough, mastoid troubles, or weak eyes, and sometimes still startles the internes of metropolitan hospitals, but had its darker uses. Urine could be employed to soften the malice of an enemy or to convert a wench's friendship into passion. Saliva was all but omnipotent in the avoidance of hostile spells and the working of your own. These were products of the living; the tokens of the dead were also powerful. This dim world responded to everything that was tainted with death. The touch of a corpse's hand would cure wens and many other disorders and served too as an infallible detector of spirits. Grave trees and gallows trees furnished amulets of known virtue, together with fragments of headstones, cerements, and coffins. To these were added the possessions of animals prescient of death, the eyes of wolves and cats and owls who saw so clearly by night, feathers of jaybirds who paid toll to Satan, thigh bones of buzzards, the nude tails of moles, knuckles of pigs who had rooted in graveyards. Monstrosities, too, must be sovereign; cauls, quaintly shaped stones, pieces of meteorites, two-headed calves, hunchbacks, whatever was striking or mysterious.

There was, in short, little in the natural world that could not be converted to the control of the unseen and little that did not serve sometime to reveal it. Most revelations, of course, were of death; and, again, the perception of animals was subtler. The howling of a dog, notoriously, portended death: lest the message might be directed at you, you were wise to take off your left shoe and turn it around, or lay it upside down at your bedside. If the cur barked without reason or chose the back yard to howl in, this too signified the imminence of death. So, too, did his wallowing before a door, when he was obviously measuring some one's grave; if he lay half over the threshold, the meaning was the same, or if he crawled along the ground on his stomach. The beast was troubled, observe, for his fine snout had smelled the odor of spirits and of death. All animals, in fact, shared this divination; they were persons a little ruder than humanity and a little nearer the unseen, such speaking kin as Uncle Remus told of. The horses who were prey to witch riders and therefore must have their manes or tails plaited, saw and smelled the passage of spirits down wind. When a person was ill his horse would be observed for prophecy; if the horse neighed twice after midnight the man would die. The lowing of cows carried the same message. The snakes knew and when a rattler slid away from you, he was fleeing the knowledge of your death. A mouse came by night to gnaw your clothes when you were marked for death. The very beetles in the sand trembled to your doom. Stars fell to put their mark on you and your garden died with you. Then some one must go tell the bees of your passing, or they too would pass.

Thus the lore of slaves. The world was ominously corrupted with malevolence looking toward the terror of death, but time had heaped up a variety of defences and forewarnings in which the slaves were always busy. They were vigilant to inform children and the boys who lived with them wholly shared their dreads. Childhood was thus seasoned in miracle and terror.

On page 54 of "Tom Sawyer", Huckleberry Finn wanders into immortality swinging a dead cat. He proposes to use it to cure a wart, for which rain water in a hollow stump is also efficacious, if employed with the proper ritual and incantation.

A bean will magically dispose of warts, too, when sprinkled with blood and buried at a crossroads — where vampires cannot pass — at the proper phase of the moon. The cat is hexen: it is approved by Mother Hawkins, a witch, and its power is associated with the corpses of wicked men and with the devils who possess them. Tom, leaving school, crosses water to baffle pursuit, and then, because a lithomancy fails him, is aware that a witch has been at work. A prescient doodlebug, who conceivably has reported the unseen world to many slaves, refuses to bear witness. That night — like all the world, Tom was not sane at night — his nerves are tortured by the perceptible movement of spirits, patently alert for the death foretold by the ticking in Tom's wall and the minute howling of dogs. Then the spirit of Hoss Williams, at his grave, is aware of Tom and Huck whispering together while their lungs choke, and faintly, far off, they see the approach of devil fire when the fiends come to take their property. The night of horror spins on. The boys take to earth in the old tannery, where presently a dog howls, a stray dog brought hither by his foresight of death. After agony, it transpires that the auspice is not on the boys, for the dog howls in the moonlight and he faces Muff Potter, who must surely die. And so must Gracie Miller, for a whippoorwill entered her house and sang. That Injun Joe's false oath does not draw down a thunderbolt must mean that he has sold his soul to the devil — which brings the Faustus legend to St. Petersburg by way of the Ewe-speaking people of the Congo. Moreover, red gold of the Spanish Main is watched by ghosts, and when the search for treasure on Still-House Branch is baffled by witches, the seekers move on to the haunted house on Cardiff Hill. Spirits are abroad there, and ominous owls, and a baying hound. The opinion of Huck Finn prefers corpses: "Dead people might talk maybe, but they don't come sliding around in a shroud, when you ain't noticing, and peep over your shoulder all of a sudden, and grit their teeth" — which seems a ghastly knowledge for a boy. And Huck has dreamed of rats, a fearsome omen but tolerable since in this dream they did not fight.

Cannon and quicksilver assist the search for the drowned

bodies of the boys, who were safe enough from drowning since they had charms made of rattlesnake tails. Drowned men, understand, float on their backs, whereas women lie face downward in the water, and this is Pliny come to Hannibal through the slave trade.

One sixteenth of Roxy was black and that fraction did not show. It bubbled in her veins, however, running the dark knowledge of her world. David Wilson, the pudd'nhead, made a necromancy with glass slides, which Roxy would not approach unless she could find a horseshoe for defense. Wilson was clearly a witch. . . . Yet the complete picture is that of the Hawkins children guarded by Uncle Dan'l, who was so devoted to them that when the Lord of vengeance came in a chariot of fire, he offered himself in their place. His life was consecrated to the children and so too was his religion. They had pillowed their heads on his shoulder night after night, till "the air was filled with invisible spirits and . . . the faint zephyrs were caused by their passing wings."

So children grew up in terror. Huck Finn "heard an owl, away off, who-whooing about somebody that was dead, and a whippoorwill, and a dog crying about somebody that was going to die; and the wind was trying to whisper something to me, and I couldn't make out what it was, and so it made the cold shivers run over me. . . . Pretty soon a spider went crawling up my shoulder, and I flipped it off and it lit in the candle; and before I could budge it was all shrivelled up. I didn't need anyone to tell me that that was an awful bad sign." He was so scared he most shook the clothes off of him. The emergency was grave. He turned around three times, to set the dull-witted witches on the wrong track, made a cross on his breast to intimidate them, and tied up a lock of his hair with thread for further antisepsis. Yet anxiety remained, for this conjuration, though effective after the loss of a horseshoe, might have no relevance to the death of a spider. It was Huck's misfortune frequently to go astray with spells and charms. All his misadventures, all the long wanderings of his saga, spring from the return of old man Finn — which could have been averted if Miss Watson had permitted him to toss over his shoulder some of the salt that he had spilled. That he survived the menace of the unseen world was due wholly to Jim, a Negro, who was expert in manipulating it. Witches rode Jim one night but mostly his skill outwitted them. He owned a hair ball from the fourth stomach of an ox, in which a spirit lived and with which he could do magic. The hair ball could prophesy but when a hex was on it there were other means of divination. Birds and chickens, whose routine forecasts were the weather, beheld always the future's pattern. These had their lore, common enough to Jim, who was versed in all signs. Knowledge reached him from the Sussex downs, so that he knew you must tell the bees when their owner died; he had observed, too, that bees would not sting idiots. Dead men must not be talked about, lest they come back and ha'nt. He knew the loathsome prescience of snakes and how to work homeopathy with their flesh. He "druther see the new moon over his left shoulder as much as a thousand times than take up a snake-skin in his hands." Competence at reading dreams also armed him against spirits, for dreams were a symbolic language, the key to which unlocked a man's past and future, dredged up dark secrets, and suggested a system of re-education that would change one's destiny. So he had a professional sympathy with the Duke of Bilgewater who could find water and gold with a divining rod and had traveled widely about America, dissipating witch spells.

The slave's world was dominated by the terror of death. No sunlit landscape lacked its oppression of unseen malevolence. The air vibrated with the will of ghosts and witches to do evil to the luckless race of men. It was a world that stank of death and shuddered with its terror. The mind was spellbound, obsessed, conditioned by the presence of corpses, their will to evil, and their power. Till a child could not venture beyond candlelight without dreading the touch of clammy hands.

Critics of Mark Twain profess to be bewildered by noticeable irregularities of his nervous system, which for explanation require the parable of America destroying its artists; and by his lifelong preoccupation with a Calvinist creed already vanished in his boyhood, which can be explained only by probing the unconscious, by way of his books, for the frustration of his genius.

It is not granted here that the nervous instability of Mark Twain needs explanation. But if it does, explanation does not require the assistance of a literary theory. A nervous organism that has been racked from its beginning by the Negro's midnight magic need not depend on American contempt of art for its discords. And the religion against which Mark Twain was perpetually in revolt is, if the religion he writes and talks most about can be accepted as the one he objects to, the religion of the slaves.

The effort here is to determine how such a book as "Huckleberry Finn" gets itself written, or what shaped the talent of Mark Twain. . . . There was an idyll of sunny river towns with the forest and prairies beyond them. There was the rush and clamor of America becoming something it had not been. There were the two facets of democracy. There were the melancholy, the music, the laughter, the terror, and the magic of the slaves.

IV

THE DANDY AND THE SQUATTER

FOR the first twelve years of Samuel Clemens's life no source of information is open to a critic or biographer except Clemens's books and the memories of old men. Of the latter, the only valid one is his own and this, admittedly treacherous, is made more undependable by his books. They obviously were shaped by his experiences and seem to have been shaped first by the experiences of his boyhood. But though the books of Mark Twain were conditioned by experience, guessing that any given incident in them actually happened to Samuel Clemens is a precarious business. It is essential to distinguish in some measure the imaginative artist Mark Twain from the historical personage Samuel Clemens. Creation works its chemistry, necessarily transforming the crude stuff of experience into art. It seems likely that the memory of Samuel Clemens, in his old age, included something that was the creation of Mark Twain — as the works of Mark Twain, the artist, demonstrably supplied old friends with biographical data about Samuel Clemens.

No attempt is made here to determine just what, in the memory of Samuel Clemens and of his friends, was fact and just what was imaginary. Such an attempt would be, at the highest possible level, merely guesswork.

One item, as example. In his old age, Samuel Clemens remembered a glamorous incident, one that symbolized the boyhood of young Sam and of the Tom Blankenship who grew into Huckleberry Finn. The boys desired money and possessed one coonskin, whose value was ten cents. They took it to Selms's[1] store at Wild Cat corner, where they converted it into cash. Then, going around to an open window, they stole the coonskin and sold it to Selms again. They repeated the theft and sale till "John Prince, Selms's clerk, said: 'Look here, Selms, there is something wrong about this. That boy has been selling us coonskins all afternoon.'" Search revealed only one coonskin in the store. And "Selms himself used to tell this story as a great joke.". . . The incident symbolized the picaresque boyhood of Sam and Tom. It brought back to the aging Samuel Clemens the flavor of that vanished past. The data were circumstantial: names, places, dialogue all give it the ring of truth. He perceived that it was truth and convinced his biographer, so that the story appears in Mr. Paine's biography. And yet, detail for detail, the story was old in American folklore when Sam Clemens was born, had been told of every sharp-dealing personage whom the folk elevated to heroism, and had reached print in the works of Davy Crockett. It is a product of frontier humor, an item in the folklore to which Sam Clemens was born — so at home there that Mark Twain instinctively bestowed it on Sam Clemens.[2]

The memories of old men are precarious. Mr. Paine carefully winnowed them for his presentation of Samuel Clemens's

[1] So spelled in Paine. The masthead of the Hannibal *Journal* shows that the true spelling was Selmes. See p. 87.

[2] The earliest attribution of the feat to Crockett which I have found is in the anonymous "Sketches and Eccentricities" (1833. Tenth edition, 1837, p. 75). It is repeated in the "Exploits and Adventures in Texas" (1836. English edition, 1837, p. 5), and the "Life of David Crockett" (1855. Evans edition, 1859, p. 239).

boyhood, and the boy he shows is unquestionably as near as any one will ever get to the boy who really lived. It is safe to accept that figure in its form and in the outline of its conduct. But when any one, Mr. Van Wyck Brooks or another, constructs a literary theory out of specific details of that boy's life, he forms it entirely from guesswork.

The boy of Mr. Paine's biography is, at twelve years, energetic and picaresque, mischievous and moody. He is formed in the image of Tom Sawyer. He has the gift of laughter. His health is exuberant but undependable. He has lived through a good many of the adventures he is later to put into books and has observed or heard about a good many more. And that is all.

John Marshall Clemens died on the 24th of March, 1847, when Samuel was eight months short of twelve years old. Sometime after May, 1848, Samuel Clemens was apprenticed to Joseph P. Ament, who owned a printing shop in Hannibal and edited the *Missouri Courier*, a weekly newspaper.

These two facts would need no scrutiny, if Mr. Van Wyck Brooks had not made them the cornerstone of his theory. He finds in the circumstances of Samuel Clemens's apprenticeship the events that determined the development of Mark Twain and settled on him the weight of a lifelong frustration. The apprenticeship, Mr. Brooks decides, his mother's use of his father's death to discipline him, was the psychical trauma that made Mark Twain a prostituted artist, a conformer, and a victim to American materialism.

The facts, as stated, do not justify the interpretation. For justification, Mr. Brooks is forced into theory — and into the memory of Samuel Clemens during his last years, after the works and habits of Mark Twain had clouded it. That memory contained three different versions of the apprenticeship. Of these, one was not available to Mr. Brooks when he wrote "The Ordeal of Mark Twain." The other two were. He selected one and ignored the other, wholly omitting to mention it. One wonders what principle of selection guided him. One concludes that the principle was merely this: in a conflict of evidence, that evidence shall be chosen which supports the theory in course of elaboration.

The version of his apprenticeship which Samuel Clemens remembered on March 29, 1906, is the one which was not open to Mr. Brooks and the one which is most factual. It says merely, "I was taken from school at once upon my father's death and placed in the office of the Hannibal *Courier*,[3] as printer's apprentice, and Mr. Ament, the editor and proprietor of the paper, allowed me the usual emolument of the office — that is to say, board and clothes, but no money."

On January 9, 1906, Mr. Albert Bigelow Paine began the audiences with Mr. Clemens which eventually produced the official biography. In the course of these audiences, fifty-nine years after the event, Mr. Clemens told Mr. Paine the version of the apprenticeship which appears in the biography and provides Mr. Brooks with the cornerstone of his theory. According to this dramatic memory, Jane Clemens made use of her husband's death to reform her son. Mr. Paine, in the passage which forms the basis of Mr. Brooks's book, says:

The boy Sam was fairly broken down. Remorse, which always dealt with him unsparingly, laid a heavy hand on him now. Wildness, disobedience, indifference to his father's wishes, all were remembered; a hundred things, in themselves trifling, became ghastly and heart-wringing in the knowledge that they could never be undone. Seeing his grief, his mother took him by the hand and led him into the room where his father lay.

"It is all right, Sammy," she said. "What's done is done, and it does not matter to him any more; but here by the side of him now I want you to promise me — "

He turned, his eyes streaming with tears, and flung himself into her arms.

"I will promise anything," he sobbed, "if you won't make me go to school! Anything!"

His mother held him for a moment, thinking, then she said:

"No, Sammy; you need not go to school any more. Only promise me to be a better boy. Promise not to break my heart."

[3] So Mr. Clemens consistently remembered it. Ament's paper was really called the *Missouri Courier*.

So he promised her to be a faithful and industrious man, and upright, like his father. His mother was satisfied with that. The sense of honor and justice was already strong within him. . . .

That night — it was after the funeral — his tendency to somnambulism manifested itself. . . . He walked in his sleep several nights in succession after that. Then he slept more soundly.

The memory of Samuel Clemens had provided him with a scene from melodrama. The other witnesses, Jane Clemens and Pamela, were dead. No way of testing the story existed. It convinced Mr. Paine, who supplies the actual dialogue. One may say of it that it is the only incident in Samuel Clemens's memory which endows Jane Clemens with dramatic technique, that the properties of the open coffin and the dreadful oath suggest the imagination of Tom Sawyer, and that the language attributed to young Sam gives him a greater maturity than one expects at eleven. Still, there it is, the official reason for Sam's apprenticeship to Mr. Ament. One might assume it as true, after mentioning the existence of a contradictory version. But even on that assumption, the scene seems hardly a sufficient explanation of everything that thereafter developed in Samuel Clemens and in Mark Twain.

In Mr. Brooks's hands, however, the scene tells the whole story. It creates Mark Twain and damns him. By promising to be a better boy, young Sam has thrown away his birthright as an artist (undetectable in anything available to biography). John Marshall Clemens, dying, has molded in the shape of respectability a boy who might have been the greatest of American writers. Jane Clemens, the goddess Nemesis in linsey-woolsey, seals on him the mark of the mother-image, and creates the retribution of self-betrayal for this acceptance of false values, thus strangling genius in its twelfth year.

Who is sufficiently the master of signs and portents to read this terrible episode aright? One thing, however, we feel with irresistible certitude, that Mark Twain's fate was once for all decided there. That hour by his father's corpse, that solemn oath, that walking in his sleep — we must hazard some interpretation of it all, and I think we are justified in hazarding as most likely that which explains the most numerous and the most significant phenomena of his later life. . . . What was this remorse; what had he done for grief or shame? "A hundred things in themselves trifling," which had offended, in reality, not his father's heart but his father's will as a conventional citizen with a natural desire to raise up a family in his own likeness. Feeble, frantic, furtive little feelings-out of this moody child, the first wavering steps of the soul, that is what they have really been, these peccadillos, the dawn of the artist. And the formidable promptings of love tell him that they are sin! . . . And his mother stamps there, with awful ceremony, the composite image of her own meager traditions. He is to go forth the Good Boy by *force majeure*, he is to become such a man as his father would have approved of, he is to retrieve his father's failure, to recover the lost gentility of a family that had once been proud, to realize that "mirage of wealth" that had ever hung before his father's eyes. And to do so, he is not to quarrel heedlessly with his bread and butter, he is to keep strictly within the code, to remember the maxims of Ben Franklin, to respect all the prejudices and all the conventions; above all, he is not to be drawn aside into any fanciful orbit of his own. Hide your faces, Huck and Tom. Put away childish things, Sam Clemens; go forth into the world, but remain always a child, your mother's child! . . . Your mother imagines her heart is in the balance — will you break it? Will you promise? And the little boy, in the terror of that presence, sobs: "Anything.". . . It is perfectly evident what happened to Mark Twain at this moment: he became, and his immediate manifestation of somnambulism is the proof of it, a dual personality. If I were sufficiently hardy, as I am not, I should say that that little sleep-walker who appeared at Jane Clemens's bedside on the night of her husband's funeral was the spirit of Tom Sawyer, come to demand again the possession of his own soul, to revoke that ruthless promise he had given. . . . His "wish" to be an artist, which has been so frowned upon and has encountered such an insurmountable obstacle in the disapproval of his mother, is now repressed, more or less definitely, and another wish, that of winning approval, which inclines him to conform with public opinion, has supplanted it. The individual, in short, has given way to the type. The struggle between these two selves, these two tendencies, these two wishes or groups of wishes, will continue throughout Mark Twain's life, and the poet, the artist, the individual, will make a brave effort to survive. From the death of his father onward, however, his will is definitely enlisted on the side opposed to his essential instinct.[4]

[4] "The Ordeal of Mark Twain", pp. 40, 41, 42. The dots, throughout, are mine and indicate elisions. To avoid confusion, I have left out dots used by Mr. Brooks to represent ellipses in his thought.

Thus Mr. Brooks's tears. The wild play of assumptions — the assumption that boyish mischief was really the beginnings of art, the assumption that Sam Clemens had ever rebelled against "respectability", and the assumption that there is some relation between the boy's promise to his mother and his future conduct — will be examined later. It suffices here to point out the confidence with which a theory elaborates a few casual memories, probably fictitious, into a final judgment. And to inquire why Mr. Brooks did not mention another memory, which contradicts this one.

For in 1909, Samuel Clemens remembered otherwise his apprenticeship to Mr. Ament. He published this remembrance in *Harper's Bazaar* for February, 1910, in an article called "The Turning Point of My Life", which forms a part of "What Is Man" in his collected works. As three years had passed since he had remembered the other version, we might suppose that the reminiscences of a man seventy-four years old had grown more unreliable. On the other hand, he was writing with complete solemnity about "the change in my life's course which introduced what must be regarded by me as the most important condition of my career." He was examining the course of his life in an effort to determine its possible meaning — and we might suppose that the effort would hold him to the rigid truth. Truth or not, it was what Samuel Clemens believed in 1909.

According to this version, his apprenticeship followed an attack of measles to which he had deliberately exposed himself. An epidemic of the disease came to Hannibal and "the village was paralyzed with fright, distress, despair." The agony of fear grew intolerable to Sam Clemens. "At some time or other every day and every night a sudden shiver shook me to the marrow, and I said to myself, 'There, I've got it! and I shall die.'" He determined to end the ordeal. He stole away from home, crept into bed with a playmate, and acquired the infection. "Everybody believed I would die." But "on the fourteenth day a change came for the worse and they were disappointed."

In 1909, Samuel Clemens solemnly declared: "This was the turning-point of my life. . . . For when I got well my mother closed my school career and apprenticed me to a printer. She was tired of trying to keep me out of mischief and the adventure of the measles decided her to put me in more masterful hands than hers. I became a printer and began to add one link after another to the chain which was to lead me into the literary profession."

That is a straightforward account of how Sam Clemens came to be apprenticed to Mr. Ament. It should be mentioned that in this account he says he was twelve and a half years old when his father died, whereas he was a year younger; that elsewhere in his "Autobiography" he assigns the episode of the measles to 1845; and that Mr. Paine gives it still another date, saying it "occurred when he was very young." Nevertheless, that is the way he remembered the circumstances of his apprenticeship in 1909, in as solemn an effort as he ever made to tell the truth about himself. Since he was the only surviving witness of the circumstances, this account seems fully as valid as the one which does such service to Mr. Brooks. Skepticism rejects them both: they are unverifiable. Still, in the creation of a theory, it would have been proper to take the last one into account.

The ascertainable fact is that Ament came to Hannibal sometime in the latter part of May, 1848. He had been publishing the *Missouri Courier* in Palmyra. Between May 18 and June 1, he bought the Hannibal *Gazette,* with which he merged the *Courier.* The merger continued as the Hannibal *Gazette* until October 12th, after which the name became permanently the *Missouri Courier.* The known length of Samuel Clemens's apprenticeship is two years. It was unquestionably served under Ament and ended with the establishment of Orion's Hannibal *Western Union,* whose first number was printed on October 10, 1850. The apprenticeship to Ament, thus, could not possibly have taken place until fifteen months after the death of his father.

The circumstances of his apprenticeship seem to me unimportant; the fact itself, as he said in 1909, the most important one in his life. Important, that is, for the development of Mark Twain, the writer. He became a printer and learned how to

write. He became a journeyman and wandered, in the tradition
of the trade, over a good part of America — during years vital
in the formation of his personality and vital also in the formation
of American society. And as a printer he worked for years on
newspapers, rural, frontier, and metropolitan — and so observed
the development of the kind of literature he was to write. Mark
Twain the humorist and Mark Twain the realist were the creation of newspapers.

To record the sequence, therefore, seems desirable. The
discoveries of the Reverend C. J. Armstrong and Professor Fred
W. Lorch have filled the hiatus in Mr. Paine's account and
have corrected some of its details.

Young Sam was apprenticed, then, to Joseph P. Ament of
the *Missouri Courier*, some time in 1848. In 1850, his moonstruck older brother Orion, a journeyman printer who was to
become Washington Hawkins in "The Gilded Age", came back
to Hannibal from St. Louis, where he had been working at his
trade. A young man of vast and yeasty visions, he proposed an
editorial career, established a weekly newspaper called the Hannibal *Western Union*, and took Sam from Ament's office to
work for him. The earliest number of Orion's newspaper recovered by Mr. Armstrong is dated October 10, 1850. It lasts as
the *Western Union* till August 28, 1851. The following week,
on September 4, it becomes the Hannibal *Journal and Western
Union*, the combination probably representing the purchase that
Mr. Paine records. On September 9, 1852, it becomes merely
the Hannibal *Journal;* that title remains till the last issue under
Orion's editorship, September 21, 1853. During the last six
months of its career under Orion, it was merely the weekly edition of Orion's most foolhardy project, the Hannibal *Daily
Journal*, a daily newspaper in the town that could not support
both his and Mr. Ament's weeklies.[5]

Young Sam set type on all these ventures of Orion's. He
was nearly eighteen when, in June, 1853, he left Hannibal and
went to St. Louis, where he worked as a compositor on the

[5] Armstrong, C. J., "Mark Twain's Early Writings Discovered" in *The
Missouri Historical Review* for July, 1930.

Evening News. By August 31 of that year he had moved on to New York, where he was employed as a job printer. On October 26, he was in Philadelphia, "subbing in the *Inquirer* office." Through the spring and summer of 1854, after a visit in Washington, he worked for the *Ledger* and the *North American* in Philadelphia. By fall he had returned to St. Louis and gone over to Muscatine, whither Orion had transferred his career and where Sam set type for Orion's Muscatine *Journal.* Soon afterward, he went back to St. Louis and the *Evening Post.* In the spring of 1855 (probably) he went to Keokuk, where Orion, having abandoned his editorial career, had set up as a job printer.[6] Sam worked for him as a typesetter till some time in the fall of 1856 — some time not later than October 18, the date of the first Snodgrass letter from St. Louis. By November 14, he was in Cincinnati, working once more as a job printer. He stayed there till April, 1857, when, starting down-river for the Amazon, he met Horace Bixby and decided to become a pilot.

Piloting put an end forever to the printer's trade. Thereafter, he was to write for newspapers nine years, from 1862 to 1871, but always as a reporter, an editor, or a correspondent. After April, 1857, he did not again stand at the case. The trade had had almost exactly nine years of his life, had taught him a characteristic style, and had exhibited to him the forms and themes he chose to make his own.

We are concerned, for the moment, with the Hannibal *Journal,* whose masthead announces that it is "published by O. Clemens, on Hill Street, near Main, a few doors west of Selmes' Buildings", and whose terms were "One Dollar, if paid in Advance; if not paid within Six Months, One Dollar and Fifty Cents; if not paid within Twelve Months, TWO DOLLARS." Sam was fifteen when he first went to work for Orion; he was nearly eighteen when he left Orion to begin his experience as a tramp printer. This is the period of the slight, exuberant, sandy-haired boy singing at the case, "If I ever git up I'll stay up if I kin", smoking furiously, sparking the maidens of Hannibal,

[6] Lorch, Fred W., "Mark Twain in Iowa" in *The Iowa Journal of History and Politics* for July and October, 1929.

serenading them with a guitar, writing, "Love Concealed" to
"Miss Katie of H——l" and "The Heart's Lament" to "Bettie
W——e of Tennessee", and lampooning "Local" (probably
Ament's successor) in paragraphs signed "A Dog-be-Devilled
Citizen" and "W. Epaminondas Adrastus Blab." It was the
period of adolescent growth, to which may well be assigned the
memories of Jim Wolf and the Tomcats, Alexander Campbell,
and the "Jesus H. Christ" episode. It is the period when he first
took notice of the life around him and of its infinite resources for
the wit of a young printer's devil who had a flair for words. Most
significant of all, it is the period when he undertook to show the
larger world that the youth who amused Hannibal had his
qualities.

Mr. Benjamin Penhallow Shillaber was the author of much
verse which fluctuated between a mediocre archness and a
nauseous sweetness. He was also the creator of Mrs. Ruth Partington, a Yankee widow whose comments on the times endlessly
amused America. At this distance, Ruth Partington — together
with her mischievous son Ike and such intimates as Professor
Wideswarth and Mr. Blifkins — seems intolerably depressing.
Her literary parentage was Charles Dickens and Joseph C. Neal.
She was also in the lineage of the Yankee moralizing that eventually achieved Doctor Holmes's Autocrat and of the verbal
atrocities put in the mouth of Mrs. Malaprop. To read her to-
day requires an indurated doggedness, but in the Fifties she was
famous. America found infinitely laughable such whimsies as
this instruction to Ike Partington: "You should learn, dear, to
bemean yourself before folks; because without good behavior, a
man may be ever so imminent for debility, but will never be inspected."

A great part of the widow's career was conducted in the pages
of the *Carpet-Bag*, a humorous weekly which Shillaber published in Boston from 1852 to 1853. The publication, though
short-lived, had an extensive popularity. Its circulation was
national and it was particularly well received along the rivers.
It had wholesale agents at Cincinnati and Louisville and was

distributed in St. Louis by R. E. Edwards and Company, 3 North Fourth Street, and R. Cheney and Company, 115 North Fourth Street. The village papers joyfully accepted it, filling their columns with quotations from it, acknowledged and un-acknowledged. Among the printshops where it was a permanent exchange was the Hannibal *Journal*. Orion Clemens found much of its contents amusing enough to furnish out his own columns.[7]

Shillaber himself wrote a good part of the contents of the *Carpet-Bag*. So did his associate, Charles Graham Halpine, who was to become the creator of Private Miles O'Reilly. He had the support of Boston's tiny — and only — Bohemia, and drew contributions from their prototypes at Pfaff's, then giving New York its first experience of light reading. It ranged still farther afield, for the Southerners sent in their notes on native scenes, and from California came sketches by Captain Horatio Derby, "John Phoenix." Finally, in 1852, the *Carpet-Bag* employed a young compositor from Skowhegan, Maine, named Charles Farrar Browne. Young Browne also contributed sketches to the *Carpet-Bag* under the pseudonym "Lieut. Chub": he had not yet invented the exhibitor of moral waxworks whom he was to call Artemus Ward.

Browne probably set type for some of the issue of May 1, 1852. This number contained an unsigned drawing by John Phoenix, called "The New Uniform." There was a typical bit of Southwestern humor in a sketch by Colonel Tuggs called "The Maine Law Out West", whose denunciation of enforce-ment agents has a poignant familiarity in 1932. One C. B. B. added to our literature's extensive collection of tales about amateur productions of Shakespeare. "Snooks", either Shilla-ber or John C. Moore, reported "the great speech of Mr. Batkins of Cranberry Centre, concerning the unconstitutionality of doughnuts." This was bucolic humor, Yankee variation, and pro-duced laughter by such spellings as deown, neow, reout beer,

---

[7] The number of issues missing from the files discovered by Mr. Armstrong prevents me from making a scholarly assessment of Orion's clippings from the *Carpet-Bag*. Between March 4 and June 3, 1852, with five weekly issues miss-ing, the *Carpet-Bag* is quoted four times. This is perhaps the average frequency.

passel, and catawampously. There was doggerel in defence of
Lola Montez and a noble poem by Shillaber called "The Old
Image Maker." Professor Wideswarth, one of Shillaber's crea-
tions, contributed another poem, and Ruth Partington's boy Ike
behaved atrociously at school. There was a news story about
Kossuth's visit to Mt. Vernon, wanly humorous sketches by Fred
Freequill and E. Goethe Digg, N.G., and a rash of abominable
puns and conundrums. But also there was a sketch called "The
Dandy Frightening the Squatter." It dealt with Hannibal, Missouri, and it was written by some one unknown to the *Carpet-Bag*,
some one who signed himself "S. L. C." [8]

This is the earliest bit of literary work by Samuel Clemens
yet uncovered. It precedes by four months the Dog-be-Devilled
Citizen's attack on a rival editor, and by an even year Rambler's
poems "To Miss Katie of H——l" and "To Bettie W——e of
Tennessee." If the fragmentary files of Orion's newspapers discovered by Mr. Armstrong are ever filled out, the missing numbers may be found to contain still earlier sketches,
but it seems likely that "The Dandy Frightening the Squatter"
was the first appearance of Sam Clemens outside the family
paper. He remembered and described to Mr. Paine two humorous anecdotes which he wrote in 1851 and which were published
in the *Saturday Evening Post*. These can never be identified,
even if his memory was exact, and in my opinion, as well as
Franklin J. Meine's, that memory referred to this appearance
in the *Carpet-Bag*.

"The Dandy Frightening the Squatter" introduces Hannibal when it was little more than a wood yard. A steamboat stops
there and "a spruce young dandy, with a killing moustache",
observes a "tall brawny woodsman" leaning against a tree. Desiring to amuse the passengers, the dandy thrusts a bowie knife
into his belt, takes a horse pistol in each hand, and strides ashore
to accost the squatter. " 'Found you at last, have I? You are the
very man I've been looking for these three weeks! Say your
prayers!' he continued, presenting his pistols. 'You'll make a

[8] Credit for this discovery belongs to Franklin J. Meine of Chicago. See his
book, "Tall Tales of the Southwest."

capital barn door, and I shall drill the keyhole myself.' " The heroic squatter looks at him for a moment, then knocks him into the river. The dandy is rescued but sneaks away; the squatter takes the knife and pistols. As the dandy leaves, the squatter shouts, " 'I say yeou, next time yeou come around drillin' keyholes, don't forget your old acquaintance.' "

Samuel Clemens's first literary effort is a humorous sketch contributed to a humorous newspaper. Its material is the characteristic frontier life of Hannibal. It is typical of the newspaper humor of the South and Southwest that was the first vigorous realism in American literature. It was the sort of thing that Sam Clemens, printer's devil and journeyman printer, had seen flourishing in the little weeklies that came to the exchange desk. Its *genre* was the native expression of the frontier. He began writing it in his first experiment and he continued writing it all his life. This literature of the frontier requires examination.

The frontier, according to Messrs. Frank, Brooks, and Mumford, had no folk art. Of the folk arts developed by the frontier, perhaps the richest was its stories. We deal here with a shy thing, which can be perceived in the twentieth century only where a traditional, wholly oral form of narrative is set down in print. Printing, of course, immediately and irrevocably changes the art. It gives the stories sophistication, polish, and the strange new shape of type. The border ballads of the seventeenth and eighteenth centuries suffer the same alteration in the broadsides, Percy's "Reliques" and their innumerable successors. We are at the disadvantage, then, of dealing with a different and sometimes a lesser literature. Yet much of the true folk art can be perceived in its printed memorials. Italics faintly suggest the intonations of these legion narrators, who learned their art from their companions and predecessors. The printed form reveals the careful structure of narration cunningly devised for pause and emphasis, for the slow preparation of climax, for the point that becomes a dénouement, a resolution, or a coda. It was an infinitely versatile art form; and, what is more important, an art sharply and autochthonously American — unique. To the eyes of any one but a theorist, and especially to any one who reads American literature, however superficially, the American is universally a story-teller. How the observation has escaped recent critics and historians of our literature remains, in 1932, the most amazing of all literary puzzles. For from the beginning it did not escape the hundreds of travelers among the Americans — who universally set it down first of all in their notes. It did not escape our own writers when they first presented Americans in plays cr in essays comfortably imitated from the *Spectator*. It did not escape those writers whom even the intellectual read, Cooper, Paulding, Hawthorne, Melville, Simms, Kennedy, Cooke.

The literature was redolent of the frontier. It was born of frontier leisure and frontier realities. By camp fires on the shores of lakes and rivers or on the plains, among the forests, or under the shadows of peaks; by the fires that blazed in skin tents, log lean-tos and cabins, sod huts, and trading posts; in the taverns, stores, groggeries, and meetinghouses of the frontier continent; on the decks of rafts, scows, flatboats, broadhorns, and steamboats — wherever frontiersmen met for conversation, this literature flourished. It obeyed the laws of folk art everywhere: in so far it was a universal literature. It had a corrosive humor — not the humor of "The Mabinogion" or of Tyl Eulenspiegel, its nearest analogues, but a humor derived from an instinctive realism: in so far it was an American novelty, something new and unique. It created folk heroes — not a great many but its own. Some of these it elaborated from historical fact: — Girty and Boone of the forests, Mike Fink and Colonel Plug of the rivers, Hare and Murrell of the outlaw trail, Colter and Hugh Glass and the lost trappers, and Jim Bridger, Jim Beckwourth and Kit Carson of the fur trade; Davy Crockett, Old Hickory, and Honest Abe of the hustings. Some of them it created whole from its own inner nature, Annie Christmas, Paul Bunyan, Jim Henry, Pecos Bill, even Frankie and Johnny and their myriad followers. Yet the existence of heroes must not distort one's ideas of this folk literature, whose overwhelming emphasis is upon the folk themselves. It is a literature of oral anecdote, whose purpose is the embodiment of character and the revelation of a point, whose aim is the entertainment of listeners, and whose origin is the life immediately at hand. The literature exists for drama, for humor, and for satire. It is the frontier examining itself, recording itself, and entertaining itself. It is a native literature of America.

Through the three decades of the common man following 1828, this literature reached its height. It was enormously male — emphatic, coarse, vivid, violent, uproarious. A great part of it, too, was bawdy. It had its conventions and technique. It had its channels of transmission and it had its immortality. One specimen only, for the type and process. Among the earliest emergences from oral tradition into type was David Crockett, member of Congress from western Tennessee. The backwoods newspapers endowed him with scores of anecdotes already traditional in the folk literature and by 1833 it was possible to make a book of them. Those who care to may find in "Sketches and Eccentricities of Col. David Crockett" legendary anecdotes by the dozen which have clustered about other, later notabilities. A frontier tradition was the humor implicit in calling a man ugly. The features of frontiersmen had been comic from the Kentucky Licks to the Three Tetons, where such diverse heroes as Daniel Boone and Jim Beckwourth celebrated the convention. Crockett, being a folk hero, must have his ugliness. As Bardolph's nose had saved Falstaff a thousand marks in links and torches, so Davy Crockett's paralyzing grin economized powder and lead. He could bring down a raccoon by grinning at it. Once the paralysis seemed unavailing; he grinned for a long time without bringing down his coon. His record remained secure, however, for investigation showed that he had mistaken a knot in an oak tree for a coon and had grinned all the bark off it.

The tradition embraces at least one man in every frontier settlement. It attaches to most popular heroes. Old Hickory, whose celebrant Davy Crockett was, became an Ugly Man to the delighted admiration of the common man. Old Tippecanoe and Old Rough and Ready must necessarily be Ugly Men too, for the production of votes. The tradition grows. Out of the folk humor rises the lovely vision of gifts and prizes, so that

the Ugly Man is awarded shotes or quarter sections for his pre-
eminence. Somehow a horn-handled knife enters the scheme. It
is bestowed on an Ugly Man, to be his property till he shall meet
an Uglier Man, whereupon honor will require him to hand it to
his vanquisher. American folklore, remember, records an anonymous stranger approaching Abraham Lincoln in a Washington
horse car. After the traditional inquiries, the stranger hands
Mr. Lincoln a horn-handled knife. It had been given to him
long before, with instructions to give it to the first man he met
who was uglier than he. But the convention was a generation
old in 1851 when Johnson J. Hooper burlesqued it in "A
Night at the Ugly Man's", by having "a level peck of buck-
horn handled knives" showered on Bill Wallis, the Ugly Man,
from the decks of a passing steamboat.

The leisurely, frontier, waterside village of Hannibal was
everywhere permeated by this anecdotal humor, which derived,
remember, from the realistic observation of character. It was
the frontier's experience and the frontier's idiom. All family fire-
sides, all meeting places of men, and in particular all stores and
wharves, made stages for its exhibition. The rich life of America,
and of the common man who composed it, was refracted through
a fine lens which was no more than an anecdote that richly
drawled a narrative of the frontiersman in action, paused for suspense and enjoyment, and built up a climax toward the laughter
of an audience. Samuel Clemens was born to this humor, realism,
and philosophy. All his life he was a story-teller, in the manner
and idiom of the frontier. He entertained audiences from the
platform; more richly and less chastely he, like Lincoln, entertained the audience of his private friends. It was his drama, his
life, and Mark Twain, its creation, was a riverside frontiersman
who, for the world's entertainment, exhibited a frontiersman's
observation of the world.

Samuel Clemens went to work for the newspapers of Joseph
P. Ament and Orion Clemens. The exchanges of the whole frontier and most of America besides came to the printshop, and he
saw this oral literature set in type. Thereafter, though at the
labor of great study, it is possible to follow him. There is no

need, here, to list the ephemeral papers that, coming to a Hannibal printshop, impressed on Sam Clemens's mind the idea that the oral literature might be also a printed literature — that these observations and this humor looked well in type. They sprouted like fungi, like Orion's own papers in the villages of two States, and after a few months or a few years they died. They mightily boomed the real estate of a hundred Herculaneums and Constantinoples. They made a mechanism for the common man's politics, battling to the death over conflicting platforms and the morals of candidates. They warred upon each other. They perished — but meanwhile they set down the literature of the frontier. Let them be anonymous here, since only an occasional St. Louis *Reveille,* New Orleans *Delta* or *Picayune,* *Arkansas Intelligencer,* or Nashville *Union* left any mark on the national life. They may be satisfactorily anonymous, since one more noteworthy than any of them is available to students. It was the *Spirit of the Times,* a sporting weekly edited in New York by William T. Porter of New Hampshire, that, fostering this *genre,* developed highest and spread farthest the literature of the frontier.[9]

The first interests of the *Spirit of the Times* were those of a country gentleman, — "the turf, agriculture, field sports." But in the course of chronicling these activities it began also to set down the life in which they existed and so came to the "literature and the stage" of its subtitle. Its circulation was national, but was top-heavy in the South and the old Southwest. The literature which it sponsored naturally reflected the interests of these sections. Porter might, for dignity, pirate the serials of Dickens and Thackeray only a few weeks tardily, but his enthusiasm was the frontier literature of his friends, hunting companions, and most numerous subscribers. Under his direction the *Spirit of the Times* fostered the humor of the frontier newspapers, brought it to focus, multiplied its production, and became its principal mouthpiece.

The emergence of Davy Crockett into print has been noticed. It made a formidable model. An even more influential and surely

[9] See Appendix A.

a finer model for the transference of folk literature into deliberate art was provided by Augustus Baldwin Longstreet's "Georgia Scenes", which appeared in the *States Rights Sentinel* of Augusta and other Georgia newspapers beginning in 1832, and which achieved book form in 1835. Longstreet, an editor, a college president, and a parson, was — inevitably — a frontier raconteur of widespread reputation. So far as any man may be credited with the discovery that this realistic humor of the backwoods was the material of literature, the distinction is Longstreet's. He, at any rate, set down his yarns and observations in print. They were enormously popular, running through many editions in the succeeding thirty years: they became the source and the model of innumerable successors. They were, too, enormously good: in some respects, Longstreet's successors never equalled him, in many respects they never surpassed him, and his book remains to-day vital and absorbing — the frontier's first permanent work.

"With 'Georgia Scenes'," Mr. Meine says, "Longstreet established a pattern that had a profound influence on all subsequent humorous writers of the South." They swarmed at once into print, following his path. The newspapers bristled with their works, anonymous hundreds, pseudonymous other hundreds. By February, 1845, Porter could write, in his preface to the first collected anthology of them, "A new vein of literature, as original as it is inexhaustible in its source, has been opened in this country within a very few years, with the most marked success." He rightly asserted the preëminence of his own paper in this development, saying that "the correspondents of the *Spirit of the Times* comprised a large majority of those who have subsequently distinguished themselves in this novel and original walk of literature." His selection of contributors for individual mention shows the catholic and versatile appeal of his paper. He names as contributors: Colonel C. F. M. Noland of Arkansas; T. B. Thorpe the artist; Colonel Mason; Captain Martin Scott (whom a frontier anecdote immortalized, after it had previously added glamour to Boone and Crockett); General Gibson, Major Moore, General Brooke, "and a host of other gallant officers of the U. S. Army, whom we are not permitted to name"; Audubon, Timothy Flint, Albert Pike, Charles F. Hoffman, Catlin, Mrs. Kirkland; "ex-Governor Butler and Mr. Sibley, the Indian agents"; J. M. Field, Mr. Kendall of the *Picayune*, "and several others whose identity we are not at liberty to disclose." In 1851, six years later, he "boasted eighteen correspondents in both houses of Congress."

In a characterization of this newspaper humor there must be mentioned, besides those on Porter's earliest list, a number of later, more distinguished writers — most of whom indeed were occasional or frequent contributors to Porter's weekly. With Longstreet on the *States Rights Sentinel* was William T. Thompson. He wrote, in this *genre*, a great many sketches which appeared in several papers, principally in the *Southern Miscellany*, and were later gathered into three books. The continuity of the literature is shown by Thompson's introduction of Joel Chandler Harris to the Savannah *News* in 1871. A lawyer, Joseph G. Baldwin, produced the memorable "Flush Times of Alabama and Mississippi." Another lawyer, who was also an editor, Johnson J. Hooper, created Simon Suggs and contributed his adventures to Hooper's own paper, the *East Alabamian*, and to the *Spirit of the Times*, together with many other sketches of the same kind. One must mention T. A. Burke, "Madison Tensas", John S. Robb, Sol Smith the actor-manager, and finally the robust and distinctive creator of Sut Lovingood, George W. Harris of Knoxville, whose versatile activities included service as a newspaper reporter and as the captain of a steamboat. These, with the names quoted from Porter's list, and a few of his correspondents whom he did not name, are the most noteworthy practitioners of frontier humor, all, in fact, who are relevant to our purpose. But their significance is chiefly that of their category, and one must persistently remember that they were only the more prominent of literally hundreds of humorists whose writings formed a great part of the material published in hundreds of newspapers all over America, and especially on the far-flung frontier.

The importance of this literature for history is its complete embodiment of frontier society. No aspect of the life in the simpler America is missing from this literature. The indigo tub and the bearskin rug are here, as well as the frontier gentry's efforts to speak French. In the solitude of the upper rivers, trappers practice their ferocity on Indians or notably slaughter elk by running them to death; in the solitude of hither-Illinois, Ole Bull meditates on his art. Jackson, Van Buren, Harrison, Benton, Taylor, Tyler, Douglas, and such worthies entertain the electorate; so do such humbler worthies as Big Bear of Arkansaw, Kit Kuncker, Dick McCoy, Billy Warrick, and Cousin Sally Dilliard. The panorama of religion passes: camp meetings, christenings, Millerism, Mormonism, spiritualism. So does the comedy of the land — claim jumpers, false locators, Regulators, auctions, surveyors, roof-raisings, husking bees — and of the law courts, the bench and bar, sheriffs, muster days, legislatures, election campaigns. The folk boil over in Texas and the literature swarms with dragoons and infantry, recruits, West Pointers, and Rangers. Itinerants pass by, those strange travelers from abroad, peddlers, actors, singers, mesmerists, prophets, temperance agitators, physicians, census takers, circus clowns, bear leaders, accordionists. The folk labor at their vocations in the fields and woods, the doggeries, the still-houses, the swamps, the bayous; at the spinning wheel, the loom, the churn. They frolic always, and if Betsy Smith, the fair offender, isn't married to John Bunce, why, jedge, "we oughter been, long ago.". . . Cataloguing is futile. Here is the complete life of the frontier.

The importance of this literature for criticism is that, humble as it is — a sort of rudimentary art on or just below the threshold of literature — it finally ripened in Mark Twain. In 1860, a young Ohioan whose kin had piloted steamboats on the rivers but who felt that the one value of the West was its two contributors to the *Atlantic Monthly*, made obeisance in Concord before the author of "The Scarlet Letter." Mr. Hawthorne perceived young Howells's shame and expressed great interest in the West, desiring to see some part of the country on which the damned shadow of Europe had not fallen. Books had usually more being in Hawthorne's mind than men or landscapes, and what he truly wanted was a book which had escaped that damned shadow. Howells had shuddered away from this humble literature; Sam Clemens had not. From his earliest days he read books which were a continent away from the damned shadow of Europe and, a continent away from the shadow, he lifted the *genre* into immortality.

It is not only that Mark Twain never became anything but a humorist, realist, and satirist of the frontier; he never desired to be anything else. His earliest writing was a natural, an inevitable expression of this small art. It expressed him and the life he saw. He went on to the bucolic contests of editors in Hannibal and in due time he wrote the Snodgrass letters in this form. From the pilot house he mailed frontier whimsicalities to the New Orleans papers. Then he was in Virginia City, and the Mark Twain who gigantically amused the readers of the *Enterprise* and became the Wild Humorist of the Pacific Slope merely grew out of the printer's devil at the Hannibal *Journal*. It was the same printer who finally brought a machinist into Arthur's court, filled St. Joan's France with Mississippi witticisms, and made the angel Satan a companion of Joe Harper in Eseldorf. But it was also the Hannibal printer who wrote "The Adventures of Huckleberry Finn."

V

THE RIVER

SAMUEL CLEMENS slowly takes shape. By 1857 we have, of actual fact, his letters to the Keokuk *Post* and the better part of thirty-five pages of letters to his family, and about one-fourth of that portion of the "Autobiography" which, in 1932, his executor and estate have thought appropriate for the public taste. Mr. Paine's biography has used up one hundred and fifteen of its seventeen hundred and nineteen pages. Mr. Armstrong and Mr. Meine have recovered the sketches earlier than the *Post* correspondence. There is nothing else. Something of what is said about him up to now may be derived from fact; most of it must remain inference and conjecture. From April, 1857, onward, however, it is possible to follow him in his books and the stream of private letters rapidly increases. Hereafter, this account will not without specific notice deviate from the facts ascertainable from the sources or from other material, duly documented.

The letters to the Keokuk *Post* require no more than classification. They are wholly of their type: newspaper humor in the
form of travel letters by an illiterate bumpkin. They are almost
the only excursion of Clemens into humor based on misspellings.
They contain nothing new, original, or individual. The collections listed in my Appendix A contain some twenty or thirty
specimens indistinguishable from these letters and the uncollected columns of the papers swarm with the same thing. The
letters of Thomas Jefferson Snodgrass, the bumpkin's name, are
nearest, perhaps, to Thompson's sketches about Major Jones, but
enormously cruder and more commonplace. Their humor goes
no further than misspelling, stock situations of ignorance and
embarrassment, and such hoary clichés as the speed of a railroad
train which, "Mr. Editors . . . made a rail fence look like a
fine tooth comb." They investigate the comic possibilities of re-
telling Shakespeare in the local idiom — which seems to be a
permanent plague, even in the smartest weeklies of to-day. They
allow the bumpkin to confuse stage catastrophes with actual
danger, a device which has been a part of English humor since
"The Knight of the Burning Pestle", which was to do Mark
Twain sturdy service later on, and which, in the Snodgrass
letters, he unquestionably imitated from Sol Smith's reminiscences in the *Spirit of the Times*. There is also an economy in
the exchange of Bible tickets, which are bartered at Sunday-
school.

The letters are wholly devoid of interest and amusement.
They have a single importance: they reaffirm the conclusion
enforced by "The Dandy Frightening the Squatter" and the
sketches in the Hannibal papers. Clemens's earliest impulses led
to the production of humor and nothing whatever suggests any
literary impulse or desire of any other kind. Yet it is Mr. Brooks's
strange thesis that Clemens really wanted to be Shelley.

The common man had staked out his promised land, crisscrossed it with his plows, and gathered in its first fruits. Flush
times had lasted almost twenty years. America had grown un-
believably rich. The new lands poured out their harvests, the

new factories multiplied beyond belief, the new railroads accelerated the progress of wealth into geometrical ratios, and hundreds of millions of dollars in new gold came eastward from California. So, in the heart of the continent, frontier society disappeared, and with it economic and social simplicity, ease and leisure, and the mood of pioneers and experimenters. Prophets came down but infrequently from the hills now, and the little communities of the consecrated, which had everywhere glazed American geography with the bright hues of hope, flickered out. Communisms of herbs or pear trees, of affinities, or of spirits perfected in the kingdom of God no more raised their ashlars on prairie soil. They were of yesterday, together with the angel Moroni and William Miller's mathematics and Sister Flavilla's white limbs flickering through storm and darkness toward the mountain top.

Life grew showier, noisier, hastier, and the Big Bear of Arkansas was only a memory in the canebrakes. The nation, accelerated, tricked itself out in vulgar ways. The flush times roared more stridently down the Fifties and then happened upon catastrophe. For though wealth had increased beyond computation and the nation's resources were inexhaustible, the genius of America has no capacity for economic organization and no feeling for the world abroad. The summer of 1857 found Great Britain heavily involved with American finance and production. The strain tightened, and then strange new fungi of the flush times, such as the Ohio Life Insurance Trust Company, collapsed. The genius of America saw no way to support them and other fungi came to grief — Erie, Reading, Illinois Central, Michigan Central. This was a panic. Thousands of firms failed. Banks closed. The common man, who had become a wage earner, starved over wide areas. Crops did not move. The Cabinet expected a revival of business. . . . And in the mist and tumult perished the flush times, an era, an American phase. New Jerusalem was over. America faced disunion and nationality and a new age.

But Cotton was King and in the South something of the old era lived on a little while. Samuel Clemens, of the flush times, took a boat out of Cincinnati, bound for the Amazon and great fortune.

On the *Paul Jones* the ambition of boyhood in a river town reasserted itself and, abandoning the Amazon, he apprenticed himself to Horace Bixby, a master pilot. This was in April, 1857. With Bixby, and with other pilots when Bixby was on the Missouri, he served his seventeen months' apprenticeship on the *Alex Scott* and the *Pennsylvania*, "Railroad Line" boats which connected with the Illinois Central and so hastened the end of the steamboat's prime; on the *Crescent City*, and the *New Falls City*, and on other boats anonymous in history. On September 9, 1858, he was licensed to practice this craft and became the partner of Horace Bixby. We can follow him on the *City of Memphis*, the *Alonzo Child*, the *Col. Chambers*, and the *Edward J. Gay;* he seems to have been regularly employed but his other boats are nameless now. Later, when he was famous, the customary legends grew up in the profession, and newspaper reporters could always find a veteran who was willing to say that he was an inferior pilot. The notion was worth repeating in the *American Mercury* as late as 1926.[1] Mr. Bixby, his master and partner, said otherwise, and, though the point is immaterial, it seems likely that he was a competent journeyman in this skilled trade.

He was not quite twenty-three when he was licensed. He practiced his trade until the spring of 1861, when, before his third year was complete, more than four years after his apprenticeship, the Civil War put an end to it.[2] He became an irregular soldier, in one of Missouri's extemporized guerrilla organizations, and soon afterward left for the far West.

The first of a series of deaths that were to be poignant in his memory, and were to fester throughout his life, occurred during his apprenticeship. His younger brother Henry died when the *Pennsylvania* was wrecked and Sam Clemens held him-

---

[1] Childs, Marquis W., "The Home of Mark Twain", *The American Mercury*, September, 1926.

[2] The exact date is not recoverable. "Life on the Mississippi" does not give it, and Mr. Paine found nothing definite.

self responsible for the tragedy. The shock was great and Mr. Paine says that his hair was partly gray thereafter — which is surely wrong, for its sandy auburn had no silver in it fifteen years later, when he was lecturing in the East. But the shock passed and for the most part those four and a half years on the river were an exuberant period. The flush times were ending in the noise and color of the steamboat age. Sam Clemens had come to a position of authority. "In the West," said Monsieur Dureau, the Americans "frequently give balls on the steamboats and they celebrate many of their marriages there. The line from Cincinnati to Louisville is renowned for its nuptial chambers. The Americans frequently make voyages on the steamboats to pass the honeymoon at a pressure of six or eight atmospheres. They love the noise and smoke, and the hissing of the steam makes music in their ears." [3] He had been a journeyman printer, but now he could live spectacularly at a pressure of six or eight atmospheres, and the noise and the smoke of the flush times were gorgeous, and the hiss of steam made music in his ears. It always did thereafter.

He is out on the icebound Mississippi, sounding for the channel. The yawl is caught in the gorge and swept downstream. A great bonfire on an island thaws him out but next day there is more sounding to be done, and when at last he is hoisted on board the *Maria Denning,* he and his companions and the yawl's cordage are sheathed in ice till they look like rock candy. He is on the *City of Memphis,* "the largest boat in the trade and the hardest to handle", and he swaggers before older pilots whom the hard times have kept out of work. He lets "the d——d rascals get a glimpse of a hundred-dollar bill peeping out" from his wallet. He swaggers before Orion, the moonstruck elder, who once would not let him buy a gun but is now happy to accept support. In New Orleans (where Eliza Ripley did not admire the gilding of steamboats and expressed her disdain of swaggering pilots) there are ten-dollar dinners in the French Quarter, admiring walks along the Vieux Carré, boating in the bayous and journeys "in the cars" to Lake Ponchartrain. Per-

[3] Dureau, B., "Les États-Unis en 1850", p. 81.

haps, too, there are excursions through the dimness of Gallatin Street. . . . Aunt Betsey Smith is advised to take the *Ben Lewis*, where mention of Sam Clemens will put Carter Gray, the pilot, at her service. Tom Hood's letters have interested him, though their humor is inferior to Orion Clemens's, but "my *beaux ideals* of fine writing" are "Don Quixote" and the "Citizen of the World." It is fine to drink coffee with burnt brandy in it, finer still to investigate the clairvoyant Madame Caprell, who feels that Sam Clemens might win distinction as an orator but will return to the trade of writing, at which he has surely had some practice. And he is "in a bad way again — disease, Love, in its most malignant form", though at table "still terrible as an army with banners", and, Aunt Betsey, " — the wickedness of this world!". . . A painting "The Hut of the Andes" is very fine, with a page of description overblown. And the girls allow him to embrace and kiss them, though Jane Clemens, on a holiday, disapproves. Jane is, however, "perfectly willing for me to dance until 12 o'clock, at the imminent peril of my going to sleep on the after watch." A Miss Castle, and a cousin, Ella Creel, are gay and glow for a moment, caught thus in March, 1860, dancing the schottische on the hurricane deck, with the pilot who a little while before was Horace Bixby's cub.

On the decks of the steamboats and in their cabins and pilot houses, the American race offers itself to the observation of Samuel Clemens. During the off watches George Ealer plays his flute and discourses about Shakespeare. Voyagers exhibit the whole reach of experience till there is, he says, no one in books or out of them whom he has not first met on the Mississippi. Above all, there is the talk of men. It is a constant stream in Mark Twain's books, and a good part of it was heard in early evenings while the *Alonzo Child* or the *City of Memphis* went booming down the spring floods. Tales of feuds and voyages, of mistaken identities, piracies, murders, hangings and lynchings, monstrous twins, hypocrisy, revenge, ghosts — much that his tropical imagination was to play with all his life originates here. Why not? The vitality of these people and times is all but inconceivable. The steamboat age perfectly expressed America. Even the débris through which it passed was vital and eloquent — the dens at Helena and Natchez and all the waterside slums; the shanty boats with their drifting loafers; the boats of medicine shows, daguerreotypers, minstrel troupes, doctors, thugs, prophets, saloon keepers, whoremasters. The squatters on the banks and the unbelievable folk of the bayous. It was a cosmos.

And for the first time cosmopolitanism enters the mind of Sam Clemens. All this was education. Frontier boyhood and the simplicities of a tramp printer merge into a maturity weathered by this infinitely variegated experience. He perceives much more: the damned human race is clearer to him. Much that is constant in his books — much of what is valuable — comes from this clear perception. One understands much better now the river rats, squatters, and no-accounts who will be so completely set forth in "Tom Sawyer", "The Gilded Age", "Huckleberry Finn", and "Pudd'nhead Wilson." A new light is cast on the idyll of St. Petersburg and one is surer about the gentilities also: the parlors, the chivalrous barbarisms of the South, the ways of men in packs, the measure of courage and kindness in an animal only imperfectly distinguished from the apes. One has at last that clear perception of the difference between what men are and what they pretend to be which will be the core of one's books. But with it, the boundless gusto in them, the dispassionate perception of apehood not in the least lessening a delight in the variety of man's nature that is the eventual Mark Twain. . . . Late in life, he is back at Hannibal, watching the villagers emerge from church. An old man who was a boy with him in Tom Sawyer's gang, deaf now and amiably unconscious of his voice, gestures toward the citizenry and bellows "Same damned fools, Sam," in an ecstasy of appreciation. For Sam they were always the same damned fools, perceived and stated, but in nothing abhorrent.

Criticism has been uncomfortable about "Life on the Mississippi", the mature expression of these four years. That is because it has found the realism of the belated second part hard to reconcile with the idyllic first part. Eight years elapsed between the writing of the two parts and in the second he could not recapture the glamour of the first, which is romance. The capacity for idyll-making gave us these gorgeous chapters but also it has gravely betrayed the critics, who interpret the first part of the book, "Old Times on the Mississippi", as the truth about the river and about the deepest of Mark Twain's desires.

That it was the second, that it fulfilled his hypothetical desire for creativeness, seems to be only one of those convenient assumptions that make easy the elaboration of theories. Clemens had a magnificent gusto for experience of all kinds. That he enjoyed piloting is obvious. That the color of these years with America at white heat should sometimes, in later life, convince him they were the truest expression of his nature is natural enough. No one could experience the flush age of 1857–1861 on the river without remembering it glamorously. He could therefore write to Howells, while the excitement of the *Atlantic* articles was on him, "I am a person who would quit authorizing in a minute to go to piloting, if the Madam would stand it. I would rather sink a steamboat than eat, any time" — without, in so doing, necessarily revealing the deepest cravings of his unconscious mind. The fact is that over the whole period of his life these years of piloting were in his thoughts far less than the romance of "Old Times" would indicate. Allusions to them as experience and desire in his letters are markedly infrequent, and in his autobiography quite as markedly so. He seems to have thought about them, in later life, rather less than about the years in Nevada, for instance, or in California. Nor can we discover in his books any influence of this assumed consummation. The years on the river did indeed complete his perception of the river folk and of the human animal; in that their effect is everywhere patent. But of the piloting itself, of this mystical fusion of creation with desire, nothing exists in the books that any person can dig up.

The truth is that "Old Times on the Mississippi" is not at all of Samuel Clemens but altogether of Mark Twain. On October 24, 1874, he wrote Howells, in answer to a request for further articles for the *Atlantic,* that he could find nothing that would do. Mailing the letter, he went out with Twichell for "a long walk in the woods" and "I got to telling him about old Mississippi days of steamboating glory and grandeur as I saw them (during five years) from the pilot house. He said 'What a virgin subject to hurl into a magazine!' " The riotous imagination of Mark Twain was touched off. His genius was wild, explosive, and undisciplined. All his life similar casual accidents plunged him into fevers of creation, some of which worked out into books, more of which shook the earth for a while and then came to nothing. This one, quite without forewarning or preparation, generated a masterpiece. The experience, the impulse, the opportunity, and the legitimacy were integrated, as they so seldom were, and the frenzy of creation, set in motion by a walk in the woods and Twichell's remark, worked out in the romance.

Realism was at work eight years later, when he wrote the remainder of the book, and sufficiently explains the difference between the halves. But it is essential now to point out how far realism is incomplete in both halves, and especially in the first, which has been thought so significant. For, if this experience on the river is held to be completely harmonious with Mark Twain's soul, then that soul had very little in common with Shelley's.

The flush times made the steamboat age, which perfectly reflects them. These florid palaces, garishly painted and gilded, pine smoke belching from their stacks, seized America in the bulk and set it afloat on the rivers. It was not altogether an America of spiritual loveliness, nor were the boats wholly instruments of creative fulfillment. The trade of steamboating was carried on in a competition which was typical of the age and far worse than anything the pioneering railroads achieved. It was an American commerce, without conscience, responsibility, or control. The financial returns it offered were so great that, whatever happened to boats, crews, or passengers, owners might count on profits. The proverbial frequency of disasters rested on snags, groundings, and lack of skill to some extent, but more than all else on fraudulent jerry-building and inferior material. The soundly built boat was the exception, a product of occasional pride or responsibility; the average boat was assembled from inferior timber and machinery, thrown together with the least possible expense, and hurried out to snare her portion of the unimaginable profits before her seams opened or her boiler heads blew off. Once launched, she entered a competition ruthless and inconceivably corrupt. No device for the fraudulent capture of freight and fares was overlooked. Everything that chicanery, sabotage, bribery, and malfeasance could devise was a part of the commonplace mechanism of the trade. The very poetry of racing rested on the commercial basis of profits to be made from reputation and superior speed. And racing is the cleanest aspect of the trade. The government, the States, and the insurance companies devised regulations for construction, upkeep, manipulation, loading, and tariff, and established services of inspection and enforcement. American commerce knew how to meet these tests and the bribery of officials was the routine of captains, engineers, and pilots. It was the ecstatic climax of unregulated competition, when a business prevailed over its rivals on pseudo-Darwinian principles. An examination which presses beyond the romance and the spectacle finds an economic reality hideous with cutthroat tactics. Of all this there is no hint in "Life on the Mississippi", and yet Clemens was for four years a part of this trade in greed and corruption. To be misled by his romanticizing it, to discover in a business that was the consummation of American materialism an assurance that what he most desired was, in the secret recesses of his soul, this same American materialism, is a triumph of subtlety. There was also much more about the steamboat age that does not appear in "Life on the Mississippi." Or rather, there is much about it that appears only indirectly in a book which, whatever it may be, is not a description of the steamboat age.

The effect of the years on the river is visible, I have said, in Mark Twain's perception of the human animal. This was, in essence, a confirmation and clarification of his earlier life.

It is to be found in other books, wherever he is scrutinizing reality. It is to be found only a little in "Life on the Mississippi", and not at all in its earlier, romantic part. In the second part it exists in the discussions of Southern manners and ideas, of feuds, of gentility, and of squatters. But these are merely the annotations of "Huckleberry Finn", which he was writing at the time, and of "The American Claimant", which was in his mind. For the rest, he was making romance about the Mississippi by concentrating on the infinite skills of the pilot's trade; and it is as romance, as the *genre* of "Tom Sawyer", that the book lives. It ignores the conception of the steamboat age, and though it chronicles a good deal of its garishness and stridency, it chronicles only what is spectacular in them.

There is, for instance, no hint of the squalid venery of the steamboats, which were consistently a habitation for the loves of travelers, river rats, and frontiersmen. Harlots of all degree, New Orleans courtesans in the grand manner as well as broken-down yaller gals no longer useful to riverside dives, were habituées of the boats. They and their pimps and all the machinery of bought protection, of display and sale, of robbery and murder were a constant in the trade. The book makes no mention of them. It probably would have made none in any case, since the amenities of literature in its time forbade, but its whole drift forbids also. There is no mention, either, of the parasitism that was also constant in the trade. The skin games, the frauds, the robberies, the gambling, the cozenage, the systematic organization of the sucker trade are wholly absent from its pages. To read the autobiography of George Devol is to perceive at once that the river as it was is not the river of Mark Twain.

It was, however, the river of Samuel Clemens and in due time, though not in this book, it would have its effect on Mark Twain. Meanwhile, it is essential to understand that Clemens experienced these years in the steamboat age. . . . He abundantly entered into its life. Also, he mastered another skilled trade. Not even romance, which could distort its importance,

could overstate the intricacy and subtlety of the trade. He had
been a printer; he became a pilot. Quite adequately he took his
steamboats along their channels, in storm, flood, and darkness.
When the war put an end to piloting, he had already had more
of the experience of America, and had been more intimately a
part of it, than any one else in American literature. Even more
was to follow.

Also, he had been "always scribbling." There is no possibility that this scribbling comprised anything more than anecdotal humor, conceived for the amusement of friends and designed for publication in the New Orleans newspapers. Nothing
could have been much different from the Snodgrass letters or
much better than them. Nothing has been recovered and nothing can possibly be important. Except the burlesque of Isaiah
Sellers, which eventually was to give Sam Clemens the nom-
de-plume Mark Twain.

In American literature, the Civil War has been mostly a department of oratory. Writers who fought in it made little of
it. There were always tears when veterans assembled before
footlights and rhetoric climbed skyward for the production of
votes. Robert Ingersoll set the blood beating in men's ears,
or professional sergeants touched a viscous pathos in remembrance of drummer boys, or the soughing of "The Fair God"
stopped for a moment and the memories of General Wallace
scrawled a page or two whose rhythms bore the authentic impress of men dying in orchards. Other generals quarreled endlessly with one another, or demonstrated the asininity of the
high command, or produced an endless trickle of books which
suggested that it was wrong to entrust sovereignty, Union or
Confederate, to upstarts who were clearly not gentlemen. They
are not pretty books. Charles Francis Adams, Jr., a combatant,
shared his brother's distress at the war's monopolization by the
vulgar and dedicated much of a historian's career to defining
revolution in terms of his family. One veteran broke through
rhetoric and statuary to something true: the war is there for
those of strong nerves, suspended in a clear medium, and our

successors for a long while will be reading the curt brutalities of Ambrose Bierce.

Noncombatants, on the whole, did a little better by the war than the active. From Georgian and Carolinian newspaper offices, from the weeklies of New England and the Middle States and the crisper journalism of New York, competent writing flowed steadily and names here first made known turned sometimes to the war in later years. They were best, no doubt, in John T. Trowbridge's visitations to empty battlefields after Appomattox, in the elegiac poetry of the South, and in the careers of humorists. These last, even in war time, made a profitable matter of derision from lyceum platforms and thus created a "Confedrit X Roads" or the plight of wax works confiscated in Richmond, devices that paid handsomely. They were entertaining in the stress of war, a little less so when the emotions had to be reinvoked in peace, and one reads them now between embarrassment and shame.

But American literature in the three decades following '65 was created mainly by men who, of military age in war time, found matters of greater moment than campaigning under arms. Nothing is challenged or supported by that fact, which casts no light on either literature or war. Merely, the war did not greatly disquiet most of our authors. It appears in the letters of William James as a concern about the good looks of officers at Pensacola, where Kitty Temple may encounter them, and an amused pleasure in a photograph of a "bully-boy", General Sickles, which James sends to his sister Alice as part of "a great anthropomorphological collection."

So that Sam Clemens in the summer of 1861 was not betraying the heroics of literature when a brief enlistment among the irregulars contented him. Later, he was to decide that the tinsel grandeurs of Sir Walter Scott had infected the whole South with romance and so brought on the war. In the glamour of this romance as it overspread Missouri in early '61, he joined the Marion Rangers, an impromptu collection of young Confederates. Chiefly, he "was full of unreasoning joy to be done with turning out of bed at midnight and four in the morning for a while: grateful to have a change, new scenes, new occupations, a new interest." The holiday lasted while the Rangers made grandiose night marches, listened to the declamations of Colonel Ralls, and swaggered among girls. Marching grew irksome, however, and the military diet began to pall, while a realization that they were combatants and so subject to hostile attack slowly impressed itself on "this herd of cattle." The amorphous war began to take a crude shape, irregular organizations coalesced into something of military semblance, and the Rangers dissolved. Sam, a second lieutenant with a sword, suffered from boils and had sprained an ankle. After his organization was demobilized, he lay humiliatingly at the house of a Mr. Matson and limped into the cornfield when a negro boy on picket duty shouted the approach of possibly hostile squads.

That was his war service as a commissioned officer in the Confederate Army. It had a pleasant confirmation in 1926 when Mr. Quaife published the reminiscences of Absalom Grimes, who also belonged to the Marion Rangers. War in Missouri proved unlike its prototype in "The Talisman", and chance converted Lieutenant Clemens to the Union cause when Orion was appointed secretary to the new Territory of Nevada. He might otherwise have lain in secret till his wounds healed and then joined some more bellicose successor to the Rangers, entering the border warfare that terrorized Missouri through five years. Or, failing the Quantrill motif, he might have imitated Ab Grimes's slinking between the lines with Confederate mail. Or still less gloriously, he might, like Sam Bowen, have safely served the Union Army as a river pilot while he served its opponents by assisting the transport of spies.

But he went West. So that the war meant to him only the abortive effort at the secession of Washoe, excited moments at a telegraph office when rumors of battle came through, the flour sack that was auctioned for the Sanitary Commission and plunged him into a duel, and with the years a slowly deepening reverence for Ulysses Grant. Then in 1885 he published in the *Century* "A Campaign That Failed", a reminiscence of his enlistment in the Marion Rangers. He said quietly that this picture of "Bull

Run Material" had its place in history, and so it has. There is more of the war in these youngsters, subject to glory and panic, than in most of the heroics that the *Century's* War History reveals. No glamour clouded Lieutenant Clemens's vision as he looked back over a quarter-century to that herd of cattle; and, happily, no typical impulse toward burlesque marred his writing. The sketch remains a lonely realism about the gathering of the militia clans in the confused days of '61, a perfect expression of Missouri's Civil War. The scared, excited boys go about their apprenticeship in fratricide and Sam's war literature seems likely to be permanent.

But, even looking backward in 1885, he found the war less important than the tug of his inheritance that drew him, in complete obedience to the American wandering, farther toward the West.

VI

WASHOE

I<small>T</small> was noon mark in the West. Perihelion. Sam Clemens, printer, pilot, soldier, traveling the Wells-Fargo stage route, passed along the nation's oldest trail. It had begun at the falls line of seaboard rivers. It had reached western beaches now, the frontier's farthest boundary, and it was deep with the ruts of many years. An English poet passing this way lamented a great dearth in this country: there were, he complained, no ghosts here. No literary ghosts surely, but a company in spectral buckskins, travel-stained, derisive, and not soft. You had your choice among whole regiments of wraiths: Meriwether Lewis and William Clark; Nat Wyeth and Benjamin de Bonneville, and Jed Smith and William Ashley, and Samuel Parker and Marcus Whitman and Jason Lee; ghosts out of our mythology, Kit Carson and Tom Fitzpatrick and Hugh Glass and Jim Beckwourth and Old Gabe; Uncle Dick Wooton and Bill Williams and Lucien Fontenelle; ghosts grown legendary before they were yet ghosts, like Kit and Jim and Gabe — like John C. Fremont and Pierre-Jean De Smet. Or ghosts of a humbler rank, the thousands stung by God's gadfly, crowding westward through dust and sleet and alkali for Oregon. *Pasó por Aqui!* Passed this way the fur trade and manifest destiny and the Oregon migration. Passed this way also the Mormons — sweat-stained and dogged, their eyes dazed with desert sun and New Jerusalem beside the Great Salt Lake, commanded by the Lion of the Lord, feeding on manna and quails, the true God himself a pillar of cloud before them by day and of fire by night, when they halted in the desert and formed their wagons in circles, to bury their dead perhaps or to praise the true God with frontier quadrilles to frontier music plucked from strings. Passed this way also the drums and tramplings of '49. And those lesser tramplings that succeeded them.

It was not, please, it was not a shameful passage, nor was there anything humble in these ghosts. Sam Clemens followed the migration of his folk and was merged in the myth and legend and fable of America. Up the valley of the Platte, past Scott's Bluff and Chimney Butte and Independence Rock, past Devil's Gate and Poison Spider Creek, past the Sweetwater to South Pass and over the Bad Lands to the ruins of Fort Bridger and thence to Echo Canyon and so to the Salt Lake House and wines and clear water and mountain trout in the kingdom of Brigham Young. It was not a mean pathway of inconsiderable folk.

Sam Clemens was absorbed in the passage. He was free of the interminable routine of piloting, free of the war, and bound on Western adventure in obedience to his heritage. It was holiday. He remembered "the gladness and the wild sense of freedom that used to make the blood dance in my veins on those fine overland mornings." So he went on from Great Salt Lake City and left the stage for good at Carson City, having progressed from a country of fable to the reality of the mines, from cloudland to Washoe.

A gentleman said it was the damnedest country under the sun. Sam agreed with him at first, remembering magnolias and

live oaks and lush river bottoms to the deprecation of this emptiness and thin air. An authority described the town as a mere
accident, the climate as hurricanes and snow, and the drinking
water as a dilution of arsenic, plumbago and copperas that had
to be heavily rectified with alcohol. The birds that flew over
the land, Sam said, with a nod in the direction of General Sheridan, had to carry their provisions with them; he found the
Carson River's trickle contemptible, and the sunrise stench of
sagebrush offended him. Yet there was bravado in mingling
with these bearded men and living in a frame shack papered inside with flour sacks. Then the desert began to exert its influence. The mountains became an acceptable substitute for the
Mississippi. Soon he climbed to Lake Tahoe, which "throws
Como in the shade." Thereafter one hears no more about desola-
tion.

But, on the mineral frontier, these bearded men were hammering out an epoch. On October 25, 1861, two months after
Sam's arrival, Pamela Clemens learns that if Cousin Jim
Lampton were in Washoe with three thousand dollars, it would
not take him six months to make a hundred thousand. Cousin
Jim was to become Colonel Sellers, the archetype of American
optimists, the complete symbol of dazzled eyes. But that was
in the future, and after two months in Washoe, Sam really believed that this country would make the fortune of a talent
like Cousin Jim's.

Two months of winter prospecting in the Humboldt country follow. Then Bob Howland comes back from Esmeralda,
and he is Sam's partner in the Horatio and Derby ledge. This
will soon be a big thing, so big that Sam laments his inability
to buy out all the shareholders; and if conceivably the ledge
should fail, the water rights will be worth a fortune. That is
in February, 1862. The Pyramid Lake campaigns against the
Indians rioted through western Washoe in March and April,
with disgraceful massacres, scalping, and the bluster of heroes
who had finally to be subdued by vigilantes, but they are worth
only a curt paragraph in a letter to Orion, and an allusion to
Cousin Sally Dilliard of the frontier press. Sam, now in Es-

meralda, can give no more space to Indian wars, for he will strike the Horatio and Derby ledge by July, needs the Live Yankee deed, can't work the Red Bird or the Governor claims while they are under snow, but has recorded them and the Douglas, and has thrown away the Pugh as nothing but bed-rock croppings. A man named Gebhart has been shot while trying to defend a claim, the mills are not worth a damn, and Orion must send forty or fifty dollars immediately. A month later he is willing to wait two years for a fortune but, though his other claims will make him rich by '63 or '64, only six weeks need elapse before the first dividend from the Monitor ledge, of which "money cannot buy a foot" of his holdings, for "I know it to contain our fortune." Then Orion's speculation in Mountain House is commended as a big thing, and Sam needs one hundred dollars to keep open the Flyaway and has not a single cent. A few days later he understands the killing of Gebhart, for his Wide West claim has been jumped by armed men who are in the hole and mean to die for it. To-morrow these roughs are to be driven out by force.

This last became the story of the blind lead in "Roughing It", a quintessential recording of Washoe lusts in which the whole era is compressed. There is the miner, squalid in beard and faded jeans, squatting beside a sick man in a windy cabin, mechanically attending to the invalid's needs while his own mind plays through a gaudier delirium. "I was altering . . . the plans for my house and thinking over the propriety of hav-ing the billiard-room in the attic . . . I was trying to decide between green and blue for the upholstery of the drawing room . . . I was content to put the coachman in a modest livery." In Washoe the sick man groans and wails, filling "the odd chinks with the most elaborate profanity that strong convictions and a fine fancy could contrive." But in New Jerusalem, "I was systematizing the European trip . . . whether to cross the desert from Cairo to Jerusalem by camel, or go by sea to Beirut and thence down through the country per caravan. Meantime I was writing to the friends at home . . . directing them to look up a handsome homestead for my mother . . . and also direct-

ing them to sell my share of the Tennessee land and tender the
proceeds to the widows' and orphans' fund of the typographical
union, of which I had long been a member in good standing."
He leaves the sick man convalescent and, still bemused by silver-
land, returns to the blind lead. Reality comes corrosively: in
his absence the claim has been relocated and the vision dies
like a skyrocket. "We would have been millionaires if we had
only worked with pick and spade one little day on our property."

The yarn is true to the mining career of Sam Clemens in
that febrile spring and summer of 1862. "Millionaires!" The
image flickers along the mind's horizon as ceaselessly as the
undulations of the heat mirage above Washoe. His overcharged
nerves relieve themselves in oaths and threats. "The Clemens
Company — all of us — hate to resort to arms in this matter
. . . but I think that will be the end of it nevertheless." (American literature contains so very few books by men who have experienced an emotion so violent as an impulse to kill.) He
flames against Orion's gullibility — "sending a man fooling
around the country after *ledges*, for God's sake!" An "if" slowly
tarnishes the vision: "if we strike it rich." Fortune is farther off
and he wonders how in hell he can live three months on a hundred dollars. The question is urgent. He had written jovial letters to the *Enterprise*, now removed to Virginia City. Signed
"Josh", they had delighted Washoe, and it may be that the
earlier trade of correspondent may support him on the road
to millions. Orion is to barter Sam's literature among California
papers, mentioning the respect in which New Orleans has held
it. The savage battle between quartz and fever endures another
month. Then abruptly the offer of a steady job writing news
for the *Enterprise* arrives and puts an end forever to Sam's silver
mining. He writes Pamela that he has never thought of returning to the river and never expects to do any more piloting
at any price. His livelihood must be made in Washoe and so
he leaves Esmeralda for Virginia City, mining for journalism,
and discharges at Orion a savage blast of disillusionment. Tell
B, he says, that "the 'endless snows' have all disappeared and
in their stead . . . the mountains rear their billowy heads

aloft, crowned with a fadeless and eternal verdure; buds and fountains and trees — tropical trees — everywhere! — and the poet dreamed of Nevada when he wrote:

'And Sharon waves, in solemn praise
Her silent groves of palm.'

and to-day the royal Raven listens in a dreamy stupor to the songs of the thrush and the nightingale and the canary — and shudders when the gaudy-plumaged birds of the distant South sweep by him to the orange groves of Carson. Tell him he wouldn't recognize the d —— d country."

This break in his career has had psycho-analytical attention. Sam walked sixty miles of the way from Esmeralda to Virginia City. No reason for the hike is mentioned in his letters, which merely announce it and direct Orion to tell the *Enterprise* that he is coming, and it may be that Sam was only saving stage fare. But Mr. Paine, without offering evidence, says that "he had gone into the wilderness to fight out his battle alone." Presumably this means that Sam was reluctant to give up the vision of millions from silver for a wretched twenty-five dollars a week from reporting. One can understand the reluctance, if indeed it played any part in this unimportant walk; and this was probably the emotion that troubled Sam, if any did. He wrote in "Roughing It": "I had been making such an ass of myself lately in grandiloquent letters home about my blind lead and my European excursion that I did what many and many a poor disappointed miner had done before; said 'It is all over with me now, and I will never go back home to be pitied — and snubbed.'" That seems true enough. But Mr. Brooks is able to discover in this alleged hesitation about joining the *Enterprise* the artist in Mark Twain rebelling against his future degradation. "This reluctance shows us that in becoming a humorist he felt that in some way he was selling rather than fulfilling his own soul." He had foully betrayed himself, Mr. Brooks thinks, by trying to make a fortune from hard rock; now the greater betrayal of writing humor for a newspaper raised up a psychic dam and the condemned artist in Samuel Clemens made this protest before going out to die.

A passage in beautiful thinking, unrelated to fact.

James Fennimore, alias James Finney, was known as Old Virginia, from his birthplace and his talent for containing one of its products. He had briefly owned the Ophir, one of the most fabulous portions of the Comstock, but had sold it for "an old horse, a pair of blankets, and a bottle of whisky." History would have made more of him but for this self-indulgence; still, he has his permanence, for he gave the camp its name. It had been called indifferently Pleasant Hill, Mount Pleasant Point, Ophir, Ophir Diggings. Finney stumbled, one evening, and broke a bottle of the refreshment known as tarantula juice that was in his pocket. Rising, he stoically sprinkled the remaining drops of it on the site and said, "I baptize this ground Virginia." He then disappeared forever, but the place was named.

The town sprawled on the slope of Mount Davidson and gazed eastward through clear air to the Humboldt Mountains, one hundred and eighty miles away. Across emptiness one saw desultory rainstorms flash and gloom along those ridges, but in between was only the striated white and olive of the desert. Northward were the Castle peaks and, a thinner line beyond them, the wavering purple outlines of mountains southward from the Carson River. Eastward, and lower, the rounded top of Sugar Loaf permitted glimpses of the Carson's valley with Forty Mile Desert beyond it, naked in intolerable sun. Then the Humboldt peaks curved in again, mere illusion, and closed the circle of Washoe. A high town, naked to the west, parched by desert sun, stripped by the Washoe Zephyr which came whooping over the summit of Mount Davidson two thousand feet above.

Virginia City was the mineral West in a new phase. California gold had mostly lain in creek bottoms and the detritus of spring run-offs, so that any one could loosen it with a shovel or a fire hose and wash it out in a rocker or a tom. A vast democracy marked the takings in the gold fields while they lasted;

though, as always, the impressive fortunes were made not by the
miners, but by storekeepers, Yankee or Jew, who sold them
supplies, at a price, and bought their dust, at a discount. But
Washoe silver was imbedded in the fundamental rock, which
implied capital to work it. A traditional figure vanished, the
miner who sang about the washbowl on his knee and sat for those
astonishing chromos by Bret Harte. He came to Virginia City
in great numbers, but he lacked money to develop his claims
and so went to work below ground at four dollars a day. His
employers were, for the most part, the same storekeepers who
had trimmed him so competently in the Sierras. An engaging
caste. Their marbles gleam flawlessly between evergreens and
the Pacific sky; they have done a splendid pillage in European
art shops; and princelings have contributed the refinement of
a more ancient banditry to the blood of Yankee tinmen, Irish,
and ghetto Jews which was first ennobled by short-weight sales
to miners along the Stanislaus. Washoe eventually bred up its
own millionaires at the shaft-head but its first phase belonged
to Californians who took their profits and moved on toward
the construction of railroads. One may now consult rare books
through their bounty and college boys might as well be pension-
ers to their bereavements, no doubt, as to the megalomania of
petroleum wells.

Their shafts were hundreds of feet down when Sam Clemens
came to Virginia City. The city climbed the mountainside by
steps, its inclined streets crisscrossed by avenues that were like
levels of a terrace. Also, it sank gradually, for it was built on
a shell of rock above a timbered void. The mines were a honey-
comb; not many shafts caved in from above, but they were
kept from doing so only by the long sacrifice of Washoe forests.
Beams held the earth stable, more or less, but the city streets
were rocked all day by the detonation of blasts under the hollow
rim. Rocked, too, by the crunching of stamp mills and by the
endless procession of ore wagons. Narrow, filthy, and parched,
the streets lay open to the desert sun, to the Washoe Zephyr,
and to the sand storms that ripped westward from Forty Mile.
They were as defenceless against fires, which three times levelled

the whole city and which were prevented from a daily repetition of the cleansing only by the volunteer fire companies, foci of politics and social discourse.

A noisy, violent, incredible city. Elsewhere in the West the miner labored in inaccessible gulches and, for a bust, made infrequent pilgrimages to the big town — Denver, San Francisco, Helena. But here hard rock and the big town met in one continuous bust. The West consummated itself. When the shift ended, miners boiled out of the shafts, paused only to note the day's fluctuations on the ticker, and then diverted themselves in ways that were invented for them. The tender-minded have been repelled by these amusements, which were, simply, a loud show. The miner at his ease mingled with the traffic of the streets, the ore wagons, the stages, the scavenger Piutes, Chinese with mountainous piles of firewood erected on the backs of burros or bearing laundry baskets on their own heads, the blare of bands while fire companies and militia paraded with nickeled axes or purely decorative bayonets above red flannel shirts, plumes and sabers and fasces swaying to the procession of threescore lodges marching in aprons or tin armor or yashmaks to the funeral of Buck Fanshaw. They fought a way through this strident crowd and a hundred palaces received them. These were "bit houses" where every drink, regardless, cost the short or the long half of a quarter-dollar; or "two-bit houses", Mayfair, where one paid the full quarter for any refreshment, ranging through beer and whisky and lemonade to blended confections and vintage wines. As the Comstock climbed its blazing pathway, the barrooms became a Western art. Packed in freight wagons, mirrors and rare woods came up Mount Davidson for the adornment of gin mills. Crystal and mosaic and jewel work dazzled eyes used to squinting in the flare of shaft lamps. The polite world everywhere follows the serious money: Washoe drew sculptors on the grand tour to carve bawdy figures in ivory or marble toward whom the miner gestured his invitations. Painters down on their luck or merely alcoholic were washed inland from San Francisco: some grew, later, to formidable reputations which neglected to list signed frescoes in Washoe bars. These were the accompaniment of a fine art, the plain song of American drinking, which first invaded Europe with our imaginative compounds. Its professors came to Washoe from gustatory centers in the East or from San Francisco. They came, mostly, in the rush for claims; they stayed to preside over bars of mahogany and ebony, to stand before heaped crystal and to obscure authentic masterpieces in oils or tempera while, with infinite craftsmanship, they compounded the multiplicity of drinks necessary to a heroic age.

The palaces blended with scores of dance halls, melodeons, parlor houses, cribs. Mark Twain's elderly memories included the swirl of Etta Booth's crimson frock amidst the dancing of two or three hundred men, half of whom wore handkerchiefs on their arms to symbolize femininity. Etta was, he remembered, with her mother, the only woman in the room. The memory was pretty but unreal. *Hetæræ* accompany the fine arts in association with quick money. They came to Virginia as soon as the true value of the Comstock was perceived. They constituted, no doubt, a deplorable source of gambling, pleasure and embroilment. They were not soft-spoken women, their desire was not visibly separable from the main chance, and they would have beheld Mr. Harte's portrayal of them at Poker Flat with ribald mirth. But let them have a moment of respect. They civilized the Comstock. They drove through its streets reclining in lacquered broughams, displaying to male eyes fashions as close to Paris as any then current in New York. They were, in brick houses hung with tapestries, a glamour and a romance, after the superheated caverns of the mines. They enforced a code of behavior: one might be a hard-rock man outside their curtains but in their presence one was punctilious or one was hustled away. They brought Parisian cooking to the sagebrush of Sun Mountain and they taught the West to distinguish between tarantula juice and the bouquet of wines. An elegy for their passing. The West has neglected to mention them in bronze and its genealogies avoid comment on their marriages, conspicuous or obscure, but it owes them a here acknowledged debt for civilization.

These palling, Virginia City offered still a myriad delights.

The mines were a lush country for the strolling players, who had followed the rush to California and now played a long circuit through the Sierras and beyond. A half-dozen legitimate houses flourished on the Comstock, besides a score of more dubious enterprises in the bars and cribs. Miners packed them nightly to the footlights and showered their silver dollars with catholic taste on every moment of illusion. San Francisco's Italians sang "Norma" and "Somnambula", the "Barber of Seville" and "Trovatore" for them, and all the doleful, forgotten passions of that kind; the flannel-shirted wept, with sympathetic glances at the boxes where the *hetæræ* sat, and to-morrow buried a Tom show under other dollars in recompense of little Eva's ascension, or, justly, applauded the gymnastics of grunting seals on the same stage. Any romance would do, any rapture compounded of tinsel and red fire. The Renowned Basiliconthaumaturgist sent white pigeons fluttering from a silk hat or performed the great Japanese Papillonaceous Puzzle taught him at the court of Prince Satsuma; the flannel shirts cheered him with their silver hail and, after him, tragedians presenting select programs from Shakespeare and the Bowery, baby stars lisping ballads of the war in cute skirts, spirtualists who summoned Napoleon from the great deep, and French importations who were adept in the cancan. The minstrels, in the wake of Uncle Tom whom they savagely burlesqued, fluttered their lavender swallowtails in endless dances, now resuscitated for the applause of moderns, and sang a matured balladry rich with topical illusion. It was a climax for the minstrel troupes, a native extravaganza of high merit. Tambourines accentuate the music of banjos and fiddles. Bones clack as Mr. Interlocutor courteously responds to Sambo and Mr. End-man in a rapid persiflage of comment on American life, in no way credulous or uninformed. The blacked chorus forms, gorgeously raimented, and Auntie, will your dog bite — no chile no, while the walk-around begins or the solo dancers perform to melodies then undergoing transmutation in the jubilees. . . . It was all glorious to hard-rock men. Glorious, too, the light tunes of the burlettas, when choruses of girls in fleshings paraded for the eyes of men who had crossed the

continent for the silver they bestowed on these nymphs. The
tinsel moment was beyond price, whoever produced it. The
triumphs of Macready, Forrest, Booth rocked these frontier
boards in smaller apings. War melodramas, with tranquil in-
terpolations in song or tableau or fusee; Shakespeare and Con-
greve and Sheridan; farces of Irishmen, Yankees, and whiskered
Englishmen; the myriad high romances of the East. The brawny
leaned forward in their chairs, straining for this gossamer dream.
At last Adah Menken bared her memorable body except for
an apologetic shred of gauze and, strapped to the wild stallion
of Tartary, was borne, white, violable and orgasmic, to the
upper flies. She consummated in melodrama the lust of an era
and a locality born of melodrama. The Comstock's adoration
of her concealed nothing of its basis. Her body was beautiful and
to the Comstock it symbolized infinite desire. So thousands of
adventurers violated her in this mimic cruelty and the writers
of the *Enterprise* performed prodigies of infatuation. Sam
Clemens did her the homage of submitting his new writings to
her criticism; he made a conundrum about her hand, which
drooped fragilely from her yellow silks, and went out to write
a confessed enchantment that spread over the continent. She
was a paroxysm, the climax of Washoe theatricality.

But graver entertainment, too, followed the money to Virginia. The translator of the "Arabian Nights", then traversing
this un-English barbarism to overhear the death-rattle of the
United States, gaped at the presence amidst sagebrush of lyceum
lecturers who had entertained almost genteel audiences in Boston. The Comstock was as attentive to Free Soil Jeremiahs and
alumni of Brook Farm as to Topsy or the purveyors of the cancan. They ranged from Horace Greeley, at the era's beginning,
to Schuyler Colfax and Samuel Bowles toward its end — in-
terspersed with geologists, globe-trotters, mathematicians, re-
vivalists, mystics, seeresses, war heroes, and senators on tour.
No deposit from such intelligences seems to have been left on
the journalist's mind, but such persons as Orpheus C. Kerr and
Artemus Ward also followed the money hither, and it is possible that he learned something from them. . . . Meanwhile,
outside the theaters and lecture halls, the Comstock provided

diversions for other tastes. The embryo of the Wild West Show was here: also, on fête days, the social combat of fire companies spraying each other with high-pressure hose or charging massed ranks with Roman candles. The bear-and-hound games of the frontier were here enriched by the Mexican refinement of bulls. Terriers matched against badgers vastly entertained the miners, who were also, of course, enraptured by cock fighting. Hingston, Artemus Ward's manager, saw a pleasant variation of the latter. One gave the impresario a dollar and undertook to pull a cock's legs off with a single jerk. If he did, the bird was his; if he didn't, the dollar belonged to the proprietor. Hingston observed that the tortured cocks made no sound. "They can't," his guide explained; "they are too much absorbed." . . . Let the game signify the more robust amusements of Sun Mountain.

It was, flatly, a robust town. The gently bred have recoiled from it in pages that express a horrid shock. The parthenogenesis of an artist is hard to reconcile with this excitement, blowing stridently through mountain air. Yet Virginia City completely satisfied Sam Clemens, whose letters boundlessly express his contentment. What is more, the city, filling the measure of his frontiersman's heritage, gave him and his writing a permanent shape. This seems no matter for apology; the business of criticism is description.

So one must patiently note this final incandescence of the westward surge. Washoe was another cosmos. Flush money brought all conditions of society westward, and the venturer in Washoe saw reproduced against a background of sagebrush the same cyclorama of the human race that had been so prodigally displayed on the Mississippi.

Notably, the West was fecund in the production of men. There is here no need to dwell on the most repulsive class, the toughs.[1] Human life was cheaper than most commodities on the

---

[1] I have described some of them in "Brave Days in Washoe", *The American Mercury*, XVII, 66 (June, 1929). A number of sentences from that essay appear in the present chapter. Any one interested in the Washoe bad man may cultivate him at delightful length in Sam P. Davis's "History of Nevada", 1913, 2 volumes.

Comstock, but violence of this sort was no novelty to an ex-pilot
or a native of the society that at the moment was conducting the
border warfare. In Washoe, a code of the duello existed: two
of Sam's colleagues on the *Enterprise* had stood up at the proper
distance, offering themselves to formal gunfire, and he himself
was finally forced out of the State because he had sent and
acted upon a challenge. Manslaughter in a fair fight carried with
it no social stigma whatever, and in the city streets, unmolested
by the law and unavoided by the citizens, walked hundreds of
men who had settled arguments by the one invincible syllogism.
But Washoe was of the West, and the West was notably cold
toward the swaggering bullies who terrorized the Southwest
and, developing a tradition of murder, gave fiction and the
screen their Bad Men. The overheard pistol shots that ex-
plode in Sam's letters represent the disputes of amateurs, not
the applauded tableaux of professionals. The West promptly
expunged professionals by means of vigilance committees, such
as Virginia City's Six Hundred and One. It is necessary, only, to
mention Jack Davis's organized stage robbers who, when progress brought rails to Carson City, performed the first train
robbery in history; and who gave the art of fiction a scene that
seems likely to be immortal when, finding champagne and *hors
d'oeuvres* in a stage they had plundered, they served an extemporized banquet to their victims. These only, and the coroner's jury which commended Henry Vansickle, a private citizen,
for his efficient disposal of Sam Brown, a Bad Man who had
been laboring to establish locally the tradition of the Southwest.
The jury inspected the perforated remains and decided that
Sam Brown had come to his death from "a just dispensation of
an all-wise Providence." Sam Clemens made use of the verdict.
So did Alfred Henry Lewis, and through Lewis, it entered the
lowly art of "Western stories" where doubtless it will remain
for ever.

   With Washoe millionaires, American legend achieves a
new image. Several of the more engaging were, during Sam's
stay, still hacking at the fundamental rock for four silver dollars a day, but the image, from Comstock's first strike to the

end of the Big Bonanza, is of one piece. Colonel Dave Buel, as sheriff of Hangtown, could deliver a prisoner from a mob of lynchers, facing them down with six potential shots from a Colt's against a thousand, and with the same tranquillity bow himself out from the royal box of Eugenie and Napoleon III at a Paris fête. The scene flickers across a score of forgotten novels, merged with Jim Nye's reception by the Sultan, who paraded thirty thousand troops for Jim's inspection. They flare through Europe, these caliphs of Western treasure caves, the world a bauble tossed among them in innocent grandeur. They are perfectly recorded in "Roughing It", "The Innocents Abroad", and "The Gilded Age", and criticism should be gentle with them, a little while. The Comstock rocked with their warfare, the incredible millions of the stakes energizing the ganglia of the world's finance. The incredible millions drew to alliance with them decorous inheritors of Eastern States, whose nostrils quivered uncontrollably but who could so far control disdain as to share profits with the bounders or to marry a daughter into the Comstock without qualms. They drew also the constellation of Washoe lawyers, unquestionably the brightest in America, who created for the caliphs' amusement the subterranean warfare of the courts. Simply, a State existed for the disputes of millionaires about incredible wealth. Rich tailings accompanied the warfare; to be a judge or even the foreman of a jury offered prospects that few ledges apart from the Comstock could equal. The battles of theft and bribery and subornation made another spectacle in the country of spectacle, and Washoe at last defined itself in legal terms. Zinc Barnes survived the arrows of Piutes to become a captain in these more exhilarant campaigns and in a moment of disenchantment phrased the specifications for an honest man. An honest man, Zinc said, was a son of a bitch who would stay bought.

It was *Kriegspiel* to the caliphs. Mills, Baldwin, Hearst, Mackay, Flood, Fair, Sharon, Lent, Buel, Jones, Ryan, Daly, — they were nabobs in the Western manner. They would not be frightened; no one bullied them. Millions were mere counters. What they desired, after a while, was the heat lightning of the game more than the chips that recorded its fluctuations. Whether in the hard rock itself or in the markets that kited its symbols, they engaged in a contest of wills. Power was their function, and the smooth effectuation of desire. They had a code — even a friendship. They sent Uncle Jim Fair to the Senate because a silly wife wanted him there, though they knew the ass he would seem. They honored one another's drafts in time of panic, omitting to imitate Eastern gentlemen in packs. Their loves were cyclonic and they were superstitious about their stars. They withdrew at last from Washoe, to crown Nob Hill with wretched palaces. Then the glories of the East and Europe became their perquisites. The gentlemen made room for them, nostrils now perfectly accommodated to the aroma. Sons and daughters were vulgar as their fathers never were, blending without effort in the plutocracy. Grandchildren are princesses now, or partners in the profits of sweatshops, and the memory of the founders endures chiefly on stock farms. The caliphs had loved horses. A thoroughbred also would run till his heart burst for no more tangible end than to win a race.

The Western manner formed: cool, detached, unimpressible. Perhaps a theory would find an analogy in desert air which dissipates half lights and presents the true outline of objects undistorted. Uncle Billie Lent uttered his epitaph: "Tell the boys I think I've bested as many as has bested me." John Mackay made comfortable the last years of his favorite actors, anonymously: he tossed rolls of gold eagles into the genuflecting laps of Irishwomen in trouble; but when the city caught on fire, "Damn the church, we can build another", though he was devout enough. Then Lincoln needed Republican votes for his war measures, and Washoe, a sovereign State, sent specimens of its mintage to the Senate. They are not forgotten there, though Washington's drowsy afternoon now hears no rumor of Leland Stanford and his California colleagues. Bill Stewart was the Comstock's creation. A local proverb, perceiving Stewart's manner, drawled its appreciation: "If heaven forsakes the poor miner, he'll be turned over to Bill Stewart." Gunmen had not dismayed Bill in Washoe: he was not troubled by Sumner,

Stevens, and such personages. He tamed Secretary Stanton in one withering interview. He saved Mr. Lincoln's war program at vital emergencies and in payment was asked along on occasions about which the uninvited great lived to lie deplorably. Chandler, Conkling, Carpenter came to depend on Bill's formidable warfare. Free silver slew him in the end, but he had given his State a spacious name; and, it is worth remembering, he had sponsored the Fifteenth Amendment and had defeated the Force Bill of Henry Cabot Lodge.

In recognition of a Washoe friendship, Stewart made Sam Clemens his Washington secretary, when the *Quaker City* returned from Palestine. Sam burlesqued him, later, and Stewart wrote a page or two of resentment in his memoirs. Another friend of Sam's, John Percival Jones, also instructed the Senate in Washoe's quality. Jones was a millionaire several times over, from the Comstock; he was less practiced than Bill Stewart in Washoe oratory, though the Senate listened when he talked; but he was fully as learned as Old Bill in the dispassionate wisdom of the West. He was President Arthur's confidant; Conkling and Cameron relied on his friendship; he came to admire McKinley, and he uttered one of the few recorded tributes to Mr. Harrison. Term after term, his quiet, almost pedantic realism was a firm thing in that chamber of rhetoric. He, too, disliked Cabot Lodge. "Senator," he once said to this elegant vanquisher of Lydia Pinkham's son, "I have heard many of your speeches and I have read all your published thoughts." The Comstock drawl dipped suavely toward offence. "It is a pleasure to me to tell you that you are an eloquent speaker; that with your epigrams and metaphors, your logic and figures of speech and your speaking the exact words needed to make clear your thoughts, it is a pleasure to read your books. Only — " this was history's assessment made known by a hard-rock man, in whose blood ran none of the inheritance that could justify reproof to Cabot Lodge — "only, Senator, you have never come down to earth. You don't know a blessed thing in the world of how a poor man goes to work to make a living and to feed his babies."
. . . The years drew the Comstock atoms together again. In

October, 1889, Joe Goodman, once editor of the *Enterprise*, was implored by his illustrious reporter to approach Senator Jones and sell him a hundred thousand dollars' worth of stock in the Paige typesetting machine, into the development of which Mark Twain had put his entire fortune. Goodman made the effort and for two years Jones and John Mackay coquetted with this mirage. It was the most intricate machine ever constructed but the hard-rock millionaires were sounder in their appraisal of it than the hard-rock humorist. The scheme gutters out, in April, 1891, in an unpleasant page of another letter to Goodman, who suspects, unjustly, that the Senator has been practicing Comstock methods on Mark Twain. A prosecution is mentioned. For the dignity of old friendship, it is pleasant that no suit was filed. . . .

Unimpressed, drawling, immeasurably acquainted with the world, the Washoe statesmen exhibit quintessentially the nature of the West. Let Orion Clemens's chief, James W. Nye, sum them up. He went with Bill Stewart to the Senate, where chance or design gave him a desk next to Charles Sumner, who was in full stature what Mr. Lodge, a little dwarfed, came afterward to be in the Brahmin culture. Jim Nye was not awed. Sumner began to greet him across an abyss of superior birth and consecration. "Good morning, Senator Nye," he would say, with Mt. Vernon Street's perception of the uncouth, and, "Good morning, Senator Sumner," Nye would answer, a hard-rock man. In time the Brahmin softened. "Good morning, Mr. Nye," he would say, and Jim would equably give him back, "Good morning, Mr. Sumner." The Westerner's formidable qualities in debate slowly dissipated the chill. Till at last, Nye related, "I went in one morning and Sumner said, 'Good morning, Jim,' and I said, 'Charlie, my boy, how are you?' "

The frontier was American energy in its highest phase. Here on the eastern slope of Sun Mountain it attained a final incandescence. The sulphurets of silver created an era at once unique and a consummation. Great wealth in hard rock and speculative stocks, the chaos of frontiersmen seeking it, the drama of their conflicts, the violence of their life, the spectacle of their pleasures, and above all the rhythm of destiny shaping the national experience — there seems no reason to deplore this. It was the end and fulfillment of a process that had begun on a gaunt shingle where Plymouth woods met the December sea. It is perhaps time to stop regretting the behavior of molecular forces.

One may say, at least, that Washoe perfectly satisfied and agreed with the compositor-pilot-prospector who here came into his heritage. It was Washoe that matured Sam Clemens, that gave him, after three false apprenticeships, the trade he would follow all his life, and that brought into harmony the elements of his mind which before had fumbled for expression. In the desert air a writer grew to maturity. Sun Mountain brought him to recognition of himself. In Washoe he took the name that is known more widely than any other in our literature and will be known as long as any. It was in Washoe on February 2, 1863, that Mark Twain was born. Not, one thinks, by chance.

He went about this gorgeous spectacle completely enraptured. Every one knew him, he told Jane Clemens, and he fared like a prince wherever he went. He added that he was proud to say he was the most conceited ass in Washoe. . . . Nurtured on the drama of frontier life, deeply dramatic in his own impulses, he found this Western drama infinitely absorbing. The *Enterprise* was a nerve center of the spectacle. He had constantly the pride of being privy to Washoe's secrets. The paper had enormous power; he took his share in it, intoxicated. His pulse beat in time with the feverish pulse of the Comstock. He owned feet in a hundred shafts, negotiating them rather than drawing his negligible salary when he needed funds. More speculations were pressed on him, in gratitude for mention in the paper or in the mere exuberance of Western friendship. His ripening personality, the slow drawl of his wit, the splendor of his imagination drew men after him. He became a Comstock personage, welcomed, deferred to, courted. And he dipped as delightedly into Washoe life — Chinatown, the palaces, the theaters, the brick houses, the minstrelsies, the lodges, the processions, the mines. He was letter-perfect in the West. And always, when the presses stopped, there was the throb of stamp mills and the shudder of the blasted earth, the rumble of ore wagons snaked through narrow streets by the tribe of bull-whackers, a harmony of the West's noises, the white gold of desert sun shining through dust.

His writing expressed the Comstock. Expressed it — and enraptured it. Fantastic, male, fortissimo. "The Empire City Massacre" and "The Petrified Man" carried his name eastward and westward, and deepened Washoe's pride in him. The jovial war of editors, familiar enough in Missouri journalism, here acquired the Western drawl, derisive and extravagant. The boys assaulted each other in columns of wonderful abuse; they then joined arms and sang the night away at one palace or another, perfectly combining war songs and Sazerac cocktails. Mark went up to Carson to report the Legislature. Western lawmakers perceived his kinship. He became an unacknowledged legislator, which should please admirers of Shelley, or in American, a lobbyist. He could swing more votes than any one else in the Territory; he could make or break a bill at his pleasure. Washoe appreciated his flavor and declared him Governor of the Third House, with monstrous ceremonies of convocation and address. Mark stood before them and made a speech, not recoverable, and received a gold watch engraved for His Excellency.

The scene contains a spacious, grave absurdity. The applauding hundreds burlesquing their own institutions, enjoyably commenting on themselves, is altogether of the West. It is of a tissue with the West's perceptions — an extravaganza in terms of the superlative. And Mark in no particular unaware of the crowd's admiration, portentously addressing a convocation of farce — it is completely of his mind as well. A tradition of humor already old here shows itself. Mark Twain was not sharing it by accident.

It was especially an era of fellowship. What has confused commentators on Mark Twain is his obvious enjoyment of a time and place which theory requires to be repellent. Simply, theorists can make nothing of an artist's absorption in this vigor. Their inability has resulted in an occasional distortion of evidence not wholly pleasant to observe. . . . Please, it is possible for a young man to like a spectacle in which he has a leading part. It is possible for him to enjoy vitality and excitement, when he shares them. It is possible to find satisfaction in friendship. Mark Twain's books amply record this serenity. They, perhaps, must be suspected, since a gratuitous necessity attributes to them the poison of frustration? Then I offer the neglected book of a man who shared the Comstock with Mark Twain and who is exempt from suspicion of that poison. It has appeared on no bibliography of Mark Twain before the one that accompanies this preface, yet it completely expresses the Comstock. Charles Carroll Goodwin, remembering the friendships of that day, did not scruple to call his Comstock colleagues stately souls. The rhetoric may be something less than fashionable, but that is the way Judge Goodwin remembered them, after years filled with the West. It is most unwise of any one to develop notions about Nevada, or Mark Twain's years there, without taking Judge Goodwin's "As I Remember Them" into account. Let this paragraph announce the complete worthlessness of Mr. Brooks's chapter on Washoe.[2]

There was Joe Goodman, three years younger than Mark, the formidable proprietor of the *Enterprise's* glory. He had differed in Washoe's journalistic fashion from Tom Fitch, a

---

[2] This is as good a place as any to express, besides my sense of the value of Judge Goodwin's books, my immediate indebtedness to them. I have freely used all three of them, but owe most to the one cited in the text. This chapter and the next lean heavily on "As I Remember Them." They lean, too, on my own memories of C. C. Goodwin. When I first went to work on a Western newspaper, late afternoons in the office were sometimes made memorable by the presence of a white-haired gentleman who smoked stogies and reanimated the West for our young glamour. Literature has heard nothing of this frontier editor; the West, which is undiscovered by literature, will not forget a career of brilliant and daring controversy. A colleague of Goodman, Daggett, DeQuille, and Clemens on the *Enterprise,* he was already a veteran of California journalism. Thereafter where the West was turbulent, Mr. Goodwin was on hand. The forces of the developing West were titanic; their story remains untold. When polite literature at last discovers it, this man's courage and leadership will belatedly have their due. Let him be, here, a memory of summer evenings when the linotypes have stopped, of tobacco mingling with the odor of ink and damp newsprint, while a veteran of the West talks about the giants.

rival editor, and had shot it out with Tom at twenty paces.
Journalism was satisfied and the two embraced; Fitch limped
thereafter but Joe had lost only a lock of hair. There was Rollin
M. Daggett, gray, obese, cynical. His character, Judge Goodwin says, was a little shopworn. He would rather be right, he
announced, than be President; Goodwin gently said, "We all
feel that way about you, Mr. Daggett," and the great fat man
roared his pleasure. He gave himself freely the pleasures of this
world, but alcohol did not soften the edge of his satire. He
hurled the *Enterprise* at villainy and corruption in high places.
Men went looking for him armed; he gave public notice of his
office hours. A dairyman objected to Daggett's attack on his
methods. The Comstock manner showed itself when Daggett
turned on him: "As I walked along the high board fence by
your corral, I heard your cows gnawing bones, and when I
turned the corner they looked up at me and growled like dogs."
He wrote challenge after challenge for Mark Twain, when
Mark's dispute with Laird of the *Union* reached the tension that
made a duel obligatory. He loved courage and when the wires
brought the historic word that, at the Little Big Horn, the
Sioux and Cheyenne had paid their long debt to George Armstrong Custer, Daggett had no sympathy for the whites. The
Sioux were warriors: "Big fellows, Roman noses, fighters. I
am proud of them." He went to Congress, then to Hawaii as minister, and died at last a complete idol of the West. His prose
was formidable: orotund too often but capable of immense ef-
fectiveness. They could write, in Washoe, and when need was,
Daggett could produce a poem of occasion that needed no apology in the East.

There was Rice, "the Unreliable", who conducted the
Union's periodic appraisal of Mark Twain. Their insults amused
the Comstock, and the two of them tirelessly searched out Virginia City's pageantry. They denounced each other in print and
then took a holiday at Steamboat Springs to cure a cold, or in
San Francisco to experience sheer ecstasy. "Rice says: 'Oh no
— we are not having any fun, Mark — Oh, no. I reckon not —
it's somebody else — it's probably the gentleman in the wagon.'

. . . When I invite Rice to the Lick House to dinner the pro-
prietors send us champagne and claret and then we do put on
the most disgusting airs." . . . There was Steve Gillis, ninety-
five pounds, half horse and half alligator. Steve was to stand
up with Mark at that culminating duel, but he shot off a bird's
head and exhibited the corpse as Mark's handiwork and the
duel faded out. A man of volcanic loyalties and quick temper,
tireless in adventure and attack, who led Mark finally to Jackass Hill. . . . There was William Wright, Dan DeQuille,
whose pseudonym unquestionably inspired Sam Clemens's, and
who also wrote history about the Comstock. Dan taught Mark
more than a little. His "solar armor" hoax probably produced
the Petrified Man; it was only an item in Dan's endless succession of fantasies. Listen to Judge Goodwin: "Dan was the most
winsome of men; no man was ever more honest or conscientious;
he was gifted in a hundred ways; he was one of the most efficient
and valuable men that ever wore out his life in a newspaper office.
. . . He was above both bribes and bluffs; no man could ever
corrupt him; no man could scare him."

That was the measure of these newspaper men in hard rock.
An immense courage, an immense gusto. Simply, this spectacle of
Washoe amused them. There were exciting days, and nights of
male fellowship. They were young and the West boiled about
them. It is possible to recover something of that enchantment
when Artemus Ward comes riding through Devil's Gate to
exhibit his "Babes in the Woods" to Washoe.

I had no sooner achieved my room in the garret of the International
Hotel than I was called upon by an intoxicated man, who said he was
an editor. Knowing how rare it was for an Editor to be under the blight-
ing influence of either spirituous or malt liquors, I received this statement
doubtfully. But I said:
"What name?"
"Wait!" he said, and went out.
I heard him pawing up and down the hall outside.
In ten minutes he returned, and said:
"Pepper!"
Pepper was indeed his name. He had been out to see if he could re-

member it; and he was so flushed with his success that he repeated it joyously several times, and then, with a short laugh, he went away.

I had often heard of a man being "so drunk that he didn't know what town he lived in" but here was a man so hideously inebriated that he didn't know what his name was.

I saw him no more but I heard from him. For he published a notice of my lecture, in which he said I had a dissipated air.

But other editors were kinder to Artemus. The "Genial Showman" was at the summit of his reputation, then the greatest fame an American humorist had attained. It is a little difficult, to-day, to understand that fame. A faint pleasantry still exists in the figure of his traveling showman, but one cannot explain why that succession of labored jokes, puns, and strained similes embedded in misspellings, seemed so universally laughable as it did. The first letter is something of a classic, a flash of caricature completely achieved, but nothing in the four volumes that follow it has its flavor. Artemus remains merely a fashion of our ancestors, an object of antiquarian interest only. But even at this distance one perceives that he had the gift of friendship. Something in his gentle madness excused the labor of his witticisms and the odium of his practical jokes. He made men glow.

So the fraternity of the *Enterprise* welcomed him and his stay lengthened to three orgiastic weeks. Goodman and De Quille and Mark Twain showed him the town. With Mark he explored the muggy channels of the mines and the alleys of Chinatown with their opium halls and oriental merchandise. Then they met somewhere and yarned the night away while the Comstock glowed with fellowship. They lasted, these symposiums, while it was still possible to talk intelligently; then Mark and Artemus went out to see dawn come up over the desert, or to walk over the terraced roofs of the city. Mark must not think of himself as the only chastely humorous writer onto the Pacific slopes, Artemus wrote back from Austin, where he had gone to exhibit the Babes. The phrase suggests something of those evenings and the letter is headed "My dearest Love." In the same letter he promised to write to the *Sunday Mercury* of New

York "a powerfully convincing note" — doubtless about some project of presenting Mark's humor to a wider audience. He recurs to the "miscreants of the [Virginia City] *Union*," who "will be batted in the snout if they ever dare pollute this rapidly rising city with their loathsome presence", but Mark is to give his love to Joe and Dan. Artemus mournfully records a grievance: "Why did you not go with me and save me that night — I mean the night I left you after that dinner party. I went and got drunker, beating, I may say, Alexander the Great in his most drinkinist days, and I blackened my face at the Malodeon and made a gibbering idiotic speech. God-dam it." It had been a handsome evening in Virginia City. Artemus pensively adds, "Some of the finest intellects in the world have been blunted by liquor."

He went on to Salt Lake City and was soon in London, where he died. The Comstock exists in that letter from Austin. One feels the earth quaking from the subterranean blasts and hears, outside the window, the passage of ore trains and the thunder of the stamps. It may suggest why, always afterward, Mark looked back on Washoe with a perceptible nostalgia, a sense of something glorious lost forever. The loss shows plainly in a letter of 1871 to Thomas Bailey Aldrich, eight years after that Christmas Eve dinner with its turkey, champagne, and laughter. The reminiscence glares "out from murky corners" of his memory and, in Buffalo, time is annihilated while Mark looks back to the irretrievable Comstock and recalls the fragrance of its nights.

Just at this moment a picture flits before me: *Scene* — private room in Barnum's Restaurant, Virginia, Nevada; present, Artemus Ward, Joseph T. Goodman (editor and proprietor *Daily Enterprise*), and "Dan De Quille" and myself, reporters for same; remnants of the feast thin and scattering, but *such* tautology and repetition of empty bottles everywhere visible as to be offensive to the sensitive eye; time 2:30 A.M.; Artemus thickly reciting a poem about a certain infant you wot of, [Aldrich's "Baby Bell"] and interrupting himself and being interrupted every few lines by poundings of the table and shouts of "Splendid, by Shorzhe!" Finally, a long, vociferous, poundiferous and vitreous jingling of applause announces the conclusion, and then Artemus: "Let every man 'at loves his fellow man and 'preciates a poet 'at loves *his* fellow man, stan' up! — stan' up and drink health and long life to Thomas Bailey Aldrich! — and drink it *stanning!*" (On all hands fervent, enthusiastic, and sincerely honest attempts to comply.) Then Artemus: "Well — consider it stanning and drink it just as you are. . . ."

VII

WASHOE TAILINGS; AND JACKASS HILL

No frontier is marked between the Western landscape and a country of fable. Sawtooth and desert, the land is habituated to mirage: fantasy has been a native amusement to its inhabitants. I give you, gentlemen, Old Gabe: Jim Bridger.

The scout was fifty-nine and wholly weatherworn when, in 1863, Captain Humfreville of the United States Army made use of him, like many other soldiers, as a guide to mountain trails and an interpreter of Indian warfare. The expedition went raiding through the South Park of Colorado and then wintered at Fort Laramie, where Humfreville could intimately observe this mountain man. This was twenty-eight years after the rendezvous at Green River, when Marcus Whitman had extracted the arrowhead from Jim's shoulder, and forty-one years after Jim's entrance to these scenes with General Ashley's expedition. He had survived the far West, through its entire existence, by virtue of a skill never surpassed on this continent, a functional adaptation of the American organism. He was the West: hard, laconic, competent, a trail-breaker, an explorer of untraveled lands, — which is to say, a master of circumstance, a mountain man. How many hundreds of Indian widows had hacked off joints of their fingers in commemoration of braves prey to Old Gabe's rifle can never be discovered — nor how many scalps fringed his annual buckskins, how many dramas he had shared, how often the unimpassioned malice of the country essayed to destroy him. Merely a lifetime in the hazard and delight of the far West: years in the unspoiled country, years more while the nesters reaped the harvest sown by mountain men, and now years while paid police made use of his wisdom.

Humfreville found him self-contained. Jim ate when he was hungry and slept when he was sleepy. He waked before dawn, blew embers to flame, and roasted some meat. Fed, he would then in the hours before sunrise beat a tin pan with a stick and sing Injun for his contentment. The music inconvenienced neighboring sleepers and some gentler way of entertaining Old Gabe had to be found. Humfreville invoked literature. The camp proved to contain a copy of "Hiawatha", and the mountains now witnessed a spectacle. Jim sat beside a fire, hugging his knees and listening to Mr. Longfellow's trochees about the Ojibwa. He was not often pleased: the story was a lie and lies should exist in the purer medium of talk, not in print. Moreover, the Injuns devised by Mr. Longfellow were — well, Jim had spent forty-one years among Injuns. When tension grew uncontrollable, he would leap to his feet and stride about, cursing Mr. Longfellow in the rhythms of the West. "No such goddamn Injuns ever lived," he said — and may be granted some critical authority. But the reading had shown Jim a new pleasure, though he had never bothered to learn the alphabet. He asked what was the best book ever written: Captain Humfreville specified Shakespeare's. Jim camped beside the Overland trail till an emigrant train produced a copy of the plays, which he bought for a yoke of steers worth $125. He then hired a sutler for forty dollars a month, to read to him. For hours at a time he would listen to this poetry under the Wyoming stars. It im-

pressed itself on a mind that had memorized the geography
of the whole West, but in the end he abandoned it. He had
tolerated everything till the sutler reached Richard III, but this
was too much. There was another violent outburst and Jim re-
signed: he wouldn't listen to any more talk about a man who
was mean enough to kill his mother. Thereafter, though he went
back to singing Injun while he thumped a mess kit, he frequently
amused himself by quoting long passages from Shakespeare. He
gracefully interlarded them with oaths, as Mark Twain did
afterward in the person of George Ealer, when presenting his
thesis, "Is Shakespeare Dead?"

Poetry thus failed Jim Bridger, but he entertained Humfreville and later chroniclers with narratives of his adventures in
the country of fable. He had first wandered into it, perhaps,
where the incredible landscape of ochre and vermilion rock
chaotically broken by the dun and lavender of sagebrush sloped
into the greater incredibility of Colter's Hell. John Colter was
a liar his life long, for describing his find, and so was Old Gabe,
his first follower: the peaks and canyons, the geysers, hot pots,
and obsidian of Yellowstone Park must clearly be a creation of
legend. Here, at least, Jim found his peetrified forest. Sagebrush and spruce were turned to stone, erect, luxuriantly leaved.
Everywhere the foliage to its minutest bud was peetrified, and
these orchards of stone ripened and bore fruit. Jim had wandered
among the trees and filled his pockets with rubies, sapphires,
emeralds, diamonds plucked from these branches. A shy fauna
crept among them, peetrified rabbits, antelope, sidewinders. The
air was sweet with the peetrified perfume of stone flowers and
musical with the peetrified songs of peetrified birds that flitted
from bough to bough. The whole world was stone here and
once Jim, in flight from enemies, tried to leap a narrow canyon
and failed. He expected to plunge horribly to the bottom but
found himself sustained in thin air. In these parts the law of
gravity was peetrified. . . . A neighboring province held a river
that was hot at the bottom and cold on top: in winter, sometimes, venturers broke through the ice to die in fiery agony below.
There was also the invisible mountain. One day the meat supply

was low and Jim sighted a grazing elk. He fired: the elk grazed peacefully on. Jim reloaded and fired again, missing a second time, incredibly. A third and then a fourth time his infallible rifle failed him; the West had seen nothing more impossible. When Jim Bridger missed his aim, life was no more than wormwood. He seized the weapon by the barrel and rushed toward the elk, which at least could be clubbed to death. He came crashing into a solid wall; picking himself up, he discovered a vertical barrier of clear glass with the elk still grazing on the other side. He then noticed that the ground was strewn with the bones and bodies of birds that had flown into it. The glass mountain made a perfect lens, so that the elk he had sighted was twenty-five miles away. Hundreds of pilgrims with the wagon trains listened to this marvel: the mountain, Jim told them, was three miles around at its base but no one knew how high, for its top had never been seen. . . . One measured the height of mountains, according to Jim's formula, by boring a hole from the summit till salt water was reached and then plumbing the hole. Another mountain handsomely served him, though so far away that its echo took exactly six hours to come back. Retiring at night, Jim would shout "Time to get up" in its direction and then go to sleep in the secure knowledge that he would be waked on time. The pilgrims gaped, hearing these tales; this chronicler of mountains must have lived in the West a long time, to become so learned in its wonders. Jim spat. Yes, a long time. His gaze moved toward some purple eminence on the horizon, the Grand Teton perhaps. A long time. When he'd first come, that peak thar had been a canyon six thousand feet deep.

He suffered pilgrims not too gladly. They had come into this solitude, which had been made safe for them by him and a thousand other buckskinned gentlemen now mere ghosts, and they were such fools! A dour mood would sometimes possess him. What could these lice know of a country they had ruined? So, black and formidable, he would sit for hours among them, unable to hear their questions, replying, when they shook his shoulder, in sign language. Best to be deaf and dumb among these scavenger coyotes. Or, in the midst of authentic tales of battle and desperation — this Odysseus in fringed leggings had spent forty years in a war of conquest — he would remember the stupidity of the coyotes. The tale would somehow shift to an occasion when he had been forced to flee from six Injuns with no more armament than a revolver. His horse was fast but slowly the Injuns began to overtake him. Five times, as the pursuit came within range, Jim turned in his saddle and wiped out the leading Injun. One redskin was left — and one cartridge in the gun.

"We wus nearin' the edge of a deep and wide gorge. [Humfreville takes this for the Grand Canyon of the Colorado, but it is a lovelier gulch in the country of fable.] No horse could leap over that awful chasm. I turned my horse suddint an' the Injun was upon me. We both fired to once, an' both horses wus killed. We now engaged in a han'-to-han' conflict with butcher knives. He wus a powerful Injun — tallest I ever see. It was a long and fierce struggle. One moment I hed the best of it, an' the next the odds was agin me. Finally — "

The scout paused and his eyes turned away from the crowd of awestruck pilgrims. He had forgotten them for the legends of cloudland. But they recalled him to his tale.

"How did it end?" they asked.

Odysseus looked gravely at them. "The Injun killed me," he said.

Jim Bridger's geography is cousin to the world's myths. The peetrified forest was a province on a map which listed Thule and Taprobane, the Sacred Promontory and the Aromatic Cape. Its fauna neighbored comfortably with unicorns and griffins, the Scythian lamb, the ants of the country eastward from Dardæ or westward from Santa Fe, ants smaller than dogs but larger than foxes, which heaped up gold and defended it against adventurers. Its flora mingled with the *arbo secco* which Marco Polo passed safely by, the rain tree of Peru, the dark mandrake which screamed when it was pulled up and so killed any unfortunate who undertook the rape. A land on the horizon, under

the shimmering of mirage — Ophir, Tarshish, the incense country, the province of Gog and Magog or of Prester John.

It was also Western America, peopled by a hard-bitten race.
And everywhere it exhibited their realism, its borders hardly
separable from township lines laid down by the unimaginative.
One traveled nowhere in the West without learning its history.
Washoe, for instance, was perfectly acquainted with the year of
the Big Snow, when for seventy days a foot of snow fell every
day till there were seventy feet on the level. Jim Bridger, passing through the valley of his greatest admiration, found his next
year's victualling problem easily solved. The buffalo had all
been buried under the snow. Jim had only to heave their car-
casses into Great Salt Lake; pickled and cured, they served him
for a long time, but that was why the Wasatch and the Humboldt
Mountains were now empty of buffalo.

The year is not to be confused with the Year of the Two
Winters, another meteorological wonder, or the Winter of the
Blue Snow, or the Year the Rain Came up from China. These
were all chronicled in old talk, items in this accompanying fantasy. Long before, Davy Crockett had recorded an immemorial
explanation of the prairies in mid-America. There were no trees
there, the folk explained, because they had been eaten away.
Opinion differed about the culprits. The race of mammoths were
sometimes held accountable, or, it might be, a horizon beast of
the hippogriff species. These, called the ligniferous animals,
might sometimes be surprised while they were grazing; they
had fed widely over the prairie States, gnawing down the trees,
and their saliva was so deadly that it poisoned the roots forever. The frontier of legend moved westward with the folk
and the country that came to be known as Washoe and Deseret
was also treeless. Clearly some agency had been at work here
too. The ligniferous animals had not survived the alkali passage;
this barrenness was most likely the work of the Munchies, those
white Indians who built vast cities that were always just beyond
the second range of peaks on the horizon but walled off by a
sheer canyon cliff which no one could ever climb. They were
the inheritors of the lost cities of Cibola, these Munchies. One

could never find the palaces they now dwelt in, but those they had abandoned could be seen in the Mesa Verde country and elsewhere, tall, intricate apartment houses of adobe. They were probably Welsh in origin, some commentators thought, or related to the Fair God of the Incas or, as the natives said, descended from the Children of the Sun. One of their marvelous cities was on the southeastern edge of Brigham Young's dominion. Brigham, who spoke of sending an ambassador to them, believed that they were a fragment of the emigration from Jerusalem that had brought the True Church of Jesus Christ to America and had conducted a golden age here before dissension arose and they degenerated into the Lamanites. . . . Sunset reddened on the cliffs and there were always explanations of this country.

Then finally Paul Bunyan, who had finished logging off North Dakota, was held responsible for the desert, and all explanations gathered around him. He came in from North Dakota to this, the He-Man Country, bringing Johnny Inkslinger and Babe the Blue Ox. He scraped up what was left of the earlier winter's Blue Snow and Babe hauled all of it, four hundred and sixty-five loads of one hundred and ninety-six cubic tons each, to a mountain basin whose blue depths were thereafter known as Crater Lake. He put up Mount Hood as a watch tower from which to superintend the work of his bully-boys. Mr. Rainier and Mr. Puget wanted Seattle to have a harbor and Paul obligingly dug Puget Sound for them. But he found in Washoe and Deseret a logging problem that put a strain on his ingenuity. The timber here consisted entirely of stonewood trees, which blunted the axes of Paul's crew. He met the crisis by inventing for them a double-bitted ax, one edge of which whetted itself against the stonewood as the other bit in. But the weather grew oppressively warm and lo!, this proved to be the Year of the Hot Winter. Paul's bully-boys fell asleep on the scorched hillsides, whose stonewood trees yielded no shade. The inventive Paul contrived a timber scythe and through all that torrid winter swung it himself against the stonewood trees. They were all felled by spring, and Washoe and Deseret were thereafter barren of timber. But Paul's exertions in the Year of the Hot Winter had made him sweat excessively. The gigantic perspiration rippled down the mountainsides to the plateau beneath, where it remains to this day as Great Salt Lake.

Fantasy as one element in Washoe humor should now be plain. Uncle John Gibbons drove the Belmont and Austin stage for the Pioneer Company. He was benign to tenderfeet, calming the apprehension of one of them with this comfortable reassurance: "Don't be scairt; the Pioneer Company's rich and responsible, and if you git killed they'll pay all you're worth, without buckin' or sweatin' a ha'r." Crossing Smoky Valley one day, he saw ahead of him what he took to be the sudden gathering of clouds known locally by its Shoshone name, Pogonip. As the stage went on, however, he saw that the cloud was composed of living creatures. He whipped the team into it but the wheels stalled. It was a gigantic flock of sage hens — sage hens above, below, in front, on all sides, as far as Uncle John could see. The team was "throwed back on their ha'nches jest as if they had butted clean up agin a stun wall" and, for the first time in Uncle John's career, the United States mail was late. He borrowed axes from a prospector but the two of them were unable to chop a road through this swarm. The prospector then rode away for drills, fuse, and giant powder, which conceivably would clear a trail. The flock rose in time, however, and were gone when the prospector returned. Uncle John's story, like so many others, got itself accepted by Eastern and European scientists, who were vigilant to explain Western marvels. . . .

Such incidents were routine. Fossils blasted out of the shafts would come to life and these snails or hoptoads from geological time would crawl and slobber in the pages of the *Enterprise*. One, outraged, bored back into the rock it had been chipped from. A man slept in the lower half of a bunk whose upper half was occupied by a Comstock millionaire. Thereafter he fell ill with strange aches which medicine could not relieve, but he recovered after going to a Turkish bath, where he sweated out silver to the value of $417.92 which his pores had absorbed from the millionaire. An acquaintance of his had been in Deseret during one of the plagues of grasshoppers that periodically afflicted the Mormons. They grievously damaged the Saints but were great stuff for their chickens. The chickens ate them by the peck, till at last feathers disappeared and legs elongated; spitting their obscene tobacco juice, the chickens now hopped through the air toward the destruction of Mormon crops.

Such events happened on the borderland of fable, the unmarked frontier between Washoe and fantasy. Another element enters. Sam Bass and anonymous hundreds of his kind brought "all the way from Pike" the mode of the canebrakes and the great river. A customer enters a Virginia City restaurant and gives his order: "Give me a baked horned toad, two broiled lizards on toast with tarantula sauce — stewed rattlesnake and poached scorpions on the side." When John Percival Jones first ran for the Senate, he was offered the assistance of a worthy who described himself as "the Tarantula from Calaveras, a warhorse from the hills, and a fighter from Hell." A ferocious-looking person won several hundred dollars from a quiet man at poker, and seemed to have won a little ambiguously. The meek one withdrew but something in his demeanor led the spectators to suggest the desirability of the winner's departure. He laughed. "Why, gentlemen, you don't know me. You don't know who I am. I'm the Wild Boar of Tehama! The click of a six-shooter is music to my ear, and a bowie knife is my looking glass — " Here the meek one came back, lugging a fowling piece. "But a shotgun lets me out," said the Wild Boar and dived through a window. In these passages the immemorial idiom of bear hunters and boatmen, the tall talk of the older frontier, comes to Washoe. The climax of the Wild Boar perfectly adapts it to the far West. Tall talk, in "But a shotgun lets me out" acquires the sharp edge of realism that is the West's manner.

This is the meeting place of the fauna out of fantasy and the Big Bear of Arkansaw. The hide of the Big Bear, who had lived "at the Forks of Cypress on the Mississippi", made a bedspread large enough "to cover my mattress and leave several feet on each side to tuck up.". . . It was "a creation bar, and if it had lived in Samson's time, and had met him in a fair fight, it would have licked him in the twinkling of a dice box." Well, there were large and dangerous bears in Washoe too, and ways of taming them. A grizzly treed some prospectors one day and wanted to devour them at his leisure, but one of them somersaulted over a limb to where a shotgun loaded with shrapnel stood ready. He fired both barrels into the gaping mouth. The bear sat down on his haunches and began "retchin' kinder violent like, and pretty soon he began to puke up slugs and old nails and door hinges and other trash" that had been loaded in the gun. The prospectors looked at his tongue, felt his pulse and sympathetically held his head. They said he was the sickest-looking bear in Washoe; then they put a lariat on him and led him to Virginia City. . . . They would throw groundhogs into the Carson; catfish would swallow the groundhogs which, being energetic, would eat their way to freedom and so deliver fresh fish to their captors. But Washoe catfish were art lovers and could be lured into nets by the whistling of niggers. Perch, on the other hand, were remarkable for affection and loyalty. Uncle John Gibbons had one which he fed on bread and molasses and which would leap out of its pool to cuddle in Uncle John's hand while he stroked its back. Uncle John was called to his old home, forty-three miles away. After a period of longing, the perch followed him there afoot but collapsed under the strain and hung itself to Uncle John's door, passing a willow through its gills before dying. Mountain trout were maternal; you paused at the Carson or the Truckee to watch one suckling her young and felt yourself a little softened by the sight. . . . The western bestiary was hardly marvelous, however, for the Washoe climate might be held accountable for anything. It produced a variety of white sage that was efficacious in the growing of hair; cattle ate the sage and then Washoe butter had a beard. A girl ran a needle in her foot; later it came out, a little rusty, through the head of her granddaughter. The Mormon grasshoppers grew so large in this climate that chops and steaks from them were broiled in the restaurants. Vegetable marvels were, of course, a commonplace; they have been everywhere in America.

Washoe turnips reached such dimensions that when you pulled them up artesian wells spouted in their place. They were, like the animals, kin to Big Bear's possessions. What had been taken for cedar stumps and Indian mounds on his place were really beets and tater hills: he was of the opinion that "planting in Arkansaw is dangerous."

Exuberant vitality is evident. The West, remember, roared for a while. They were hard-rock men in Washoe and their jokes were robust. One of them who typically took his pleasure where he found it came upon a casual affray and without inquiry waded in. A participant broke a bottle over his skull but when bystanders revived him he sighed in ecstasy: "Boys, it's gorgeous. I've found a perfect paradise." They found Old Daniels overcome with drink and laid him away in a convenient coffin. Waking, he at once understood what had happened. "The day of resurrection! Yes, the day of resurrection, and I'm the first —— out of the ground." [1] The Biblical thread weaves through this humor; one hears, for instance, of "the old rancher down in the Valley of Gallilee, who brought in the hungry and thirsty old bummers and guttersnipes." Religious imagery riots in the jokes, only a moment away from Captain Stormfield and Eseldorf. It tickled the hairy-chested, this perversion of King James rhetoric; it was part of their emphasis. They loved liquor and fighting; they would fight any one, a rattlesnake, if called upon, and give it first bite. They loved displays of hardness. Their diversions have been listed earlier; another is of record, the legend of William Tell transported to Sun Mountain. Swaggerers sometimes shot eggs from each other's heads; the feat required nerve and its untidiness was pleasant. A bald man once pasted his egg on with flour. Or wayfarers might stop at a tavern near Austin and observe a loaded shotgun in the corner. The innkeeper would explain that he fired one barrel to call his guests to dinner; the other was in reserve, to collect with. A tale tells of a saloon keeper who asked whether a customer knew Mr. Popper. No: the stranger had heard of Mr. Popper but had never met him.

[1] Supply the nomenclature of Zinc Barnes.

" 'No?' said the saloon man. 'Well, you ought to make his acquaintance. He's a nice agreeable gentleman. I never saw him until night before last when he came in here about twelve o'clock and took a drink. He is a man who makes himself at home with you at once. Why, he had hardly been in here five minutes before he drew out his six-shooter and began shooting holes through the pictures, the lamp, and other little notions about the place, just as familiarly as though he and I had been boys together. Nothing cold and distant about him! He's a charming fellow — charming.' "

Familiar rhythms are discernible in the quotation. It is minted of the Comstock. It contains the gentle absurdity, the explanatory, fantastic patience that are indisputably Mark Twain's. One could pass it off as Mark's without difficulty. But it isn't Mark's; it is Dan DeQuille's.

A story about Old Virginia's antic moods may or may not be fact — one is skeptical because a cognate yarn involving the eating of raccoon under the pseudonym of possum is a widespread item of the folk humor — but is certainly expressive of Washoe. In time of scarcity Old Virginia killed a skunk, which he cooked and presented to his companions as a fisher. They feasted on it, expressing their enjoyment of its flavor. The meal finished, Virginia produced the animal's pelt. The resultant vomitings were held infinitely laughable through years of Comstock humor. It is not a lovely thing, but it expressed another element of this robust life. The phenomenon of spewing produces laughter in innumerable witticisms of the period. The ailing bear may be recalled; one more example must suffice: a boy fell ill and developed a fever proportionate to the climate, a fever so high that when he was induced to swallow eggs and milk he vomited up custard. A violent humor, appropriate to violent life. It extended to corpses. Death in picturesque, horrible, or exaggerated forms was a source of laughter. Bodies of the lynched, the murdered, and the grotesquely killed are stock devices in this humor. Washoe here contributes nothing unique, except individual forms of cruelty, for nothing is more permanent in the national humor than this interest in death. It is not specifically of the frontier: only ignorance of popular humor in the weeklies, the broadsides and ballads, and the myriad other mouthpieces of the folk could localize it on the frontier or ascribe it to sectional differences. Nor is it an American phenomenon. The world's humor has always dealt grossly with death. Critics would have been better advised to remember Falstaff, Panurge, Tyl Eulenspiegel, and uncounted thousands of their kind before diagnosing an American inadequacy by means of death-fantasies. Humanity gesticulates this defiance at its gods. What is humor?

Similarly Washoe's innocent scatology. Another universal. The folk are everywhere bawdy and obscene. The verbal humor of copulation and other physiological functions is eternal and it is the least diluted form of folk art. The antiquarian who at last surmounts the all but insuperable difficulties in his way and gives us a study of the bawdy American folk will endlessly amuse himself and do art an immortal service. Two reasons restrain this preface from studying from that angle the folk in mid-America and Washoe: to disentangle the local from the universal would take too long and we are concerned with Mark Twain's books, not his conversation. It is known that the river and the West gorgeously enriched this department of his talk. Known too well, perhaps, since reminiscence and mere gossip now father on him every obscenity that drifts about the clubs of America. But the proprieties of his time kept him from writing this kind of humor, if indeed he ever felt an impulse to put it in his books, which is not demonstrable. Implications are mentioned later; here it is enough to state the fact.

The circumference of the far West is now completed. Simplifications are precarious: this one may be gently urged. Western humor flowed from an undeluded perception of the country and the race who exploited it; the West mitigated nothing of the perception. What counted was first the knowledge of humanity unsoftened, and then the delight that vigorous metabolism could take, unfrightened, in this knowledge. An assent, an acceptance, is implied but an assent without surrender. The rest is merely good nerves. . . . The gale that howled over Mt. Davidson and was locally said to bury a creek five miles away under fifteen feet of hats, must be the Washoe Zephyr. The burros that balked and sang throughout the Territory must be Washoe canaries. An honest man was a son of a bitch who would stay bought.

The wisdom of the Mississippi frontier found its function on the farther frontier. The shaping of Mark Twain was finished.

Writing in an established tradition, Dan DeQuille described in the *Enterprise* a Comstock invention, called "solar armor", whose purpose was to make more tolerable the summer heat of the desert. It consisted of an India-rubber suit to which an air compressor was attached. One started the machinery when too hot and stopped it when an equable temperature was attained. But a defect in the apparatus proved fatal. Wearing his armor, the inventor started across Death Valley one morning at a temperature of 117°. He did not come back. A searching party went after him and found him only four or five miles out — frozen to death. The compressor, which he had apparently been unable to stop, was still at work and an icicle eighteen inches long hung from the corpse's nose. . . . A characteristic Washoe joke — a solemn, factual description of absurdity. The miners laughed. Then the story moved eastward and crossed the sea. The London *Times* saw the promise of such an invention and hoped for its early perfection. Her Majesty's Government, in a two-column leader, was invited to equip Tommy Atkins with this Yankee armor, for service in India and other British tropics.

This was the sort of thing that jovial hours in the *Enterprise* office produced. The cosmic fantasy of Washoe is in it, together with the frontier's tall yarning. What completed its tang was its acceptance by the East and Europe: the West thus satisfactorily commented on the world at large. And, of course, it was exactly what Mark Twain was writing in the *Enterprise*.

"The Petrified Man" recounted the discovery of a human body turned to stone. Scholars came to look at the marvel and decided that it had attained its present condition at least three hundred years ago. Thereupon the Humboldt coroner convoked his jury, which decided that the "deceased came to his death from protracted exposure." The jury then undertook to bury the discovery and found that it could be dislodged only by blasting, which the coroner "with that delicacy so characteristic of him, forbade . . . observing that it would be little less than sacrilege." The corpse's hands had turned to stone in the immemorial gesture of derision. . . . Washoe again astonished the world. Solemnly the yarn went forth. It "penetrated territory after territory, state after state, and land after land, till [it] swept the great globe and culminated in sublime and unimpeached legitimacy in the august London *Lancet*." One tailing of the Comstock lode. . . . Quite as characteristic was the "Empire City Massacre" of October, 1863. One P. Hopkins, this narrative said, had been driven insane by the stock-rigging of California mining companies of which he was a shareholder. In his frenzy he had killed seven of his nine children, murderously assaulted the other two, and then killed and scalped his wife. Thereupon he had cut his throat "from ear to ear" and, carrying the bloody scalp of his wife, had galloped four miles to Carson City before falling "in a dying condition in front of the Magnolia saloon." [2] Other stupendous details titillated the Washoe nerves, and this yarn also victimized the California newspapers, which reprinted it with expressions of appropriate horror. One aspect of the "Empire City Massacre" should be noted. To its coarse and bloody details and to its fantastic exaggerations was added another quality: social reproof. Mark Twain was rebuking the practices of California speculators. Social satire thus makes its appearance at the *Enterprise* office, completely embedded in the native joke.

The two hoaxes are recoverable because their success spread them over other papers. The destruction of the *Enterprise* by fire has made Mark's routine diversions all but extinct. Probably no complete file of this Washoe paper exists: single

[2] So runs the version printed in Mr. Paine's "Appendix C." In "My Bloody Massacre" ("Sketches New and Old") Mark Twain describes another detail — absent from Mr. Paine's quotation. Mark sits in a restaurant, watching a miner who is at breakfast reading the *Enterprise's* account of the massacre. At last the miner turns to his companion and says, "Jim, he b'iled his baby, and he took the old 'oman's skelp. Cuss'd if *I* want any breakfast."

copies of it are great rarities. The occasional sources that have been available to this preface exhibit only an agreeable acceptance of all the Washoe themes. Horace Smith looks in a mirror at Governor J. Neely Johnson's: "finally it cracked and Horace Smith's reflection was split right down the center." The Governor's party gives The Unreliable a chance to eat and drink without charge; his consumption is listed, and "I am of the opinion that none of his ancestors were present when the five thousand were miraculously fed in the old Scriptural times. I base my opinion on the twelve bushels of scraps and the little fishes that remained over after that feast.". . . Mr. Perry, Marshal of Virginia City, is accorded a long, wearisome biography. The founder of his family "was the property of one Baalam." The Marshal won a battle on Lake Erie, opened Japan to the Occident, and invented the famous Pain Killer. He is credited with the writing of poems which consist of famous lines scrambled (a device which interested Mark Twain for a long time). The size of his feet is noted. "In 1853, during a great leather famine, many people were obliged to wear wooden shoes, and Mr. Perry, for the sake of economy, transferred his bootmaking patronage from the tanyard which had before enjoyed his custom to an undertaker's establishment — that is to say, he wore coffins." Mr. Perry, it appears, paid six bits to have this biography written. Somehow this sort of thing seemed amusing in Washoe. . . . There is a long account of church services in Carson City, with some attention paid to Sheriff Gasherie. The Unreliable is observed to be indifferent to the contribution box. . . . The Unreliable sends a challenge to Mark, who names "boot-jacks at a hundred yards." The Unreliable falls into intoxication; while it lasted "he did nothing but sigh, and sob, and snuffle, and slobber, and say he wished he was in the quiet tomb. . . . Then rose up this young man and threw his demijohn out of the window and took up a glass of pure water and drained it to the dregs. And then he fell to the floor in a swoon." His condition excites Mark's pity: in expression of it, Mark "went and bought him a beautiful coffin and carried it up and set it down in his bed and told him to climb in when his time was up." But the Unreliable only has a series of fits.

Wan enough. Merely the journeyman pieces of a frontier humorist, working in the material at hand.

One sketch needs a longer pause. "Ye Sentimental Law Student", also written for the *Enterprise*, describes Mark's finding a valentine on the summit of Sugar Loaf. It had apparently been written by a lawyer who was incompletely articulate. It blended "the beautiful language of love and the infernal phraseology of the law in one and the same sentence." Mark thinks that the Unreliable may have written it:

To the loveliness to whom these presents shall come, greetings: — This is a lovely day, my own Mary; its unencumbered sunshine reminds me of your happy face, and in the imagination the same doth now appear before me. . . . Lying prone upon the earth in the verge of the distant horizon like the burnished shield of a giant, mine eyes behold a lake, which is described and set forth in maps as the Sink of Carson; nearer in the great plain, I see the Desert, spread abroad like the mantle of a Colossus, glowing by turns with the light of the sun, hereinbefore mentioned, or darkly shaded by the messenger clouds aforesaid. . . . And about said sun and the said clouds, and around the said mountains, and over the plain and the river aforesaid there floats a purple glory — a yellow mist — as airy and beautiful as the bridal veil of a princess, about to be wedded according to the rites and ceremonies pertaining to, and established by, the laws or edicts of the kingdom or principality wherein she doth reside . . . I have declared and made known, and by these presents do declare and make known unto you, that the view from Sugar Loaf Peak, as hereinbefore described and set forth, is the loveliest picture with which the hand of the creator has adorned the earth, according to the best of my knowledge and belief, so help me God.
(Signed)
SOLON LYCURGUS
Law Student and Notary Public in and for the said county of Storey and Territory of Nevade.
To Miss Mary Links, Virginia (and may the laws have her in their holy keeping).

Fantasy, travesty, and extravaganza meet in this passage and yield to burlesque. It is pedestrian enough — no one who here reads it for the first time will find it amusing — but it contains a mood that was to become Mark Twain's. It is thoroughly expressive of Washoe humor: this wild mingling of rhetoric and derision of rhetoric has the Comstock seal. One ventures to insist on this quality of sagebrush and thin air. And yet it also looks backward to the mid-American frontier. The exchanges that came to the Hannibal *Courier* and its successors had widely dealt with the absurdities of legal phraseology and its application to other themes. It was an invention of the newspaper humor and Mark had enjoyed it innumerable times. The anecdotes of Sol Smith so pleased him that echoes of them are scattered through his work and Sol Smith had several times played with this conceit. But, when he wrote this valentine, his recollection of predecessors was even more exact. There can be no question that he had read John B. Lamar's widely circulated sketch, "Polly Peablossom's Wedding." The correspondences are striking and Lamar's extemporized wedding ends with this formula: "You and each of you do solemnly swear, in the presence of Almighty God, and the present company, that you will perform toward each other, all and singular the functions of a husband or wife — as the case may be — to the best of your knowledge and ability so help you God!" [3] Two frontiers meet in the Lycurgus valentine and the humor that Mark Twain will write all his life is almost formed.

[3] "Polly Peablossom's Wedding" was probably first printed in the *Family Companion* late in 1842. This was "a magazine issued monthly at Macon, Georgia, and edited by" William Tappan Thompson, the author of the Major Jones papers, "and Sarah Lawrence Griffin." (Quoted from T. A. Burke's editorial note to "The Unclad Horseman" on page 24 of his collection, "Polly Peablossom's Wedding.") The sketch was reprinted in the *Spirit of the Times*, February 4, 1843, where it was dated "Macon, Georgia, 1842." From the *Spirit of the Times* it unquestionably radiated through the frontier press, for its popularity continued. It remained sufficiently well known to give Burke's anthology, in which it was the first item, its title in 1851. In the same year Lamar included it in his book "Homespun Yarns." If Mark had escaped exposure to it in its first decade, the widespread popularity of these two books was enough to bring it to his hands.

Not quite completely. His Washoe work contains in embryo the fantasy, the burlesque, the satire, and the irony that will henceforth occupy him. But it is only that. Its complete uncouthness would no doubt have yielded to experience and in time he might have become a larger John Phoenix — a funny man. He would have been little more, developing the qualities exhibited in his Nevada sketches. There remained one further discovery for him to make. He had to be more than a mere funny man. He had to find a way of converting this humor of his to the embodiment of his perception of character. He had left Washoe when he found the clue. It was waiting for him on Jackass Hill and it was to be drawn from the treasury of the earlier frontier.

So few American writers have felt strongly enough about anything to face the muzzle of a pistol on its behalf. There was a moment when White Jacket would have attacked his captain and so risked death before a firing squad. The curious parallel between the apprenticeships of Herman Melville and Samuel Clemens thus receives another reinforcement, but the literature contains no comparable integrity of conviction. . . . It seems clear that Mark Twain actually did appear at a designated place on a Washoe hillside to make good his published opinion of Mr. Laird. Elderly reminiscences of Mark and Steve Gillis provide comic aspects, but the intention was severe enough. The duel ended in apologies, not gunfire, but it sufficed to hurry Mark Twain out of Washoe, his final apprenticeship completed.

Even here, however, folklore has overgrown the fact. Mark himself, Steve Gillis, and other chroniclers seem to have remembered details of a mock duel that flickers through frontier humor. Bill Gillis, before he died, remembered the story through a good many pages, with circumstances of names (misspelled as was Bill's habit) and the inevitable bit of wadding which struck Mark's opponent and added the climax of imagined wounds. Once more, American legend interweaves itself with fact.[4]

[4] Some one should chart the progress of this mock duel through American humor. The ingredients of the story seldom vary. Two people quarrel and their friends egg them on to a challenge. The friends then determine to turn the duel

It was late May, 1864. The Army of the Potomac bled stubbornly on the way to Petersburg, and Ulysses S. Grant, who was to become Mark Twain's greatest reverence, seemed likely to go the way of the army's earlier commanders. Spring looked toward the summer of national despair. Mr. Lincoln made plans for ending the war before a Democratic President, probably General McClellan, could withdraw from it. Greenbacks went lower still. The Cabinet busied itself with politics and treason. Somehow, reports of even greater treason and despair in the Confederacy were not widely credible in the North. . . . The Adams family insisted that to reconstitute staffs and Cabinet from the gently born would suffice, but at last began to understand that this emergency measure could not be adopted.

The West was winning the war by providing quarter sections for deserters to occupy and borrow debased currency on. It also endeavored, by kiting stocks, to corrode the national solvency which its gold and silver managed to hold steady. It was a province in farther Gaul without hysterical concern in bloodshed, though it wept easily and emptied its pockets at

into a practical joke by loading the pistols with wads only. In one variant, both antagonists are kept in ignorance of the joke and a double hilarity is produced by their reluctance on the field of honor. In another, one of them is made a partner in the fun and, at the discharge of the pistols, falls forward screaming. Chicken blood is sometimes employed to give the joke poignancy. At other times, as in Bill Gillis's version, a wad strikes the wounded man and gives realism to his screaming. The story is as widespread as any I have found in American humor and it is attached to the biography of other historical personages besides Mark Twain. One historian even holds it responsible for the anti-duelling statute of a middle western State.

The Bill Gillis here mentioned is William R. Gillis, who appears briefly in Mark's "Autobiography" as the younger brother of Jim and Steve — with an imaginative genealogy which Bill does not claim for himself. During the last years of his life he was custodian of the "Mark Twain cabin" on Jackass Hill. In 1924 the *Banner* of Sonora, California, published his 96-page pamphlet, "Memories of Mark Twain and Steve Gillis", a pathetic specimen of an old man's garrulity. Bill contributed his remembrance of the only greatness he had ever known. The intention was disarming, but he remembered much that had never happened, and, of the rest, remembered everything wrong. The slightest familiarity with Mark Twain chronology or California history suffices to exhibit impossibilities on nearly every page and contradictions from one page to another. The pamphlet becomes an item for collectors but is useless to

Sanitary Fairs. Its most intimate participation would come later, in reminiscences.

With Steve Gillis, Mark Twain left Washoe ahead of a warrant for his arrest, and the national agony is not worth an allusion in his letters or such of his published writing as can be recovered. Soon after their departure, the speculative structure of Washoe collapsed. The shafts were down as far as known methods could sink them, subterranean waters filled them, and the ore ran thin. The Californians had taken their millions; the Big Bonanza and most of the native caliphs were still to come.

In San Francisco, Mark became a reporter on the *Call*. The *Enterprise* had acquainted him with social satire and the moralist of occasion was already twitching his pen. San Francisco provided abundant themes. Also, the city's second Bohemia drank Mexican wines and delighted one another in the *Era* office or basement restaurants. An articulate Bohemia, whose importance has diminished. Prentice Mulford wrote pleasantly but be-

either biography or criticism. In 1930, however, A. and C. Boni republished it, with further reminiscences apparently by Bill and an Introduction by Cyril Clemens, the president (under Mussolini) of The Mark Twain Society. As "Gold Rush Days with Mark Twain", this larger book received a certain respect from reviewers. The pamphlet had been reprinted with its typographical errors, chronological discrepancies, and obvious absurdities untouched. Or even improved upon — since Dan DeQuille, who had mostly been spelled correctly in the original and had never gone further astray than Dan De Quill, became in the new version both McQuill and M'Quill. So far as I could follow the book through the reviews, no one remarked on these ambiguities. No one pointed out that Mark was made to be in California and Nevada when he was in Jerusalem, Washington, and the Middle West. No one observed that both he and other characters were made spectators of events which no geographical elasticity could have made possible for them. No one even bothered to correct the spellings of historic names. May reviewers deal as benignly with the errors in this book — though a certain indifference to Bill's may be forgiven them since his publishers did not bother to check the manuscript and Mr. Cyril Clemens, himself apparently the author of a biography of Mark Twain, omitted the same precaution.

"Gold Rush Days with Mark Twain" has, however, one value. The additional matter, which consists mostly of stories attributed to one J. W. E. Townsend, further attests the durability and wide dissemination of the newspaper humor which embodied the folk tales of the frontier. Gillis says, erroneously, that Townsend was the original of Bret Harte's "Truthful James."

longed rather to the Los Angeles tradition, his talents tending toward the philosophy of Bahai. Charles Warren Stoddard, halfway between "Typee" and grass-skirt cinemas, was a Byronic incompetent who gratefully accepted the rebukes of Bret Harte and whose humility commended him later to the protection of Mark Twain. Joaquin Miller, part Barnum and part Elbert Hubbard, may have been there at this time. He remembered being there when the circumstance had acquired distinction, but his mind was inventive. Certainly he was wrong when he remembered Artemus Ward among this company. Now anonymous poets and romancers filled out the circle but its importance centered in the Secretary of the Mint, the Professor of Literature at the University of California, who contributed poems, burlesques, and an occasional romance to the *Golden Era* and the *Californian*.

Bret Harte had visited the gold fields, he had even ridden stagecoaches among them, in the capacity of express messenger, for a period of some weeks. The syrupy tales that he spun out of this acquaintance drifted opportunely before a public relieved of war and facing westward. They were prettily written, between laughter and kind tears. They informed readers enamored of sentiment that even in the Sierras the simpler virtues were imperishable and that humanity remained capable of sweetness on the Pacific slope. So America awarded these romantic Mexicans, quaint miners, and heartbroken harlots the applause and the sobs with which it annually welcomes the announcement that hearts are golden after all. Our literature thus acquired "Far Western fiction", a pattern of platitudes and conventions seldom broken since 1869. Mr. Harte had presented to us a code of behavior attributable to God's out-of-doors and the lonely peaks. He had invented a dialect even more meretricious, which is current still among his inheritors. Few besides Mark Twain have ventured to dissent from either code or dialect; fewer still have been recognized as dissenting and no dissent has availed much, which is the history of realism in our fiction. Sentiment and fashion abundantly repaid him for a few years, after which he spent a lifetime pathetically rewriting his success. But he had given the nation the nicest possible lens through which to scan its western boundary.

He was not, even in personal behavior, a Westerner. A kind of envy corrodes his letters to his nearest friends — plus a certain frankness in confessing his disasters. He had no generosity; even his praise sneers. He endured fame more eagerly than competitors and grew steadily more covetous of other men's success. No warmth was in him, no capacity to accept a friend's advancement with pleasure. Envy deepens through his relationships, becoming in the end mere bad temper. He seems to have kept no friends, at least in America; what finally ended all his friendships was not so much the loans he forgot or the hospitality he flouted, so much as it was his acetic malice. That proved, finally, the end of Mark Twain's patience. They were congenial enough in California, where Harte was the elder talent appropriately deferred to. Both were famous when they came east, and at Ober's, the whole of Boston's Montparnasse, Harte could not withhold a sneer at Mark's advancement. Thereafter his quoted allusions to Mark are sinister. A collaboration expires in a sulphurous page of Mark's letters. Mark, as a publisher, personally underwrote advances to Harte and had a quarrel over the stage rights of "Gabriel Conroy" for his pains. Every one lent him money, a species of endowment. Mark's subsidy to the art of Western fiction reached three thousand dollars, while relations still endured.[5] It seems possible that he wrote Harte on his birthday, sending all his notes back, and "B. wrote one of the most brutal letters he ever saw." If Mark was not that man, some one else whom Harte owed the same amount received this characteristic treatment. Yet what precipitated the final break was Harte's criticism of Mrs. Clemens while a guest at Mark's house.[6] When he died, William Dean Howells, the gentlest of American chroniclers, felt constrained to defend the memory of one "who belonged to our youth which was glad, and knew it",[7]

---

[5] "Letters and Journal of Thomas Wentworth Higginson", p. 330.

[6] Letter to me from Albert Bigelow Paine, supported by the testimony of others who do not consent to my naming them.

[7] Howells, "Letters", Vol. II, p. 157.

and for this defense the conscience of this fine gentleman was troubled. He wrote to Mark, "I am glad that the half-truth of the 'B. H.' didn't quite seem to you a half-lie." [8] It was an epitaph to a literary charlatan whose tales have greatly pleased the second-rate.

Aside from Harte, no one in this society appears superior to the literature of Washoe. A recent immersion in all this forgotten rhetoric, at least, discovered more vitality in Henry Mighel's "Sagebrush Leaves", from Carson City, than in anything published at the Golden Gate. A practiced humorist, with the authority of his *Enterprise* success, Mark Twain took his place among the company without diffidence. San Francisco was, says Idwal Jones, infinitely amusing, and Mark was now a comfortably paid bachelor in a position of celebrity. A gay time, and he had the gift of gayety — swinging all his life from extremities of depression to sheer delight. A glimpse shows him pausing in doorways with Steve Gillis to sing "The Doleful Ballad of the Neglected Lover", which belongs to the uncollected erotica, or producing chords on a banjo or guitar while he sings about an old horse named Methusalum, from the river balladry, for the entertainment of the *Golden Era*. Washoe had not given him a fortune from hard rock but it had confirmed his true bent; he is, in these San Francisco moments, a contented man.

His writing, in the *Era*, the *Californian*, and the *Enterprise* (whose staff he soon rejoined as San Francisco correspondent) continues the sort of thing he had done in Virginia City. The purposeful satirist develops somewhat: social reproof is oftener present. Here, if anywhere, one should find justification for an academic cliché. The classrooms are committed to a belief that Mark Twain's humor developed in imitation of John Phoenix, Artemus Ward, and, still more amazingly, Petroleum V. Nasby. Is it necessary to point out that Nasby's misspelled puns and personal libels in behalf of the Republican Party are without echo anywhere in Mark Twain? To Ward he owed, at this moment, a popular epithet: he was called "The Wild Humorist

[8] *Ibid.*, p. 179.

of the Pacific Slope", whereas Artemus had been locally chris-
tened "The Wild Humorist of the Plains." Later a few phrases
of Ward's reappeared in his mind — they are listed farther on
— but of Ward's manner, his approach, and the content of his
humor nothing of Mark's possesses anything at all.

Geographical accident brought to California, some ten years
before Mark, Captain George H. Derby of the United States
Army, who wrote then amusing burlesques under the name of
John Phoenix. Geography and priority appear to compose the
whole case for the professors, whose trade requires the assumption that originality in literature does not exist, everything being reducible to "sources" or to "influence." It may be that John
Phoenix's pallid extravaganzas suggested the scheme of Bret
Harte's "Burlesque Novels", though if influences are to be
traced, unquestionably Phoenix found his clue in the periodical
humor, specifically in the *Spirit of the Times*. It may be that his
burlesque Fourth of July oration suggested the "Josh" letter
to the *Enterprise,* of which only the opening sentence is preserved. It may be — but permit me to doubt both instances.
Phoenix did not invent burlesque for American humor, and all
that he has in common with Mark Twain, even at this stage, is
the writing of burlesque. Burlesque was a fashion and both drew
on it freely. Mark nowhere echoes the phrasing of John Phoenix
and nowhere makes use of Phoenix's point of view. Already, the
greater included the less: when Mark wrote burlesque it was
both funnier and more pointed than anything in Phoenix. Both
found grand opera, legal phraseology, and assemblies of women
subjects to their taste — as scores before them had done in the
periodicals — ; the academic are here desired to produce evidence of influence. Phoenix could have used "The Great Beef
Contract" of Mark's later stay in Washington: what he would
have failed to do with it may be suggested by the endless struggling of his reconnaissance of the route from San Francisco to
Mission Dolores. They shared a Western laughter at repellent
sights, and if Mark extracted amusement from drunken vomitings, Phoenix could dwell pleasantly on a boy's picking his nose
— probably he had not read Aristophanes. Phoenix reached no

higher in realism than such Pike County talk as "We buried him thar on the Peacus River we did and as we went off these here lines sorter passed through my mind." Even then, a sentence of dialect sufficed Mark Twain for the rendition of character. It occurred to both of them to burlesque bad poetry, especially bad love lyrics: Phoenix hardly invented the practice. His work was somehow amusing and even to-day an occasional line seems less dreary than the rest, but he suggested nothing whatever to Mark Twain, whose burlesques were now mostly in the public interest. The academic findings of source and influence may be dismissed.

In California, through the two and a half years following May, 1864, Mark's work grew surer and grew, also, broader in scope. It is possible to discover, or perhaps to imagine, an acceleration in both developments after the interlude at Jackass Hill. If not imaginary, this acceleration may have been due to the success of "The Jumping Frog." Be that as it may be, all the rest of Mark Twain's books are embryonic in what he had written by December, 1866, when he went east. Washoe and California had finished what the mid-western frontier and the Mississippi had begun. These casual pieces outline the future: the humorist, the social satirist, the pessimist, the novelist of American character, Mark Twain exhilarated, sentimental, cynical, angry, and depressed, are all here. The rest is only development.

The letters to the Sacramento *Union* about the Sandwich Island, together with the lectures that supplemented them and gave him still another trade, hold in solution "The Innocents Abroad" and "Roughing It", which became one matrix of his work. A passage which the *Californian* reprinted from the *Union* on April 28, 1866, is the "Innocents" completely wrought. Half a column contrasts the sun and foliage and leisure of Honolulu with the "mud-colored brown stone fronts", and "the combined stenches of Sacramento Street, Chinatown, and Brannan Street slaughter houses" of San Francisco. In excellent prose the idyllic mood spins on. He reaches the "brilliant transparent green near the shore, bound and bordered by a long white line of foamy spray dashing against the reef, and further out the dead blue water of the deep sea, flecked with white caps and on the far horizon a single lonely sail — ." Here he is interrupted by a fellow voyager who has been reading over his shoulder, a Mr. Brown. Says Brown "Yes, and hot. Oh, I reckon not — only 82 in the shade. Go on, now, and put it all down, now that you've begun; just say 'And more santipedes and cockroaches, and fleas, and lizards, and red ants, and scorpions, and spiders, and mosquitoes and missionaries' — oh, blame my cats if I'd live here two months, not if I was High-you-muck-a-muck and King of Wawhoo [Oahu], and had a harem full of hyenas! [Wahine — women]." The formula, already exposed in the letter from Humboldt quoted on page 120, repeats itself tirelessly in Mark's books. Brown is the prototype of the Doctor who distresses guides in "Innocents", and of a long line of invincible realists who make war on rhetoric and sentiment, Mark's own as often as not. The Sandwich Island letters, too, are speckled with anecdotal interludes, with the sequences of satire, eloquence, and burlesque that remain constant in all Mark's travel books. Also America is told plainly about the course of civilization and holy work among barbarian tribes.

These letters are, except for "The Jumping Frog", the highest reach of his California period. The rest continues, only a little subtilized and a little socialized, his Washoe manner. Drunkenness is frequently a source of merriment. He writes of astronomy, as Phoenix had, and calls Adah Menken "the Great Bear." He mingles one text with another — "John Smith (My Dearest and Sweetest:) Soap Boiler and Candle Factor; (If you love me, if you love) Bar Soap" — a device which he had employed for Solon Lycurgus and which he found serviceable all through his life. He converts burlesque to the service of morals, as he did too often later on. He reproves the stock-market speculations of bishops and perceives that patriotic oratory makes a good target. He conducts editorial controversies. He attacks poetic nonsense and purple fiction. He deplores the ethics of American business and fears that the advance of the industrial revolution may destroy leisure. Ben Coon, the original of Simon Wheeler, is discovered prematurely on March 18,

1865, some months before the composition of "The Jumping Frog", and then, two years later, Simon Wheeler reappears in "Jim Wolf and the Tom Cats." On May 6, 1865, Tom Sawyer slumbers in a column of prose.

Inventive energy is apparent. These sketches present a current of humor without much pattern or direction. Pattern and direction appear, finally, in "The Jumping Frog," but on the way Mark found a number of incommensurable themes and methods that would remain with him, mostly to his detriment. He found also a number which he discarded but which have reappeared. In an account of a meteoric shower, itself a burlesque of scientific jargon, and in the various exploits of Mr. John William Skae, he played with a peculiar kind of *non sequitur*, of chains of association apparently quite mad — a kind which I have been unable to find earlier than Mark Twain in American humor. He tired of it soon, finding it a little adolescent, but in his middle years he explained, apropos of Whitcomb Riley, that it was a humor native to America. He lacked expositors. No one was at hand in 1865 to explain that this madness represented a cleavage, a dissociation, and that the surface flux of his *non sequiturs* overlaid profundity. Exegetics has recently made clear that the unconscious has a way of its own and that these absurdities compose something trenchant in the relief of buried impulses. The explanation has no doubt comforted Mr. Sullivan, Mr. Benchley, Mr. Stewart, and their imitators. . . . Five years after Johnny Skae thus lived without the solace of Freud, Beau Twain and John Morgan Twain and Guy Fawkes Twain were alluded to in Mark's first autobiography, an anticipatory plagiarism of Trader Riddell.

Earlier than some of these journeyman pieces, but later than most, a crystallization had occurred. These were, for the most part, tailings of Washoe ore; but at Jackass Hill, Mark Twain came to maturity.

It was the social critic, the satirist, that fled from San Francisco. His *Enterprise* letters had dealt savagely with corruption in San Francisco government. When Steve Gillis shared a bar-

room fight and Mark went his bail, the police undertook to
return his attentions. Steve having returned to Virginia City,
Mark left hastily for the hermitage of Steve's brother Jim, in
the Tuolumne country. Mr. Paine gives the date of his arrival as December 4, 1864.

It was the geography now known as "the Bret Harte country." Well, Harte's memory for the emotions of Charles Dickens had given the Stanislaus its distinction in literature. The
spate of '49 and the succeeding years had passed across these
hills and valleys. The authentic passions of the gold rush
had been enacted here, creeks had been dammed and diverted,
hillsides had been washed away. The earth had given up its
gold and the rush had passed on, leaving the hills to restore
their passionless beauty. A dwindling race lingered on, the incompetent and the disappointed, melancholy men who had
failed to find gold and could not bear to go home. The pathos
of these aging miners who declined through eccentricity to
madness lingered in Mark's mind. In most of his books one
or another of them pursues some illusory woman or bonanza.
Sometimes, as in "The Californian's Tale", with a mawkish-
ness hardly endurable.

Jim Gillis, whose cabin on Jackass Hill was Mark's retreat
from politics, did not belong to this rejected caste. Jim was a
twentieth century, post-war liberal wrought in hard rock. The
industrial revolution, he thought, was destroying humanity: the
machine age was crushing individualism. So, the most skillful
pocket miner in the hills, he accepted the as yet unborn philosophy of Mr. Stuart Chase: he produced according to his needs
and for the rest dwelt idyllicly among his friends and his books,
scornful of the search for fortune and the turmoil of San Francisco. Out of an anecdote which Mark Twain told Mr. Paine
about Jim and which is alluded to in the "Letters", Mr. Van
Wyck Brooks constructed one more prodigy of conjecture.
Some one asserted that the wild plums of the countryside were
inedible. Jim contradicted him and cooked a batch. They were
— and are, in the knowledge of every Westerner — violently
caustic, but Jim had said they were excellent and he must make

good. Through some days he ate them, while Mark and Dick Stoker jeered. To Mr. Brooks this meant "the same over-determination that led them [the pioneers] to call their settlements by such names as Eden, like that wretched swamp-hamlet in "Martin Chuzzlewit", that made them inveigle prospectors [9] and settlers with utterly mendacious pictures of their future, that made it obligatory upon everyone to 'Boost, not knock', a slogan still of absolute authority in certain parts of the West." Jim Gillis thus becomes a Rotarian because he backed his guess. It is not safe to entrust humor to Mr. Brooks.

When inquiry is substituted for theorizing, it becomes plain that Jim Gillis was a gentle, unworldly pocket miner of literary and scientific tastes. His cabin on Jackass Hill housed a considerable library, to which Jim added on his annual visits to San Francisco. It was hedged around by hills and forest, with whose inhabitants Jim was perfectly acquainted. He knew where the quail nested and would whistle them to him, or lift the unfrightened mother from her eggs while he stroked her feathers. He could answer the call of any bird, and a page of Judge Goodwin's shows him going out at dawn to practice this art. Something of St. Francis existed in him: he was sure that he conversed with these birds and with the squirrels and chipmunks. (That is why my guess is that he, more than Dick Stoker, is in the character of Dick Baker who so signally joins the Mississippi folklore to the West in Mark's work.) He lived there among the pines and chaparral. When the bottom showed in the locker, the hills found him practicing his trade. For the rest, Dick Stoker and casual wayfarers sufficed — these and the lengthening shelves of books, the papers brought by infrequent mails, and endless evenings of poetry or speculation. Infinite leisure had acquainted him as perfectly with the language of poets as with that of quail. It was a tranquil life, remote from the world. He has found the Indies in Walden woods. He had loved the wood rose and left it on its stalk, and far or forgot to him was near.

[9] Purely for the information of a Westerner, the well-informed are invited to send me word of an instance when prospectors were "inveigled" in the West.

We are in Jim's debt for a moment when the Western manner flashed through his detachment, a moment worth giving this wider circulation. Among the casuals who came to Jackass Hill was Bret Harte, before America had heard of him. He lived with Jim for a while and then, departing, took with him the first of the series of loans that history finds co-extensive with Harte's career. The tradition that Jim became Harte's Truthful James is strong and the overtone of derision in these poems, — they attached the idiom "which the same" to Western literary dialect forever — suggests its truth. Bret Harte had no memory of Jim, or of the loan, when some time later after Harte's rise had begun Jim called on him at the *Era*.[10] Jim speaks:

He received me very stiffly and coldly and showed very plainly that he was bored by my presence. I was not dressed like a bridegroom and my hands had not been manicured that day. I retired in as good order as I could and all that night was thinking what a deuce of a fraud this old world is. But next day I went back to the newspaper office and said to him, "I would like that fifty dollars which you got from me, Mr. Harte."

He touched a bell, a messenger came, to whom he said. "Please tell Mr. —— to send me a check for fifty dollars." The messenger soon returned and handed him the check. He endorsed it and handed it to me. I took it and said, "Don't misunderstand me, Mr. Harte: I was glad to give you that money. I have been glad every time I have thought of it since, thinking that it was a real favor to you. I did not loan it to you. I gave it to you, marking it off my books. I have rejoiced to hear of your success since, and came here yesterday for no purpose except to congratulate you. Your reception changed my mind in some respects.

"Before I fell asleep last night my soul was saying to me: 'Gillis, is it true that you permitted a dirty scrub to get the best of you?' That is why I came back this morning. We are even now. Good morning, Sir."

The stay on Jackass Hill was another of the pastoral interludes, like the visit to Tahoe and the Sandwich Island trip, that Mark came to look back on nostalgicly. A sentence in a letter to Jim of 1870 records "our dismal sojourn in the mud and rain of Angels' Camp", but the "Autobiography", the record of the visit in the works, and the anecdotes which Mr. Paine

[10] I follow C. C. Goodwin. A vaguely recognizable account appears in Bill Gillis's book.

sets down are wholly idyllic. Mark boasted later that he here acquired another trade, Jim Gillis's. He practiced pocket mining desultorily but had no time to learn it well and no taste for its enormous labor — as several vivid pages reveal. Mythology provides an anecdote which shows him refusing to carry the final bucket of water that would have revealed a fortune and which both Jim and Mark seem to have believed in later life. The imaginative drama of his autobiography seems the truer interpretation. But, pocket mining abandoned, Mark was free to loaf about the countryside. He could visit the Carrington girls and sing "Araby's Daughter" to them. He could debate the nature of bird language with Jim and Dick. He could listen to their endless speculations. He could play billiards on the rickety table at Angels' and listen to the conversation of the hopeful, the speculator, the disappointed, and the intoxicated. It is known that Mark talked pyrotechnically; it is obvious that he listened quite as well.

The frontier was a passageway down which came all of America — all its conditions, histories, and castes. The westward tide had here, on the farthest beach, washed up a story from the earlier, the midwestern frontier. One of the boozy hangers-on at Angels' was Ben Coon, who, Mr. Paine says, had been a pilot on the Illinois river. And Mr. Paine sets down, from Mark's notebook, this item:

"Coleman with his jumping frog — bet stranger $50 — stranger had no frog, and C. got him one: — in the mean time stranger filled C's frog full of shot and he couldn't jump. The stranger's frog won."

It was a folk tale. There is no evidence that Mark had heard it before Ben Coon repeated it, but his demonstrable familiarity with both the folk humor of the frontier and its utilization in print make it extremely likely that he had. He seems not to have read the variation of it that Samuel Seabough had already printed in a California paper — from Ben Coon or from some other earlier teller of midwestern yarns.[11] In the *Overland*

---

[11] Seabough's story appeared in the San Andreas *Independent* for December 11, 1858. In "The Origin of the Celebrated Jumping Frog of Calaveras

Monthly for April, 1929 (the "Mark Twain number", inspired by Mr. Cyril Clemens), Mr. Fremont Older tells a version of the yarn which Bill Gillis had told him. This version has Bill's customary errors of chronology and its circumstances and details are flatly contradicted by the entry in Mark's notebook, but it has a certain suggestive value. This yarn is frankly from a negro source. Colored Man has a frog named Henry Clay, on whose jumping he is willing to make bets. Nigger Man derides him. Colored Man finds a frog for Nigger Man to bet on, but in the meantime Nigger Man pours some buckshot down Henry Clay's throat. Nigger Man christens his frog Jim Polk, when it is found, and Jim Polk wins the contest.

Bill Gillis remembered otherwise in his own book and said that Mark "gathered data" for the story at Angels' Camp. The story which he told Mr. Older appears to be a collaboration between Bill's memory of Mark's story, which his book indicates he had not read for many years, and some cognate negro yarn still deeper in his memory. His book shows that he had heard much negro yarn-spinning, and some version of the frog story may well have been included in it. His own rendition, however, names the frog Henry Clay, which is a reminiscence of Mark's Dan'l Webster, not a name which negro story-telling would have invented. His character, too, uses buckshot and this absurdity would have been impossible to negro lore.

Bill's story, however, suggests the existence of a negro variant, and it is probable that one or more existed. The scholarly journals amply demonstrate that negro fancy made use of white stories and that negro stories in turn furnished the germ of a good many folk tales otherwise authentically white. The story is one of shrewdness, or outwitting, and this is a favorite theme of negro folklore, of frontier folklore (may one add, of Yankee lore as well?), and of Indian folklore. There was a common interchange of all three folk arts on the mid-Ameri-

County" (San Francisco, 1931), Mr. Oscar Lewis reprints a still earlier version which he has discovered in the Sonora *Herald* for June 11, 1853. That both stories stem from the common root is obvious. Neither has any literary importance.

can frontier, so that the legends of Kit Carson, for instance, include details attributable to mighty hunters, red and black. No desire exists here to discover the original story, but merely to point out its existence in the vein that composed Mark Twain's finest ore. It was American folklore here wrought into literature, a truism that hardly needs recording, since it is declared in every line of "The Celebrated Jumping Frog of Calaveras County." But, mostly, critics of American literature have neglected to read that story.

If Ben Coon's yarning at Angels' Camp did not refresh Mark's memory of a story heard in its natural state along the wharves of Hannibal or on the deck of a steamboat, it may very well have reminded him of some printed variant. Of these, the likeliest is the one reprinted in my Appendix B, "Frogs Shot without Powder" by Henry P. Leland.[12] This appeared in the *Spirit of the Times* for May 26, 1855. At that time, Mark, in Keokuk, was still a printer and unquestionably read the *Spirit of the Times* — his memory of other items from it can be shown. It may be that he read Leland's story on its appearance, or in one of the reprintings which it probably had in the Western press. Or he may have read it in "The Grey-Bay Mare", a collection of Leland's sketches probably first printed in 1858 and sufficiently popular to be reprinted as late as 1870. He may have read it in one place or another. At least Leland's more famous brother thought that he did. Charles Godfrey Leland wrote in his "Memoirs", "He [Henry Leland] published two volumes of tales, sporting sketches, etc., with Lippincott in Philadelphia, which are remarkable for originality. One of them was subsequently written out by another distinguished author in another form. I do not say it was after my brother's, for I have known another case in which two men, having heard a story from Barnum, both published it, ignorant that the other had done so. But I would declare, in justice to my brother, that he told this story, which I am sure the reader knows, quite as well as did the other." The reference is unmistakable, no other

---

[12] Once more, my thanks to Franklin Meine, whose long assistance to me began by his calling my attention to this story in the *Spirit of the Times*.

of Henry Leland's sketches being recognizable in any work of a "distinguished author."

The Leland sketch attests the nature of this story, a folk tale of the Mississippi frontier. Its variations are numerous, but the residue is a frog whose gullet is so filled with shot that he cannot jump. The sketch, too, pleasantly exhibits a setting in which the story must have been told innumerable times, in which Mark Twain may well have heard it first. It is low water on the Mississippi, so low that the boat must travel with infinite slowness and must tie up at night, so low that a frontier aphorism is recalled of the conscientious man who refrained from drinking water since every drop was required for navigation. A wood-lot owner is paid for fuel with two dozen bottles of Bourbon. This apparition of the backwoods precipitates a session of yarning in the saloon, to which the pilot, who is off duty, contributes the story of the frog. . . . This is a typical stage for the production of frontier humor and the story is a typical specimen of frontier folklore.

Mark Twain appreciated the nature of the yarn and found in it nothing to be proud of. When "The Celebrated Jumping Frog of Calaveras County" had achieved a national celebrity, he complained to his mother: "To think that, after writing many an article a man might be excused for thinking tolerably good, those New York people should single out a villainous backwoods sketch to compliment me on! 'Jim Smiley and His Jumping Frog' — a squib which would never have been written but to please Artemus Ward, and then it reached New York too late to appear in his book. But no matter. His book was a wretchedly poor one, generally speaking, and it could be no credit to either of us to appear between its covers."

Once more, Mr. Van Wyck Brooks, by ignoring what the context says, is able to point out its significance for theory. He sees "in that letter the bitter prompting of his creative instinct, in rebellion against the course he has drifted into" — the writing of humor, which Mr. Brooks so passionately resents. But, of course, what Mark plainly set down is his chagrin that the East should have singled out for praise "a villainous backwoods sketch" instead of "many an article a man might be excused for thinking tolerably good", which he had written before "The Jumping Frog." And nothing he had written before it was anything but the humor that offends Mr. Brooks. His creative instinct had produced, and his desire was to have preferred to this villainous backwoods sketch, such triumphs as the boiling of a baby and the scalping of a woman by a madman, the discovery of a petrified man with his thumb touching his nose, conundrums like "Why was Napoleon when he crossed the Alps like the Sanitary cheese at the Mechanics Fair?", the portrayal of a drunken man "spitting on his shirt bosom" while a child kisses "his poor blossomy face", and the fight between Governor-elect Low and Governor Leland Stanford, in which Stanford hit Low's head "in such a way that the crown thereof projected over his spinal column like a shed" and Low "sent one of his ponderous fists crashing through his opponent's ribs and in among his vitals, and instantly afterward he hauled out poor Stanford's left lung and smacked him in the face with it." . . . The letter reveals no bitter prompting of his creative spirit. It merely attests, as scores of later letters do, the inaccuracy of his self-criticism.

With this "villainous backwoods sketch", the anecdotal folk humor of the West reaches a kind of climax, and Mark Twain, in the characters of Simon Wheeler and Jim Smiley, and in their story, achieves a blending of his inheritance with his individual gifts that for the first time expresses him.

This anecdotal humor derived from the realistic observation of character. It was the frontier's experience and the frontier's idiom. The life of America was refracted through a fine lens which was no more than an anecdote that drawled a narrative of the frontiersman in action, paused for suspense and enjoyment, and built up a climax toward the laughter of an audience. Mr. Meine says that "The Jumping Frog" is the end of a development, not the beginning of one, and Mr. Meine is quite right. Behind this yarn of shrewdness triumphing over skepti-

cism is a whole generation of newspaper humorists, wholly forgotten now, who delighted in the vigor of Western life. Behind
them, in turn, are other generations of anonymous story-tellers
— of the West perceiving itself, delighting in itself, and commenting on itself by the mouth of the folk. A good many cur-
rents meet here. We neighbor with Dakota priests when the
stranger "prized his mouth open and took a teaspoon and
filled him full of quail-shot." When Smiley's mare comes "ca-
vorting and straddling up and scattering her legs around limber,
sometimes in the air, and sometimes out to one side among the
fences, and kicking up m-o-r-e dust and raising m-o-r-e racket
with her coughing and sneezing and blowing her nose" — we
are at the very threshold of Uncle Remus. And, of course, the
whole tale is organic with the frontier which speaks in, for
instance, "It might be a parrot, or it might be a canary, maybe,
but it ain't — it's only just a frog", as the frontier spoke and
loved to hear itself speak. . . . Of its *genre*, the story is an
accomplished masterpiece.

But the hilarity is gone from it now. That it holds embedded
this complete expression of its kind preserves it for literary
history, but no one will ever laugh at it again as all America,
in the actual presence of the life it wrought with, laughed at
it in the closing weeks of 1865. A quieter pleasure takes the place
of that excitement.

Simon Wheeler never smiles, never frowns, never changes
his voice from the gentle-flowing key to which he had tuned his
initial sentence. But, "fat and bald-headed", with "an expression
of winning gentleness and simplicity", he begins to speak. "Rev.
Leonidas W. — H'm Reverend Le — well, there was a feller
here once by the name of Jim Smiley, in the winter of '49 — or
maybe it was the spring of '50 — I don't recollect exactly."
. . . A chemistry of imaginative literature has taken place.
The first of the creatures who, of all American fiction, have the
vividest life, has acquired life in those words. The tale moves
on and Simon Wheeler and Jim Smiley exist. Till the last words
that Simon speaks, with their announcement of a tale about

Smiley's "yaller one-eyed cow that didn't have no tail, only just a short stump like a bannanner", a tale which like Mamilius's story of the man who lived by a churchyard is never to be heard except in John Charteris's library — there are actually before us living creatures in whom one cannot doubt. Mark Twain had found his art.

VIII

CRYPTORCHISM

"In despite of Mr. Clemens's desire for better things, he was still a man untrained and unpolished; the customs of the frontier still held him fast."
— MRS. THOMAS BAILEY ALDRICH, "Crowding Memories", p. 152.

HE left San Francisco at the end of 1866 and the frontier, having completed him, was done with him forever. His first book, composed of "The Jumping Frog" and other Western sketches, was out on May 1, 1867. A week later he was lecturing at Cooper Union on "Kanakadom" from the stage that had announced another notable frontiersman to the East. In June the *Quaker City* sailed for the Mediterranean and Palestine. She was back in mid-November and while Mark wrote correspondence for three newspapers and a syndicate, he essayed to be Bill Stewart's secretary. Then the American Publishing Company of Hartford, whose prosperity was derived from religious books, offered him large royalties on a volume to be made up from his *Quaker City* letters to the *Alta Californian*.

April, 1868, saw him hurrying to San Francisco, to make

terms with the *Californian*. He lectured there and, triumphantly, in Washoe. Then James Redpath set the seal of authority on his elocution and he roamed the circuits through the East and Middle West till the end of the spring season of 1869. "The Innocents Abroad" came out in July and began a circulation which, of American books, only "Uncle Tom's Cabin" has exceeded. He had bought a third of the Buffalo *Express* by fall and was again lecturing for Redpath. In November he faced his first Boston audience and met Howells, who had reviewed "Innocents" for the *Atlantic Monthly* and so sanctioned its intrusion on New England. When he saw that review, he told Howells, he felt like the woman who was so glad her baby had come white.

In February, 1870, he married Olivia Langdon of Elmira. On the authority of Mrs. Aldrich, she was "a slender, girlish figure with the little touch of appeal which long confinement to a sick-room brings." Mark continued as an editor of the *Express* and began a year's engagement with the *Galaxy* to which he contributed a monthly department of humorous sketches. "The Innocents Abroad", meanwhile, had swept the world. "Mark Twain's Burlesque Autobiography" followed it, while Mark was meditating "Roughing It." John Hay expressed to John Bigelow his dislike of this wretched pamphlet's notoriety, and of "Innocents": "The public mind is curiously apathetic nowadays. It seems impossible to do anything with it except by narcotics and buffoonery. Mark Twain's and William Morris's [the third volume of "The Earthly Paradise"] are the two successful books of last year. They laugh at one and go to sleep over the other — two luxuries they are willing to pay for. . . . I have suffered from this temporary disease of taste. I have written one or two poems in our Pike County language and I am nothing but 'the author of' them henceforth until people forget them." Gentility had not yet submerged Mr. Hay, who was at last to surround the authorship of "The Breadwinners" with a secrecy quite as neurasthenic as Henry Adams's.

The stay in Buffalo was shadowed by the deaths of Olivia's father and of a friend. Langdon Clemens was born prematurely in November, 1870, and Olivia's fragile health failed. They went to Elmira for the summer of 1871 and, the *Galaxy* engagement closing, Mark worked on "Roughing It." The child's feeble health diminished and Olivia's was not renewed. Mark sold his stock in the *Express*. In October they moved to Hartford, where they were to live until 1891.

Hartford possessed a literary society almost as locally celebrated as Boston's. Like Boston, too, Hartford was well-bred.

There was a cockleshell in Howells's cap when he made that fragrant first visit to New England. Thereafter he experienced no impulse to remove it, though the time came, as he grew old, when his veneration could be a little tempered by realism. Even then his reminiscence suffered the same limitation that afflicts his fiction, and Doctor George M. Beard, who in 1880 described "the American disease" may explain both insufficiencies. But in 1860 young Howells's piety was unflawed. There existed a Diaspora and lingering in this exile he had devoutly longed for Jerusalem. He came now, justified by the appearance of his verse in the *Atlantic*, and it was possible, on the steps of the Temple, to believe that pioneering Ohio might be redeemed. He came — and had to acknowledge to Doctor Holmes that he had confused Unitarianism with Universalism.

In the kindest way the Doctor explained the difference, amazed to learn that in Ohio the well-born were Presbyterians, and in the kindest way the Doctor was always explaining such differences. There was a conviction that the Saturday Club repeated the distinction of The Club: a sentiment, perhaps in obedience to his best-known pseudonym, selected Doctor Holmes to inherit Samuel Johnson's authority. He accepted the obligations: had he not described to Yankee farmers the absurdity of their theologizing at a time when Boston had reconstituted Jehovah? God now contributed to the successors of the *Dial* or was at most a subtilized essence capable of description by Emerson; but surely it was provincial of the farmers to dispute about Him. The Doctor's whole literature, such of it as does not state the importance of Harvard College, consists of such rebukes to Yankee narrowness. The farmers are persistently told, through

more than forty years, that things are ordered more satisfactorily
in Boston. Holmes had his share of the nostalgia for England
which is integral in the New England mind, but no other awareness of geography disturbed him. England aside, the world
consisted of well-born Boston and those farmers who must be
scolded for their crudity. He corrected them for forty years
and a whimsicality which is endurable for a while degenerates
into a loathsome archness.

The Autocrat — only Boston could beget a minor essayist
capable of gravely accepting the designation — went about his
village with no intention of abating that archness. A mercantile
system had partially overcome a preoccupation with metaphysical guilt, so that the local intelligence felt itself freed, and had
prospered sufficiently to create inheritable wealth, so that the
local families felt themselves well-born. Descendants of obscure English burghers with a talent for legalistic religion —
or, as Barrett Wendell once suggested, of English Jews who
had changed their names and accepted Christianity for a while
— thus composed a kind of aristocracy. It was a kind which
wavered a little in response to its religious compulsions and
still more in obedience to its inherited commercial values —
which for two centuries have exposed a core of cold brutality
whenever high winds have disturbed the surface. Still, out of
commerce had come ennoblement and Boston, whose architec-
ture resembled the shabbier portions of Chelsea and Hyde
Park, acknowledged the presence of patricians. The more resplendent, the doges, confined their public functions to founding
charities or institutions for the service of commerce and went
on making sure their succession in finance, the tradition of their
models. They abandoned literature to the second order of distinction or to the wayward, the unadjusted, the crippled, or the
blind.

It was this caste and its capital village that Holmes explained.
It is perhaps necessary to point out the objective existence of
his criteria. The Boston which he celebrated really existed. It
was a civilization and Holmes's function was to interpret it
to the farmers and, by the medium of schoolbooks, to the Dia-

spora. This archness, this feminine drollness and inquisitiveness and snobbishness, moving rapidly among the subjects proper to refinement, was an expression of this civilization. In his generation a literature came to be and of that literature he was the metropolitan arbiter. A nervous sprightliness, an intelligence which was quick and flexible though never deep, overlay and sometimes managed to conceal both his vestigial Calvinism and his Brahminism. He was a literary self-consciousness and the village accepted his authority. Tea and dinner — at Mrs. Fields's, even breakfast — became occasions of accredited intellect. His cape graced the reception halls of houses attributable to Bulfinch, or to the influence of McIntire, and the Doctor talked to his admirers. If the talk becomes pontifical and condescending, if the Doctor preens endlessly before a mirror of his self-satisfaction, the admiration of the village is sufficient excuse and he hurt no one. He talked through the years, inexhaustibly, the rippling of his mind a sort of wit. Boston listened, awed by this native Horace, so unimaginably dwelling on the Hill, so unimpeachably born.

He talked on. His wit is not recoverable to-day and seems to have consisted chiefly of similes. Emerson called him an illustrated magazine with twenty thousand accurate engravings, and that seems, finally, to have been the basis of his fame. Elderly people, he said, will suddenly shut up their faces like an accordion. A New York scribbler, an upstart of probably undistinguished parentage, who denied that Boston was our literary capital, was only a stick of sugar candy and another one was not even a gumdrop. At a dinner table Mrs. —— had been picked clean as any duck for the spit and then roasted over a slow fire. George Bigelow was able to use all his talent, like some cooks — give 'em a horse and they will use every part of him except the shoes. . . . No objection is made to this preciosity — except that its reception by the village made the Doctor vain. Nothing could be said of him, Mrs. Fields acknowledged, that he had not said of himself. He fluttered whimsicalities over a teacup and literature was what the Brahmins wrote and life was dinner with watered Madeira on Mt. Vernon Street and the nightly gatherings of Bostonians before lecture platforms from which incurable schoolmasters read papers on the soul.

But not quite. To several of these gentle minds came, late in life, a dimly felt, uninterpreted sense of something missed. The Doctor felt it and the closing paragraphs of Howells's portrait suggest his puzzled regret. Perhaps, after all, there had been something in America, in humanity, that lay beyond the genealogical tables of the Doctor's Hub. He cannot be blamed for failing to find it. The village descended, after all, from the Congregations. A supercargo's diary has here and there a leaf ripped out by pious sons, and merchants who retired from their countinghouses at forty would not have found it decorous to recall girls of Tahiti or Hong Kong or Batavia, whom first mates of twenty had found delightful when the ships dropped anchor across the world from Boston pump. Fayaway for boys who sailed their ships beyond the reach even of British envy, but for men homeward bound — only Priscilla. . . . In the Autocrat's lectures on anatomy, archness has sometimes a curious turn. But anything Bohemian distressed Doctor Holmes and for years he spoke fiercely of a New York literary fellow who had asked him to dine in a basement restaurant.

Holmes completely expressed the village amenities. Conversation, lectures, and propriety composed the highest phase of this literature, which had strangely begun as a Newness looking toward the redemption of society. Francis Parkman understood that the noun in Howells's title, "The Rise of Silas Lapham", referred to the acceptance of Lapham's daughter by a well-born Bostonian. Such acceptances and the consideration of man's eternal home substituted, in the Boston literature, for experience of life.

The Emersonian philosophy, then well along toward its eventual fulfillment in Christian Science, dissented from the amenities but purely on the plane of moral thought. The Yankee farmer did not offend Emerson, who perceived that the farmsteads of Concord begot a horse sense hardly to be encountered at the Saturday Club. Yet for the imperatives of village decorum he could substitute only further moralizing. In Emerson the

New England mind freed itself for a space of guilt, but he never left the pulpit. As the author of "Self-Reliance" he felt the duties of emancipation and at the Saturday Club would puff a cigar through two hours of talk, though Holmes believed that smoking paralyzed the will. Two and sometimes three wines appeared at those dinners, in further recognition of freedom's obligations, and they pleased at least Longfellow and Lowell. They were intended, these gatherings, to bring together the fruitful minds of the village and its suburbs — to give genius its mutual hour. Yet the genius of New England was a genius for formalizing, for abstraction, for insulating the mind from mortality. They talked about citizenship, the qualities of greatness, the nature of the soul, and what one must do to be saved. They accepted in their fellowship merchants and professional men from the larger Boston: no hæmoglobin was added to their own minds but the civic affairs of Massachusetts received a needless anointment with morality. They added scientists and heard bulletins from a research they believed worthy in intent: Holmes and Emerson versified pious generalities as a result. They were village internationalists and whatever Lucretius or the Buddha had said about the soul was immediate in their minds, but they basked in an assurance of provincial distinction and they knew nothing whatever about mankind. They had the awareness of talent, though they magnified its dimensions, but they devoted it to the perfection of amenity and to the amelioration of a religion already obsolete. The most annoying of them were merely parish prigs who mistook good breeding for distinction and knew no other standards, for literature or behavior, than the New Year's cards on Beacon Hill. The best of them gave America an authentic literature, but erred by expecting to study the universe within an hour's walk of Concord Green.

The martial rhetoric of Charles Godfrey Leland earned him an invitation to the Saturday Club [1] in the dreary close of 1861. The studious generalizations at last hit upon a typical question

---

[1] Leland calls it the Atlantic Club, but that organization was quiescent in 1861, and his context clearly indicates the Saturday Club.

and the savants wondered if any man had ever written "a complete and candid autobiography." One may imagine the progress of the topic, debated with the inevitable antiphony of hypothesis and exegesis. After a while Emerson suggested that Rousseau's "Confessions" met the requirement, but Leland declared it full of untruths. For plain candor, he thought, it was surpassed by Casanova's memoirs. He had puzzled the Harvard degrees, for "of this work . . . neither Emerson nor Lowell, nor Palfrey nor Agassiz, nor any of the others present seemed to have any knowledge, until Doctor Holmes, who was more adventurous, admitted he knew somewhat thereof."

Between Boston and Concord, a paradox in a society wholly absurd, Cambridge literature produced a genuine charm. No coefficient to Cambridge society appears to have been derived, and the undertaking would balk the genius of Sainte-Beuve. Its impregnability, though less brutal than Boston's, has proved more durable. What formed the unity, what forms it to this day with the petticoats of 1900 furnishing forth the gowns for Thursday concerts at Sanders Theatre, is beyond exploration. These people were the inconspicuous relatives of Boston, Salem, and Newburyport; their high endeavor existed in graceless frame shacks, mostly unpainted and empty of the craftsmanship brought to Mt. Vernon Street by the East Indiamen; they nourished their culture in an insularity never lightened by commerce or politics or wealth. The secret of their hegemony eludes analysis, unless it is explained by their conviction that Harvard College has some importance in the world. Still, there they were and the breakdown of Calvinism, which had been accompanied in Boston by some awareness of the world and in Concord by a vigorous new life, produced in Cambridge only another, more stringent system of amenities. The commands of the moral will had been at least a living voice. Silenced, it left to Cambridge a single imperative, good taste. The debacle of Yankee literature is the triumph of this imperative.

Yet Cambridge held one skeptic, Henry James *père*. An alien to this culture, he was nevertheless its only mouthpiece of self-criticism. Where else had New England produced one capable of agreeing with Carlyle's designation of Bronson Alcott as a "terrible old bore"? He suffered Alcott without gladness. The Seer volunteered to talk with Mr. James over the heads of an assembly and began by announcing Divinity's presence in his paternal line. The shifting of Mr. James's leg no doubt gave emphasis to his rebuttal, "My dear sir, you have not found your maternity yet. You are an egg half-hatched. The shells are yet sticking about your head." He probably endured humbly the Seer's decision that he was damaged goods and would come up damaged goods in eternity. He seems to have distinguished but imperfectly between Alcott and Alcott's prototype. Emerson, he found, was quite incapable of satisfying his mind. He considered that the title of Emerson's lecture, "Philosophy of the People", must be a joke. "It would be no less absurd for Emerson himself to think of philosophizing than it would be for the rose to think of botanizing. Emerson is the divinely pompous rose of the philosophic garden, gorgeous with color and fragrance. . . . Philosophy *of the people*, too!" Cambridge is not chargeable with the Swedenborgianism that softened the edge of his disbelief, but may be accounted a party to his futility. And if Cambridge courage makes vigorous the career of his son William, it was the Cambridge amenities that formed the novels of his other son.

Cambridge contained also Longfellow and Lowell and their presence makes more striking the paradox of this earnest town. They and a few like them, professors mostly, had a riper and wider culture than the town or its allies. They lived richly. Elmwood and Craigie House were not the parlors of village squires. When Longfellow forgave Joaquin Miller his quid of tobacco on the ground that he himself might have been capable of it at twenty, he dissociated himself from the whole province. He lived in literatures whose very existence was concealed from the province. The literary life all about him nourished itself on water or on Doctor Holmes's blossoms of Bohea; Longfellow surpassed even the Cotton Whigs in the study of vintages. His judgments were colored by a wider world. It was a world of propriety, gently antiquarian and genteel, but it escaped from

Massachusetts Bay. He lived deeply and he was — if the word is not too weary — an artist. Of his fellowship only Whittier and Hawthorne comparably deserved the designation and Longfellow's art is more harmonious, more fully integrated, than theirs. There seems no reason to deny him that simple justice on the ground that the poetry he wrote is not the poetry we venerate in the 1930's.

James Russell Lowell was a finer talent, a more vigorous mind, and a great tragedy. He had begun as a member of the Newness and his talents had ripened in a desire for social justice. An instinct for the roots of life had led him to the very farmers whom Doctor Holmes sniffed at from the Hill. In the "Biglow Papers" he had achieved an expression of New England at its best — the desire of righteousness perfectly wrought in the humor, the realism, and even the dialect of those granite-ribbed farms. He had created the *Atlantic* and given it distinction. Europe had weathered his mind but, in his earlier phase, without winter-killing it. He remained as cool among its social traditions as amidst its literature. Like Longfellow, he translated Dante and admired the wines of France; like Longfellow he, at first, refrained from obeisance before the lineage of baronets. He could write with disgust of English ways and for years he alone, of all this academy, kept in touch with the exuberance of American life. The "Fable for Critics" attests an enthusiasm for a literature too undignified for the Saturday Club, but his interests were still more lively than these ephemeral poets. He bought and seems to have read appreciatively the popular fiction and humor of the uncouth Fifties,[2] and this warmth toward the rude America is without parallel elsewhere in New England, since Emerson's tolerance was merely another function of the Oversoul. Cheap localism was no part of Lowell's mind. He could

[2] Such items of the popular humor described in my Appendix A as the Harvard College Library possesses it owes to the collection of Evert Jansen Wendell and to the library of James Russell Lowell. Lowell's interlineations and occasional marginalia in these volumes are my authority for the statement in the text. When he passed a favorable public judgment on "The Jumping Frog", therefore, he spoke with an authority that no critic since him, especially in this generation, has possessed.

speak bluntly to John Bull and, just as bluntly, he could describe America as the Land of Broken Promise. He could silence the Saturday Club with a caustic truth. When Emerson remarked, "We have met two great losses in our Club since you were last there — Agassiz and Sumner," Lowell burst out, "Yes, but a greater than either was that of a man I could never make you believe in as I did — Hawthorne." His youth had as great an expectation as any in our literature. Satire and the furtherance of social integration would have fulfilled him — if he had gone, perhaps, no farther away than Whittier's Amesbury. But he declined into criticism, pedantry, and what, in New England, passes for aristocracy.

Cambridge, it may be, overcame him. Even in his later adolescence the priggishness of the town circulated the love letters of Lowell and Maria White in manuscript. The applause of the village became increasingly essential, especially as poverty and grief made him dependent on Harvard College. The standards of the village fastened more tightly upon him. The "Biglow Papers", the Commemoration Ode, yielded to apologues in which the gentility of Massachusetts was passionately vindicated. Morality engulfed him and the familiar shrinking appeared. Ibsen, Howells says, he would not know, nor the Russians, and he abhorred the French naturalists. These spoke too directly of experiences that Cambridge could not consider refined. He immersed himself in Calderon. He read Fielding inexhaustibly, but in the privacy of Elmwood. Mrs. Fields reports him: "He said he could not tell his boys at Cambridge to read Tom Jones, for it might do them harm. . . . Thackeray and the rest were pleasant reading, very pleasant, and yet how could he tell his class that he read Tom Jones once a year!" Life must subject itself to the convictions of Brattle Street, and that it did not was, in the end, more the content of America's Broken Promise than any failure of the national intent. He corrected people. He scrutinized them, querulously eager to detect vulgarities. Another stay in Europe rectified his earlier dissent. He began to shrink from Americans. They lacked birth and behavior. Conductors and cabmen failed to exhibit the deference that inferiors had in England and too many people wanted to shake hands. He began to dress in English fashions and he practiced the civilities to which, after his ambassadorship, he attributed the British Empire. Yankee grocers at Harvard Square could now grin a little when Mr. Lowell took off his hat on entering their shops. He ended in the longing for English ways and the shame at the province's failure to adopt them that seems to be, ultimately, the grave of the New England mind.

No accusation is made here that this province was deficient in charm, kindness, learning, or integrity. The civilization of Massachusetts Bay has failed to perish under the attacks of young men who mistake undergraduate chatter for revolution and this preface is not concerned with deploring the Yankee in American history. It points out merely that the manners of these writers were perfect, that they were gentlemen, and that their lives were rich in ignorance of the world outside. That, perhaps, explains their charm and their insufficiency.

For by now, by 1870, the system of amenities dominated the province — and through the province, the literary standards of America. The province itself was beginning to die. The Diaspora had drained its energies, the Civil War had dissipated what remained, the Irish and the trust funds were exerting their strangulation. A code of gentility, the twilight of its religion, remained its last authority over America. And this code was based on a parochialism, a provinciality, that was insulated from the world, and on a propriety that shrank from every kind of vehemence. Transcendentalism silenced Calvin but substituted for him a bloodless preoccupation with ethics. Its imperative degenerated from conviction and experience to nothing more than good taste. Good taste, too, as interpreted by village moralists who knew nothing of mankind and who devoted themselves to elaborating mere abstractions. The culture which through them informed America was encapsulated from the realities of American life and closed tight against everything passionate and disturbing in human experience. It was a cryptorchid culture and the literature that expressed it was cryptorchid.

On November 20, 1868, the dinner table of James T. Fields heard a startling suggestion. James Parton believed that the *Atlantic* could be made more popular. It should have, he thought, more articles connected with life than with literature and he suggested that "a writer named Mark Twain be engaged." The suggestion reveals a historian's alertness to the contemporary spectacle and the tireless journeying of "The Jumping Frog." Also it contains a menace, the first and distant trumpet of the Goths. Already one lacking citizenship was assistant editor of the *Atlantic* and before two years had passed the dreadful hosts were at the gates. Bret Harte and "a writer named Mark Twain" had come East.

"Tennessee's Partner", "The Outcasts of Poker Flat", "M'liss", "The Luck of Roaring Camp", and similar items in saccharinity, some of them sanctioned by the *Atlantic*, had created a brummagem reputation, and their composer's progress across the continent was attended by bulletins in the nation's press. He was introduced by the Howellses with a party that was "generally allowed to be one of the most brilliant ever given in Cambridge." Let Mrs. Howells describe the issue: "There has been a perfect furore over Bret Harte's writings among nice people here, and he was received with open arms. One day he dined at Lowell's, the next at Longfellow's and the next they both dined at Agassiz's. One evening he went to the Fields', but they had to refuse invitations from every quarter — especially he, from clubs and associations." These houses, primly closed to local writers whose birth lacked distinction and incapable of opening to Mark Twain, received Harte as late as 1875, though his financial transgressions had proved painful. Mrs. Fields interrupted her veneration to record that Fields and Osgood would probably advance him no more money except on a basis of *quid pro quo*, and he contrived a sizable misunderstanding with the *Atlantic*. Even more distressing was the episode when Harte lectured from a Boston stage while a deputy sheriff sat in the flies, waiting to attach the receipts.

The extent of the province's homage may be measured by its forgiving that episode and its silence when Harte, given the final accolade of an invitation to deliver the Phi Beta Kappa poem at Harvard, showed an exact appreciation of the honor by reciting a burlesque. The amenities were outraged but even outrage was forgiven him. His acceptance by the province is not attributable solely to Cambridge's instinctive preference for the second-rate. What the province perceived in him was a confirmation of itself. An Easterner, a mere sojourner in the goldfields, a schoolteacher and the son of schoolteachers, he vindicated this system against the challenge of the living America. His mind, Mrs. Fields recorded, was "full of the grand landscape of the West, and filled also with sympathetic interest in the half-developed natives who are to be seen there, nearer to the surface than in our Eastern cities." No more specific statement could be made of Harte's solace to this culture — to those for whom Mrs. Howells had found the phrase "nice people." At the moment when New England dominance went down before the emergent America, he came filled with sympathetic interest in the half-developed natives who had overthrown the dominance. His sympathy, embedded in sweet tales, greatly comforted the nice people. Story after story assured them that the natives were dreadfully crude, that behind this crudity were the virtues admired along the Mill Dam, and that finally the Westerners deserved only a sentimental, humorous disdain. It was clear that Mr. Harte belonged among the nice people and that the caste had nothing to fear from the amazing nation. In gratitude for that assurance, even carelessness about debts could be forgiven him.

But with Mark Twain the amazing nation itself came to Boston pump. It was not possible to misinterpret his qualities. In him the village confronted a civilization that had no value whatever in common with its own. He was no Howells making a pilgrimage to his spiritual home. He was no Harte gracefully asserting the inferiority of the conquering frontier. He was the frontier itself and he had already, in "The Innocents Abroad", derided most of the holy objects in Howells's temple. Howells, if ignorant of the difference between Unitarianism and Universalism, had eagerly accepted correction. Mark Twain was not able to perceive that the difference amounted to a damn. He was, that is, a savage.

It was as a savage that the province received him. To this day Cambridge believes that he customarily appeared there drunk, and Mrs. Thomas Bailey Aldrich was sure that he was drunk when her husband brought him home to a dinner she could not force herself to serve. Hers were the eyes of the village and as she sat there, "fragrant with the odors of Presbyterian sanctity", shuddering with the double affront to her femininity and her gentility, a society of decorum and fragility shrank from the frontier. His very hair and mustache announced anarchy. His sealskin coat affronted propriety, for the fur was on the outside whereas the village only sanctioned it as a lining. No scrupulousness had been expended on his clothes, for his trousers were brown, his waistcoat gray, and his cravat violet. The experience of Mrs. Aldrich needed no further evidence that the man was drunk but the judgment was heavily reinforced by his behavior. He swayed on his feet, he omitted to sit upright in his chair, his hands gestured widely, and his voice had a soft drawl such as a lady could never have encountered. He was, completely, an insult to refined womanhood — which moved at once toward reprisal. Womanhood controlled genteel society by means of the tyranny of congealment, the righteousness of offended purity. Mrs. Aldrich sat there and froze, her eyes accusatory, her mind preparing the tannic rebuke with which American women corrected their males. The word was bridle — she sat there bridling. She was a lady of the period. She had grown up in a genteel society. And while even Aldrich's vivacity went down before her righteousness and even Mark's conversation faltered, it may be that Mark was remembering a scene in a Virginia saloon with the boys of the *Enterprise* pounding out applause with wine bottles while Artemus Ward reeled about and recited Aldrich's "Baby Bell."

How could the province understand him? It took its tone from sheltered gentlemen whose experience included no single item of his. They were children of an immense provincialism, immutably virginal. They had studied, they had traveled, they had philosophized — wrapped forever in the swaddlings of Yankee morality. Emerson indeed had conversed with the hillside farmers and Thoreau had worked with the roadmenders, yet the poetaster who had invited Doctor Holmes to dine in a restaurant to which one entered down a flight of steps had affronted the Doctor's respectability. To this innocence now entered a man who as a boy had played with Negroes and deckhands and raftsmen, who as a printer had been little better than a tramp, who had spent years on the decks of steamboats, who had gone soldiering with guerillas, who had joined the westward surge and gone to work in hard rock. He had observed nightriding and lynching, the flogging of slaves, reiterated murder. Commonplaces of lust and corruption, of violence and subornation and cruelty, of human squalor and human depravity which had been implicit in his mind since childhood had never, even by rumor, entered this aseptic society. He had conversed with murderers and harlots: it was not possible to imagine Doctor Holmes engaging his sprightliness with either. In the Emersonian rhapsodies it is sometimes admitted that the stuff of divinity may lapse somewhat and a man may fail to resemble in all particulars the divine archetype. The frontier, in the person of Mark Twain, spoke more directly of the bastards of the devil. Passions of whose very existence these gentle minds had never heard had rioted in Mark's soul. He had experienced the frenzy of a silver rush; a sizable number of men had died in their boots under his immediate observation; he had backed his opinion with a duelling pistol; he had, or symbolically remembered that he had, traveled fifteen hundred miles for the calm purpose of shooting an enemy. Clearly, this was not Mr. Longfellow.

He was detached, careless, irreverent. He was not only ignorant of the intangibles which this society valued — ignorance, if properly allied with humility, could have been forgiven him — he was indifferent to them. Most of all, he was untutored: his discipline had been only that of reality. His learning, his interest, his absorption was wholly in the spectacle of man. And to this hegemony man had always been infinitely less important than man's eternal home.

He was anarchy. He had derided a culture which these people venerated: he had even derided the veneration, and "The Innocents Abroad" was perhaps a burlesque of Mr. Longfellow's travel books, as it was clearly a burlesque of their type. He had guffawed at reverend traditions. He had denounced picturesqueness as poverty. He had mocked simple faith as superstition. He had laid hands of violation on literary and artistic traditions toward which these people had yearned from childhood, and what might be forgiven Mr. Swinburne as eccentricity (though culpably immoral) became, in a backwoodsman, sheer blasphemy. No greater comfort could be derived from his domestic opinions. Transcendentalism, now dead, had counselled a forthright anarchy, yet the dissent of even Emerson remained an abstraction and it was not refined to call a Congressman a thief. The years brought a succession of plain statements from the backwoods pen. These were as distressing as his more personal incapacity for reverence. Finally, there was the long gallery of his portraits — the characters of the Americans unretouched. These looked intimately at the human race, which New England has always preferred to examine through the pink mist of allegory.

There was no possibility that he could be welcomed.

They did, of course, their earnest best. Colonel Higginson met him in 1874 and recorded that he was "something of a buffoon, though with earnestness underneath." This solemnity was occasioned by a dinner for Wilkie Collins. Later, the Colonel was a guest at Mark's house in Hartford, where "when I heard him say grace at table it was like asking a blessing over Ethiopian minstrels." But "he had no wine at his table and that seemed to make the grace a genuine thing." The shock, the paralysis of comprehension, is plain. Higginson, like Mrs. Aldrich, like a good many of the more flexible, yielded in time to the personality that seems to have been the most glamorous of our literature, but the amelioration was the work of years. Mrs. Fields — her mind was more robust than most of those to whose chronicle she devoted it — experienced the same amazement. Like all of the province she could at first merely gape. She was able to accept him earlier than most because she felt that she detected in him "a desire for growth and truth in life." His aims were high and so his lying on the floor while he talked did not offend her. She thought that she perceived a moral earnestness and she was a Yankee. But he looked too steadily at facts and, again, she was a Yankee: she shrank from his realisms about the nation. He was aware of no sentiment of patriotism and that troubled her. He considered living in the conceivably better governed England and that distressed her. He described the collapse of democracy and she felt that "so much earnest endeavor of our statesmen and patriots cannot come to naught." . . . The national life had slipped away from this province — its first expression in literature could be only an offence. The criteria failed and the judgment of the province was epitomized by Lowell's: he thought that the curve of Mark's nose signified Jewish blood and so lost interest in him.

History provided a distillation of essences on the evening of December 17, 1877. A company which the Boston *Daily Advertiser* described as "without doubt the most notable that has ever been seen in this country within four walls" assembled to commemorate the twentieth anniversary of the *Atlantic* and the seventieth birthday of John Greenleaf Whittier. Mr. Houghton, the banquet's begetter, had had some difficulty in persuading Whittier to attend. The poet preferred the conversation of Amesbury. He failed somewhat to enjoy Boston's approbation of itself and he would have to write a poem for the occasion, which would be interfering with the function of Doctor Holmes. There was, besides, a sounder objection: "I shall have to buy a new pair of pants." He yielded, however, and Boston prepared for its adoring hour. The scene recalled to the *Advertiser* "the one of Shakespeare and his friends."

Later, it developed that certain spiteful persons had withheld their reverence. On December 19, Mr. Houghton found himself addressed in the *Herald* by Mrs. L. B. Barrett, the State Secretary of the Women's Christian Temperance Union. Her organization had resolved its "deep pain and regret" that

Mr. Houghton's firm had thought it necessary "to give countenance to a custom which in its observance has brought dis-
honor and disaster to so many homes", by serving wines. The
crime had been the more heinous, in that many people might
believe that Whittier, "an advocate of the great cause so dear
to the hearts of Christian men and women of the country, had
abandoned his lifelong conviction on this subject." And Mrs.
Barrett, in her own person, annotated the resolution. "Is it
possible that you, who have known so intimately the eminent men
of a generation and more, can have forgotten how many of their
lives have been shattered, how many bright hopes and expecta-
tions have been destroyed, by the social customs to which, in
placing liquors upon the *menu* of last night's banquet you
have given public sanction?" She confessed "unexpressible
pain", and she hoped that Mr. Houghton would thereafter
"do what you can for a cause which is doing so much to bless
mankind."

One sort of genteel female having expressed herself, another could not abstain. On the twentieth, the *Advertiser* carried
a communication from "Parnassusville", signed "A Few among
Many." The guests at Mr. Houghton's dinner were announced
to be contributors to the *Atlantic*, but no taffeta had rustled on
the floor. "Some of us," A Few among Many announced, "feel
as though our mothers had received a slight; a few of us have
cried and many stormed." She then stormed some more. "Who
had earned a seat at Whittier's own right hand? Who but Harriet Beecher Stowe, one of the chief contributors to the *Atlantic?*
And Harriet Prescott Spofford, Rebecca Harding Davis, Gail
Hamilton, Elizabeth Stuart Phelps, Mrs. Whitney, Harriet W.
Preston and Louisa M. Alcott — were they not 'to the manner
born'? Among the sweet singers ought Rose Terry and Lucy
Larcom, Celia Thaxter, Florence Percy and 'H. H.' to have been
overlooked? . . . Yet this is Boston, that sat on her three hills
and ruled the world! And these are just the Bostonians — so
broad, so liberal, and so just. . . . Hopeless as seems the task,
we must still seek an explanation of this unseemly state of things.
Was it because 'women are angels' that the contributors belong-

ing to that celestial class were not invited to nor mentioned at a banquet in honor of a total abstainer before whom were set (in delicate compliment, of course) eight kinds of wine? [3] Was it because Eve, being first in transgression (a tempter in chief at the first dinner), her sons determined she should nevermore sit down beside them at the convivial board? Or was it that *prestige* of sex is not yet offset by the chivalry of justice even among the liberals? If it were not Boston we should say 'I wot it is through ignorance ye did it.' But, as it is, we dismiss the subject with the mild reproof in sorrow not anger, 'My brethren, these things ought not to be!' "

These exhibits of refined womanhood practicing its fury — they were early specimens of a rage that was epidemic in later decades — were still unwritten, however, at the hour of the banquet. Whittier, presumably in his new pants, sat at Mr. Houghton's right hand, and seems to have borne without pain the portrait of himself, "set in a luxurious gilt frame and wreathed with a wealth of ivy", at which he had to stare all evening. It was a climax of provincial adulation and the village awe is contained in the *Advertiser's* footnote that "the trio — Whittier, Emerson, Longfellow — gave a reverend, almost holy air to the place." The village felt that way — Boston honestly considered them holy — and the reporter set down his further amazement at seeing Longfellow actually strolling among the guests and talking with them.

They had reached the Burgundy by ten-fifteen, the doors were opened to many who had clamored outside, and Mr. Houghton rose to announce the rhetoric. He spoke briefly of the *Atlantic,* which, he considered, "while thoroughly New England in its instincts and traditions . . has been as broad and powerful as even its great namesake, the Atlantic Ocean, in its influence on American literature." The assertion remains true, in several ways. Having manufactured it, Mr. Houghton introduced Whittier, who spoke charmingly and ended, "because my voice can only be heard above a breath", by asking Longfellow to read his poem for him, with the hope that at "his ninety-ninth anni-

[3] The lady's ardor betrayed her mathematics. Six wines were served.

versary some of his younger friends will do as much for him."
When Longfellow had finished, the ritual passed into the hands
of Howells, the editor of the *Atlantic*.

A kind of progress has occurred. The sentiments hurled at
the head of this sane Quaker retain all their fulsomeness and
absurdity at their annual repetitions in the 1930's, but the doggerel that accompanied them would not now be thought literature, and that is hopeful. Mr. Howells read it in quantity, but
first he made his genuflection. The *Atlantic*, he said, "may
be almost said to have embodied American letters." A writer
"cannot even die without leaving it a rich legacy of
manuscript." Appearance in it makes us "naturalized Bostonians." He had justified his own past and now undertook his
duties.

General Magruder's letter spoke of the "radiant genius and
mellowed fame of the gifted bard." Aldrich's produced "brave
and sweet old poet", Bryant's "eminent poet and excellent man."
Doctor Holland thought that, with the others, Whittier helped
"to save the American nation from the total wreck and destruction of the sentiment of reverence" merely by living among us
and the effect on the public mind was "in the highest and sweetest degree salutary and salvatory."

Another Westerner echoed Howells's fealty:

> What though no kith or kin of mine
> Came with the Mayflower o'er the brine?
> (I know not — the dear Lord only knows,
> No wide-branched family record shows.)
> Grudge me not local pride — aye, much
> In him, New England! French and Dutch
> (We also fled for conscience sake,
> From zealot sword, revival stake,)
> Was I not taught by thy wise rule,
> In the great Western Yankee school?
> Was I not shaped by thine and thee
> In almost all that now makes me?
> So while my pulses warm and stir
> I truly am a New Englander.

This was Mr. Piatt, who possessed the sentiments proper to the West. On behalf of another inferiority, R. H. Stoddard bared his head:

> I represent the South;
> She put her heartiest words into my mouth;
> And through a democrat makes her amends.

Much other dame-school poetry and much further oratory struggled against the Beaune in this warmth of common admiration. Yet this was a Boston moment and its crest would come only with the personage whom the *Advertiser* had observed "sparkling with vivacity for all who greeted him." Years of these testimonials were behind him when he rose to give this dinner the archepiscopal blessing. The *Advertiser* noticed that "the contributors cheered as if they were all intimately acquainted with him", and the irrepressible archness commenced:

> I believe that the copies of verses I've spun,
> Like Scheherazade's tales, are a thousand and one —
> You remember the story — those mornings in bed —
> 'Twas the turn of a copper — a tale or a head.
>
> A doom like Scheherazade's falls upon me
> In a mandate as stern as the sultan's decree:
> I'm a florist in verse, and what *would* people say
> If I came to a banquet without my bouquet?

Gaslight struck glints from the spectacles above the narrow Yankee nose. His cheeks were like a rose in the snow and the eager voice danced over the accents of the verse. He was so amiable; the occasion was so comforting, so sweet!

> How we all know each other! no use in disguise;
> Through the holes in the mask come the flash of the eyes;
> We can tell by his — somewhat — each one of our tribe,
> As we know the old hat which we cannot describe.

That was quite as true as it sounded. So he glanced at Longfellow:

We shall say "You can't cheat us — we know it is you —
There is one voice like that, but there cannot be two,
Maëstro, whose chant like the dulcimer rings
And the woods will be hushed while the nightingale sings.

A dulcimer having been discovered in the Craigie House, the bouquet designated Emerson:

And he, so serene, so majestic, so true,
Whose temple hypæthral the planets shine through
Let us catch but five words from that mystical pen
We should know our own sage from all children of men.

Lowell was absent, but "no distance can dim" his bright image:

Do you know whom we send you, Hidalgos of Spain?
Do you know your old friends when you see them again?
Hosea was Sancho! you Dons of Madrid,
But Sancho that wielded the lance of the Cid!

The poem reached a climax with "the wood-thrush of Essex . . . so fervid, so simple, so loving, so pure." Whittier was "Holy George Herbert cut loose from his church" and the verse moved sweetly to its close in commercial metaphor. It had listed those who counted in the tribe and had affirmed their sanctity. The florist in verse had displayed his wreaths and sprays, honest, artless, superbly innocent. No planets shone through. He had expressed his little world.

The great had spoken — Emerson had read "Ichabod", commemorating the poet-politician's most conspicuous error of judgment. Fervor increased, if appositeness diminished, as Mr. Howells progressed down his nicely graded list. . . . A disarming scene. The province swung censers at its saints. It was quintessential of New England, of New England's genius and her patrician ignorance of the world beyond her hills. . . . Mr. William Winter brought some syrupy rhetoric to an end and Mr. Howells rose again. He introduced "the humorist who never makes you blush to have enjoyed his joke, whose generous wit has no meanness in it, whose fun is never at the cost of anything honestly high or good but comes from the soundest of hearts and clearest of heads. Mr. Clemens, gentlemen, whom we all know as Mark Twain."

Mark had listened to the florist in verse. He had heard all these lethal alleluias. A reporter of the Boston *Globe* — who alone among the newspaper men there wrote about this as a gathering of literary people and not a congregation of angels — observed that he smoked a corncob, while Mr. Emerson held his cigar "between his thumb and forefinger and sipped it fastidiously, with an air of greatest respect." Another reporter had asked him for his manuscript and he had promised it, "if you will put in the applause in the right places, especially if there isn't any." . . . He smoked a corncob through this long Te Deum. He had stared over dim pikestaffs into the murk of river storms, he had battered Washoe quartz with a pick, and from nothing whatever in the cauldron of frontier life had he turned away. He was seated here, six chairs farther down the scale than Colonel Higginson, who was soon to shudder at a scene in Mr. Howells's "Lady of the Aroostook" on the ground that "it was only necessary for a refined woman like the heroine to know the *fact* of a man's intoxication and not the *facts*, in order to have a revulsion of feeling toward him." He was able to remember being jailed for drunkenness.[4] He was able to remember — nothing that this virginal assembly could imagine, everything that was untranslatable to them. He was a humorist. A humorist grounded in the frontier, a way of life not remarkable for reverence toward persons who became holy by writing verse. A way of life, a mode of perception, to which an honest man was a son of a bitch who would stay bought.

He stood up. . . . How would it be to bring the florist, the sage, and the Maëstro to the Sierras?

Another existence begins when "in the voice of one who is secretly suffering" the proprietor of the lonely cabin says, "You're the fourth — I'm going to move." It is an existence which is able to say to one of the consecrated, "Beg your pardon, Mr. Longfellow, if you'll be so kind as to hold your yawp for about five minutes and let me get this grub ready, you'll do me

---

[4] Private but unimpeachable information.

proud," — that, when Mr. Holmes declaims, "Build thee more stately mansions, O my soul," is able to reply, "I can't afford it, Mr. Holmes, and moreover I don't want to."

"Mr. Emerson was a seedy little bit of a chap, red-headed. Mr. Holmes was as fat as a balloon; he weighed as much as three hundred, and had double chins all the way down to his stomach. Mr. Longfellow was built like a prize-fighter. . . . They had been drinking, I could see that."

And when Mr. Holmes yelled, "Flash out a stream of blood-red wine!" the existence was getting worked up: "Looky here, my fat friend, I'm a-running this shanty and if the court knows herself, you'll take whisky straight or you'll go dry."

So, in transalpine America, where the foothills shaped toward the Sierras, Emerson and Longfellow and Holmes began to play euchre. Mr. Emerson said that he was the doubter and the doubt; he passed and dealt again. He produced a right bower, but Mr. Longfellow, thanking his worthy friend for the lesson he had taught, fetched down another one. "Emerson claps his hand on his bowie, Longfellow claps his on his revolver, and I went under a bunk." But Holmes, who weighed so much, "rose up, wobbling his double chins, and says he, 'Order, gentlemen: the first man that draws I'll lay down on him and smother him!' All quiet on the Potomac, you bet."

The Wild Humorist of the Pacific Slope had been able to imagine Emerson carrying a bowie knife, Longfellow carrying a revolver, and the two of them on the brink of using their weapons. He was capable of still hardier pioneering.

They were pretty how-come-you-so by now, and they begun to blow. Emerson says, "the noblest thing I ever wrote was 'Barbara Frietchie'." Says Longfellow, "It don't begin with my 'Biglow Papers'." Says Holmes, "My 'Thanatopsis' lays over 'em both." They mighty near ended in a fight. Then they wished they had some more company, and Mr. Emerson pointed to me and says:

> "Is yonder squalid peasant all
> That this proud nursery could breed?"

He was a-whittling his bowie on his boot — so I let it pass. Well, sir, next they took it into their heads that they would like some music; so they made me stand up and sing "When Johnny Comes Marching Home" till I dropped — at thirteen minutes past four this morning. That's what I've been through, my friend. When I woke at seven they were leaving, thank goodness, and Mr. Longfellow had my only boots on and hisn under his arm. Says I, "Hold on there, Evangeline, what are you going to do with them?" He says, "Going to make tracks with 'em, because —

'Lives of great men all remind us
We can make our lives sublime,
And, departing, leave behind us
Footprints on the sands of time.'

As I said, Mr. Twain, you are the fourth in twenty-four hours — and I'm going to move; I ain't suited to a litterary atmosphere.

Throughout the speech Doctor Holmes was observed to be writing busily, with an air of intent preoccupation.

The first paralysis appears to have existed chiefly in the nerves of Howells. A search fails to reveal the anger which the Boston papers are traditionally said to have expended on the offence. On the 18th of December, the *Transcript* briefly debates "the taste or lack of it in Mark Twain's use of those distinguished names" and ends by conceding that it had elicited "hearty fun." The next day, as the sense of shock travels over the village, the *Transcript* is firmer: "The general verdict seems to be that Mark Twain's speech, though witty and well worked up, was in bad taste and entirely out of place. As one critic puts it, if the three gentlemen named in his remarks had been entertained in New York, and a speaker had said what Mark Twain did, Boston would have felt insulted." Thereafter, the *Transcript*, with all its contemporaries, abandoned the topic and devoted its resentment to the feminists and prohibitionists who had criticized a village ritual.

Offense was not even profound among the personages. The shock was shattering, of course: they had been used to the homage of lecture-goers, the self-satisfaction nicely embodied in the florist's bouquet, and a violence from the frontier had exhibited impersonators of them playing cards and drunk. But their gentleness was equal, almost, to absolution. Longfellow wrote the letter of a gentleman in answer to Mark's abasement. No offense had been offered him and he had taken none; it was a pleasant dinner and Whittier had enjoyed it. Miss Ellen Emerson (she had recently, at the Fields's dinner table, had to ask the meaning of the word "æsthetic"), confessed her pain, though her brothers and her father had found parts of the speech quite funny. She was not offended: she was disappointed. She wanted Mr. Clemens to feel that his contrition became him very much and had earned him forgiveness. And Doctor Holmes was very kind. He had heard some questioning whether "even in fun it was good taste to associate the names of the authors with the absurdly unlike personalities attributed to them." He was willing, prettily, to consider it an open question. Two of his friends had "stoutly defended it against the charge of impropriety." That was the Doctor's inevitable way. . . . What they suffered from, these fragilities, was not offense. It was stupefaction. It was the bewilderment of stunning and incredible discovery. It was the experience of an impossibility: at a parish supper in honor of a gifted bard whose presence in new pants saved the American nation from the total wreck and destruction of the sentiment of reverence — in the midst of this *gemütlichkeit* had come the revelation of a mind, a territory, an American civilization which, glancing at Mr. Longfellow, could tell him to hold his yawp.

Offense existed, apart from the *amour-propre* of Doctor Holmes, in the society, the civilization, which these amazed poets summarized. Howells's neurasthenia and the black silence which Mark remembered expressed this people and its shock. The village, in simple fact, witnessed blasphemy. It was in the village that excommunication was pronounced and it is there that heresy is remembered. A relative of Mr. Longfellow, in 1930, spoke of the gross insult offered to his kinsman and so recorded the final sentiment of a small society about a way of life that differed from its own.

What is sought here is description. To resent or deplore the genteel tradition is a waste of sentiment. History consists of facts, not of regret. That the settled society of eastern America met the shock of the differing West in various ways is a fact. That in the latter half of the nineteenth century the fetish of good taste did substitute duty for other criteria of behavior and literature in the governing levels of American life is a fact. It is not a simple fact, as a good many ambitious efforts to analyze it have embarrassingly revealed. It is not a local fact attributable to some loathsome defect in the American race, as the history of England and continental Europe attests. And certainly the emotion that has been spent in rebuking it is infinitely silly. It has been announced on fairly sound authority that you cannot indict a map. It would seem equally obvious that you cannot, with much sense, denounce a century or a people.

So far as any simplification is trustworthy, this one may be ventured upon: the course taken by the literary career of Mark Twain was inevitable. That career epitomized the experience of the West in American history and nothing very much different from what actually happened could have happened. The West has, in the larger outline, shaped American political history. In the larger outline, the West has had little formative effect on American cultural history. It has, in the main, accepted the education and the standards of the East. To suppose that any other outcome would have been possible is to exhibit — as a succession of recent critics have exhibited — either an ignorance, a naïveté, or a romanticism incapable of dealing satisfactorily with the materials of history.

It is to be observed, then, that the writing of Mark Twain suffered a little, here and there, from the convention of verbal delicacy which, once in the East, he seldom resented and never questioned. His writing suffered much more from his accepting material and themes of interest to the genteel tradition instead of confining himself to his native interests — though this assertion rests on the hypothesis that something else might have been possible and is rendered exceedingly dubious by the presence in Mark Twain's nature of impulses toward these alien themes that may have been as authoritative and profound as any that he had. The books of Mark Twain, then, in these two particulars, suffered from the conflict of Western life with the genteel tradition. Both must be examined in detail — for the purpose of description, not lamentation. There will then be time to explain, as no one has hitherto bothered to explain, that they also profited from the conflict.

He was a humorist. He had had no formal education. His life had been spent in activity, away from what are known as artistic pursuits. He had had no discipline whatever in systems of æsthetics. The society that had formed him was mobile, not static. He had had no experience of continuous and ripening tradition. His mind flashed, sometimes, with a brilliance, a penetrating illumination that is unmistakable genius. No impulse, no experience existed to coördinate these movements: he had no capacity to control the imagination that was warmer and more human than any other in our literature or to sustain it in the labor of prolonged creation.

He came East and he accepted tuition. That is a complete description of what happened — as it is an epitome of Western experience. He accepted, to the small extent of which he was capable, with no awareness of any surrender, the dominant criteria of his age. Criticism could spare itself much nonsense, as the books of to-day's theorists recapitulate those of yesterday's, if it considered this a fact of natural history, repeated in the persons of many of the theorists, and not a betrayal of a point of view that was when Mark Twain came East as yet unborn. Much further nonsense could have been avoided if criticism had discovered how little the acceptance of those criteria altered what he was and how little it affected his books. But that would have necessitated reading Mark Twain, whereas criticism has preferred to theorize about him and to read Mr. Brooks.

One conduit of tuition was Olivia Clemens. She had suffered "the American disease", being prostrated for two years with a hysterical paralysis. She was completely of her generation in the neurasthenia that afflicted her throughout her life, driving her into repeated "collapses." Neurasthenia seems to have been, over wide areas, a concomitant of gentility. No time is available here for further description — the works of Doctor Beard and Doctor Weir Mitchell may be referred to and Mrs. Howells may serve as well as thousands for comparison. No time is available, either, for explanation, but the one theory which this preface ventures upon may be offered as a theory. The folkways, as this century advanced, shaped an ideal of purity and propriety. Consent has selected the Queen's name to designate it and Mr. Furness's "Genteel Female" is prescribed to any one who may desire to consider the ideal more extensively. The ideal found a convenient summary in a letter of Barrett Wendell's in 1881: "It seems to me that the nature of our women is too high and pure easily to be lowered, or corrupted, or even injured. From things that they ought not to think of — I mean things that you and I would not like them to think of — they turn away of themselves. . . . I think we can trust them with anything with which they are willing to trust themselves." Theory suggests that the tyrannical righteousness which refined American womanhood wreaked upon its husbands and sons may have been an act of revenge, dictated by the ideal, for its violation in marriage. Theory then supposes that much of the neurasthenia among refined womanhood during Victoria's last forty years may perhaps have sprung from the acceptance of this revenge acquiescently by husbands and sons. It may be that the female nervous system thus repaid its own betrayal. . . . Theory only, please: no structure will be erected on it.

At any rate, Olivia was neurasthenic and was completely drilled in the gentilities of her sex and era. Throughout his career, Mark Twain submitted his manuscripts to her — gladly. As gladly as Mr. Sinclair Lewis is said to have submitted the manuscript of "Main Street" to the correction of Mr. Cabell.[5] It is likely that he resented some of her deletions. A furore in the 1920's rested on one marginal note quoted by Mr. Paine which accused her of steadily weakening the English language.

[5] "Straws and Prayerbooks", pp. 50–51.

The "Letters", however, exhibit a willing pride in her super-vision, whereas Howells suffering a similar supervision — it appears that to gentility even Howells might seem coarse — complained of "the merciless excisions of Mrs. Howells." Lit-erature is thus poorer in that Tom Sawyer must say that the Pain Killer griped Peter's bowels, rather than his guts; in that Huck Finn must be combed all to thunder instead of all to hell; and in that feminine oaths are elsewhere substituted for the pro-fanity of the frontier. Literature would have had to forego them quite as thoroughly without intervention by Mrs. Clemens. Mr. Gilder, who represented the liberal, the bohemian taste on the *Century*, in opposition to Mr. Buell, who was the office purist, performed his editorial duty by making changes which "were mainly those in the direction of good taste, the deletion of slang and coarseness and the softening of all expressions or statements likely to offend." The folkways had hardened against offence and nowhere in America would an editor or publisher have permitted in print much of what Olivia Clemens may have de-leted in manuscript. In 1867, the date of "Sut Lovingood", the expression "sons of bitches" in Longstreet's "Georgia Scenes", which had survived reprinting through the Forties and Fifties, became "critters", the form which it still retains. (This was twenty-five years after the same change in the same context in the English editions.) Nor is there evidence that Olivia had many horrid words to contend with. Mark's literary vocabulary on the Pacific coast is just what it was in the East. The conven-tion seemed to him quite sane and he had not violated it.

The total of these merciless excisions could not have been great, Olivia Clemens could not have greatly weakened the English language, and they would not have survived even if they had escaped her. They shared the destiny of similar im-pulses throughout the literature of the era. The opinion may be advanced that we are not much poorer for their censoring: the context is plain, always, and sympathy can supply the phrase. . . . If Olivia threw her gentility against scenes of vomiting and disembowelment, which became less common in the later books, we are in her debt.

If she had wholly withheld her hand, propriety would still have done its surgery on Mark Twain. He came East and accepted tuition. The editor of the *Atlantic*, the custodian of the genteel tradition, became his confessor. It was Howells, most often, who read his proofs. It was Howells with whom he endlessly talked and corresponded about the offices of literature. It was Howells whom he admired as the greatest writer of his era and to whose ideas about writing he devoted himself. Let no injustice be done Mr. Howells. He was the strongest force in a generation that raised American fiction to the level of literature. He taught his inheritors, who have acknowledged their superiority to him, both the art of prose and the material of fiction. He revealed their trade, its possibilities, and its methods to a good many gentlemen still alive who have devoted to his disparagement a good many pages that echo his phrasing. He preserved, for historians as well as artists, an era, a phase of America, more completely, more honestly than any other who treated it. He was, however, of the era. A fine courage observable in his nonprofessional activity failed to show itself in his fiction: in common with his adopted culture, he shrank from vehemence and passion. His disordered nerves show here, as they do not show in his public actions — and to neurasthenia was added the pilgrim's reverence for Jerusalem, whose culture it was not possible to doubt in any way. The inconceivability of any dissent, the reverence with which he accepted the tradition in its entirety, exists in his confessed emotion toward Lowell: "I used to falter at his gate, and walk up the path to his door with the same anxious palpitations I felt when I dared to call upon the girl I was first in love with."

He denies the *Atlantic* to a verse play by a protegé of Norton's: "I no longer wish to be put in pain about a woman's virtue, or to ask that suffering from others. It's odious; all the tragedy went out of that situation long ago and only the displeasures remain." His children, he acknowledged, were his censors; if he wished to be wicked, he hoped they would be his safeguards. By act of dedication, his fiction recorded the "kindlier aspects" of life, avoiding whatever might put him, or his

readers, in pain. It was a literature of the genteel tradition. . . .
This was the confidant to whom, throughout his career, Mark
Twain submitted his enthusiasms. As late as April, 1906, their
letters record the progress of Mark's books and his unwritten
books, and record also Howells's doubts, cautions, and correc-
tions. It was the "Autobiography" in 1906; it was the "Fable
for Good Old Boys and Girls" in 1874. He would have the
profanity out of "Tom Sawyer" in a minute. Some twenty words
in "The Prince and the Pauper" seem "rather strong milk for
babies", and Howells will correct them in the plates. "But such
a thing as that on p. 154, I can't cope with. I don't think such
words as divil or hick (for person) and basting (for beating)
ought to be suffered in your narrations." He felt haggard after
reading the manuscript of Orion Clemens's autobiography and
wrote what amounts to a full statement of his dreads and his
influence: "The writer's soul is laid *too* bare; it is shocking. I
can't risk the paper in the *Atlantic;* and if you print it anywhere,
I hope you won't let your love of the naked truth prevent you
from striking out some of the most intimate pages. *Don't* let
anyone else even *see* those passages about the autopsy."

Mr. Howells was, as the Bostonians died, the principal literary personage in America. He perceived the importance of
Mark Twain and thought that "we others shall be remembered
merely as your friends and correspondents." Only, this genius
came a little maculate with evidences of the frontier which
Howells had fled from, and these must be removed. Mark
sometimes loved the naked truth too strongly, wrote too intimate pages, and used words which ought not to be suffered in
his narrations. In the person of Howells, the tradition of gentility corrected him. And Mark was grateful.

He sought correction from others besides Howells. He was
a Westerner: he desired instruction from the masters of his
trade. So on July 7, 1889, Edmund Clarence Stedman thumbs
a manuscript copy of "A Connecticut Yankee in King Arthur's
Court" and answers Mark Twain's request for criticism and suggestion. It is, on the whole, he believes, a great book. "It isn't
so learned and pedantic as 'Pantagruel' and it doesn't need to

be — but why it should not be preserved somewhat as Rabelais' work has been . . . is more than I can see." [6] Nevertheless, there is some exaggeration, and this, suggesting Mark's very early manner, should be toned down. There is danger that the Protestant Episcopal church will be offended. "Damned and welcome" is a trifle out of tone. And three times, on pages 34, 119, and 120, Mr. Stedman has horribly encountered the word "sewer." Clearly, in something that is comparable to Rabelais, such offensiveness cannot be endured.

Three years before Mr. Stedman's deletion of sewage and exaggeration from Pantagruel, the editor of the *Century* mailed a letter, with inclosure, to Mark Twain. . . . With Mr. Gilder, the problem of nineteenth-century refinement may be clearly posed. To attack him with any of the catchwords which the twentieth century has employed to indicate its dislike of its immediate predecessors would be absurd. The man's intelligence, courage, and integrity are beyond question. He was, in his times, a liberal — even a reformer. His career included unremitting warfare on the public abuses of the age. He was a civilizing force, and as the editor of our most noteworthy magazine, his influence for the further civilization of America was, simply, tremendous. Only, a mind that suffered few illusions about its times was incapable of dissenting from one of the folkways. Mr. Gilder accepted the dominant literary criteria of his age. . . . He wrote Mark Twain, on January 8, 1886, that he was venturing an indiscretion. A superintendent of public schools in the West had complained about the *Century's* publishing Mark Twain. Mr. Gilder, for Mark's instruction, inclosed his answer to the gentleman. He wanted to send it, he said, as a sample of what often happened in his office. It may serve the same purpose here.

[6] Just thirty-one years before a cheap sneer of contemporary criticism, Stedman foresaw the asininity that has been repeated in most critical surveys of the last decade: "*Some* blasted fool will surely jump up and say that Cervantes polished off chivalry centuries ago, etc. After a time he'll discover, perhaps, that you are going at the *still existing* radical principles or fallacies which made 'chivalry' possible once, and servility and flunkeyism and tyranny possible now." The passages quoted here and in the text appear in the second volume of Stedman's "Letters", pp. 370–372.

Mr. Gilder wrote to the superintendent:

We understand the points to which you object in Mark Twain's writing, but we cannot agree with you that they are "destitute of a single redeeming quality." We think that the literary judgment of this country and of England will not sustain you in such an opinion. I ask you in all fairness to read Mr. Howells' essay of Mark Twain in September number of the *Century* for 1882. To say that the writings of Mark Twain are "hardly worth a place in the columns of the average county newspaper which never assumes any literary airs" seems to us to be singularly untrue. Mr. Clemens has great faults; at times he is inartistically and indefensibly coarse, but we do not think any thing of his that has been printed in the *Century* is without very decided value, literary and otherwise. At least, as a picture of the life which he describes, his *Century* sketches are of decided force and worth.

Mark Twain is not a giber at religion or morality. He is a good citizen and believes in the best things. Nevertheless there is much of his writing that we would not print for a miscellaneous audience. . . .

The work of which the schoolmaster had complained, and for which Gilder had had to plead Mark Twain's good citizenship, was an American masterpiece, "The Adventures of Huckleberry Finn." Selections from it had appeared in the *Century* for December, 1884, and January and February, 1885. Gilder's alterations in the text, and especially his omissions,[7] summarize the standards of gentility.

The selection printed in the January number is merely a short bit from Chapter XIV, in which Huck and Jim discuss kings. It is textually unchanged. The other two comprise Chapters XVII to XXVIII, with a small part of Chapter XVI and two sentences of Chapter XXIX. The action involved is the Grangerford-Shepherdson feud, the arrival of the lost Dauphin and the Duke of Bilgewater, their activities in Arkansas, and their impersonation of the English heirs. The text is considerably shortened for magazine publication, but it is striking that the

[7] No account is taken here of omissions made for the sake of brevity, or of the omission of the Duke of Bilgewater's corruption of Hamlet and Huck's garbling of English history. These last two items seem to me to have been left out on the single ground that they weren't funny, and I am interested only in the objections alluded to in Gilder's letter to the Superintendent.

longest passage wholly omitted is that which records the shooting of Boggs and the attempt to lynch Colonel Sherburn. It may be that this vanished from the *Century* in obedience to a foreman of make-up — but one doubts it. Gilder's literary judgment was unimpeachable: he cannot have misunderstood this climax in American realism. But it looked too closely at themes and characters ungraced by refinement — it would not do for a miscellaneous audience. It was strong milk for babies.

Gilder's letter held that Mark was not a giber at religion. Still, he deleted the preacher's exhortation at the camp-meeting. Mark was allowed to describe this hysteria but quotation was realism and could not be borne. The Dauphin's piety is also denied a miscellaneous audience; he is not allowed to say "Thish yer comes of trust'n to Providence. It's the best way, in the long run. I've tried 'em all, and ther' ain't no better way." Huck is not permitted to observe that hogs like churches because of the cool puncheon floors. He is also forbidden to remark, when the duke and the king weep over Peter Wilks, "both of them took on about that dead tanner like they'd lost the twelve disciples."

Even Huck's grammar is occasionally rectified and his spellings are sometimes corrected — as when Gilder translates "forrard" by "forward." Such expressions as "Dern your skin", in which an earlier correction by Olivia or Howells may be guessed, are offensive to the *Century* and are omitted. Huck's acknowledgment that he was "in a sweat" is coarse and so it disappears. A possible offense to refinement lurks in Jim's suggestion that meteors are stars that had "got spoiled and was hove out of the nest": the suggestion disappears. A similar mephitiphobia deletes Huck's admission that he knows "the signs of a dead cat being around." Huck is forbidden to observe that "people always blows them [their noses] more at a funeral than they do at other places except church", and a possible gibe at morality is averted by the suppression of his "it's kind of natural to hide under a bed when you are up to anything private." A statement that he had no clothes on escapes, probably because the event occurs after dark, but morality is defended from an earlier admission, "We was always naked [on the raft], day or night, whenever the mosquitoes would let us", together with the explanation that Huck didn't go much on clothes nohow. When the Dauphin prances on the stage in "The Royal Nonesuch" the *Century's* readers are not informed that he is naked and an oblique notice about his decorations is withheld from them. But Gilder's staunchest protection of morality appears in his elimination of the last line of the playbill and the duke's comment:

"Then at the bottom was the biggest line of all, which said

LADIES AND CHILDREN NOT ADMITTED

" 'There,' says he, 'if that line don't fetch them, I don't know Arkansaw.' "

The description of the "one-horse town" in Arkansas and of its natives who later gape at the circus and the murder of Boggs is wholly omitted. No offense to morality or religion is discernible in this description and it lacks the violence and depravity that probably barred the Boggs incident to the *Century*. What we meet here is still another graceful avoidance on behalf of refinement. The passage in which the natives exchange tobacco and send the village hounds after a sow and her farrow is a passage of pure literature. Its two pages of dispassionate portrayal distil more realism about squatter life in rural America than the whole Midland group of the 1920's got into their books. But realism was not comfortable to the *Century's* miscellaneous audience. A study in low life which made no gesture in the direction of morality was offensive. The deepest instinct of refinement revolted from such verity: Gilder was softening for his readers a kind of realism very different from that of Howells and Henry James. His literary convictions — they were the best of his generation — would not permit this kind of study. He softened it, and in the same spirit, he softened this literature's unsentimental dealings with death. Huck might not say, "He didn't look like he was dead, he looked considerable more than that." He might not describe the coffined face of Mr. Wilks. When he hid the money in the coffin, he was allowed to say, "I tucked the money in under the lid," which sufficed for information; but he might not add, "just down beyond where his hands was crossed, which made me creep, they was so cold." He could say, "I didn't want to set her to thinking about her troubles again," but he might not complete his sentence with "and I couldn't seem to get my mouth to tell her what would make her see that corpse laying in the coffin with that bag of money on his stomach." Death, in the genteel tradition, was not permitted this barrenness of decorative piety.

The folkways undergo a slow change, which nothing much seems to affect except their own — obscure — inner foliation. These specimens of Gilder's editorial obligation toward Mark Twain exhibit a tradition enforcing conformity on an alien. No surprise should be occasioned by their operation, or by Mark's dislike of them or his surrender to them. He accepted them, Gilder says, with "full consent." He restored his own text when the book appeared, but when Gilder did a similar service to "Pudd'nhead Wilson", Mark appears to have retained Gilder's text. In so far, it is evident to our altered residues, the books of Mark Twain suffered harm from the genteel tradition.

This damage was purely verbal. The tradition may have wrought a greater damage by turning him from Pudd'nhead Wilsons and Huck Finns to knights, kings, and armored virgins. If indeed the tradition can be held responsible for this shift of interest. The doubt exists less in natural history than in literary criticism, to which this preface will now devote itself.

IX

THE CRITICS OF MARK TWAIN

A lady once asked him how he came to define Pastern the knee of a horse.
— BOSWELL.

SOMETHING — it is not necessary to explain just what — about the criticism of literature in America is latent in the fact that between Howells's review written from the proof sheets and the appearance of this preface, American opinion neglected to attempt a full-length appraisal of "The Adventures of Huckleberry Finn." A masterpiece thus remains unconsidered during forty-eight years, although the literary have devoted a thousand pages to explaining its creator in the portraiture of the artist as American and an even greater bulk of paper in calling him a mountebank. It is to be anticipated, however, that the national aptitude for commemoration assisted by the enterprise of publishers will, in 1935, observe his centennial and rehabilitate the writings of Mark Twain. A classic experiment in this revival of reputations was provided in 1919 when the liberal discovered Herman Melville's books.[1]

Few experiences could be more depressing than a study of those thousands of pages. Hardly a hundred contain anything of value to one who desires criticism of Mark Twain. It is expedient to specify. Mr. H. L. Mencken has never devoted a Preface or a Prejudice to Mark Twain but incidental paragraphs in his treatises compose a brilliant appraisal. Professor Pattee, though his opinion changes between books, has written about Mark Twain with sustained intelligence. Mr. Van Doren's article in the "Dictionary of American Biography" is sound, and Mr. Macy's chapter in "The Spirit of American Literature" says all that need ever be said about an aspect of Mark Twain's work whose existence it remains fashionable to deny. In the fall of 1931, Mr. Macy published a collection of essays by various hands, "American Writers on American Literature." Mr. C. Hartley Grattan's chapter on Mark Twain in this collection is the finest treatment of him in print.

The opinion of the official biographer is simple. To Mr. Paine, Mark Twain was a great genius and his books were great books. Defects are occasionally admitted but as who should say: the hand of the Potter shook. His critical judgment may be appraised in his pages about "Joan of Arc" or, more briefly, in his idea that "it was not Mark Twain's habit to strive for humor. He saw facts at curious angles and phrased them accordingly."

Howells, Brander Matthews, Bernard Shaw, Stuart Sherman, Archibald Henderson (in a book curiously devoted to the thesis that Mark Twain was a Southern gentleman), and anonymous pamphleteers have *obiter dicta* of some charm. The rest is worthless. For purposes of examination, it may be classified as academic criticism and politico-psychological criticism.

---

[1] Those who enjoy the exterior view of literary opinion will find amusement in examining Melville's status in liberal (American) thought in the books written by the profound before 1919 and in the reconsiderations which they wrote after they had learned about his books. The parenthesis is necessary because Melville has always been read in England.

A passage from Professor Hastings's "Syllabus of American Literature" of 1923 sums up pedagogical ideas about Mark Twain which were orthodox during the quarter-century before its composition and have been repeated since in a good many textbooks written for college courses.[2] It is quoted here because it is succinct and representative. "Heir to the devices of the earlier American humorists, who chiefly practiced a 'gigantic exaggeration and calm-faced mendacity' — George H. Derby, 'John Phoenix'; Henry Wheeler Shaw, 'Josh Billings'; David Ross Locke, 'Petroleum V. Nasby'; and Charles Farrar Browne, 'Artemus Ward'; also influenced by Bret Harte [*sic!*] and coached somewhat by his friend, William Dean Howells."

The four humorists whose heir Mr. Hastings considers Mark Twain to have been, had in common with him the intention of producing laughter. Josh Billings may without further comment be grouped with Phoenix and Nasby whose "influence" on Mark Twain has already been considered here: he had none. If any one desires a refutation not worth embarking on, let him read Josh Billings. So we may now consider the traditional influence of Artemus Ward.

It is here asserted that the minds of Mark Twain and Artemus Ward, their methods, and their effects were antipathetic. The briefest way to establish the fact that they had little in common is to examine one of the themes they shared. The doubtful may read Artemus Ward's lecture on the Mormons, his "Visit to Brigham Young", his "Mormon Romance", and Chapters 9 to 18 of his "Travels." Oppose to these Chapters 13 to 16 of "Roughing It" and the Appendix on the Book of Mormon. True, one joke is shared by both humorists and it belongs to

<hr>

[2] As, for example, Napier Wilt's "Some American Humorists", 1929. See p. XIII. It should be observed, however, that since Mr. Meine's "Tall Tales of the Southwest" appeared and his Introduction called attention to Mark Twain's place in this humor, a number of articles receptive of his material have appeared in the scholarly trade journals. Several dissertations making use of his point of view have also been announced. Professor Blankenship's book, which appeared after this chapter was written, and Mr. Lewisohn's "Expression in America", published as the proofs of the chapter reach me, both contain intelligent passages about Mark Twain. I cannot, however, wholly approve of either one.

Ward, but a difference in intelligence and intention is so evident that no space will be expended in elaborating the obvious. Mark Twain in this much resembled Shakespeare: he desired the rewards of labor, and, when he borrowed an inspiration, he improved upon it.

Conscientious study has produced these statistics. Twenty-three years after Ward had written a letter to the Prince of Wales, Mark Twain addressed one to the Queen of England: it is more amusing but retains some of the notions of its model. Mark's "Story of a Good Little Boy" and other inverted fables resemble Ward's Romances: so do Bret Harte's Burlesque Novels, but the type was conventional in newspaper humor when both were children. Mark's "General Washington's Negro Body-Servant" may be a reminiscence of the Revolutionary Soldier in Artemus's "Affairs Round the Village Green." Artemus burlesques Shakespeare and so does Mark: the annoyance is immortal and was a fixture in the newspaper humor, especially in the works of Sol Smith. When Thomas Jefferson Snodgrass in 1856 proposed to print his "Dierrea", it is unlikely that he anticipated the showman's panorama of 1859 which was called "A Grand Movin Diarea of the War in the Crymear." Artemus once said, "I was 96 minits passin a given point" and Mark found the announcement useful several times. "My wife says so, too" in "The Draft in Baldinsville", suggests Huck's "Tom Sawyer, he says the same." "Roughing It" contains another reminiscence of Ward. Artemus, jailed in Montgomery as a Northern spy, had found the table "librally surplied with Bakin an Cabbidge" so that "when I didn't hanker after Bakin I could help myself to cabbidge"; at a stage station on the plains Mark expressed his dislike of mackerel, the only dish served, and was told "Oh — then help yourself to the mustard." The dilemma was already traditional in American humor when Artemus employed it. But Ward's most notable contribution to Mark Twain may be observed when, at the Green Lion in London, Artemus proposes to the innkeeper that they attend the performance of a Trans-Mejim who "says the sperrits of departed great men talk through him. He says that tonight sev'ril em'nent persons will speak through him — among others, Cromwell." The landlord is interested. "And this Mr. Cromwell" he says, " — is he dead?"

These instances, with the two already listed, compose the sum of Mark Twain's indebtedness to Artemus Ward. It is almost wholly verbal — fifty words in the collected works. Their minds were disparate, their intentions antagonistic, their methods incommensurable. They were humorists and in the production of humor Artemus Ward was chronologically the first. That is all.[3]

Toward the close of the century New Jerusalem essayed to reappear in America. Voyagers arrived from Altruria and similar commonwealths, and Mr. Bellamy glanced backward so hopefully that he could receive a kindly patronage in 1931. At nine-forty on the evening of February 15, 1898, however, lights perished in a roaring shock and the screams of wounded men traveled across Havana Harbor. Flames leaped up and the waters that closed over the *Maine* buried the city of gold under one more resurgence of the American empire.

Twelve or fourteen years passed. Then sudden thunder, and dawn was once more crimson on golden pinnacles.[4] The Newness was here again. Three quarters of a century had something altered the ground plan of Jerusalem. Its architects were professors now, who had been seers or parsons in the 1840's; justice, not righteousness, was painted on its guidons; and the most explicit had substituted a title of Mr. Mallock's for the Kingdom of God. Psychology provided the incantations for which the Forties had only had phrenology, and the course of perfection derived from acts of Congress rather than maxims of self-reliance. Still more remarkably, the enunciation of creeds had shifted from ethics to literary criticism, so that the Orphic

[3] Popular jokes contain nothing new. The immediate instructor of Artemus Ward was Ruth Partington, who had the ages behind her.

[4] 'The Gilded Age, "the epoch of industrial pioneering . . . came to an indeterminate conclusion, by the kindness of heaven, shortly before the war of 1914" — "The Ordeal of Mark Twain", p. 54. About this time, too, a new generation of literary critics were graduating from college, well equipped with Professor Carver's economics of the group. Soon Carver blended with Veblen and no shock was experienced.

Sayings must now call themselves "Our America" and the "American Scholar" was reborn as "America's Coming of Age." But New Jerusalem is time's continuity. The American as literary critic was the same expectant man who, as preacher or pamphleteer, had made the 1840's bright with hope. He believed that society could be made perfect and that, by taking thought, he was helping to make it perfect.

Vilfredo Pareto, an Italian who achieved the exterior view of society, has provided a convenient lens for the consideration of ideas over periods of time. There may be an energic base, a sentiment, which changes slowly or not at all, and which may produce a variety of adaptive sentiments. This base or continuity, Pareto calls a Residue. The adaptive notions, logical or nonlogical, which proceed from it, he describes as Derivations. . . . A Residue persisted in American optimism from the hopeful decades to "the end of pioneering materialism": confidence in the perfectability of American society. The Derivation of 1840 relied, for this perfection, on the regeneration of the individual; the Derivation of 1912 relied on the regeneration of government. Of many glistening continuities from the earlier age to the later, only one other is relevant to this discussion.[5] A Residue distrusted art. The American perfectionist in 1840 could not admire literature unless it was dedicated to ethics: his inheritor in 1912 abhorred literature that did not devote itself to politics or economics.

Once the nature of our twentieth-century Derivations is perceived, no objection can be urged against them. The sentiments that produced a great bulk of literary criticism between 1912 and 1925 need only be recognized as what they were, a species

[5] But the collector of beautiful notions easily perceives Residues in diet, marriage customs, and tribal organization. He is struck, too, by a grouping of unrelated sentiments in both areas. The Derivations form chains of nonlogical association. In 1840, if you had the right, or orthodox, sentiment about vegetarianism, you had *ipso facto* right sentiments about marriage, government, abolition, phrenology, Graham's bread, the rights of women, and ethical culture. Eighty years later, if you had the right sentiment about pioneering materialism, you had *ipso facto* right sentiments about marriage, government, socialism, psychology, the new art, the rights of women, and self-expression. In the 1930's another series of linkages is being formed.

of religion. It had the weaknesses of religion, specifically a strong preference for emotion as opposed to thought, a selective attitude toward the data of literature which is hardly different from fanaticism, and a willingness to substitute epithet for analysis in the consideration of what it disapproved. It had also the strength of religion: fervor, the conviction of righteousness, and acquaintance with the resources of rhetoric.

The process is one of simplification. The American heritage is the accumulation of only three centuries but remains chaotic. Facing a welter of incommensurables, the hopeful mind requires categories, personifications, unities. To deal patiently with the irreconcilable, to subordinate desire to fact, to derive theory from observation, to concede the existence of insolubles — is to risk despair. It is pleasanter to embody one's sentiments in words and then apply the words to the description of the American heritage. Unity follows quite naturally from this process and simplicity is achieved. It is then possible to lay these words like bricks in a well-ordered edifice.

So, in the criticism of American literature, the word became God. Abstractions became entities and objectively existed. The Frontier, the American, the Puritan, the Pioneer, the Artist, the American Artist, Pioneering Materialism, Industrial Philistinism, and a score or two other clichés began by embodying the sentiments of critics about ideas they disliked and ended as actual, independent existences. It is important to realize that these words ceased to have any correspondence in fact: they were symbols of emotion and a little later they were persons. Mr. Herbert Croly could decide that the pioneer lived in a herd and (irrelevantly) that "the pioneer democracy viewed with distrust and aversion the man with a special vocation and high standards of achievement" without touching reality at any point. The words clanged beautifully and expressed Mr. Croly's sentiments about pioneers and Puritans, but they had no relation to fact: their meaning was a religious meaning. The words "Pioneering may in part be described as the Romantic movement in action" have a religious meaning for Mr. Mumford, but have no relation to the passage westward from the Atlantic seaboard of actual people through three centuries across a geography. The elaboration of word-entities, the construction of a logically invulnerable edifice through fifteen years and some hundreds of books, and the acceptance of this transubstantiation as a description of American history and literature is the progress of a religion.

It was historically necessary to redraw pious maps of the known world in accordance with verified fact, and a similar necessity results from the decision of New Jerusalem to study an eidolon, "Mark Twain", in its relation to another phantom, "America." A religion of perfection, expressing itself in political and economic theories, has dealt irrationally with the books that Mark Twain wrote. The assurance that people of a non-religious turn of mind are also interested in those books makes obligatory an examination of Mr. Van Wyck Brooks's treatise, "The Ordeal of Mark Twain."

In the sentiments contributed to American thought by a politico-religious system which partially established itself on this continent before 1650, several Residues may be perceived. Those which dealt with theocracy may be disregarded. Another one, which had to do with Duty, is about the only permanent characteristic of the only persons in relation to whom the word Puritan has had any historical significance. Puritans have been — so far as they were anything reducible to formula — men who were dominated by the idea of Duty. The ideas of Mr. Brooks are thus a part of the Puritan tradition.

They are, however, expressed in the Derivations of the early twentieth century. Mr. Brooks proposed a Portrait of the American as Artist. The effort was to include three principal exhibits, which would establish categories capable of holding all other specimens. There would be the Artist as adaptation to environment: Mark Twain. There would be the Artist as flight from environment: Henry James. There would be the Artist as expression or summation of environment: Ralph Waldo Emerson. The second and third of these exhibits are not relevant here but one effort was common to all three: the examination of America. Clearly, if you are describing the Artist in relation to his environment, you must study the environment. The principle seems axiomatic. Yet, if the wide acceptance of Mr. Brooks's Mark Twain did not make detailed examination of his thesis obligatory, it would be possible to dismiss him on the ground that he is ignorant of the America about which he writes.

Just as Mr. Brooks's ideas of American literature are derived from a reading of the accepted canon, without awareness of large areas which contradict his conclusions (as when he says that we have inherited no folk art) — so his description of America is derived from the logical necessities of his theory. His America is an *a priori* description dictated by the requirements of theory; apart from the evangelism of his text, it is referred only to the theories of Mr. Croly and Mr. Waldo Frank. These, in fact, with an occasional quotation from Mrs. Trollope, Charles Dickens, and the letters of American notabilities, compose the whole sanction of his portrait. In his analysis of Mark Twain, the eidolon "Frontier" has a primary importance; yet Mr. Brooks fails to consider Frederick Jackson Turner's study of the frontier, the basis of realism in any discussion, and there is no evidence that he had ever heard of it or of the investigations it begot. He had no knowledge of the frontier and considered none essential. The logical edifice of Mr. Croly and Mr. Frank was enough — since it was always possible to offer in support those portions of Mark Twain's books that seemed to justify the eidolon. . . . Thomas Huxley once protested the methods of certain fireside scientists who reviewed his books. Their only knowledge of biology, he said, came from the volumes they criticized, and he doubted the authority of the man he was informing to reject his facts.

Seven chapters of this preface have been derived from facts about the American frontier and its relation to Mark Twain's books which do not appear in Mr. Brooks's book. Mr. Brooks does not ignore them; more simply, he does not bother to learn of their existence. The logical edifice was already built; it was simpler to assert what must be true about America than to inquire what was true. So we have those curious misrepresentations of Missouri, the Middle Western border, the steamboat age, Nevada, California — brilliantly evocative descriptions, eloquent with Mr. Brooks's denunciation of what he dislikes and his exhortations for repentance, but worthless as descriptions of societies, eras, and people, and gravely misleading in the criticism of literature. Mr. Brooks's eidolon, "Frontier", superbly enlarges on the frontier which Mr. Croly, Mr. Frank and other theorists had created, but it has no correspondence in history. His Mark Twain, a product of this phantom, has existed nowhere outside his pages.

Seven chapters have been offered to correct the distortion and no rebuttal of Mr. Brooks's frontier will be attempted now. It is convenient, however, to quote two passages to illustrate his understanding of the American past. He is discussing the roots in our colonial and early nineteenth-century past out of which grew the "Gilded Age." In the course of his discussion he says: "We were a simple, homogeneous folk before the Civil War and the practical effect of pioneering and the business régime was to keep us so, to prevent any of that differentiation, that evolution of the homogeneous into the heterogeneous which, since Herbert Spencer stated it, has been generally conceived as the true note of human progress." Nothing can be done with such thinking. It represents not a superficial knowledge of America before the War but no knowledge whatever. A theory that is capable of calling the America of 1700–1860 homogeneous racially, intellectually, emotionally, philosophically, economically, or æsthetically, is powerless to describe America. Four pages later Mr. Brooks says: "As we can see now, a vast unconscious conspiracy actuated all America against the creative spirit. In an age when every sensitive mind in England was in full revolt [*sic*] against the blind, mechanical, devastating forces of a progress that promised nothing but the ultimate collapse of civilization; when all Europe was alive with prophets, proletarian prophets, religious and philosophical and humanitarian and economic and artistic prophets, crying out, in the name of the human spirit, against the obscene advance of capitalistic industrialism; in an age glorified by nothing but the beautiful anger of the Tolstoys and the Marxes, the Nietzsches and the

Renans, the Ruskins and the Morrises — in that age America, innocent, ignorant, profoundly untroubled, slept the righteous sleep of its own manifest and peculiar destiny.". . . Mr. Brooks shifts from the age he is discussing, 1840–1860, as the need of examples develops, and ends in a later period, but the passage is a characterization of America before the Civil War. Mr. Brooks later wrote about Emerson and spoke respectfully of Thoreau. He had not heard, however, of prophecy in America. He had not heard of the communisms, millennialisms, restorations, and experimental societies of the hopeful decades, nor of the energetic people who conducted them. He had not heard of one main current of American thought — probably the strongest and certainly the most characteristic — during the period he was discussing. We are desired to accept this sort of thinking as a description of the America against which is to be exhibited the figure of Mark Twain.

Inquiry into the life of the formative frontier being renounced, and the whole American past being considered only in epithet, what instrument might be used in the exploration of Mark Twain? In the Newness of the twentieth century one choice was inescapable. Mr. Brooks nowhere called his treatise "a genuine Freudian analysis of Mark Twain's unconscious motives." But Mr. Harold Stearns promptly did,[6] and there can be no doubt that Mr. Brooks undertook exactly that objective. He may, in fact, to some extent, be horribly charged with the fashion of lay analysis that raged across American biography in the ensuing six or eight years. He pointed the way to a fatally easy method of reinterpreting history, and though his effort was carried on at a level of integrity and intellectual brilliance that few if any of his successors attained, something of their frequent absurdity must be ascribed to his pioneering enterprise.

The validity of psycho-analysis as a fact-finding instrument in biography and criticism remains debatable. No opinion on the larger question need be expressed here, since if the instrument be accepted we must still require its manipulator to show his mastery of its use. One who undertakes to psycho-analyze

[6] "America and the Young Intellectual."

literature must be a competent psycho-analyst. Mr. Brooks is not. He displays no greater acquaintance with the materials and methods of his science than was common to the literary during the decade when he wrote — that is to say, the acquaintance with analytical theories to be acquired from the reading of half a dozen books.[7] He had the amateur's freedom of procedure. An analyst who attempts the exploration of a neurosis must spend months in regular study of a living man. The pattern which he eventually perceives is subject to constant reference, for correction, to the actual patient, who can never be disregarded. Furthermore, his method enforces on him the inclusion of all data and forbids him to bridge discrepancies by the use of theory. Finally, he is usually unwilling to explain a neurosis by the use of contradictory principles.

It must constantly be remembered that Mr. Brooks's patient is a dead man. The material of psycho-analysis is not the dead man's mind but his books and letters, together with the more dubious data of Mr. Paine's book about him. Over this material Mr. Brooks exercises an arbitrary and even capricious selection. His effort is not the determination of a pattern but the proof of a theory. He selects what data will support that theory and if he does not suppress those that contradict it, at least they do not find their way into his pages. Judgments that a psycho-analyst would make only after months of probing a living mind leap to Mr. Brooks's pen when he reads a single line of type — frequently not even Mark Twain's. He exhibits

---

[7] A professional psycho-analyst who has reviewed these pages in proof checks this paragraph and the next and writes in the margin. "You are not explicit enough. Do you, or don't you, mean to say that Brooks's analysis is exactly on a level with those of the parlor Freuds?" I had supposed that such a judgment would be derived from what I wrote. But let me say explicitly that, in my opinion, Mr. Brooks's psycho-analysis of Mark Twain is a species of dinner-table annotation. Between his assertion that the thwarted artist in Mark Twain avenged his betrayal by inducing Mark Twain to murder his son, for instance, and the parlor entertainer's notion that the American Radiator Tower is a phallic symbol, or his host's parrot a partial sublimation of the Œdipus complex or a master-slave constellation, or a symptom of the inferiority complex — I can perceive no important difference. And nothing in "The Ordeal of Mark Twain" is entitled to any greater consideration.

the amateur's reverence for the principle of ambivalence. This, in lay psycho-analysis, is a device for the reconciliation of contradictory evidence. It explains that a fact can be both its literal self and a symbol of its opposite, that one fact can prove a given assertion on one page and a contradictory assertion on another, that two facts which seem to indicate irreconcilable conclusions really mean one thing — the preferred thing. And finally, Mr. Stearns is quite wrong in calling "The Ordeal of Mark Twain" a Freudian analysis. It is Freudian when the basic theory can be advanced on Freudian principles. It is Jungian or Adlerian when those principles are more serviceable. The Œdipus Complex is metamorphosed into the ego's will to power when it ceases to be useful for the denunciation of American materialism, and there are times when both notions retire in favor of a racial unconscious which can explain villainies insufficiently explained by either. . . . No schisms in the orthodox church troubled psycho-analysis in American biography. Freud, Jung, and Adler were common avenues of approach to a common end. Vienna, Zurich, and Geneva thought otherwise, but in the codification of American sentiment everything was serene.

The initial undertaking of Mr. Brooks's psycho-analysis is to discover why Mark Twain, a man of genius, fame, wealth, and happy social relations was a pessimist. The presence of cynical and bitter passages in his works and letters required explanation, although no explanation of his laughter and good nature was required. The need grew out of a discomfort traditional to criticism in America: the literature of disillusionment has always had to be explained as something other than the sense of reality. At the beginning of his search, Mr. Brooks assumes that this pessimism was the product of an unconscious conflict, a sense of guilt, a symptom that Mark Twain was a divided soul. Having made this assumption, he then uses it to prove itself.

The basic conflict is derived by assumption. Mark Twain was born, Mr. Brooks says, to be a literary artist. Here the eidolon appears. An "artist", to Mr. Brooks, is a person who rebels against authority. Literature is "a great impersonal social instrument." The root of Mr. Brooks's theory is plain: it is a moralist's dislike of all art that does not demand political or economic reform. Popular psycho-analysis derives the careers of revolutionists from juvenile revolt against the authority of parents: literary theory substitutes Shelley for Samuel Adams but retains the mechanism intact.

For evidence of Mark Twain's predestined greatness as a "pure" artist Mr. Brooks offers the admissions of Mr. Paine that up to the age of twelve Mark was a mischievous child who played pranks, sometimes disobeyed his parents, and had an aversion to school. (It must be borne in mind that a great part of this psycho-analysis is applied to Mr. Paine's book, not to Mark Twain.) No further evidence is offered: none exists. Mark Twain was clearly designed to be an artist, in rebellion against the Philistinism of America, because he played pirate and absented himself from school. These diversions were "the first stirrings of the normal æsthetic sense, the first stirrings of individuality."

But Mark Twain did not become an artist. Another cliché is invoked to explain the failure. "Pioneering materialism" and the brutal frontier which contained it, "the desert of human sand", put an end to his wish to be an artist. In the person of his mother, the Puritan-Pioneer suppresses the rebel. The scene at his father's coffin, which probably never occurred, is held to be the moment of betrayal. "All those crystalline fragments of individuality, still so tiny and so fragile, are suddenly shattered; his nature, wrought upon by the tense heat of that hour, has become again like soft wax. And his mother stamps there, with awful ceremony, the composite image of her own meagre traditions. He is to go forth the Good Boy by *force majeure*, he is to become such a man as his father would have approved of, he is to retrieve his father's fortune, to recover the lost gentility of a family that had once been proud, to realize that 'mirage of wealth' that had ever hung before his father's eyes. And to do so he is not to quarrel heedlessly with his bread and butter, he is to keep strictly within the code, to remember the maxims of Ben Franklin, to respect all the prejudices and conventions;

above all, he is not to be drawn aside into any fanciful orbit of his own!"

That every statement in this exhortation is contradicted by Mark Twain's books does not impede the progress of psycho-analysis, which thereafter derives its momentum from the assumption made in this paragraph. Mark Twain, whose unconscious wish was to be an artist in rebellion against society, is to be instead a conformer, a victim of material respectability, an American business man who accepts and supports the cowardice, injustice and Philistinism of his type.

The rest of Mark Twain's career, psycho-analysis makes plain, is dictated by the mother-image. Olivia Langdon becomes the surrogate of Jane Clemens after Mark's marriage, but his life is used up in obedience to his mother's demands for conformity, respectability, and getting on in the world. For these, in turn, America is responsible — that product of pioneering materialism which Mr. Brooks is so unqualified to describe. This is the "Ordeal" of Mark Twain: that, desiring to be an artist (a rebel against society), he surrendered to the ideals of materialistic America and so betrayed his deepest self. So he suffered throughout his life from a sense of profound guilt, the product of a conflict between art and conformity. What is the mechanism by which he systematically betrayed his destiny? Well, he wrote humor.

Mr. Brooks dislikes humor.

It is convenient to repeat that all the evidence for Mr. Brooks's cardinal assumption and eventual explanation of it has been offered here: Mr. Paine's statement that he was a mischievous boy, which is probably true, and his description of the scene at John Clemens's coffin, which it is possible to reject as imaginary. If Mark Twain really wanted to be Shelley, the desire was buried deeper than any research, psychological or skeptical, has revealed. The only fact that can be recovered — it is established beyond question — is that Mark's earliest experiments with literature were humor, that he wrote humor through all the formative years of his career, and that during that time he wrote nothing but humor. He appears to have desired to write nothing else. Fact is, of course, inferior to theory in the pursuit of certainty, but psycho-analysis has opposed to it only the discovery that Mark, before the age of twelve, played hookey from school. That seems a little fragile.

The course of psycho-analysis, however, reads backward to the past and, in what happened after the betrayal, is able to discover a great deal of evidence for it. That is the superiority which the method has to the scrutiny of fact. It therefore becomes necessary to illustrate how, at every level of significance, theory utilizes what it requires, ignoring the rest, and how enthusiasm distorts evidence. The divided personality of Mark Twain and the basic conflict having been assumed, his books and Mr. Paine's may be conveniently arranged to support the assumption.

The contradictions in this process of elaboration appear on all levels, from the most superficial to the most profound. On page 5, Mark Twain's assertion that he was never ill and never tired is accepted as true: the immediate effort being to establish his vigor. On page 200, his frequent illness is asserted, because it can be urged as a flight from the repellent life of the frontier, though the earlier acceptance specifically denied illness at that time. On page 220 his admission that he was "tired all the time" is exhibited as proof of the artist's crucifixion, the period being almost identical with that of a contrary assertion accepted on page 5. An immaterial datum is thus accepted and denied at Mr. Brooks's convenience. On page 205, Mark's humor is a vehicle for his hatred of pioneer life; on page 211 it is a mechanism for acceptance and glorification of that life. On page 84 Mark despises lecturing and story-telling and revolts from the trade because it betrays the lost artist in him. On page 172 he lavishes care on lecturing and story-telling in obedience to "the voice of the artist, the prompting of the true craftsman's conscience." At one stage of the argument, Mark's naïve exposition of determinism in "What Is Man?" (it had a fashionable revival recently in Doctor Watson's Behaviorism) is a symbolic scheme which allows him to solace his feeling of frustration; later on it is a literal description of his experience. Mark dresses with fashionable care when he is a pilot on the Mississippi and this is evidence of pride in the one trade that gratifies his wish to be an artist. When he becomes a silver miner and adopts the durable breeches and boots of the silver miners, this roughness exhibits an infantile regression and a lapse from the artist's spiritual discipline. Mr. Paine duly sets down a return to fashionable clothes when Mark goes to work for the *Enterprise* but the return does not appear in Mr. Brooks's pages — a symbol of pride in the writing of newspaper humor would be inconvenient — and, late in Mark's life, when the white suit [8] gleams before crowds on Fifth Avenue, it only convinces Mr. Brooks that a vanity in clothes is Mark's pitiful substitute for pride in his creative work.

Yet such contradictions as these merely elaborate several basic ones that run throughout Mr. Brooks's book. The defeat of the artist in Mark Twain is sometimes wholly subliminal, so that Mark is never aware of it except as a contrary impulse which he cannot understand; but sometimes it is a defeat, which he recognizes and laments or despises, and sometimes it is a voluntary surrender. Sometimes love of applause and the desire to conform are the root of the neurosis, but sometimes pure commercialism and the desire to make money — a desire which at least once Mr. Brooks also specifically denies. The very pessimism that Mr. Brooks undertakes to explain is sometimes the outgrowth of his betrayal, but sometimes "his inborn Calvinistic will-to-despise human nature" — which, earlier, he did not at all possess. And, throughout the treatise, Mark's books are characterized as whatever will justify the immediate assumption — no matter how, for other justifications, they are otherwise characterized in other passages.

We observe the momentum of a thesis which derives from religious sentiments about the reformation of American life.

---

[8] The white suit has been tiresomely debated. I see no necessity for explaining it. If an explanation is required, however, and neither Mark's theatrical impulses nor his known liking for costume and color will suffice, I offer the plausible one suggested to me by Miss Mildred Howells. Miss Howells says that Mark was sensitive about his small stature and suggests that he finally wore white because it made him look taller.

Evangelical enthusiasm subordinates the data of investigation
to the necessities of the thesis. It persuades Mr. Brooks that
accuracy is not essential to criticism. His inaccuracy is of no
moment when, for instance, he habitually refers to the Nevada
silver mines as gold fields, but becomes somewhat more serious
when he offers as proof of Mark Twain's spiritual squalor passages from "The Gilded Age" which a footnote of Mr. Paine's
informed him were written by Charles Dudley Warner.
Yet this habit of informality provides most of the data that
are employed to support the assumptions of theory after they
are made. A kind of misrepresentation on behalf of theory —
the product of enthusiasm or carelessness — is so common
throughout the book that it cannot be more than illustrated
here.

He finds it convenient, for instance, to say that Mark Twain
solved his financial difficulties by going into bankruptcy: that is
a misrepresentation. The assertion that Mark Twain was a convert to Christian Science misquotes Paine and betrays its author's
ignorance of a vaguely related form of "Mental Healing."
When Mr. Brooks says of Mark Twain's birth, "it is suggested
that he was not wanted", he derives his assertion from the
word "perhaps" which Mr. Paine attributes not to John or Jane
Clemens but to the neighboring housewives who, he says, may
perhaps have thought the Clemens house already full enough —
but it is desirable to represent Mark's birth as loveless. His description of Mark's letters home during his *wanderjahr* is untrue. In the same passage, the same necessity requires him to
assert, in contradiction to the facts, that neither Mark's letters
nor his scribblings at this time were humorous. His analysis
of "The Gilded Age" is profoundly misleading. His only source
for the Nevada episodes is Mr. Paine and the effect of his careful
selection is misleading. His decision that Samuel Clemens
adopted the pseudonym Mark Twain for various subliminal
reasons, among them a practical man's shame of the impractical
pursuit of authorship and an artist's shame at degrading himself
by writing humor, ignores the whole convention of humor and
journalism in America at the time — as well as the practice of

Swift, Addison, Steele, Thackeray, and Dickens, whom it might be difficult to explain on this basis. He misrepresents Jane Clemens's attitude toward Mark's writing — and also contradictorily reports it in two places. He accepts a palpable misstatement of Paine's about the Nevada letters without checking it by the letters themselves. He says that Anson Burlingame's materialistic advice was responsible for the *Quaker City* trip, whereas Mark had contemplated a similar voyage before he met Burlingame. He accepts a momentary notion of Mark's about smoking which helps to damn Olivia, in flat defiance of an enormous bulk of evidence open to all the world. He says that Mark spoke of himself "in public to the end of his life" as a Presbyterian, which simply isn't true. The episode of the Paige typesetting machine in Mr. Brooks's account has little relation to the facts; his treatment of Grant's "Memoirs" is fully as careless.[9]

In his effort to prove Mark Twain ignorant of literature and even hostile to it, Mr. Brooks seriously misrepresents his knowledge and taste: only dry statistics from his books can check the accusation, but I have made them and they refute it. The psycho-analysis of Mark's affected laziness on page 166 is a distortion of the facts and a painful demonstration of Mr.

---

[9] Nevertheless, Mr. Brooks does not do common sense the violence of suggesting that Mark Twain wrote the "Memoirs." That absurdity was begotten, in our day, by Mr. Burton Rascoe, who said flatly in the *Bookman* that Mark was Grant's "ghost writer." Mr. Woodward, in his life of Grant, handsomely confessed that he had read every word of the "Memoirs" and did not believe the allegation. Well, I've read them also — twice — and I do not believe it, either. I have even made a long investigation to determine whether Porter, or Badeau could have had any share in their production. No evidence can be found that calls into question Mark Twain's account in the "Autobiography." Grant wrote his own book — in its entirety. My first reading encountered a number of passages whose turn of phrase suggested Mark Twain, and I considered the possibility that, in seeing the book through the press, he had been unable to withhold his hand. Then I found the passages intact in the *Century*, for which they had been prepared before Mark knew that they existed and where they appeared before he saw them. The phrasing was not Mark's but Grant's. Grant had been near the common humor in America, on the frontier and in the army. In this small way he was subject to the influence that produced Mark Twain.

Brooks's helplessness in the presence of humor. Recurring to Nevada in Chapter IX, Mr. Brooks again misrepresents the frontier, through ignorance, and Mark's attitude toward it, through enthusiasm. His theory then compels him to show that the artist in Mark despised practical jokes and the infinitesimal point is made in defiance of the authorities he has accepted. "Almost infinite repression" of Mark Twain is next discovered in Washoe and what Mark did and wrote there is necessarily rejected. A page or two later the necessity of proving that Mark did not write satire — one of the most constant elements in his work — produces the assertion that "in Nevada or in California he was prohibited, on pain of social extinction, from expressing himself directly regarding the life about him." One explanation may be that Mr. Brooks neglected to read what Mark wrote in Nevada and California. The collaboration in "The Gilded Age", which Mr. Brooks had already failed to describe correctly, is distorted on page 228. In fact, most of Mr. Brooks's references to the books of Mark Twain do them violence. He considers in detail only "The Gilded Age" and "Life on the Mississippi" and his reporting of them has singularly little relation to what they actually say. For the rest, Mark Twain's books appear only fragmentarily in "The Ordeal" and are mainly used as the data of psycho-analysis.

But everything is a datum of psycho-analysis. Pudd'nhead Wilson's aphorisms are, on various pages, whatever they need to be for theory. One of them which condemns heaven is held to mean that Mark deceived himself when he thought he liked Joe Twitchell; in the same way, his dislike of Jane Austen must mean an act of revenge on Howells, who also wrote novels. Huck Finn and Tom Sawyer are identified as Mark Twain and so is Pudd'nhead Wilson — but somehow Roxy, Nigger Jim, and Colonel Sherburn are not. Edward J. Billings, the frustrated artist in "Captain Stormfield" is inevitably Mark Twain: the Jersey barkeeper is not, and neither is Tom Canty, Miles Hendon nor the Connecticut Yankee, who are identifiable as Mark on the same evidence. Colonel Sellers, who was drawn from Mark's uncle, is Mark; but Washington Hawkins, taken from his brother, is not. Lord Berkeley and the Stranger are Mark — identifications made, like the rest, on mere assertion — yet we are not permitted to see Mark describing himself in Brigham Young or Satan.

Psycho-analysis of the betrayed artist explains Mark's superstitions on page 22, and then on page 79 attributes clairvoyance to this buried poet. We are here desired to believe that the artist in Mark kept him from finding silver or gold and the suggestion explicit here is implicit in the treatment of his business failures. Ambivalence solves an awkward dilemma on page 139. An unfinished manuscript which Mr. Brooks has never seen is confidently explained on page 192. A fine expertness in profanity, as well as Mark's Elizabethan experiment, proves to be related to the frustrated artist, though no explanation is attempted of the geographies and trades in which it was acquired. The famous drawl is really a compensation for the repression of Mark's desire to tell the truth in satire: the vocal mannerism of a population is disregarded for the sake of theory. So, too, is the demonstrable fact that Mark drawled before he wrote. His volcanic rages derive from the familiar betrayal.[10] Mark was a Baconian because the betrayed artist could solace itself by denying originality to Shakespeare: whether the same mechanism explains another literary Baconian, Walt Whitman, is not made clear. And "the natural man, the suppressed poet, registered its tragic protest, took its revenge, against a life that had left no room for it" — by murdering Mark's son and trying to murder his daughter.[11]

[10] Mr. Brooks is, as yet, the only psychiatrist who has studied Mark Twain in print. It remains possible for some one with a different set of first principles to discover that Mark suffered from manic-depressive insanity.

[11] In a morose mood, Mark accused himself of having produced the boy's illness by exposing him to cold air. At another time he said that he absently let go the handles of his daughter's go-cart when it stood on an incline. Mr. Brooks treats these accusations with the gravity quoted in my text. A pretty problem in the analysis of literature is presented by the success of one attempt at murder and the failure of the other. What weakened the natural man, the suppressed poet, when he essayed the later infanticide? A study in the frustration of frustration is suggested —or perhaps criticism may invoke Malicious Animal Magnetism.

At the risk of ennui, it is essential to repeat that the items listed in the foregoing pages are not the sum of distortion and misunderstandings in "The Ordeal of Mark Twain", but merely representative examples. From the point of view of one who is familiar with American history and has made a detailed examination of Mark Twain's life and books, Mr. Brooks does not appear qualified to report Mark Twain and pass judgment on him. When "The Ordeal of Mark Twain" was published, Mr. Carl Van Doren, a lonely voice, inquired whether Mr. Brooks was able to understand his subject.

The answer may be reduced to a single demonstration. On page 162, Mr. Brooks asks, "How, then, are we to describe Mark Twain's literary character?" As a basis of description, he offers several quotations from Mr. Paine. Mr. Paine, who was able to narrate the adult life of Samuel Clemens with accuracy and great literary charm, was able to bring to the criticism of Mark Twain only the most rudimentary ideas about literature. Nevertheless Mr. Brooks accepts them. Mr. Paine speaks of Mark as "given rather to elaboration than to construction" — "most of his characters reflected intimate personalities of his early life" — "he was always greater at these things than invention." In one sense the first of the assertions was true, as Chapter XI of this preface demonstrates, but in the sense which Mr. Brooks accepts, it was not true. The other two assertions were profoundly untrue. Mr. Brooks accepts them, however, and goes on: "Are not these traits, which are indisputable, the traits of a mind that has never attained to creation in the proper sense, a mind that has stopped short of the actual process of art?" He then answers his question affirmatively.

It is silly to dispute about words and idle to inquire what Mr. Brooks may mean by creation and the actual process of art. One remembers that the mind here assailed created the almost endless population of characters that move through Mark Twain's books with, somehow, more illusion that these phantoms live than can be derived from any other books in American fiction. This mind created St. Petersburg and Dawson's Landing. It produced "Life on the Mississippi" and "Pudd'nhead Wilson." It created "The Adventures of Tom Sawyer" and "The Adventures of Huckleberry Finn." It made a world and filled it with living creatures. If this is not creation, if it is not the actual process of art, then one is not troubled by the possibly mystical meaning the words may have for Mr. Brooks.

New Jerusalem is time's continuity. In "The Ordeal of Mark Twain" a religion applies its mode of thinking to Mark Twain and adds one more wall to an unrealistic edifice which is intended to be a description of America. It exists as a part of a logical structure, on which further masonry may be erected as the city of gold lifts its pinnacles. These sticks and stones, being once in place, make unnecessary any further consideration of Mark Twain's books when it is desirable to refer to Mark Twain in later ideology about Our America. In the twelve years since the book appeared, it has supplied the assertions about Mark Twain in other books that proceed from the same religion. Their reference is never to Mark Twain but always to Mr. Brooks. It would be impertinent — and doubtless wrong — to assert that Mr. Mumford and Mr. Josephson, for instance, have not read Mark Twain. Still, their treatment of him in "The Golden Day" and "Portrait of the Artist as American" has no relation to what he wrote but only to what Mr. Brooks wrote about him. The logical edifice progresses in their work but discussion has moved away from what actually appears in the books of Mark Twain, and, that being true, the point of view here expressed is profoundly uninterested in considering them.

X

THE BIG BEAR OF ARKANSAW

MARK TWAIN was a frontier humorist. His literary intelligence was shaped by the life of the frontier and found expression in the themes and forms developed by the humor of the frontier. Time's erosion simplifies much: it is now clear that Mark Twain, Henry James, and William Dean Howells wrote what is important of American literature in their period, and it is not Mark Twain's humor that gives him this permanence. For the future in America he is the author of "Roughing It", "The Gilded Age", "Life on the Mississippi", "The Man Who Corrupted Hadleyburg", "Pudd'nhead Wilson", "The Adventures of Tom Sawyer", and "The Adventures of Huckleberry Finn." [1] But these books exist as satire and realism to which the frontier humorist attained. They are the humor of the frontier in its greatest incandescence, realizing its fullest scope and expressing its

[1] It is not my desire to establish a Mark Twain canon. It will become clear that, in my opinion, a number of fragmentary pieces share the qualities of these books.

qualities on the level of genius. In them an American civilization sums up its experience; they are the climax of a literary tradition. But from the laughter of anonymous frontier story-tellers to the figure of Huckleberry Finn a clearly traced line exists, and Huckleberry Finn could have been arrived at along no other path.[2]

Simplifications are dangerous. Frontier life across a nation and during three generations was extraordinarily complex. The humor of frontiersmen grew out of that life at every level, so that an attempt to find unity in it would be folly. The same folly would attend an effort to explore the mind and books of Mark Twain in the interest of consistency. It is possible only to discover certain continuities in both. They obey no principle of simplicity; some of them are irreconcilable.

It is convenient to begin with the frontier humor character-ized in Chapter IV as anecdotal narrative. Its origin was the life at hand; its creators were the people who lived on the frontier, and, I have said, its overwhelming emphasis was on the folk themselves. In American literature, fantasy and realism exist side by side. In the same way, burlesque and extravaganza, which are theoretically derived from fantasy, are hardly to be separated from satire, a derivative of realism. There is at all times a current of mythology that produces the wilder activi-ties of Boone and Crockett and Beckwourth, Mike Fink and Paul Bunyan, the flora and fauna of Jim Bridger's country, Uncle Remus's dark tales, the ballads of riverside and crib-house love and their kin in folksong of all kinds. This is a constant element in frontier humor, a continuity. It is most prominent at the level of folklore, but may be observed throughout the newspaper

---

[2] To avoid disputing about words, I refuse to define humor. Such definitions seem to me to become metaphysics and in that subject I have no present interest. We all attach some meaning to the word "humor" and enough meaning is com-mon to our usages to be immediately recognizable. Beyond that recognition I do not care to go. Perhaps, however, I may save dissenters some speculation by an-nouncing that I am familiar with the theoretical analyses of humor. Merely, I cannot see that they are serviceable here.

humor that is our immediate interest. If any one cares to relate to it the humor of exaggeration, which as burlesque is one of the largest areas in our field, no dissent need be expressed.

Nevertheless, a larger area in this emergent humor is the realistic portrayal of character.[3] The exuberant frontier delighted in burlesquing and caricaturing itself, but its steadiest pleasure came from merely depicting itself. The substratum is the simple joy of anecdote — anonymous hundreds embodying their experience in narratives devised to produce recognition and laughter. The desire to produce laughter is the motive that begets the anecdote. It was the motive that made Samuel Clemens a literary person, Mark Twain — the motive that is constant in his work, interrupted only because the process of expressing it revealed opportunities that momentarily promised other pleasures.

The anecdote was oral. Before he existed as a recognizable person, the American was a story-teller. The conditions of frontier life richly encouraged him. He told stories endlessly, though he was incapable of the precious impulse that makes Mr. Sherwood Anderson describe himself as a teller of tales. His storytelling was the foremost art of his civilization and the men who first confided it to type were raconteurs before they were writers. Something of the earlier, more ingenuous art exists in its sophisticated development — so that the rhythms of speech, of voices skillfully preparing effects, are widely recognizable on the printed page. These rhythms are sometimes so apparent in Mark Twain's work that several critics have identified in them a residual influence from his lectures. They are not, of course, a product of the lyceum. They go back to the basis of his humor: they

---

[3] Miss Constance Rourke's "American Humor" is by far the most important book ever written in the field. My present study is concerned solely with the newspaper humor of the Southwestern frontier, and differs in a few respects from Miss Rourke's characterization of that humor. My emphasis is on its realistic aspects, its delight in character and self-portraiture, but I do not mean to deny or disregard its other elements. In fact, Chapters VI and VII examine other aspects in detail. Miss Rourke prefers to emphasize the other aspects, without denying or disregarding its realism.

record his presence in crossroads stores, on sunny wharves along the river, in the saloons and pilot houses of steamboats making downstream voyages by daylight above no bottom. They declare unanswerably the assurance that his roots go down deep into the common life of America and are nourished by the native blood of the folk.

But that the humor of the frontier, specifically the anecdote of character, rests on a basis of folklore does not mean that its emergence into print is in any particular unconscious. The newspaper humor that becomes its vehicle is not a symbolism shaped by some mystical pattern in the folk mind, but the conscientious work of writers, frequently intelligent and sometimes very talented, who knew quite well what they were doing. Longstreet declared his intention of recording what he had seen. He broke a way for, literally, hundreds of successors who faithfully observed the precept of their model. It was his desire, and theirs and Mark Twain's, to produce laughter by exhibiting what they had seen and heard in the world of reality.

Following Franklin Meine's lead,[4] students have agreed to call the frontier anecdote a "Tall Tale." The phrase competently describes a good many species and if the adjective is not italicized, will do to describe them all. It is a narrative of a length dictated by the necessities of newspaper publication, usually based on the life immediately at hand, and working through the realistic portrayal of character toward the desired end, laughter. It is a distinct *genre*, the frontier newspaper's contribution to American literature. It was the occasional amusement of hundreds of amateur writers — the lawyers, doctors, soldiers, travelers, merchants, actors and scientists whom William T. Porter describes in a passage already quoted. It became the medium of a good many more nearly professional writers — Longstreet, Baldwin, Thompson, George W. Harris, Hooper, Field, Robb. Finally, it was the first and commonest vehicle of

[4] Let me repeat here an announcement made in Appendix A. The most convenient way of checking what I say of frontier humor is to read Mr. Meine's "Tall Tales of the Southwest." At my suggestion, Mr. Meine included in that volume a number of sketches very relevant to this discussion of Mark Twain.

Mark Twain's humor and it produced the characteristic framework of his books.

When he wrote "The Dandy Frightening the Squatter",[5]
his earliest recovered sketch, he was utilizing the humorous
anecdote — the tall tale. The Snodgrass letters manipulate
the device in theaters and railroad cars. Significantly, the tale
is here sometimes used, as in "The Empire City Massacre", to
carry satire. The tale moves readily through the Sandwich Island letters. It exists purely in "Jim Wolf and the Tom Cats"
and in much of what found its way into the *Californian*. It reaches
a climax, of a kind, in "The Celebrated Jumping Frog of
Calaveras County." By now Mark Twain's humor has been colored by the farther West, and in this tale he manages for the
first time the creation that gives life to what has been only figure-
heads, but the vehicle of both humor and creation remains the
narrative taught him by the newspapers of the frontier.

At hardly any time may he be said not to have used it. As
late as "Joan of Arc" the Paladin is embroidering the narrative
with yarns that are in the strict tradition.[6] About half of the
"Autobiography" consists of anecdotal reminiscences told solely
for the sake of the story. This fact is significant; it indicates the
truth about Mark's use of the device. He took the humorous anec-

[5] In *American Literature* for November, 1931, Professor Fred W. Lorch,
whose articles on Mark Twain in Iowa have been very useful to this preface,
presents a possible "source" of "The Dandy Frightening the Squatter." He has
discovered in the Bloomington (Iowa) *Herald* of February, 1849, a sketch
called "A Scene on the Ohio", which in turn is credited to an issue of *The
Elephant*, a comic magazine of the year before. The sketch has a striking
similarity to "The Dandy", but does not impress me. Source-hunting is the
most profitless of literary occupations, and, in the field of humor, is wholly
absurd. There is no such thing as the "source" of a joke. Mr. Lorch believes that
"A Scene on the Ohio" may have "served Mark Twain, either consciously or
unconsciously, as the framework for his story." True, it may have, although
Mark was only thirteen when it appeared. But why this sketch in particular?
Mr. Lorch admits, quoting my contribution to Mr. Meine's Introduction, that
these stories traveled widely through the frontier press. Further study will unquestionably reveal earlier and earlier versions of this story, which is only a type-
specimen of "The Stranger Discomfited" or "The Braggart Worsted." The basic
idea is hoary in frontier humor. Why try to track it down?

[6] For example, Chapter VII.

dote, combined it with autobiographical reminiscence, and so achieved the narrative form best adapted to his mind. His imagination was rich and vivid, but incapable of prolonged creation. He could not sufficiently objectify his material to give it the discipline of form. His fiction is episodic — as loosely constructed as the picaresque romances of eighteenth-century Spain or France. Form, as a reasoned and achieved technique, was not possible to him. The mode of creation that expressed him was a loosely flowing narrative, actually or fictitiously autobiographical — a current interrupted for the presentation of episodes, for, merely, the telling of stories. It is in these stories that the best of Mark Twain exists, from the humbler level of the Jumping Frog, to the episodes in "Huckleberry Finn" that are shot with fire. The oral anecdote thus becomes a narrative interlude, a sophisticated art form charged with the expression of genius.

But this is also, of course, the method of his travel books, which require a moment's examination. "The Innocents Abroad" is Mark Twain's discovery of the method. It is both a travel book and a burlesque of travel books. In deriding three decades of sentimental homage to Europe, Mark was not breaking new ground. The assertion of which criticism has been so fond, that in "Innocents" adolescent America at last dares to assert its commercial Philistinism against the civilization of the Old World, proceeds out of ignorance. A tradition of dissent from the romantic treatment of Europe — Samuel Fiske's "Dunn Browne Abroad" [7] and Theodore Witmer's "Wild Oats Sown Abroad" will do for specimens — had been well established by 1860. Not novelty but superiority gave the book its distinction.

"The Innocents Abroad" is structurally an autobiographical narrative. Descriptive passages, most of them in the windy rhetoric he elsewhere satirizes, interrupt the narrative from time to time but its steady progress is accomplished by means of stories. Some of them are brief, unelaborated anecdotes, in no

[7] Also published as "Mr. Dunn Browne's Experiences in Foreign Parts."

way different from the type out of which they proceed, but others already show Mark's perception that this form can be utilized for more intricate effects. . . . The Pilgrims are in Paris. On page 107 Mark is shaved by a wigmaker; in one form or another the anecdote had already amused a good many audiences in the frontier press. On page 113, A. Billfinger becomes Ferguson and begins a series of anecdotes whose purpose is usually satirical. A few pages of descriptive writing follow and then a burlesque of Abélard and Héloïse leads into another traditional story, the tourist's attempt to get an American drink. The passage is typical and the point need not be labored; stories of guides, other shaves, other drinks, the purchase of gloves and souvenirs, burlesqued legends, reminiscent passages that exhibit pictures of Missouri and Nevada, happenings in catacombs and in the desert — the momentum of the book derives almost exclusively from anecdote. It is Mark Twain discoursing in the manner of the pilot house; he has found a technique completely adapted to his qualities.

The same framework produces "Roughing It", "A Tramp Abroad", "Life on the Mississippi", and "Following the Equator." The narrative interlude is organically developed in these later books; possibilities are more thoroughly realized. When, in "Roughing It", Bemis recounts his experience with the buffalo bull or Johnson describes his interview with Brigham Young, the device has come a long way from the Doctor gazing at a signature and asking if Christopher Columbus is dead, but it rests on the same base. The book moves throughout by this motive power. Sometimes the intent is a mere mechanical joke, as in the story of the Mexican Plug; sometimes, as with the flood-bound bully, Arkansas, or Captain Ned Blakely's lynching of Bill Noakes, it is a means for presenting in silhouette a lifetime or a civilization. It creates melodrama in the Wide West lead and expresses the essence of a national experience. And it constantly makes articulate Mark Twain's delight in the variations of the human race. Mr. Ballou tastes the water of the Humboldt and remarks that "it was too technical for him"; he has been added to a gallery of living portraits. The Sanitary

Flour Sack moves its procession across Washoe. Scotty Briggs visits the parson and asks him to preside at the funeral of Buck Fanshaw. Jim Blaine — "tranquilly, serenely, symmetrically drunk" — begins his story about Grandfather's old ram. Dick Baker, a momentary figure given life so abundantly that he gives life to his cat, Tom Quartz, reaches into the bestiary of Uncle Remus and brings the narrative device close to perfection.

But it seems desirable to select still another story of Baker's for consideration. He is Dick Baker in "Roughing It", when he talks about Tom Quartz. By "A Tramp Abroad" he has become Jim Baker — which shows more plainly that Mark was remembering Jim Gillis, the dour pioneer of Mr. Brooks's imagining. Mark thinks of him at Heidelberg, one afternoon while he is walking in the woods. He falls into "a train of dreamy thought about animals which talk, and kobolds, and enchanted folk." Quite naturally. He was treading earth over which the shy people had crept for centuries, when they were no longer gods but only the friendly or spiteful creatures whom the brothers Grimm have dedicated to children. And at Hannibal his own childhood had understood animals which talked and kobolds and enchanted folk, desirable in the stories that Uncle Dan'l told before the fire and Uncle Remus repeated, or dreadful in their darker traffic across new graves. So he is not surprised when a raven begins to caw at him derisively. "However, I made no reply; I would not bandy words with a raven." So the raven summons a friend and the two discuss him "as freely and offensively as two great naturalists might discuss a new kind of bug." After a while the two call in another friend and all three squall insulting remarks. "They were nothing but ravens — I knew that — what they thought of me could be a matter of no consequence — and yet when even a raven shouts after you 'What a hat!', 'Oh, pull down your vest!', and that sort of thing, it hurts you and humiliates you, and there is no getting around it with fine reasoning and pretty arguments."

So, in the hills above the Neckar, the Tuolumne country comes back into his mind. "Animals talk to each other, of course. There can be no question about that; but I suppose there are few people who can understand them; I never knew but one man who could. . . . He was a middle-aged, simple-hearted miner who had lived in a lonely corner of California, among the woods and mountains, a good many years, and had studied the ways of his only neighbors, the beasts and the birds, until he believed he could accurately translate any remark they made." This is Jim Baker and we learn his opinions about the grammar, articulation, and the stage presence of various animals. In Jim's opinion, bluejays are the best talkers in the animal creation.

You may call a jay a bird. Well, so he is, in a measure, because he's got feathers on him and don't belong to no church perhaps; but otherwise he is just as much a human as you be. . . . A jay hasn't got any more principle than a Congressman. A jay will lie, a jay will steal, a jay will betray; and four times out of five a jay will go back on his solemnest promise. The sacredness of an obligation is a thing which you can't cram into no bluejay's head. . . . You think a cat can swear. Well, a cat can; but you give a bluejay a subject that calls for his reserve powers, and where is your cat? Don't talk to *me* — I know too much about this thing. . . . Yes, sir, a jay is everything that a man is. A jay can cry, a jay can laugh, a jay can feel shame, a jay can reason and plan and discuss, a jay likes gossip and scandal, a jay has got a sense of humor, a jay knows when he is an ass just as well as you do — maybe better. If a jay ain't human, he better take in his sign, that's all. . . .

So Jim Baker tells a story about bluejays.

When I first begun to understand jay language correctly, there was a little incident happened here. Seven years ago, the last man in this region but me moved away. There stands his house — been empty ever since; a log house, with a plank roof — just one big room, and no more; no ceiling — nothing between the rafters and the floor. Well, one Sunday morning I was sitting out here in front of my cabin, with my cat, taking the sun, and looking at the blue hills, and listening to the leaves rustling so lonely in the trees, and thinking of the home away yonder in the states, that I hadn't heard from in thirteen years, when a bluejay lit on that house, with an acorn in his mouth, and says, "Hello, I reckon I've struck something." When he spoke, the acorn dropped out of his mouth and rolled down the roof, of course, but he didn't care; his mind was all on the thing he had struck. It was a knot-hole in the roof. He cocked his head to one side, shut one eye and put the other one to the hole, like a possum looking down a jug; then he glanced up with his bright eyes, gave a wink or two with his wings — which signifies gratification, you understand — and says, "It looks like a hole, it's located like a hole — blamed if I don't believe it *is* a hole!"

Then he cocked his head down and took another look; he glances up perfectly joyful, this time; winks his wings and his tail both, and says, "Oh, no, this ain't no fat thing, I reckon! If I ain't in luck! — why it's a perfectly elegant hole!" So he flew down and got that acorn, and fetched it up and dropped it in, and was just tilting his head back, with the heavenliest smile on his face, when all of a sudden he was paralyzed into a listening attitude and that smile faded gradually out of his countenance like breath off'n a razor, and the queerest look of surprise took its place. Then he says, "Why, I didn't hear it fall!" He cocked his eye at the hole again, and took a long look; raised up and shook his head; stepped around to the other side of the hole and took another look from that side; shook his head again. He studied a while, then he just went into the *de*tails — walked round and round the hole and spied into it from every point of the compass. No use. Now he took a thinking attitude on the comb of the roof and scratched the back of his head with his right foot a minute, and finally says, "Well, it's too many for *me*, that's certain; must be a mighty long hole; however, I ain't got no time to fool around here, I got to 'tend to business; I reckon it's all right — chance it, anyway."

So he flew off and fetched another acorn and dropped it in, and tried to flirt his eye to the hole quick enough to see what become of it, but he was too late. He held his eye there as much as a minute; then he raised up and sighed, and says, "Confound it, I don't seem to understand this thing, no way; however, I'll tackle her again." He fetched another acorn, and done his level best to see what become of it, but he couldn't. He says, "Well, *I* never struck no such a hole as this before; I'm of the opinion it's a totally new kind of a hole." Then he begun to get mad. He held in for a spell, walking up and down the comb of the roof and shaking his head and muttering to himself; but his feelings got the upper hand of him, presently, and he broke loose and cussed himself black in the face. I never see a bird take on so about a little thing. When he got through he walks to the hole and looks in again for half a minute; then he says, "Well, you're a long home, and a deep hole, and a mighty singular hole altogether — but I've started in to fill you, and I'm d———d if I *don't* fill you, if it takes a hundred years!"

And with that, away he went. You never see a bird work so since you

was born. He laid into his work like a nigger, and the way he hove acorns
into that hole for about two hours and a half was one of the most exciting
and astonishing spectacles I ever struck. He never stopped to take a look
any more — he just hove 'em in and went for more. Well, at last he
could hardly flop his wings, he was so tuckered out. He comes a-drooping
down, once more, sweating like an ice-pitcher, drops his acorn in and says,
"*Now* I guess I've got the bulge on you by this time!" So he bent down
for a look. If you'll believe me, when his head come up again he was just
pale with rage. He says, "I've shoveled acorns enough in there to keep
the family thirty years, and if I can see a sign of one of 'em I wish I may
land in a museum with a belly full of sawdust in two minutes!"

He just had strength enough to crawl up on to the comb and
lean his back agin the chimbly, and then he collected his impressions
and begun to free his mind. I see in a second that what I had mistook for profanity in the mines was only just the rudiments, as you may
say.

Another jay was going by, and heard him doing his devotions, and
stops to inquire what was up. The sufferer told him the whole circumstance, and says, "Now yonder's the hole, and if you don't believe me,
go and look for yourself." So this fellow went and looked, and comes back
and says, "How many did you say you put in there?" "Not any less than
two tons," says the sufferer. The other jay went and looked again. He
couldn't seem to make it out, so he raised a yell, and three more jays come.
They all examined the hole, they all made the sufferer tell it over again,
then they all discussed it, and got off as many leather-headed opinions
about it as an average crowd of humans could have done.

They called in more jays, then more and more, till pretty soon this
whole region 'peared to have a blue flush about it. There must have been
five thousand of them; and such another jawing and disputing and rip-
ping and cussing, you never heard. Every jay in the whole lot put his eye
to the hole and delivered a more chuckle-headed opinion about the mystery
than the jay that went there before him. They examined the house all
over, too. The door was standing half open, and at last one old jay happened to go and light on it and look in. Of course, that knocked the mystery galley-west in a second. There lay the acorns, scattered all over the
floor. He flopped his wings and raised a whoop. "Come here!" he says,
"Come here, everybody; hang'd if this fool hasn't been trying to fill up a
house with acorns!" They all came a-swooping down like a blue cloud,
and as each fellow lit on the door and took a glance, the whole absurdity of
the contract that that first jay had tackled hit him home and he fell over

backward, suffocating with laughter, and the next jay took his place and done the same.

Well, sir, they roosted around here on the housetop and the trees for an hour, and guffawed over that thing like human beings. It ain't any use to tell me a bluejay hasn't got a sense of humor, because I know better. And memory, too. They brought jays here from all over the United States to look down that hole, every summer for three years. Other birds, too. And they could all see the point, except an owl that come from Nova Scotia to visit the Yo Semite, and he took this thing in on his way back. He said he couldn't see anything funny in it. But then he was a good deal disappointed about Yo Semite, too.

The story exhibits a good many aspects of Mark Twain's humor. It is a narrative interlude in "A Tramp Abroad", an anecdote of California told reminiscently in the Neckar hills, a passage in which the argument of the book halts while Mark Twain is overhearing the talk of men who are leisurely and entertained. Its material comes from the Negro's bestiary, interstitial with the life of his boyhood in Hannibal; and in this way the humor rises from fantasy, from the imaginative myth-making of the slaves and the frontier. But also, Jim Baker, the narrator, exists; he is a creation from the world of reality. He lives, and no fantasy has gone into his creation, but only the sharp perception of an individual. His patient, explanatory mind actually works before our eyes and no one can doubt him. His speech has been caught so cunningly that its rhythms produce complete conviction. Fantasy is thus an instrument of realism and the humor of Mark Twain merges into the fiction that is his highest reach.

Beyond this sort of thing the narrative interlude does not develop in the travel books, except as it becomes a vehicle of satire. As Mark's audience grew, he became an accepted commentator on life, government and morals. This is also in the tradition of the frontier, a product of leisurely talk and of realism. Chapter XI scrutinizes the backwoods philosopher; here it is enough to observe that commonly, in the manner of Lincoln, he expressed himself by means of a tale.

Jim Baker's story about bluejays illustrates another aspect

of Mark Twain's humor. Some who read it here may feel that the last four sentences mar the effect of a passage in pure humor. They strain toward a joke and, escaping from the clear medium of the tale itself into burlesque, they are a blemish it is possible to regret. Well, that also is typical of his humor.

The humor of Mark Twain was indebted to the humor of the frontier for more than its anecdotal method. Mark must be regarded as primarily a humorist who brought that tradition to a climax. I have already expressed my disbelief in the pursuit of what are called sources, but a few instances of Mark's ability to remember his predecessors may exhibit the direct line of his inheritance.

J. M. Field's "The Drama in Pokerville" is a collection of newspaper humor, mostly anecdotal, first published as a book in 1847.[8] In its last sketch, "A Resurrectionist and His Freight",[9] a comedian who is traveling on a Mississippi steamboat informs a Hoosier rustic that the case of another traveler's contrabass contains the corpses of a woman and her two children. They are the property, he says, of a doctor who intends to dissect them. The humor of the sketch pivots on the smell of putrefying bodies and reaches its climax when, after the initiated passengers have inquired about the stench, the yokel explains it. " 'Reckon you don't know!' exclaimed the Hoosier, stepping forward, and almost quivering with indignation. 'Know! certainly not' said the Captain. 'Well, you've got that box TOO NEAR THE STOVE, *that's all.*' "

In January, 1879, Mark was in Munich, assembling the book that was to become "A Tramp Abroad." As always, the manuscript was gigantic: he had written nine hundred pages before he got his trampers out of Heidelberg, where the trip began. He reported to Joe Twichell a vast interest in the book and "a consuming desire to work" on it. Twichell had told

[8] The dedication and preface are dated June 7, 1847. The copyright notice, however, is dated 1846. Mark may not have seen it until its 1858 appearance in "Major Thorpe's Scenes in Arkansaw."

[9] "A Resurrectionist and His Freight" was first printed in the St. Louis *Reveille* for March 9, 1846, and was reprinted in the *Spirit of the Times*, March 21, 1846.

him a story about a butcher which, Mark felt sure, would find its way into the manuscript. Also, "I'm putting in the yarn about the Limburger cheese and the box of guns, too — mighty glad Howells declined it." Four days later he had less confidence in the story and wrote to Howells: [10] "I have rung in that fragrant account of the Limburger cheese and the coffin box full of guns. Had I better leave that out? Give me your plain, square advice, for I propose to follow it." Though no letter survives, Howells seems to have given his plain, square advice in the form of his earlier rejection, for the story of the cheese and the coffin full of guns waited another twenty-three years before appearing as "The Invalid's Story" in Mark's "Merry Tales." It is essentially the tale that had appeared in the Forties, more intricately wrought and given the benefit of Mark's dramaturgy, but still grotesquely awful in its insistence on smells. A gentleman sets out to take the body of a friend to his home in Wisconsin but a mistake occurs and a case of rifles is substituted for the coffin. In the express car a box of Limburger cheese is set on the case of guns, near a red-hot stove. The expressman carries on a dialogue with the corpse's custodian. " 'Friend of yours?' 'Yes' I said with a sigh. 'He's pretty ripe, ain't he?' " The expressman decides that the corpse must be two or three years old. They break a pane of glass in the door, but no relief follows. "I've carried a many a one of 'em — some of 'em considerable overdue, too — but, lordy, he just lays over 'em all! — and does it easy. Cap, they was heliotrope to him." Cigars have no effect and a bottle of carbolic acid proves injudicious. There are several vomitings. . . . The sketch is not describable as lovely, but it is immensely true to one kind of humor of the frontier and of Mark Twain.

Field's volume made another contribution. "Stopping to Wood" [11] has an account of a race between steamboats which provides most of the details of the race in Chapter IV of "The

[10] Howells's "Letters", Vol. I, p. 263. The letter does not appear in Mr. Paine's collection.

[11] First printed in the St. Louis *Reveille*, September 22, 1845; reprinted in the *Spirit of the Times*, October 11, 1845.

Gilded Age" that brings Laura into the story.[12] The long title sketch, too, may have shown him something about the small-town gentry who are so continuous a subject of his satire, and about the ways of strolling players.

Consider "The Adventures of Huckleberry Finn", the novel in which Mark Twain's qualities achieved their greatest harmony. In Chapter XXII, Huck goes to a circus and reports his awe of ladies in spangles and "rose-leafy dresses flapping soft and silky", his delight in bareback riding, and finally his great interest in a drunken stranger who ultimately proves to be the best rider of them all. The scene is firmly set in the tradition of humor. One at once remembers Partridge at Garrick's perform-ance of Hamlet; but the reference is more direct than that. The rustic who mistakes a play for reality had already appeared in the Snodgrass letters and had worked into them from a stock theme in frontier humor. The three volumes of Sol Smith's recollections, a great part of which appeared as sketches in the *Spirit of the Times* and elsewhere, have many examples of this situation. Mark was well acquainted with Sol Smith's material, but in this instance was reproducing[13] a scene which had else-where derived from Smith. "Major Jones' Chronicles of Pine-ville", one of William Tappan Thompson's immensely popular collections, contains a sketch, "The Great Attraction", which tells how a circus comes to Pineville. The scene in "Huckle-berry Finn" rests solidly on Thompson's. . . . In the pre-ceding chapter, the Duke of Bilgewater coaches Louis XVII in Hamlet's soliloquy and then composes a playbill. Both of these items are widespread in the humor of the time. One of the play-bill's numerous begetters may be seen in "The Drama in Poker-ville." Mutilations of Shakespeare can be met with everywhere

[12] Or does it? Scholarship would unquestionably say so, for the parallelism is striking: the burning of bacon and the firing of shots are final evidence. And yet Mark had seen a good many races and a good many wrecks — and the disaster of the *Pennsylvania* was indelibly stamped on his memory. Will not the historian's principle of multiple invention sometime enter the academic criticism of literature?

[13] Once more: I do not believe in plagiarism or in "sources." Such a cor-respondence as this is merely what Mark called "unconscious memory."

in this literature but most often and most amusingly in the anecdotal recollections of Sol Smith.

But the most important reproduction in "Huckleberry Finn"
occurs in Chapter XX, when the raft ties up at Pokeville, "a
little one-horse town about three mile down the bend." The
scene at the camp meeting is one of the book's climactic passages.
A dispassionate pronouncement on the damned human race is
implicit in this tale of backwoods hysteria and boozy repentance.
It presents the squatter in a cold light that is barren of the emotion which, in our day, has been expended in denouncing him —
and the effect is as complete as any achievement in American
literature. But also the scene provides an instance of Mark
Twain's literary judgment betrayed into error. Here, as in so
many other places, his imagination — or his discretion — goes
wrong and forces him out of realism, out of satire even, into extravaganza. His effect is something damaged by the repentant
Dauphin's decision to set his evil-doing among the pirates of
the Indian Ocean and his exhortation for funds with which to
convert them. A scene of corrosive realism loses credibility in
this touch and recedes into burlesque. . . . Mark Twain falls
below his predecessor. The scene is all but identical with Chapter
X of Johnson J. Hooper's "Adventure of Simon Suggs." [14]
Hooper lacks the Olympian detachment of Mark Twain and his
sketch therefore exists on a lower level, but its realism is sharper,
its intelligence quite as great, and its conviction considerably
greater. Simon Suggs repents his life of sin and deception quite
naturally. His conviction and conversion are set in the experiences of his audience and his swindling is therefore credible.
A high moment in "Huckleberry Finn" would have been better
if Mark Twain had adhered to the scene that unquestionably
produced it. The instance is memorable as the only one in which
the literature to which he belonged surpassed him in a subject
of his choice.

No further direct dependence on the humor of the Southwest need be shown — and no specimen so clearly reproduced

[14] The chapter is reprinted in "Tall Tales of the Southwest", 425 ff.

as these exists.[15] The indebtedness, the relationship, shades off into generalization. Not single items establish the fact of his instinctive participation in this literature, but the common possession of humorous devices, or points of view, of methods of perception and evocation.[16] These are to be encountered at every hand. The misquotation of Shakespeare has been mentioned. Much commoner is the rambling, irrelevant garrulity of Mistress Quickly. Simon Wheeler and old Jim Blaine are early examples of this device, which he employs throughout his books. It was a stock device and may be traced from Longstreet's old women to the experiences of Hooper's census-taker, by way of scores of humbler imitators. The tall talk of his squatter characters, notably of the raftsmen in "Life on the Mississippi", was faithful reporting of what he had heard, but precedents for its use had been established everywhere in this humor. The Davy Crockett books are fat with it; in Burke's "Polly Peablossom's Wedding" three separate sketches turn on it; and The Big Bear of Arkansaw, who created innumerable imitations, is the type-specimen of the species. No interest in Mark's humor is more continuous than his delight in foreigners' attempts to speak English — Mr. Brooks has selected it for an extended denunciation of the betrayed artist. Mark experimented with it as early as the *Enterprise* letters, made much of it in "The Innocents Abroad", and returned to it in a good many of his books as well as in such pieces as "Meisterschaft" and "English As She Is Spoke." It is as common as any theme in the newspaper humor, from Crockett's Dutchmen and Longstreet's Miss Pig-

---

[15] It is amusing, however, to note the names of the dogs, Bull Wilkerson in "Simon Suggs", and Bull Harbison in "Tom Sawyer", and the explanations of the names. Mark's "Autobiography" contains many anecdotes from this literature which occurred to him again in his last years, notably "Shifting the Responsibility" from "Polly Peablossom" and a form of the naked man story that was universal.

[16] "Mark Twain's Library of Humor", finally published in 1888 after many years of discussion, was edited by others. Mark Twain appears not to have been responsible for the selection of its contents. (See Paine.) Still, he must have suggested Hooper and William T. Thompson, for by that time they were wholly forgotten in the North. He had himself forgotten "Cousin Sally Dilliard", a favorite of his younger days.

gisqueaki through hundreds of sketches over a period of thirty years.

Yet such implements of humor as these are not the most important influence of this literature on Mark Twain's books, which are the culmination not only of the literature's humor, but of its realism as well. Not even Longstreet, Hooper and George W. Harris were capable of basing their work on the society it illuminated. They saw their characters as engaging studies in the poor white of the new country or in the emergence of a backwoods gentry, but they failed to make them inhabitants of a social system. Their accomplishment was considerable; and it may be intelligently argued that Tom Sawyer and Huck Finn could not have existed if Sut Lovingood had not been born, that the perceptions of Longstreet pointed the way to much that is fruitful in the commonwealths of "The Gilded Age" and its successors, and that Hooper staked out much land that Mark Twain came to occupy. But it remained for William Tappan Thompson, a less vigorous mind than these three, to establish a sense of the community, and, in his Pineville, to suggest, faintly, the possibilities of frontier society for interpretation by comedy. In the work of these four men the humor of the frontier became a literature. They rested squarely on the humor of their time and place, on the humbler work of hundreds among whom their roots went down, but they are this literature achieving realism. It is as the fulfillment of their beginnings, as a realist writing in the comic tradition, that Mark Twain achieves his permanence in American literature.

So far as there is any validity in literary ideas, so far as notions of influence can be accepted, these writers, with the tradition to which they belonged, gave Mark Twain a means of perception and evocation, and gave him also the material to which he applied it. A limit must be set to exposition: let the case rest on a single illustration. Behold the steamboat *Dr. Franklin,* "a very superb boat, albeit inclined to rock about a good deal, and nearly turn over on her side when visited by a breath of air in the least resembling a gale." She is commanded by Captain Summons, "a particularly clever fellow." In fact, "a clever fellow in the

widest sense of the term — a fellow that is clever in every way
— anxious that his passengers shall be comfortably bestowed,
well fed and well attended to — and *determined* that they shall
amuse themselves 'just as they d —— n please' as the saying is.
If he happens to have preachers on board, he puts on a serious
countenance of a Sunday morning — consents that there shall
be preaching — orders the chairs to be set out, and provides
Bibles and hymnbooks for the occasion — himself and officers
whose watch is below taking front seats and listening attentively
to the discourse. Likely as not, at the close of the service, he
will ask the reverend gentleman who has been officiating, with his
back in close proximity to a hot fire in a Franklin furnace, to
accompany him to the bar and join him in some refreshments!
If there are passengers on board who prefer to pass the time
in playing poker, euchre, brag, or whist, tables and chairs are
ready for *them*, too — poker, brag, euchre and whist be it! All
sorts of passengers are accommodated on the *Dr. Franklin* —
the rights of none are suffered to be infringed — all are free
to follow such employments as shall please themselves."

Mark the direct attack — the brisk, economical introduction
of Captain Summons, typical of Mark Twain's later years. Observe also the exalted, ideal justice of Captain Summons himself,
a figure quite plainly related to Captain Ned Blakely of "Roughing It", who hangs Bill Noakes after a trial whose formality
would delight Captain Summons. The kinship includes the company of patient, obstinate, garrulous tyrants who argue the
night watches away in "Life on the Mississippi" and are softened almost to poignance in the "Autobiography." Then he
speaks and the sensitive recording of individual talk that is one
of Mark's sharpest weapons is added to the humorist's affection
for eccentric ideas. Captain Summons is Captain Hurricane Jones
not quite finished, not yet completely evoked, but seen and enjoyed. Is he also a foretaste of Captain Stormfield?

On one voyage of the *Dr. Franklin*, three Methodist preachers spend their time working at their vocation: "We had preaching every day and sometimes at night; and I must say, in
justice to brothers Twichel and Switchell, that their sermons

were highly edifying and instructive." But the boat contains another company, who, "at the other end of the hall", amuse
themselves with games of chance. The circuit riders are grieved
by this depravity, an affront to the cloth, and frequently request the captain "to interfere and break up such unholy do-
ings." But Captain Summons has an austere ideal of justice.
He tells them: "Gentlemen, amuse yourselves as you like;
preach and pray to your heart's content — none shall interfere
with your pious purposes; some like that sort of thing — *I*
have no objection to it. These men prefer to amuse themselves
with cards; let them — they pay their passage as well as you,
gentle*men*, and have as much right to *their* amusements as you
have to *yours*, and they shall not be disturbed. Preach, play
cards, dance cotillions — do what you like, *I* am agreeable; only
understand that *all games* (preaching among the rest) *must
cease at ten o'clock.*"

In such a conception, humor complexly extends toward comedy. There is here a vast delight in character — in its logic, its
argument, its vision of duty and justice. There is also a sharp
visual and auditory rendering of a scene that had delighted the
narrator. This endless pleasure, this sharp rendering, the drawling voice which reproduces small modulations and adds comment to realism — all these are characteristic of Mark Twain's
humor. The sketch (not all of which is used here) might very
well deceive one who is familiar with the collected works into
thinking that it was a part of them. It isn't. It is one of the
anecdotal reminiscences of Sol Smith and was published in Porter's collection, "A Quarter Race in Kentucky", in 1846.[17]

This literature is rich with similar foreshadowings. There
was here an intense pleasure in the variety of the world — an
exuberant delight which sprang from the frontier's energy.
There was also the frontier's sharp perception — its ability to
understand behavior and the motives which produce it. These
form the basis of frontier humor which worked out in obscure
newspapers the first formidable realism and the first widespread

[17] Reprinted in "Tall Tales of the Southwest." The whole sketch will re-
pay study.

satire in our literature. What this humor required was some one native to its pleasures and perceptions who could express them on the level of genius. There is no need to detail a thousand pages which seem the half-erased, preliminary drafts of something that Mark Twain worked into better, more mature, more intelligent books. It is enough to assert that he was the culmination of a literature, the expression of this humor at its highest level. A frontiersman, a raconteur, a printer and reporter, his work was shaped by this rendition of the life to which he was native. This humor was his earliest expression and his most constant. Its perceptions and evocations, its methods and materials, its values, its deficiencies and weaknesses, were his also. It was the basis of his mind, as it was the framework of his books. He was always a frontier humorist, who devoted himself to the production of laughter. If he had not been that, he could not have become the satirist and realist who is remembered.

Humor is, like truth, a relationship among variables. Taste in jokes is a function of the folkways — or, if still graver language be required, a *liaison* among Pareto's Derivations. Certain continuities exist and it is likely that familiar climaxes, situations, actions, and surprises will produce the peculiarly simian response of laughter while time lasts. The laughter of words and of verbal imagery, however, is subject to fluctuations of time, temperaments, fashions, social orientations, religions, and, more simply still, language. A phrase attributed to Queen Victoria exhausts the resources of psychological analysis: laughter, at any given moment, is the product of amusement. The passage of a century may something change the conditions of amusement.

It has seemed desirable to assert a platitude with this much obstinacy.

He began as a humorist. He continued as one so long as he wrote. What is to-day most distressing in his work is verbal humor which the course of time has shifted from the areas of amusement. An agreeably meaningless tabulation might classify the themes of simplest amusement which have not changed since Mark Twain's time and compare them with those that have. Pimples, for instance, seem exempt from change: they are equally laughable in Aristophanes, Mark Twain, and if the association is permitted, Will Rogers. Yet it is not, to-day, possible to find the stench of corpses quite so funny as Mark Twain found it. Probably no consecutive hundred pages of his books fail to make use of this odor: it was, to his thinking, sure fire. It is less than that to-day, though not extinct; but this shift in the areas of amusement should not be assailed with subjective words. Corpses are not now within the province of "good taste" — a phase which may have something to do with humor. But the observation falls short of meaning. Millions of lowly intelligences have recently been amused by Mr. Chic Sale's discussion of backhouses, and if the revues and the smarter weeklies are a trustworthy criterion of our best intelligences, no other humorous theme of this generation is quite so sure fire as homosexuality. The good taste of Mark Twain's generation did not find amusement in coprophily, pederasty, or the diversions of Lesbos. A sanction has changed.

What most often annoys the sanctions of this period is Mark Twain's insistence on working at his vocation — on producing merely verbal jokes. Much that seemed to him infinitely funny is only painful to-day and its intrusion on better stuff is a source of resentment. In "Innocents Abroad" he will labor at a gigantic burlesque of Abélard and Héloïse which derives most of its momentum from such lines as this allusion to Canon Fulbert: "She then returned to her uncle, the old gun, or son of a gun, as the case may be." He is also referred to as a howitzer and a swivel. In "A Tramp Abroad", trying to go to sleep, "I close-reefed my ears — that is to say, I bent the flaps of them down and furled them into five or six folds, and pressed them against the hearing orifice." "An Idle Excursion" is constantly defaced by such sentences as "We saw an India-rubber tree, but out of season, possibly, so there were no shoes on it, nor suspenders, nor anything that a person would properly expect to find there." The preface to "Pudd'nhead Wilson", a formidable attempt to write fiction of the highest kind, is as distressing a passage as our literature has. Its worn burlesque of legal terms and such coinages as "Macaroni Vermicelli's horse-feed shed" are not short of infuriating. He thought that they were funny. That is, a laugh was possible and so no other value need be considered.

This necessity of getting a laugh, by verbal humor, as the begetter of the extended passages in burlesque and extravaganza that deface his finest work, is examined in the next chapter. It was the seal of his training in frontier humor. Perhaps its commonest vehicle is exaggeration, the bombast of immense vitality, his undisciplined imagination gone rankly to seed. Examples may be chosen at every level — just as they flow naturally into contexts where their presence is grotesque. Late in life, in "My Début as a Literary Person", he cannot describe the survivors of the *Hornet*, without saying of one, "He was already nearly full of leather; it was hanging out of his ears." He cannot mention the Taster to the Prince, without saying, "Why they did not use a dog or a plumber seems strange." No passage, however subtly conceived, however solemn in import, can be held safe from the intrusion of these wild jokes. That fact, and not their customary presence in his travel books, is what condemns him to-day. The violence of metaphor and overstatement, the preoccupation with drunkenness and vomiting and stench, the reiteration of physiological and anatomical phenomena, the constant heaping up of the clichés with which verbal humor in all ages has mostly concerned itself, the laboring of words and grammar and syntax, the all but intolerable repetition of commercial ideas and archly egoistic imbecilities — all these could be forgiven him, or ignored, if they were kept apart. The routine of verbal humor is or is not funny — but it is omnipresent in all ages. Mark Twain's fecundity in it, which has served to suggest many considerations to the ephemeral joke-makers of the moment as well as to such more rugged minds as Rudyard Kipling's and Bernard Shaw's, would excuse much boredom. Only — it is desirable not to incorporate mere joke-making in humor of a maturer sort and that desirability was hidden from Mark Twain.

The criticism of humor, however, has a further obligation which, during the last fifteen years, it has disregarded.

Mr. Waldo Frank relates the adventures of his soul, which were tearful, at a certain benefit performance for the blind. Mark Twain spoke there and, by the easy transference which constitutes the method of psychological criticism, Mr. Frank discovers his own emotions in Mark Twain. The speaker's words were, we learn "diffident and sad." [18] To Mr. Frank's horror, and Mark's, "everybody laughed." Mark was dismayed. He tried again but the swine laughed once more. "For five minutes, the sad soul struggled with this reality about him — this reality that would laugh." After a while he gave up — that is, he shamefully consented to be laughed at. "He stood there almost still, with his back to the rows of them who could not see, and dropped the ungainly humor from his mouth. And the audience before him snouted it, guzzled it, roared with delight." So Mr. Frank "hated this noble-looking fool."

The perfection of Mark Twain's platform manner, to which this preface has had little occasion to allude, is involuntarily certified in Mr. Frank's paragraphs. A page in the "Autobiography", dictated the morning after this benefit performance, makes clear — as was clear to the audience and must be clear to any one whose nerves are not jangled by laughter — that Mark went to the meeting for the purpose of making a funny speech, made it, and had a noble good time. It was not clear to Mr. Frank and, if it had been, would only have increased his distress. For Mr. Frank's literary ideas are of the kind that regards laughter as shameful. The paragraphs quoted refer to Mark's "painted and powdered visage of a clown" and contain the passionate and denunciatory exclamation, "Mark Twain — the humorist — America's funny man!" The emotions of Waldo Frank hold humor to be an offence.

A sensitive abhorrence of humor is also fundamental in Mr. Brooks's book. Mr. Brooks's inability was double: not only did humor offend him but he had the Puritan hatred of levity when austere work was to be done. To him Mark's humor was merely an avoidance of the artist's duty to right the world's injustices.

[18] The passage begins on page 40 of "Our America."

His prolonged analysis of this cowardice becomes only a club with which to beat Philistine America over the head. It reveals odious facts about Mark Twain and about the damnable people who coerced, suffered, and applauded him. It shows the cowardly, grasping, unjust, villainously unclean motives that dictated the form of his humor and of its acceptance. But it nowhere considers the simple fact that the humor is sometimes funny and nowhere admits the pleasure of those who have enjoyed it. Nor have the books which Mr. Brooks's called into being anywhere regarded Mark Twain as a humorist. Mr. Mumford finds Mark Twain a symptom that the Golden Day was over, and Mr. Josephson agrees that the artist as American is distressing, but one might read both books without becoming aware that the world's store of laughter had been increased. The corridors of New Jerusalem are golden. And aseptic.

There is a point of view to which the existence of laughter does not make shame imperative. From that point of view, "the painted and powdered visage of a clown" seems a very silly phrase to apply to the creator of Jim Blaine and the colony of his fellows, of the inexhaustible laughter that flows in the books of Mark Twain. So it points out that the man who says "Mark Twain is a buffoon" (or "a clown" or "a mountebank") has merely invoked logomachy to express his own emotions. He has really said "I regard Mark Twain as a buffoon", and the difference in significance is important. With some regret, the temptation to invoke a similar logomachy is resisted here. The discussion of Mark Twain could be put permanently on a plane of intelligence higher than the last decade has permitted, and with the willing or even respectful assent of theorists, if for some pages this preface should abandon the word "humor" and insist that Mark Twain had something or other to do with "the comic spirit." The need for such a verbal legitimation, however, does not appear compelling. Notice has been given that, in this book, the values of argument are disregarded.

For a fact exists. During seventy years his books have been a source of immeasurable laughter. The solemn are invited to begin an undertaking which the preparation of this essay has made necessary perhaps a dozen times — they are invited to read his collected works. Even the lowliest of the books, the earliest and crudest, will convince the solemn of this fact. No state of mind, no condition of inheritance or vocation or absorption, is a defence against it. The wan jokes offend for a while, the dreary passages of rhetoric or labored fun about long empty subjects rouse an irritation as of contrived boredom. It lapses. A style which only Ford Madox Ford has had the courage to list among the great styles of English begins to exert its effect. The intelligence of Mark Twain begins to flash its momentary lightning. Somehow, invariably, the book has changed — a physiological mystery has been accomplished, the solemn are laughing. Since 1860 no one else has needed the laboratory demonstration. All other kinds of men have responded to the richest humor in American literature by laughing at Mark Twain. That is the fact. Criticism which ignores it is absurd.

The laughter thus produced has so far been undiminished. It testifies to an inexhaustible variety of invention, an imagination, a creative ferment more various and extensive than any other in the whole extent of American literature. It signifies a mind which, however incompletely integrated, however incapable of discipline and sustained effort, however uneven and disappointing, is nevertheless the mind of a genius. He has boundlessly created laughter . . . by working at his vocation, as a humorist. That is the basic affirmation. However abhorrent the term, he is a humorist before anything else. All other American writers to whom the term is applicable are insignificant compared to him. Such a name as Josh Billings or Artemus Ward is the frail echo of now inexplicable laughter when one opposes to it such creatures as old man Finn, the lost Dauphin or the Duke of Bilgewater, or remembers the monologues of Jim Blaine or Jim Baker or Hurricane Jones, or listens for the arguments of Jim and Tom above the Sahara, or, on the upstream voyage in floodwater, overhears the passage of America.

The basis of this laughter is recognition. It is Mark Twain's absorption in the human race which he qualified with a deliberated adjective. The perception of humanity. The figure is caught in an instantaneous exposure, the voice is recorded by the most sensitive ear ever devoted to the study of American speech. And then to the consideration of this creature is brought an intelligence which is warm, infinitely understanding and sympathetic, infinitely rich with intuition, but undeluded, merciless, and final. Whether the creature is begotten in a phrase and left to die with the sentence or whether he persists through volumes long enough to be sold by subscription canvassers, he has lived. The basis of our laughter is that we have recognized him. What he is has been exhibited, what he thinks he is, what he pretends to be. A phase or a paragraph has stripped him. We have known him. And mostly we have believed in him while he has not deluded us. With the dispassionateness of God, Mark Twain has created and foredestined him.

But this is the art of the novelist, the art of comedy. That art is the basis of his humor. In even the casual, extemporaneous characterizations of his horseplay, of his sketches and travel books, the comic novelist lives in a phrase. It was his genius to give life, judged and stated, to even an improvisation, and that genius is the explanation of the laughter that has attended the history of his books. The comic novelist, working deliberately with the resources of his craft, produces the most profound and permanent effects. The reverie of Tom Sawyer projects a triumph which shall heal all the wounds Becky Thatcher has inflicted. Washington Hawkins moons homeward, picturing himself as Louise must be picturing him, "a noble, struggling young spirit persecuted by misfortune but bravely and patiently waiting in the shadow of a dual calamity and preparing to meet the blow as became one who was all too used to hard fortune and the pitiless buffetings of fate." Nothing is commoner in the novels than this interior soliloquy, a method which is supposed to have been invented by James Joyce but was not even new when Laurence Sterne employed it — but it is comedy, humor, Mark Twain working at his vocation. The comic novelist is dealing with the mind's confusion of reality with desire. Shall we require him to project above the threshold something whose roots coil deeply after the traumas of this world? Pudd'nhead

Wilson may be examined — or, equally, what injuries are soothed when Colonel Sellers sets a candle behind the mica of an empty stove or chooses turnips to protect himself against a plague? Or the Colonel nobly shares with Washington Hawkins the fortunes which his talent must reap in this amazing land — and in such passages as this, such passages as those in which the mind of Huckleberry Finn grapples with the problem of justice, pure humor makes plain why the pen of Howells, seeking comparisons, was led to the name of Cervantes. Or it escapes from the limitations of mortality altogether and Colonel Sellers expects "to acquire, complete and perfect control of sun-spots." The wrought fugue rises to climax, achieving magnificence, and, "That day, if I am alive and my sublime discovery is proved and established, I will send you greeting, and my messenger shall deliver it where you are, in the solitudes of the sea; for I will waft a vast sun-spot across the disk like drifting smoke, and you will know it for my love-sign, and will say 'Mulberry Sellers throws us a kiss across the universe.' "

Only pathology or ignorance could find such effects as these contemptible.

But disregard the themes of the comic novelist and consider the routine of humor in which no portraiture is involved. There remains the illimitable gusto of his mind dealing with spectacle. No other writer of his time touched the life of America at so many places. His mind was encyclopædic, restless, inquisitive, untiring. Criticism has said that he directed no humor against the abuses of his time: the fact is that research can find few elements of the age that Mark Twain did not burlesque, satirize, or deride. The whole obscene spectacle of government is passed in review — the presidency, the Congress, the basis of politics, the nature of democracy, the disintegration of power, the corruption of the electorate — bribery, depravity, subornation, the farce of the people's justice. Criticism has said that he assented in the social monstrosities of his period: yet the epithet with which criticism batters corrupt America, The Gilded Age, is his creation, and in the wide expanse of his books, there are few social ulcers that he does not probe. Criticism has said that he was incapable of ideas and all but anæsthetized against the intellectual ferment of the age: yet an idea is no less an idea because it is utilized for comedy, and whether you explore the descent of man, the rejection of progress, or the advances of feminism or the development of the insanity plea or the coalescence of labor, you will find it in that wide expanse. Criticism has said that he cravenly avoided offending orthodox religion: yet from his second book onward he laughed unceasingly at the American religious experience, and in "A Connecticut Yankee" formulated a literary case against Catholicism which our writers have not yet ceased to make use of. Criticism has said that the expectation of royalties made him give up his intention of laughing at England: but he wrote two books for the single purpose of satirizing England, as no other principal figure in our literature has yet done, and in defiance of the submission of his colleagues.

He boundlessly created laughter. In his books it is a stream that never stops. No one else in American literature has created so much of it, and for that alone he would be entitled to lasting gratitude. Laughter is not ignoble, nor is the small company of those who have been able to make it a living force, a mean fellowship. Because his laughter had that power, because it is an item in our uncrowded treasury of things actually created and creative, his name is not inadvisedly entered among the fellowship of Molière and Rabelais.

Finally, his laughter goes on — beyond. In his books the experience of the American race records something forever true about itself. The vision of New Jerusalem encounters the reality of the democratic nature and Mark Twain's humor expresses the moment of realization. Before him, disenchantment had existed in our literature only in the abortive, frustrated metaphysics of Herman Melville, which escape into mere delirium or mere tears. In Mark Twain's humor, disenchantment, the acknowledgement of defeat, the realization of futility find a maturer expression. He laughs and, for the first time, American literature possesses tragic laughter.

XI

THE DAMNED HUMAN RACE

THE story of Tom Canty and Sir Miles Hendon, Knight of the
Kingdom of Dreams and Shadows, might have been called "A
Missouri Democrat in the Court of Edward VI." It was an attempt to write the story of the Boss before the possibilities of
the idea were clear to Mark Twain. The confusion of his mind
may be observed in the very conception: this designedly savage
attack on the brutalities of the law, the damned human race,
and especially the damned king-worshipers was to be a book for
children! It became one. It probably had more respect from Livy
than anything else he wrote until "Joan of Arc"; it boundlessly
delighted the Clemens children, and, as both a novel and a play,
it has enraptured the very young ever since. Yet all the time,
its purpose was to expose the evils of Tudor England, with as
much of their modern perpetuation as could be managed. From
the summit of democracy's young hope, Hannibal, Missouri,
despised privilege, autocracy, and servility — and let it be known

that beyond the Western Ocean a more admirable society had been established. This was the fantastic Senator Benton visiting St. Petersburg on the Fourth of July to make the eagle scream.

The story which Mark Twain devised to carry this indignation came as near to achieving form as any other he wrote. The narrative is planned and moves along its foreseen course with few interruptions and little improvisation, by the means designed, to an end which grows naturally out of its motives and incidents. The framework is melodramatic.[1] A large part of the melodrama originates in Mark's acceptance of the fiction formulas with which he was acquainted. The novels and plays that delighted mid-century America contribute such pivotal scenes as Miles Hendon's return to his home where the resources of cowardice, covetousness and duplicity have been practiced on him, and where his heart is harrowed by the first ten minutes of half the last acts that sobbed before frontier footlights. The same resources draw the book's threads together in a good, sentimental, tub-thumping, God bless us one and all, happy ending, which includes the maiden who repudiates her lover to save his life. But do not find merely the stock situations of the paperbacks in this narrative scheme. In such episodes as that of the hermit who is an archangel and bends above the child king to avenge Henry's rape of the monasteries, we are only an instant away from Injun Joe in the graveyard and from the feud of "Huckleberry Finn." One reason why melodrama is constant in Mark's books is that his imagination had fed on actual melodrama since his infancy. A child who was educated by Negroes and had witnessed a dozen or so mobs and murders, a man who had piloted steamboats and belonged to Washoe's incandesence was not likely to impose in his fiction the minute psychological hesitations of Henry James.

Hannibal is expressing its contempt of brutality, injustice

---

[1] In this chapter and the next the words "melodrama" and "melodramatic" are used as descriptive, not condemnatory, terms. They signify violent, rapid, or bloody action which invokes suspense, excitement, horror and similar primary emotions. In this sense not only "Trilby" and "East Lynne" are melodramas but also "Hamlet", "War and Peace", "Henry Esmond", "Ulysses" and "Mourning Becomes Electra."

and the privileged orders when King Tom assails the precedents of his courts, when the Baptists are burned, when the beggars and serfs and commoners are ground between poverty and the church. The fable required, simply, a pauper on the throne and a king begging in the highways. It is for the most part ably sustained and informed by an imagination that recognizes its opportunities and does not fumble them. Indignation burns out in sentimentality at crucial places, however, and the democratic tenderness of the king and Miles is sometimes mere lushness. Also, the complacent republican derision of royal folderol — Hannibal mocking the servile beefeaters — succumbs to pageantry. The mind that was forever laughing at chivalry, and in particular its American apings, the mind that held Sir Walter Scott responsible for the Civil War, could not resist spectacle.

For the book is always Mark Twain. Its parodies of Tudor speech lapse sometimes into a callow satisfaction in that idiom — Mark hugely enjoys his nathlesses and beshrews and marrys. The "hard old Injun" which Leland detects in him supplies the circumstantial details of this narrative, as of all others — Tom's mother determining the imposture by means of habit patterns, Miles thrusting the thread at the needle's eye (a datum which had a later use in "Huckleberry Finn"). The frontier humorist labors at his vocation: Tom's nose itcheth and he desires to know the custom and usage in this emergence; Henry VIII is dead, his funeral is set for the sixteenth of the coming month and Tom remarks, "Tis a strange folly. Will he keep?" In a passage designed to flame fiercely against ignorance and superstition, Miles employs a cumbersome Latin parody of clerkship; in passages designed to deal mercilessly with kingship, extravaganzas about the First Lord of the Buckhounds or modern plumbers deflect the satire — and this is the customary blemish of burlesque. All Mark Twain. The book's complete expression of him — of his warmth and tenderness, of his imagination, of frontier humor working itself out in fiction, of Hannibal's democratic superiority, of his statecraft and republican pride and philosophy of history and his sentimentality — occurs when, after a long suspense, it is discovered that the Great Seal of England has disappeared for no more momentous reason than that a child has desired to crack some nuts.

The book is not important. Its imaginative realization is genuine and it expresses a vast number of the ideas to which Mark was born, so that many strata of the American people's thinking may be archeologically examined in it. Even more: it was never possible for his greatest talent to subside, and the people who move about its pages, whether Tudor or Midwestern, truly live. When no burlesque is stirring, long passages completely succeed, and the whole is quite as good as, say, Charles Kingsley's comparable tracts. But he had never seen its purpose clearly: the initial confusion definitely condemned it. In existing as a child's book, it has little validity for adults. And the court of Edward VI was not the happiest occupation for a man who, more than any other novelist, had experienced the breadth and depth of American life.

But how would it be if, instead of a boy, a great king were to find himself caught in England's cruelty? If, instead of the Knight of the Kingdom of Dreams and Shadows, the Round Table itself were subjected to the scrutiny of Hannibal?

American literature has been in nothing else so fecund as in political and economic satire.[2] "A Connecticut Yankee in King Arthur's Court" is the Jack Downing papers, "The Adventures of Captain Simon Suggs", the Crockett campaign documents, given the expression of genius, worked out with the ambition of philosophy and conditioned by the experience of the years between, the years when the impulse of perfectability had learned

[2] "With the exception of such badly wrought and undecisive efforts as Melville's 'The Confidence Man', Doesticks' 'Plu-ri-bus-tah' and Mark Twain's 'A Yankee at King Arthur's Court' [*sic*], 'The Theory of the Leisure Class' was the first fully molded satire that this country produced." — Lewis Mumford in the *Herald-Tribune* for January 11, 1931. Such amazing statements as this one give the measure of literary opinion in America. I can only wonder what Mr. Mumford's reading has been and what some one who is familiar with American satire — say Mr. Meine or Miss Rourke — privately thinks of such peremptory dismissal of a formidable tradition. And why "Plu-ri-bus-tah"? Doesticks himself wrote more "fully molded" satire than that wan burlesque of "Hiawatha", but he was so unimportant a contriver of satire in the period I deal with that I have not bothered to list him in my bibliography.

something about itself. It is colored, too, by sentiments that were yeasty in the national intelligence during the years of its composition when a new variant of Utopianism was evangelizing the literary Mugwumps.[3]

In one sense, it was Mark Twain's finest possibility: it combined satire, the tall tale, humor, democracy, religion, progress, and the damned human race. Its narrative scheme, a succession of picaresque episodes, was more adapted to his mind than the fitted plot of "The Prince and the Pauper." Its exposition of primitive England was backed by a long study, and the scale of proportionate values between the sixth and the nineteenth centuries, which is minutely worked out and never misapplied, represented the most complete preparation he ever made. It is his only deliberate and sustained effort to write satire — which appears elsewhere in his work as an interlude to some other pur-

---

[3] "A Connecticut Yankee in King Arthur's Court" was published in December, 1889. In that month, Edward Bellamy's "Looking Backward", published in 1887, was in its 210th thousand and was selling at the rate of 10,000 a week. Cridge's "Utopia; the History of an Extinct Planet" had appeared in 1884; and Allen's "The Key of Industrial Co-operative Government" in 1886. Griffin's "Nationalism" appeared in 1889. In 1890, five Utopian romances were published; the most popular of them was Ignatius Donnelly's "Caesar's Column." No less than eight appeared in 1891, five in 1892, three in 1893, and seven, among them Howells's "A Traveller from Altruria", in 1894. The literary consideration of Utopia then slackened, although 1898 saw the publication of five similar volumes and four more were added in 1900. This energetic exposition appears to have been a wholly American enterprise, no comparable fashion appearing in England or Europe during those years — the period of the Fabian Society's most vigorous activity. "Erewhon", the latest English glimpse of Utopia, had been published in 1872. The American movement was a literary product of the first serious conflict between labor and big business. The books were invariably written by liberals — men whose interests were with the developing Trusts but whose sympathies were with the exploited. The teaching of most of them was that accumulations of capital were bad but that strikes were simply horrid. The Trusts are rebuked, but the unions are denounced. The ideal commonwealths of Bellamy and Howells are communistic; the rest are socialistic but the vocabulary, ideology, and methods of the proletariat are studiously avoided. The books are, as my text indicates, basically a part of the Mugwump movement. Shortly after 1900, the impulse took another phase, in the "muck-raking journalism" of the period. ("The Literary Quest for Utopia, 1880–1900" by Allyn Forbes in *Social Forces* for December, 1927, discusses the subject with great charm.)

pose, or is accompanied, as in "The Prince and the Pauper", by a neutralizing purpose. The opening chapters, the direct attack, the simple, straightforward narrative that compresses much action into little space, the magnificent prose infused with his finest humor, are at the very summit of his accomplishment. Long passages elsewhere in the book equal this accomplishment — such passages contain dynamic qualities that American fiction has nowhere surpassed. Here, as in much of "Tom Sawyer" and most of "Huckleberry Finn", he is a great novelist.

One purpose is to confront privilege with humanity. Another is to display the conditions of slavery. Another is to examine religion, specifically the Catholic Church, as the begetter of slavery, the enfranchisement of privilege and corruption and injustice, the source of cruelty and superstition and intolerance — the most hopeless and tyrannical of human institutions. There are deeper purposes as well — and more trivial ones. The nineteenth century, which "turns automata into men", is vindicated and the Utopia of Mark's imagination is seen to be an affecting blend of Hannibal's small farms and the Colt's Arms culture of Hartford. Democracy's superiority to kingship and its long gain over chivalry are asserted in every chapter: the Republic is trumpeted through red fire and the burst of rockets. The folk of America, "the affluent multitude of the mass", are the creators of greatness; and it is they who, erecting beside the Mississippi the idyllic St. Petersburg, have made forever impossible injustice, cruelty, a caste system, and the exploitation of human flesh.

But also revolution is asserted as it had not been, in emerged literature, for a long time. It seems just to insist on this: throughout his Te Deum to the democracy of the frontier, Mark Twain is a revolutionist, "a Sansculotte — and not a pale, characterless Sansculotte, but a Marat." In some safety, since this England has been extinct for over a millennium, the serfs are commanded to drown their oppressors in a sea of noble and clerical blood — but the anger is not a dead passion and the line is projected forward. "This dreadful matter brought from these down-trodden people no outburst of rage against their oppressors. They had been heritors and subjects of cruelty and outrage so long that nothing could have startled them but a kindness. Yes, here was a curious revelation indeed of the depth to which this people had been sunk in slavery. . . . It could not help bringing up the un-get-aroundable fact that, all gentle cant and philosophizing to the contrary notwithstanding, no people in the world ever did achieve their freedom by goody-goody talk and moral suasion: it being immutable law that all revolution that will succeed must *begin* in blood, whatever may answer afterward. What this folk needed, then, was a Reign of Terror and a guillotine." Those commanded include the oppressed in all ages — in Victoria's England and the Czar's Russia directly, and, with some indirection, in the United States of Benjamin Harrison. Here enters the desire to speak plainly to England — an exhortation also part of "The Prince and the Pauper." Throughout, the perpetuation of the sixth century is insisted upon. The genealogies, privileges, and absurdities of the nobility are listed. The anachronisms of an outworn order are displayed. What "was to remain so as long as England should exist on earth" is examined with a controlled vindictiveness that expresses sentiments fundamental in American thinking. There is here the hope and belief of this nation in its youth — multitudes are speaking. But there is also plain talk to America. It ranges from superficial jeers at high tariffs (the many-sided book includes a complete statement of the Mugwump beliefs) and the rhetoric of Civil War generals, to the practices of corporations and the squalor of the poor whites which he was never able to avoid for very long.

So, by way of Hannibal's experience and the Catholic Church, the book comes to futility. "The painful thing about all this business was the alacrity with which this oppressed community had turned their cruel hands against their own class in the interest of the common oppressor." The damned assent in their damnation. These automata who might become men do not greatly desire to, and those who do are defeated by their stupidity, cowardice, and selfishness. Against ignorance and brutality, enlightenment can make no headway. When a young woman is flogged, the mob stands by and comments "on the expert way the whip was handled." The race "so tediously and ostentatiously and unprofitably developed" from the ape wallows in credulity and cruelty, confines its energies to occupations that would humiliate swine, destroys decency upon a hint of its existence, feeds upon malice and prejudice, brings its willing applause to the support of murder and rape and slavery which, in fact, if behavior is the criterion of fitness, are a destiny perfectly accommodated to its merits. Above all, it has codified its superstitions into an efficient system for evil. "Concentration of power in a political machine is bad; and an Established Church is only a political machine; it was invented for that; it is nursed, cradled, preserved for that; it is an enemy to human liberty." But the race does not desire liberty and will not use it except for the perpetration of intolerable corruption. So massed superstition, the race's capability for evil, brings about catastrophe. This people was offered freedom, civilization, progress, Utopia — but the Church invokes the Interdict, the slaves happily resume their shackles, first murdering and pillaging their deliverers, and civilization perishes. Out of a half-century's experience, Hannibal observes the human race and announces the end of New Jerusalem.

Much of this fable is literature. The enchantment that regards swine as ladies and gentlemen; the argument that these swine are "the only really valuable nobility the sun has yet discovered in the earth"; the noble who prays before cutting his victim's throat; the domestic manners of the Arthurians; the smallpox epidemic and the march of the slaves (though this last becomes tearful); the release of prisoners from the rack and dungeons of Morgan le Fay; the burnings and hangings; the extortions of the clergy; the common privilege of theft shared by both orders — all this is in the classical tradition of satire. Mostly, the examination of Holy Church is preserved from the slapstick that mars the other themes, and the fire in it is curiously powerful. The theme rises to Clarence's calm question: "Did you think you had educated the superstition out of this people?" On the way, it has focussed all that Mark has to say about credulity, baseness and tyranny, and this was helpful through the next decades to a number of American novelists who had learned about the harlot of Rome. Even the burlesque that the clergy inspire has its virtue. The Valley of Holiness is not the Thebaid by an expanse of irony and subtlety; yet the woman with "the white hair of age and no other apparel" who was "black from crown to heel with forty-seven years of holy abstinence from water" might have been imagined by Anatole France. It is conceivable that M. France enjoyed the entire passage, even that he learned a little from this "strange menagerie." And if converting the revolutions of a stylite to power and producing a miracle by means of pumps lacked something of suavity, he probably found in them an assurance that Hannibal and the American democracy had also an efficient means of dealing with saints and angels.

Leaving the hamlet of Abblasoure behind, after the burning of the castle, Arthur and the Boss come to a wood where a commotion catches their attention. A crowd of children, learning from their elders, have been playing mob. The travelers are just in time to release a little boy whom his playmates have hanged with a bark rope. The scene, to be immortal, would need only to appear in the works of Jonathan Swift. Satire has nowhere gone beyond it. . . . The Pilgrims tell jokes that would last through twelve centuries. The smith shouts, "Rah for protection — to Sheol with free trade!" The Yankee customarily comments on the sixth century from the point of view of Hartford. This contrived anachronism is a formula that has assisted the historical plays of Bernard Shaw. He is not the only one who has made use of the Yankee's inventions. Since 1889, before footlights and between covers, a good many persons have traveled back and forth in time-space who would never have made their journeys if, after a fight, the Yankee had not waked to "a far-away town sleeping in a valley by a winding river", and casually asked, "Bridgeport?"

Yet the book is chaos. The satirist's intention is constantly frustrated by the frontier humorist. The mere joke-maker, the parodist, the creator of burlesque and extravaganza, the improvisator horribly mangle what might have been a superb book. It should be observed that the plan appropriately admitted of some burlesque. When a hermit has died from using soap and the soap factory advertises "Patronize the elect", when the royal grant is referred to as sacred swag, when the Sieges at the Table Round are transmuted to seats on the stock exchange, when Sir Thomas Malory becomes a war correspondent or his language is ingeniously parodied, wholly satisfactory effects are produced. But Mark Twain's mind was unable to stay within such limits. His imaginative ferment demanded gigantic expression. The effects must by cyclonic — they must escape the finite altogether. There is something appalling in the energy that bombards this well-conceived narrative with jokes and caricatures that would have been dreadful anywhere but, in work designed as satire, are simply lethal. The climactic arrival of King Arthur's knights on bicycles is so true to Mark's humor that its use was inevitable. In a certain phrenetic way it is appropriate to these situations of nightmare — it does inflict on the by now shuddering personification of chivalry the final indignity of contempt. One can imagine Mark's satisfaction in the image he had created: he probably felt the serene awe of a creator who knows that he has perfectly handled a high moment. But the scene comes as a culmination of an episode during which the King of England has been shown the abuses of which he is sovereign — and satire has been extinguished by a tasteless and illusion-destroying burlesque.

At a pivotal place in the action, the King harangues his listeners about agriculture. As a device for the precipitation of the plot, this is mere improvisation — the mechanism shows through and illusion perishes. The content is only a series of jokes which Mark had used in the *Galaxy* nearly twenty years before: they were bad jokes then and, in such a book as this, they are grotesque. Any capacity for self-criticism must have extirpated them — but he had none and the criticism of his friends extended no further than drawing a line through the word "sewer" and telling him to say "Sheol" instead of "Hell." The knights in stovepipe hats, the knights wearing sandwich boards, the reproduction of garrulous frontier types in early England, the advertising campaigns, the labored perpetration of typographical humor in the Camelot newspaper, the use of lassos at the tournament — all this was immensely true to his conception of the book and immensely wrong. His impulses, his training, his intention provided nothing to show him how wrong it was, and there was no one to tell him. So the book runs on, blending a real magnificence of idea and execution with hideous jokes about the stenches of corpses and swine and unwashed bodies, a man who "had a wart on the inside of his upper lip and died in the hope of a glorious resurrection", the "mother of the German language", the chromos on the walls of Dawson's Landing, the foundlings of the nunneries, and every other lamentable travesty that has produced laughter in his other books.

The temptation to write burlesque overcame him. He could not impose form on his material. He could not for long discipline his thinking or his writing. What was required, the subordination of impulse to plan, the sustained intelligence to think through ideas till they thrust out an organic structure, was not within the possibility of his mind. The book expresses him and expresses a large part of his time — but it fails. Except for "Mardi" our fiction has nothing equally chaotic.

Since biography creates its own structure, these defects are subdued in the book which he considered his masterpiece. Part of its greater quiet may also have been caused by his suffering during the years when it was written, the years of his bankruptcy, following the failure of the Paige machine and his publishing house. The book was formidably serious in purpose and so, when it was serialized in *Harper's Magazine*, appeared anonymously. There was some thought that Mark Twain's manner would not be recognized in such passages as the reading of the Sieur de Conte's poem to Catherine, or in such sentences as "He was prouder of being wounded than a really modest person would be of being killed."

The Missouri democrat had tirelessly ridiculed romance, but had succumbed to it in many passages of the "Yankee", "The Prince and the Pauper", and other books. His inheritance in-

cluded, besides a perception of romantic absurdity, an ability to
be sometimes victimized by it. "Old Times on the Mississippi"
and "Tom Sawyer" are in their way idylls, a suspension of ridi-
cule, a willingness to believe. It is probably true that the approval of his friends assisted this willingness — but certain that
they did not create it. History had always been for him as much
a department of pageantry as of satire.

"Joan of Arc" is his capitulation to romance; it expresses
this fundamental if contradictory current of his mind. In it the
common man, the American, visits the France of Charles VII and
is converted. The Yankee had reviled hagiolatry: this life of
St. Joan is a chapter from the Golden Legend. Mark worships
her; his book is an act of adoration. And this fact is striking.
Literary deductions are usually silly and always precarious:
one is ventured upon here without conviction. It is possible to
associate with this book, which all criticism except Bernard
Shaw's has treated unsatisfactorily, a phenomenon so common
in American life that the doctrinaire have been sure it is a national trait. The book expresses a worship of muliebrity, a belief in the sanctity of femaleness, that was very common in Mark
Twain's generation. Mr. Shaw sees in Mark's St. Joan a "beautiful and most ladylike Victorian" who is "skirted to the ground
and with as many petticoats as Noah's wife in a toy ark." The
figure does have that appearance, but is also akin to the Clares
and Theresas of Catholic adoration, and even to the Virgin. But
she is also tenderly and warmly created and is neither wholly
a petticoated Victorian nor a product of mariolatry. She is most
alive as an idealization of Olivia Langdon. If the methods of
psychology were acceptable, this portrait might be held to tes-
tify to a successful love affair and a well adjusted married life.

The book is mediocre, or worse. It gives the novelist his
most gorgeous spectacles — battle scenes, mass movements, military and mediæval pageantry. The kind is not finally significant,
but in the kind Mark's effects are well achieved. The devices and
inventions of romantic fiction are employed with conclusive
skill. But there was no possibility that he would be able to dis-
sociate himself from his material or imaginatively create a medi-

æval France in any particular different from the Missouri of his boyhood. Domremy, Tours, Orleans, and the countryside around them are only St. Petersburg at a masquerade, and instead of an Injun Joe to create terror there is a functional villain, the Catholic Church. The peasants and the nobles of Joan's century are the farmers and gentry of Hannibal. The Paladin has cousins in "The Gilded Age", "Huckleberry Finn" and elsewhere; the other characters are like him in being nineteenth century. In La Hire, Mark found a person for whom a nineteenth-century understanding was adequate, and so this figure from the pilot house of a steamboat comes off rather better than he has elsewhere. Much better, for instance, than at the hands of Mr. Shaw. A reluctance which Mark shared with Shaw is visible in his reticence about Gilles de Rais.

The Sieur de Conte is a channel not only for Mark's sentiments but also for his burlesque. The Paladin's tall tales, the waterside conversation of villagers play with the themes and among the pretensions and superstitions that furnish out all the books. Narrative obligations count for little when a chance offers for Papa D'Arc, a relative of Uncle Silas's, to remember the bull that overturned some beehives. There is a show of crossroads' philosophy in De Conte's reflections but it is painful, and such effects as the composition of his poem and the occasion of its reading are just dull jokes. Thematic errors are less common than elsewhere and the most blatant routine of humor is not invoked. Still, it proved finally impossible for the humorist of the frontier press to forsake his trade.

He wrote vocational humor into his mythology, his effort to imagine fifteenth-century France only derived another idyll from Hannibal, and he was uncomfortable in the demands of tragedy, formalizing whatever could not be sentimentalized. Nevertheless, something of charm has survived through thirty-five years. If sophistication finds the book chiefly notable as an exposition of Mark's intelligence when occupied with themes not appropriate to it — the exposition needs no further data than a comparison with the treatment of St. Joan by Voltaire, Anatole France, Bernard Shaw, or even Andrew Lang — sophistication also perceives the qualities of the prose. Its color and warmth, its nervous and subtle strength, the delicacy and assurance of its effects are a durable satisfaction. The scaffolding of romantic reverie has nowhere been formed by a finer instrument. This is, as sheer writing, great. Discrimination will hereafter find in it whatever value the book may be said to have. The undiscriminating may as well read about St. Joan in Mark's pages as anywhere else. Few desire history to be anything but a procession of costumes over which chivalric banners flutter: the effects of sun and shadow across a countryside of legend are perfectly managed by this Missouri democrat on leave from his trade. Litterature has stranger paradoxes.[4]

The annoyance of art is its failure to obey the principles imposed on it by the necessities of systems. Creativeness is both unpredictable and irreducible to formula. Criticism is simplified by the construction of a pattern to which the artist may be held for judgment; whatever in his work observes the pattern may be adjudged his inner truth and unity, the rest being rejected as something less than integrated art. Such activity is metaphysical; it is amusing enough but can be accorded no validity beyond metaphysics. Such patterns and unities are subjective in the critic, not imposed by reality on the artist, who notoriously omits to observe them. The necessity for unity, for firm categories and clear lines of force, is native not to the creative mind but to the critical mind. Such compulsions have a possibly absorbing interest for psychologists; they may safely be left to analysts, professional ones for preference.

If it were sensible to regret what Mark Twain did not write instead of considering what he did, there would be point in condemning the three books just treated as an interception of some hypothetical but greater "Huckleberry Finn" which he might have written. Yet even if the qualities in them which have been

---

[4] In 1930, "Joan of Arc" was sixth in sales among Mark's books, ranking between "Tom Sawyer Abroad" and "Pudd'nhead Wilson", with "Life on the Mississippi" and "Roughing It" ranking eighth and ninth. The book has not been without literary influence: Mr. Paine has also written a life of Joan.

held desirable are ignored, the three books appear to have been inevitable. It is a fact that his occasional pessimistic damnation of the human race exists, rude, unformed, and impulsive, in his earliest work, and its clearer expression in his later work is a development, not a catastrophic change. In exactly the same way, his earliest work contains the themes and interests that developed into "The Prince and the Pauper", "A Connecticut Yankee in King Arthur's Court", and "Joan of Arc." These books cannot be regarded as an aberration, a surrender of his proper interests, or a betrayal of his genius. They were an expression of him; his mind was not subject to the simple unities of a theoretical system. They are true to him. They are also true to the conditions of his formative years — to the beliefs and interests and enjoyments and philosophies of a frontier society which also lacked simplicity.

A group may be made of books which express other fundamental interests. The comic novelist who exists, sometimes comfortably and sometimes uneasily, in these three is present in even the most wretched improvisations of the travel books. Other expressions of the comic novelist form a sequence in "The Gilded Age", "The American Claimant", "Pudd'nhead Wilson", and a number of tales and stories of which "The Man Who Corrupted Hadleyburg" is the most ambitious. For purposes of discussion, these have been separated, in this preface, from the group treated in the next chapter, but are organically related to them. They are Mark Twain's absorption in American life, the fiction that most immediately embodies the experience of which he was a part.

This examination should by now have established his inability to conceive form for his material, to abide by its discipline, and to forego the vertiginous possibilities of burlesque for the sake of satire or reality.

The idea of freaks had always seemed to him gorgeously promising. At intervals in his early work the monstrosity known as Siamese twins is employed. There were possibilities here for superhuman grotesqueness: the awe of an inspiration almost sublime may be observed. This conception might be developed cosmically. You might take this repulsive prodigy and elaborate it through aspiring levels of imagination till it gave off lightning. Let one half be called Angelo and one Luigi. You might then make one half a sensitive and timid person, addicted to virtue, endowed with æsthetic and religious impulses, a gentleman, a connoisseur. The other could be a bully and a swaggerer, rough, roistering, and dissolute. But by the practical joking of God, these natural antipathies were bound together, helplessly sharing a common body, each one subject to impulses and activities of the other which he despised. There was no parable here. Mark was not giving psychology a symbol of his divided self, nor was he commenting on the dual nature of man. He was only seizing upon what seemed a titanic possibility. He would study the absurdities to be derived from such a monster. He would keep Angelo, the delicate one, alive by reason of Luigi's consumption of coarse food. He would make Luigi vomit when he took medicine to cure Angelo, sleeping beside him. He would have the agnostic Luigi address a society of freethinkers and outrage the pieties of Angelo. He would show Angelo in flight from a duel which Luigi's pugnacity had provoked. He would display the squatters gravely debating whether this monster was made in the image of God.

The drive of Mark Twain's imagination went into this elaboration. It was a beautiful idea! It would bring into harmonious orchestration all the instruments of humor. It was gigantic. . . . Literature nowhere contains a more painful instance of mistaken genius. Adjectives are futile for description. The use of a freak as the pivot of humor is not only horrible — it is mad. But this disfigurement of intelligence, this nightmare of the imagination, became the book which embodies Pudd'nhead Wilson's cynicism as well as some of the most corrosive comment on American life ever written. It is also one of the few novels we have in which the institution of slavery creates genuine literature. . . . Mark Twain was so innocent of the proprieties that, instead of destroying the germinal extravaganza, he published it as a probably amusing appendix to the novel.

It is possible to accuse Charles Dudley Warner, who was

more habituated than Mark to the conventions of fiction, of the outrageous plot in "The Gilded Age." Possible but hardly just. Where in American fiction were there, in 1872, novels whose form grew from their interior necessities? The textbook novelists had not improved on the factitious clichés of Cooper. There was Melville. Structurally "Omoo" and "Typee" were as inorganic as "Innocents Abroad"; "Pierre" had a framework as false, sensational, and sentimental as that of "The Gilded Age"; "Moby Dick" was chaotic.[5] There remained Hawthorne, who was also uncertain about form. Just as "The Prince and the Pauper" began as "a funny and fantastic sketch", so Hawthorne was unable to decide whether "The Scarlet Letter" ought to be a short story or a novel.[6] With good precedent, he referred the question to his publisher; the book was developed to full length but the improvidence of its technical devices shows clearly. American novelists had no mature understanding of form, in fact no self-conscious technique, before Howells and Henry James.

If Warner invented the cumbersome story of "The Gilded Age", Mark Twain consented to it. Wasn't such melodrama the condition of fiction? For twenty years he had been reading novels in which female infants of mysterious parentage were hurled before the reader by expedients quite as violent as a steamboat wreck, and in which their compelling beauty produced a seduction that had to be paid for with the villain's life, leaving the seduced under obligation to die of a broken heart. He consented. It was quite impossible for this newcomer to fiction, this newspaper humorist, to do anything else. He had no reasoned philosophy of literature; it is unlikely that he ever analyzed, beyond its mere grammar, an effect of his own or any one's else; he completely lacked the discipline of art. But when, after accepting the absurd plot, he began the attack, he produced something that is, in literary history, an event of the first importance. This curious collaboration needs further exposition.

[5] A passage in "Roughing It" burlesques "Moby Dick." In the same passage occurs what may be a jeer at "Pierre."

[6] Nevertheless, theory widely asserts that "The Scarlet Letter" has the unmistakable unity of genius consequent to the sacrifice of Hawthorne's virginity.

The original idea was probably Warner's. The experience of
an Alger hero going West to make a fortune was autobiographical: like Phil, Warner had been a surveyor in Missouri. The
accessory study of gentility among the Quakers is his also, together with the treatise on feminism. Mark added autobiography, in the Tennessee land, the coal business of his father-
in-law and the treatise on politics. But also Mark provided the
matrix in which the novel is set, the backwoods of Tennessee and
frontier Missouri. In a sense this is only Longstreet's and
Thompson's Georgia; it is possible, by 1872, to find several
novels which undertook the honest portrayal of an American
scene. Nevertheless, when the second paragraph introduces
Obedstown, East Tennessee, we are on a higher level of realism
than American literature had ever before attained. As an accident
of collaboration, Mark Twain had found the medium for what
was most vital in his humor. The same accident is the first sounding of a theme which the fiction of the next twenty years in
America perceived to be its truest expression and which defined
our national literature.

Warner's intelligence was pleasant, shallow, conforming, and
unoriginal. It is Mark's that gives the book its vitality, its contradictions of sentiment and satire, its failures and its overwhelming success. He could not sustain his conceptions. They
were never unmixed conceptions but reached him as vast com-
posites of unrelated, unrelatable material, much of it at war with
the rest. "The Gilded Age" shows his mind typically at work.
Is it to be the forthright attack on disreputable and dishonorable
rich men, the ignoble poor, and political vileness that the preface
announces? That was the intention, but it is constantly frustrated
by a plot that advances on a mechanism of false sensation and
bathos, it faces the countercurrent of Mark's gusto in creating
the social scene, and lapses intermittently for the development
of burlesque and of the study in comedy named Beriah Sellers.

Nevertheless, the satire is formidably good. It must be re-
membered that the incredible Era of Grant has, besides "The
Gilded Age", no other embodiment except the novel in which
Henry Adams quiveringly perceives that civilization has col-

lapsed. In "Democracy", the collapse means the decadence which makes it possible for a gentlewoman, one of the well born, not only to know but almost to admire a person who has accepted a bribe. It is the book of a Federalist who suffers from fidgets. Adams's experience of America was thin and, properly speaking, he had no experience of democracy at all. He had only recently recovered from admiration of Charles Sumner, many years must pass before he could virilely attack his theme, and finally this perturbed Bostonian had no inventiveness in fiction. His novel is just squeamish, a mere phobia of crowds. But "The Gilded Age" is lively with the stench and tumult of its era. Few defects possible to ignorance, inexperience, and untrustworthy impulse are absent from it, but its creatures — the profiteers, politicians, and parasites — exist in three dimensions and the north light of contempt illuminates them. The satirist, in his first fiction, moves competently through the abattoir. Alone among the novelists of the time he concerns himself with the national muck. In him only exist the boom towns, the railroad builders, the Dilworth- ies,[7] the lobbyists, the gallicized Irish, society swelling to a gim- crack pretension with the manure of empire under its finger nails, the monster fungus of the gilded age.

Beriah Sellers is a deflection of satire. A creation of pure com- edy, he adds to the book's confusion by blunting the edge of de- rision. He is no less amazing for all that. He was the first fully wrought expression of Mark's talent — though a line leads straight to him from Simon Wheeler — and he remains one of the most superb. It is not only Mark that finds expression in him — not only the gusto of this imagination at ease in the superla- tive — but an experience so native to America that he has become a type. When Colonel Sellers warms himself before mica red- dened by candleshine while he promises Washington Hawkins that the adolescent nation will make them rich, when he plots the metropolis of Napoleon on Stone Landing's mudflats beside Goose Run, when his mirages glimmer in the anterooms of

[7] The book is, in some degree, a *roman à clef*. Various commentators have identified the politicians and financiers, most of whom are but transparently disguised.

Congress, something memorable has happened in American literature. A creative vitality to which no limit was ever observed
has formed a person who exists as inevitably as anything in art
and who, in existing, contains multitudes. Mark's impulses are
no more infallible here than elsewhere, and some strokes felt
to be heroically comic are only burlesque. In dramatizations,
the figure was subjected to the art of actors, and the atrocities
then begotten remain in the Mulberry Sellers of "The American
Claimant." There, the creation runs out in extravaganza that
is only humiliating — the nightmare meant to be a burlesque of
spiritualism is hardly endurable and achieves harmony in its
own lamentable terms only in the grandeur of the last page —
though even this humiliation is sometimes lightened by flashes
of the older certainty. Nevertheless the original, Beriah Sellers,
remains and seems likely to remain. It is desirable to recognize
that quite flatly: the literature that possesses him is richer than
it was up to the moment when a letter arrived at Obedstown
and Beriah Sellers concluded his "Come right along to Missouri" with "Come! — rush! — hurry! — don't wait for anything!"

The amorphousness of "The Gilded Age", satire and Sellers
at war with one another, is appalling and is not lessened by the
absurd plot, the set pieces of femininity that Mark always produced when he was studying women not of the frontier, the wild
jokes, and the chapter mottoes in strange tongues that were
distressingly supposed to be funny. But the book is nevertheless
literature. Defaced and disfigured, it is still much more than a
ruin above which an occasional column rises. It is a monument
crudely designed and eroded in its weaker places but certain to
endure for a long time yet. . . . What gives it this durability?

The question leads at this last to the core of Mark Twain.
For if the announcement of Obedstown was an innovation of
final importance to American literature, it only declared the
basic quality of genius. The village is part of a countryside that
includes Hawkeye, Napoleon, Hadleyburg, Pokeville, St.
Petersburg, and Dawson's Landing — Western rural slaveholding communities near the fringe of settlement during the

years when a boundless vigor was making America something it had not been. And these communities are born of Mark Twain's perception of humanity. We arrive at the damned human race.

It is first of all gusto. Great art seldom exists without this inexhaustible delight in its subjects — a delight that nowhere else comparably shows itself in American fiction. Whatever these creatures may be, they wholly absorb their creator. From the full occupation of a book, Pudd'nhead Wilson or Tom Sawyer, to such a mere allusion as Drake Higgins, they receive an attention in which sheer pleasure never flags. Listen to Roxy chattering with Jasper, to Old Damrell describing "a hell's-mint o' whoop-jamboree notions" in the Higgins house, to old man Finn commenting on government. There is here a steady exultation of understanding: it is the medium in which all the persons of the novels live. This gusto is without end. It is basic in Mark Twain.

It gives these persons a vividness, a reality, seldom or never encountered elsewhere in American novels. Comparisons are silly, yet it seems a reasonable procedure to set these characters against those who exist in the books of Mark's competitors. Who, of his time, may honestly be said to survive the comparison? Not, surely, the wraiths of Herman Melville's soliloquy, mere studies in metaphysical debate whose occupation is rhetoric. Not Hawthorne's remembrances of things past, who would not bleed if you broke their skin. Not Howells's careful documentations, nor James's laboratory which dissects the organism to the bone without finally laying bare the life. If this is true, the inhabitants of Mark's novels have the greatest authority in our literature. Yet there is something more, even, than gusto in their creation.

They are projected with an unsurpassed detachment. His boundless delight in them is not softened by apology nor deflected by anger. No emotion of the creator's is expended on the creation. The person is caught and fixed — in a clear medium, a medium without accessory coloration. He is infinitely understood: he is not abhorred. Whatever condemnation exists, and it is sometimes formidable, inheres in the mere fact of presentation, not in Mark's manner or his emotions. He is tranquil — imperturbable, dispassionate. He is undeluded. And so his characters are a finality of knowledge.

He glances at an apprentice blacksmith turned actor. "He was standing musing on a street corner, with his right hand on his hip, the thumb of the left supporting his chin, face bowed and frowning, slouch hat pulled down over his forehead — imagining himself to be Othello or some such character, and imagining that the passing crowd marked his tragic bearing and were awe-struck." Or at John Stavely, saddler, who rushed to attend every steamboat's arrival. "Everybody knew . . . that John Stavely was not expecting anybody by that boat — or any freight, either; and Stavely must have known that everybody knew this, still it made no difference to him; he liked to seem to himself to be expecting a hundred thousand tons of saddles by this boat, and so he went on all his life, enjoying being faithfully on hand to receive and receipt for those saddles, in case by any miracle they should come." These are mere glances but each of them states a life. No emotion intervenes. The effect may be savage to the limit of endurability, but savagery is in the character stated, not in the statement. In "Life on the Mississippi", two or three pages record an undertaker whom Lemuel Gulliver might have encountered among the Yahoos. He states himself: no emotion whatever is expended on him. "Same with Embamming. You take a family that's able to embam, and you've got a soft thing. . . . It's human nature — human nature in grief. It don't reason, you see. Time being, it don't care a d —— n. All it wants is physical immortality for deceased, and they're willing to pay for it. . . . Why man, you can take a defunct that you couldn't *give* away; and get your embamming traps around you and go to work; and in a couple of hours he is worth a cool six hundred — that's what *he's* worth. There ain't anything equal to it but trading rats for diamonds in time of famine." The presentation is without passion, it even has a serene affirmation: the effect is an extremity of contempt.

It is hardly necessary to point out the accessory arts

brought to creation. In all fiction written in English there is no greater sensitiveness to speech. There is an infinite subtlety in the rendition of dialects. Individuality, the differentiation, extends to nuances so discreet that not every one to-day can perceive them. There is also the "hard old Injun." The observation of the frontier is concentrated on minute characteristics of appearance, behavior, and thought. As a result, the character is rendered with a firmness of line and an economy impossible to go beyond. The physical world in which the creatures live, which they mostly defile, is rendered quite as sharply. Then the perception thus attested moves on to intangibles, to the relationships of these creatures.

It is here that Mark Twain's fiction attains its highest value. The community exists as it has never existed elsewhere in American fiction, and seldom in any fiction. The mail arrives at Obedstown, and "Russ Mosely he tole ole Hanks he mought git to Obeds tomorrer or nex' day he reckoned." The squatters lean and spit and condemn Si Higgins's wife for "plarsterin" her shack, till a dog fight draws their attention away. The first community fully sensed in our literature has recorded itself. . . . Dawson's Landing is more integrated, more completely fixed. Out of a bombast initiated by the Siamese twins rises, not perfectly but most memorably, a Southern river town before the war. Every level of this society is present. A countryside opulently beautiful incloses the microcosm. It is ruled by its gentry — the York Leicester Driscolls, Cecil Burleigh Essexes, and Pembroke Howards of Virginia traditions and Iroquois chivalry. It is chiefly composed of villagers, Justice Robinson, Aunt Patsy Cooper, Rowena, the casually named or unnamed mob who peer, flutter, destroy, condemn, and are ignorant. They are rendered with the inevitable sharpness: what is more, they are a whole. They interpenetrate. They are a symbiosis. Chivalry feeds ignorance; superstition is an energy of injustice; cruelty becomes self-preservation. There is, as well, kindness and simplicity, decency, hope, and heroism — the unaware pathos never absent from Mark's understanding. A civilization, an era, is here recorded. Given what passes for immortality in literature.

Not forgetting the slaves. He was probably not aware that he was bringing to literature a theme it had refused to use. Apart from him, the institution of slavery had no place in the fiction of his century. Northern novelists may have been unable to understand more than its propriety in reform: none went beyond the exegesis of Mrs. Stowe and John T. Trowbridge. The South had no realist before Mark Twain, except the humorists who have been here examined and who ignored the theme. Oratory and romance had a compulsion to defend God's providence, going no farther than the loyal defenders of their chains who, about the time Mark Twain was born, cast out the tyrant Van Buren's troops in Beverly Tucker's "Partisan Leader." Tucker's happy Negroes and their owners flicker through many lyric novels down to war time, then reappear as accessories of love stories and of the lost cause. After the war, a few thin talents did sometimes attempt an objective picture of remembered slavery, but they were submerged in the reveries of Confederate officers. Thomas Nelson Page is this sentiment achieving full expression. His example dominated his region until the next war. Cable and Harris, although romancers, had meanwhile examined slavery with less sentiment than Page, but they were ineffective — and, besides, had received instruction from Mark Twain.

So that when Uncle Dan'l and Aunt Jinny reach the Mississippi on page 19 of "The Gilded Age", they initiate something quite new to fiction. Slavery is interstitial to the life of Obedstown and its successors in the Hawkins pilgrimage, as of the other communities in Mark's world. It is a force in the lives of all these people. It has acted on the lethargy of squatters and produced something of the mob's cruelty as well as the gentry's watered chivalry. In "Tom Sawyer" and especially "Huckleberry Finn" it is the bloodstream of the community. Nigger Jim, a heroic person, is a main object of these books and, with whatever sentiment rendered, remains except for Roxy and Uncle Dan'l the only Negro who truly lives, as a person apart from the folk tales of Harris, in the literature of the nineteenth century.

In "Pudd'nhead Wilson" the institution that had furnished a living background for these other books becomes the active center. In all other places Mark Twain omitted an explicit statement of sexual relationships — though the force of implication is irresistible wherever the squatters are displayed. Here, it may be in all innocence, he states and develops a theme completely tabooed in nineteenth-century American literature, miscegenation. It is so inevitably a part of the book that critical amazement develops only retrospectively. Yet there is an intense artistic courage in this presentation of the slave Roxanna, one sixteenth negro, of fair complexion and fine soft hair, and of the son whom she bears to Cecil Burleigh Essex.

Roxy is unique and formidable. Mark's handling of her suffers somewhat from the melodrama and sentimentality that, it should be clear, were inescapable — but does not suffer much. In outline and in detail she is memorably true. She lives: her experiences and emotions are her own, and, being her own, are faithful to the history of thousands. With new instruments at its service and a generation of writers far distant from the reality, literature may make another essay of slavery — but is unlikely to go beyond the superstition, affection, malice, and loyalty of this woman. In her exist, as nowhere else, the experience, the thought, and the feelings of slaves. Even in melodrama she retains her verity. When she forces Valet de Chambre Essex to his knees, she is within reach of the preposterous, but the scene is as true, as inevitable, as her thieving and tippling. It ends with her declaration that "dey ain't another nigger in dis town dat's as high-bawn as you is", and this is grandeur. Grandeur of another kind appears in her original crime and, most evidently, in her disgust when she learns that her son has disgraced his father by ratting the duel with Luigi. "En you refuse' to fight a man dat kicked you, 'stid o' jumpin' at de chance! En you ain't got no mo' feelin' den to come en tell me, dat fetched sich a po' low-down ornery rabbit into de worl'! Poh! it makes me sick! It's de nigger in you, dat's what it is. Thirty-one parts o' you is white, en on'y one part nigger, en dat po' little one part is yo' soul. 'Tain't wuth savin'; 'tain't wuth totin' out on a shovel en throwin' in de gutter." In such passages as this and the mind of Valet de Chambre, slavery finds a profundity and a complexity of expression that it has had nowhere else. . . . It is worth noting that in "Pudd'nhead Wilson", Mark Twain adheres to the artistic necessities of his structure. The tough-minded ending, though clumsily managed, is carried out in its own terms.

Slavery as an institution and Negroes as sharers of the scene are organic in the community to which these novels are devoted. It is a whole community: the effect is totality. Several generations of American experience, a race, an era, and a society, are enregistered.

No one can read these books without becoming aware that the community set down with such creative gusto and with such detachment of manner is nevertheless condemned. The very relish of the portraiture, the very dispassionateness of the recording instrument, give greater finality to the judgment. The clay eaters of Obedstown, the visionaries of Napoleon, the politicians and profiteers of Washington; the gentry who assert their farcical nobilities and decorate their parlors in Dawson's Landing and St. Petersburg; the mob that cringes before Sherburn as it has first destroyed David Wilson and then groveled at his feet; the villagers and farmers and river rats among whom Huck Finn makes his way — these creatures are the damned human race. The intensity of their self-deception, the pettiness of their existence, the cruelty and jealousy and ignorance that are fundamental in their nature, are asserted at every moment. It is their function to hate freedom and love servility, to annihilate loveliness and individuality with equal fierceness. Though the reality of simple virtue, decency, kindness, and courage is nowhere denied, the race is in the main ignorant, stupid, cruel, and cowardly. The America here shown is not the America conceived in the hopeful dawn of New Jerusalem.

When the early 1920's found Mr. Masters, Mr. Anderson, Mr. Lewis, Miss Gale, and the now anonymous writers of the Midland repeating this appraisal with greater anger and less skill, Mr. Carl Van Doren for a moment forgot his reading. The new current in fiction, he said, represented a challenge to a traditional American sanctity, a legend that held vice and shame to be qualities of the city, whereas the countryside remained pure. These books were a Revolt from the Village. Mr. Van Doren forgot the novels to which Mark Twain's gave rise, but more notably he forgot Mark Twain's, in which the revolt, if that is not too active a word, received a finality it has never since attained.

In that fact final significance resides. It is unsafe to regard any artist as an embodiment of his time or its thought. An individual is not a symbol of his era. Yet no artist is severed from the experience of his age; one so instinctively a part of his place and people as Mark Twain could not escape repeating their history. So, in a sense necessarily qualified, his books do represent the experience of America grappling with democracy. His mind was formed in the experience that assumed democracy; his life was almost exactly coextensive with the seventy-five years of democratic experiment; his books contain a judgment on the collision between democratic ideal and democratic reality. So far as this identification is valid, they represent American experience repudiating its assumptions of democracy. They are the moment of realization. The experiment begun with so much generosity, so much expectation of success, comes to this acknowledgment of the result. The hope had been New Jerusalem: a commonwealth of justice, integrity, and warm promise. The realization was — Dawson's Landing. The vision was democracy; the acknowledgment was the human race.

In this shape the literature of futility, of disillusionment, and of defeat begins in America.

This is not to ignore the fustian of Mark Twain's counter-statements. He could rant like any politician. The repudiation is not steady; at nearly any moment the eagle may be expected to scream. Whenever, in fact, he is reducing his ideas to generalization, he is quite as likely to affirm the democratic faith as to reject it. It is in the far surer intuition of his fiction, the presentation of character, that the admission of despair is made. Here, he seems to say, is the actuality that has emerged from the ideal.

The phrased generalization, observe, relates not to the American but to the human race. He must not be required to base his fiction on a system of philosophy. His intelligence was not of a kind to undertake such an effort with distinction. In what passes as formal thought he had no power. When he turned away from the animal to consider its tools, he was as awestruck by the mirage of Progress as any platform lecturer of his time: this dominant illusion of his age was integral in his reasoned thinking. When he essayed a formal attack on religion, he produced something but little deeper than Ingersoll's "Mistakes of Moses." When he tried to form a system of his intuitions he wrote only "What Is Man?", a statement of the mechanistic view in the metaphors of John Watson's Behaviorism, and as perfectly accommodated to the minds of sophomores. It is only when he foregoes polemics and lets his intuitions take shape in character that they have importance. "The Mysterious Stranger" therefore has a greater dignity than the formal arguments. It wraps a gentle melancholy around its boys and angels and speaks from experience, not ideas. Its charm will outlast its fable and keep it alive a little while. But one must look for the final value of Mark Twain not at Eseldorf but, once more, at St. Petersburg and Dawson's Landing.

There seems to me, to face one last preoccupation of criticism, no need to probe for the basis of pessimism nor even to shrink from it. He had lived intensely; his sensitiveness was great; he had experienced rewards and penalties; he had known triumph, loss, and grief. He had shared as intimately as possible the life on which he entered judgment. In intellectual terms, he had experienced the intent of his age and its reality. I cannot see in what is called his pessimism anything but the fruit of his experience. Not even Christianity has believed that happiness is a function of mortal life — the assumption behind any dissatisfaction with a kind and generous man's announcement of reality. It is true that pessimism was so rare in the nineteenth-century literature of America, and remains so in the twentieth century, that its expression in Mark Twain has a kind of singularity. That does not seem to me a compelling argument that it must be wrong. Or, for that matter, neurotic.

A few days before he died, he wrote some instructions to help Mr. Paine through St. Peter's gate. Two of the maxims read:

"Leave your dog outside. Heaven goes by favor. If it went by merit, you would stay out and the dog would go in.

"You will be wanting to slip down at night and smuggle water to those poor little chaps (the infant damned), but don't you try it. You would be caught, and nobody in heaven would respect you after that."

It was his final judgment on the human race. But it was implicit in most of his books.

XII

THE ARTIST AS AMERICAN

This book had to begin, and must end, by accepting the conditions of its problem. The intent has been to restore discussion of a man of letters to what he wrote. Fulfillment of that purpose has required it to forego an exposition of Mark Twain in the light of eternity, about which it confesses ignorance, in order to present evidence against ideas about Mark Twain which are as ephemeral as they are ridiculous. It is already possible to believe that the period which Mr. Frederick Allen has described with great charm in "Only Yesterday" had a nature of its own, a nature about which a wise thing to recognize is that it is now dead. The period had its climaxes of awe and wonder. Not the least wondrous of them is this: that the 1920's chose to think of Mark Twain not as a writer of books but as a man who either betrayed something sacred or was betrayed by something vile. During that decade, it appears, some facts were, for the literary, too plain to see and some roads too plain to take. If the opinions of the literary during that time truly stand for the opinions of others instead of for their own wish fulfillments, a proposition which might be agreeably debated, then it is possible that countless thousands have mourned because the author of "The Celebrated Jumping Frog of Calaveras County" did not write "The Revolt of Islam", "Das Kapital", and "Men Like Gods." Literary opinion during the 1920's preferred to take that road rather than consider a fact so plain that even the steerages of westward-bound liners are aware of it. The fact that the author of "The Celebrated Jumping Frog of Calaveras County" gave to American literature its two immortal characters. Since Tom Sawyer was first seen hiding in a closet and since Huckleberry Finn came down a lane in St. Petersburg with the intention of curing a wart, they have exercised the conviction of belief over more kinds and conditions of intelligence than any other persons who have been imagined in American books.

What is creation? What is art? The second question may profitably be ignored if anything realistic can be said about the first. It would seem that to bring to the material of literature in America new areas of life and experience is creation. To inform these areas with character so vivid that it produces the illusion of experience is creation. To erect where there was nothing a world at once unique and universal, to give that world an organic structure, and to people it with inhabitants who live as themselves and as an embodiment of the American race is creation. To stamp upon that world an impression of oneself so vivid and so inimitable that it can never possibly be mistaken for the seal of any one else is creation. To fructify a waste place so that dozens of writers who come after may thoughtfully reap the excess of one's sowing is creation. And finally, to add to the slender number of imagined people who are forever themselves in the minds of readers, two more so true, so inevitable, so universal that they join the world's legends — if this is not creation, then nothing is. In the presence of such facts as these, questions of form become a mere catechism from the classroom and definitions of art mere conversation in a salon.

For it is the final authority of these two boys that they have become the possession of every one. So simple a clue as a moment's honesty suggests their importance: any one may ask himself who, of all the characters in American literature, has the greatest vitality in his mind. . . . Barrett Wendell, writing about what passes as the importance of Harvard College in what passes as literature, had a curious instant of recognition. After devoting 450 pages to the obligations of Doctor Holmes, he asked leave to treat America in fifty pages. In those fifty pages, Mark Twain had, of natural right, three sentences. Mr. Wendell alluded to "a book which in certain moods one is disposed for all its eccentricity to call the most admirable work of literary art as yet produced on this continent . . . that Odyssean story of the Mississippi to which Mark Twain gave the grotesque name of 'Huckleberry Finn'." [1] He has suffered some deprecation ever since for implying that an American Odyssey was possible unsanctified by a Harvard degree. Yet the adjective Odyssean does convey the plain truth about the two boys, not in the obvious sense that Huck Finn made a journey by water but in the fundamental sense that his life is something which the whole world shares. He and Tom have enriched the experience of those who read books everywhere. They are universal in that they have become legends, not as the expression of something fanciful or fantastic, but as the embodiment of something forever true. In them America has made incomparably its greatest communication to world literature.

[1] In Barrett Wendell's time the aristocratic tradition had not yet been debauched. A Professor Paul Shorey, who writes in the house organ of Phi Beta Kappa, exhibits the invective by means of which Humanism has become, by 1932, mere logorrhoea: "The question I submit to you [the American Scholar] is whether those who think so shall have the courage to unite in saying that the high culture, the sobriety, the common sense, the patriotism, the decency, the sober optimism of Longfellow, Emerson, Holmes, and Lowell and their immediate disciples, while we are waiting for something greater, more nearly represent the true American tradition and ideal than do the wilfulness, the incoherence, the inconsequences, and the fitful flashes of genius of Thoreau, Melville, Whitman, Mark Twain, or the trivial vocabulary, the pseudo-science, the Freudism, the anti-patriotic bias, the affected cosmopolitanism, the thumb-sucking *Weltschmerz*, the sex obsession, the un-American tragedies, of the spokesmen of the generation at the second remove from the older culture." Such an aspect as this of the thinking that calls itself decorum is just vulgar.

One of the finest passages of "Huckleberry Finn" appears not in that book but in "Life on the Mississippi." In the same way, some of the truest presentation of Tom, Huck, and Jim is to be encountered in "Tom Sawyer Abroad" and "Tom Sawyer, Detective." The latter is a trivial story psychologically related to the burlesques of detective fiction that amused Mark at the time, but as if by accident it expresses a native quality of the frontier. In this casual improvisation, Tom Sawyer is utilizing the shrewdness which proceeds from the woodscraft that the frontier found necessary for survival. It is a shrewdness peculiarly and indigenously American. It was created by wilderness life, derived from the chief skill of the Indians, and imposed as a condition of success by the westward exploration. It attained its highest phase among the trail makers of the far West, so that Samuel Parker, adventuring with Jim Bridger, Fitzpatrick, and Kit Carson, encountered the foremost practitioners of a great craft. But it was a craft essential to every one who participated in frontier life, and belongs to the very center of the American experience. It must be recognized as native to the frontier mind.[2] Most of Mark Twain's characters exhibit it as instinctively and unconsciously as they assume the presence of slavery. In this anecdote of Tom Sawyer it becomes explicit. Elsewhere Tom casually identifies a dog by the individuality of its baying or knows where to find embers protected from a cloud-burst; here he concentrates this sharp and cunning sagacity on the analysis of a situation. The decorations of the story and its set piece at the end are trivial inventions or mere repetitions of effects Mark had previously proved reliable, but the process of identification and proof is forged from something basic in America. When Tom

---

[2] The interpretation of observed circumstance — what Poe called ratiocination — is an interest of American literature that seems to be inseparably bound up with frontier life. Leatherstocking and "Nick o' the Woods" may be instanced. The realistic humor of the southwestern frontier has many tales devoted to this theme. The best of them has never, so far as I know, been alluded to in print. I therefore take pleasure in calling to the attention of anthologists a remarkable short story, one which of right would be an American classic, the tale Uncle Billy tells of the murder of Charley Birkham and the identification of his murderer in Philip Paxton's "A Stray Yankee in Texas." (See Appendix A.)

observes a flaw in Jake Dunlap's sickness, interprets the shadows at the foot of sycamores, and identifies the pattern a finger makes on a cheek, many thousand inhabitants of our history nod assent, for they have found a voice. Cornstalks have moved when all breeze is dead, marauding hoofs have chipped a stone by night, and, in the month when the willows redden, the color of dusk above a mountain creek has shown a wisp of smoke where no smoke should be.

The Dunlaps are squatters and they with all the other personages of the anecdote share the careless fecundity of Mark Twain, so that not even the absurdity of the ghosts diminishes them. That fecundity is freely expended in the much more ambitious companion piece. If "Pudd'nhead Wilson" had not been selected to typify the paradox of Mark Twain's invention, "Tom Sawyer Abroad" could stand symbol for it. The fictional framework, the balloon and its inventor, is not only fantastic, it is anachronistic in the troubled sense that threatens much else of Tom's biography. Yet the statement of the backwoods mind is here elaborated on an equality with anything that the two principal books contain. It cannot be spared from the whole of which the others are larger parts. It has, even, superiorities to them, since its serene, almost loving exploration of ignorant thought is more detailed, and since Nigger Jim is given more to do that reveals him. The sketch is, in fact, an elaborate exposition of St. Petersburg trying to grapple with an enlargement of its thinking, and in this exposition Jim is the pivot. There can be no doubt that Mark's deliberate effort was to explore the mentality of the common man.

Metaphor breaks across Jim's skull quite in vain. It is not the welkin they are in but a balloon, and an explanation fails because when Tom asserts that birds of a feather flock together, Jim falls back on the unassailable logic of experience, inquiring whether Tom has ever observed a bluebird in the company of a jaybird. Jim cannot applaud the method of Zadig, because the tale neglects to reveal what became of the camel. His theory of the Sahara as deity's waste heap after creation, triumphs over its competitors by instancing the Milky Way as the scraps of stars, and to that argument no answer is possible. When the lake proves to be a mirage, clearly it is a ghost, for Jim had seen it with his own eyes — and "forty thousand million people seen the sun move from one side of the sky to the other every day." An exquisite gradation carries the slave's thinking into the larger intelligence of Huck Finn. Huck takes pride in Tom's wide information but is obliged to correct it steadily by reference to common sense. He admires the reasoning that enables Tom to go direct to the dervish's enchanted hill and infallibly recognize the ruin of Joseph's granary. Nevertheless he must agree with Jim that two days cannot exist at the same time, for there would then be no day of judgment in England, and he enjoys the elation of proving by the map that no two States have the same color. Tom's tribute to fleas convinces him and he manages to form the idea of longitude, but is scandalized by the story of a bronze horse that flies. In an analysis that catches backwoods America in the very act of vindicating its intelligence, he demonstrates that a pyramid can't burn and a horse can't fly.

Such contexts give life to provinciality and ignorance. The thing itself is in them. The pattern, the very rhythm of thought is communicated in a realism that extends to the basis and conditions of the mind. The crossroads forum, the groggery and the steamboat wharf, swallowed in the isolation of a continent, have spoken in the way instinctive to them. A society is made articulate.

Inquiry has sometimes concerned itself with the origin of "The Adventures of Tom Sawyer." Aldrich's "Story of a Bad Boy" has been suggested and one inquirer has wondered if "Sut Lovingood" may not have been an influence. The latter idea may now be given a further persuasion for classrooms, beyond the partial coincidence of themes, by mentioning Sut's acquaintance with a doctor who desires cadavers for dissection. Either inquiry seems idle, for when he came to write "Tom Sawyer", Mark Twain at last arrived at the theme that was most harmonious with his interest, his experience, and his talents. If anything may be confidently said about the processes of creation, one may confidently say that this book, with its companion, was inevitable. Foreordination is probably a fact: if it is, Mark Twain was predestined to this work. That is one source of its finality.

The sun shines on Tom's St. Petersburg. The simplest description of his book is this: the supreme American idyll. It is also an idyll of boyhood; such incidents as the whitewashing of the fence are, like a familiar landscape, so intimate to our experience that their importance is easily forgotten. Yet, even in the century that brought childhood to the attention of literature, it had no other expression quite so true. Tom Sawyer's morality, his religion, his black avengers, his rituals and tabus, his expeditions for glory or adventure, his trafficking with buried treasure, his exaltation, his very terror — are, for childhood, immortal. That fact carries its own weight: whatever achievement resides in writing a book eternally true about children, a book so expressive of them that they accept it as themselves, is Mark Twain's achievement. Yet these are American boys and the book they live in has a validity beyond their presence for the nation to which they are native.

For in "The Adventures of Tom Sawyer" exists, as nowhere else, the since polluted loveliness of a continent. That it is now defiled, that successive generations have seen the assault on natural beauty made more effective, gives this embodiment of it a greater evocation, a greater nostalgia, for the inheritors of wasteland. Americans would not have kept its innumerable editions streaming from the press [3] unless it expressed some emotion and satisfied some need at the very taproot of American life. One need not venture very far into mysticism, or into history or literature, to find that fundamental reality. In whatever mood of poetry or psychological curiosity one examines the passage upland from the Atlantic, with whatever instrument of precision one tries to test its nature, one at once perceives that the symbolism of the Westward journey is tremendous. It has given the commonplace word "frontier" a meaning for the Americans that

[3] It is a safe assertion, even if one impossible of verification, that more copies of Mark Twain's books are bought annually than of those by any other American. That is, quite simply, what is wrong with them to some aspiring minds. "The Adventures of Tom Sawyer" stands second in the list of sales. The leader is, appropriately, "The Adventures of Huckleberry Finn."

it has had for no other people. Inseparable from that meaning and immediate in the symbolism, is the beauty of the land across which the journey passed. Whatever else the word means, it has also meant water flowing in clear rivers, a countryside under clean sun or snow, woods, prairies and mountains of simple loveliness. It is not necessary to think the literature of America a very noble literature in order to recognize the fact that one of its principal occupations has been the celebration of that beauty. Layer after layer of experience or frustration may come between but at the very base of the American mind an undespoiled country lies open to the sun.

St. Petersburg stands between the untouched forest and the endlessly flowing river — symbols in which every American will find what import he may but all of us will find some import. That still, blue shadow and that movement underlie passion, desire, and fantasy: they are the landscape as truly of our sleep, as, now that they are mostly vanished, of our reverie. So much, hesitantly, for what happens below the threshold when Tom Sawyer goes down the far slope of Cardiff Hill into forest, or at midnight shoves a raft into the Mississippi bound for Jackson's Island. Above the threshold, there is a drowsy town in a season that is always summer. Time, with the westward journey, has halted. For this moment, between forest and river, America is gracious and kind. Between those immensities the village is untroubled. It gossips around the pump or lounges a Sunday morning away at church, exalted only by temperance parades or the fantastic Benton's oration on the Fourth of July, vivified only by the steamboats that tie up to its wharves. Nothing touches this serenity. The steamboats bring pageantry, not pressure from the world outside. The village is ignorant of that world — which is hardly a rumor, hardly a dream. Life is unhurried, amidst this simple plenty of the folk.

If detachment can be tender, then Mark's is when he deals with these folk. He was as aware of Aunt Polly as any one who has come after him. The sum of pettiness is in the notabilities of St. Petersburg or in the concerns of the Sunday school — and yet they are affirmed to be a part of this enduring peace. They are disarming. They compose the living town through which the boy's enchantment makes its way, over which the cloud shadows drift toward Cardiff Hill. They are recognized as a necessary condition of the idyll that is Tom Sawyer's summer.

The pastoral landscape, however, is a part not of cloudland but of America. It is capable of violence and terror. The episodes at the core revolve around body-snatching, murder, robbery, and revenge. The term melodrama must be here used with caution. The lore of buried treasure, specifically the loot of John A. Murrell's clan, was a daily possession of the villagers. Half-breeds were common to their experience and, being of the dispossessed, were charged with crime as a matter of course — and some accuracy. Revenge, a motive of infrequent validity for most people, was axiomatic in the Indian nature. When Injun Joe addresses Doctor Robinson across the blanketed corpse and alludes to an affront put upon him, his language comes close to the thrillers of the itinerant stage, but his emotions are genuine. Nor, to boys whom slaves had instructed in darkness, was there anything unreasonable in the powers exerted in graveyards by ghosts or witches. The idyll is fulfilled in terms that belong uniquely to itself: its native horror is part of its ecstasy.

These belong to the multitudes that Mark Twain contains — that find expression through him. It is wise to remember that they are multitudes. Behind these white men and Negroes is the history of a race. Whether Muff Potter remembers the good fishin'-places he has shown to boys or Mr. Dobbins studies anatomy with the vision of practicing medicine, something speaks from the native soul. In the terrors that afflict the boys, quite as much as in the beauty that solaces them, are recorded generations who traveled darkness in the fear of the unseen. Engraftments from Africa, England, and the Apocalypse, sufficiently noticed earlier in this book, are part of the American experience here, as nowhere else, given existence in literature. Tom and Huck, shuddering in the moonlight when a dog's howl is the presage of death, are carriers of a truth struck from a whole population. The dark world of the slaves has made this gift. Yet Tom and Huck are merely actors in the foreground, behind whom the frontier community lives. There is no fumbling. The community is true.

There is that particular kind of truth. Sometimes literature forms out of the flux something realized to be a whole truth about a time or a people. Whether this literature shall or shall not be called art must depend on the caprice of its assayer: whatever else it is, it is finality. The St. Petersburg of Tom Sawyer is a final embodiment of an American experience many layers deep, from the surface to whatever depths one may care to examine, each layer true. What finds expression here is an America which every one knows to be thus finally transmuted into literature, which every one knows has never since Mark Twain had existence in type and never will again. In the presence of such a finality, technical defects, here freely acknowledged, are trivialities. It does not matter much that some of the artist's inventions are weak, that some of the situations and dialogue fail rather dismally, or that, by some canon of abstract form, the book lacks a perfect adjustment of part to part. It does matter that here something formed from America lives as it lives nowhere else.

It matters, too, that the boys and villagers of this landscape not only contain an age in which the nation shared but also record and evoke emotions unattached to that age. It is injudicious to examine the idea of universality in literature, for that also is a phrase which means merely what any critic uses it to mean. Still, Tom and Huck have been universal in this: that for half a century their adventures have fed the hunger of millions. Whether cowering in the shadows by an open grave or swimming at daybreak off Jackson's Island or digging for treasure near the haunted house, they have had authority over the belief of readers — over an audience probably more varied and widespread than any other American has addressed. On the authority of a poet whom Washoe told to hold his yawp it is asserted that a boy's will is the wind's will and the thoughts of youth are long, long thoughts — where else have they had a tongue? Whitewashing a fence, prodding a tick with a pin or dying in the greenwood to rhythms from the border balladry, Tom speaks as competently for his millions as in passages that go deeper into the untranslatable. Into that obscurity it is not necessary to follow

him. He accompanies Huck Finn to the graveyard; he is not
quite sane at night, remembering that horror; he swims the
Mississippi on an errand; he wanders through a cave from which
he can find no way into the light. During more than fifty years
his summer has had, over the world, a necessity that belongs only
to what is great in literature. It seems something more than unlikely that he will lose, hereafter, any of that necessity.

As an accessory of literature, American journalism attained
its highest reach in the February or Midwinter number of the
Century Magazine for 1885. That issue carried "Royalty on
the Mississippi" the last of three selections from "The Adventures of Huckleberry Finn." It had also the ninth and tenth
chapters of "The Rise of Silas Lapham" and began the serializa-
tion of "The Bostonians." No comparable enterprise has ever
been undertaken by a magazine.

To Mark, Howells's novel seemed "dazzling — masterly —
incomparable." But as for Henry James's, he "would rather be
damned to John Bunyan's heaven than read that." Both judgments were inevitable to him, but they neglect to understand a
coincidence that joined the two novels with his in the climax of
the national literature which followed the Civil War. The coincidence provides a yardstick for comparative measurements.

The two studies of amenities in the Back Bay are a chapter
in the amiable difference between Howells and James which
seems to have been, through the course of several novels on
intersecting themes, an almost deliberate debate. Neither went
beyond this chapter. "The Rise of Silas Lapham" is the most effective of Howells's stenotypes. After "The Bostonians" James
began to submerge in the psychological perplexity through which
only members of a school can follow him with complete belief;
it was his last confrontation of an objective world. In the two
books, two realisms, each in its way formidable, deal with American theorems — in so far as there remained, on the water side
of Beacon Street, something recognizable as American.

The paint-maker's achievement of an ethics had been preceded by two or three statements of plutocracy, which are now

forgotten and which probably learned something from "The Gilded Age", but begot a whole literature that studies the native millionaire. Its problem has lost the importance it had for Howells, who lacked Mark Twain's knowledge of business in operation. A more candid assumption, verifying Mark's, is now implicit in our thinking. Not the problem but the book's exquisite record of manners and behavior constitutes its achievement. Within the areas that Howells considered legitimate, it is a social history of unimpeachable validity. There can be no doubt whatever that, within those areas, these Bostonians are true. Within those areas, this is how they felt and thought; these are their actual impulses and problems; their life consisted of these emotions, experiences, and aspirations. The trouble is that the areas are selected by inhibition. The timidities of Howells forbade him to inquire into the deeper springs of action, or barriers to it, and from associating his people with the national blood stream. The society he so exquisitely reflects, it may be said, was in its own way ligatured away from that metabolism. Well, that is a further reason why the book remains something under glass, a specimen beautifully mounted in a museum with the gowns and embroideries of its period, a contemporary manuscript invaluable to historians who may reconstruct from it the entirety of those selected areas. But hardly a novel of America.

Howells sketched it from the life — from such models as he permitted himself. James's intention was identical but a greater reverence for what is merely literary frequently impeded him. The minor women in "The Bostonians", all of them except the veterans of reform in whose behalf it was unnecessary to invoke chivalry, are from fiction, and from cheap magazine fiction at that. Mrs. Luna's terrible archness seems to have been, in the mind of this witty man, a true kind of wit; both it and the capricious tyranny supposed to be her charm are derived from a convention, accepted also in Grace Litchfield's "The Knight of the Black Forest", which accompanied "The Bostonians" in the *Century*, and remains unchanged to-day. Literature also supplied Basil Ransom, a gentleman from the South. Experience is substituted for convention when James turns to Cambridge and Boston characters whose social origins do not demand respect,[4] and to the two principal characters of his fable. Their relations are rendered ironically and irony assists James to a more profound comprehension than Howells's. The artist's perception is signally vindicated in a triumph of intuition over ignorance. Much the finest value in the novel is Olive Chancellor's love affair with Verena Tarrant. The spinster — she was in origin merely a "Boston old maid" of tradition — understood herself no better than the brother of America's foremost psychologist consciously understood her. But a passion far from ambiguous dictates her jealousy, her courtship, her very language. She is presented with a frankness as impossible to the Henry James of 1885 as to any other writer in the America of that time. Boston had forsaken its seafaring inheritance and James had not lived in a mining camp. He could not have created Olive Chancellor if he had recognized her motives. But they are the greatest animation in a novel that is, otherwise, a minor study in the manners of a provincial society out of touch with its time and nation and denied all richness of experience except this.

Both novels are exquisitely conceived and written. Both employ a more mature technique than our fiction had experienced before them. Both, to the full extent of their powers, embody the truth about their themes sensitively studied and imaginatively projected. But both are wonderfully innocent of the world, their time and their nation. They are insulated from America. They are the genteel tradition attaining its complete expression in fiction but also irrevocably revealing its anæmia. Their impotence could be no more dramatically exhibited than by Gilder's accompanying them with selections from the novel in which nineteenth-century America exists with a vitality, a finality, and a greatness it has had nowhere else.

The kernel of "Huckleberry Finn" is in a speech of Huck's toward the end of "Tom Sawyer." At the foot of the dead-limb tree t'other side of Still-House branch, he doubts the value of finding buried treasure. "Pap would come back to thish yer

---

[4] In these persons "The Bostonians" is a *roman à clef*. It was pleasant to transport one of them from Concord.

town some day and get his claws on it if I didn't hurry up, and I tell you he'd clean it out pretty quick." "Old Times on the Mississippi", contains a passage as integral with Huck's journey as anything in his book, and "Life on the Mississippi", written over the period when Huck was gestated, has many incidents on their way to fruition.[5] The Darnell-Watson feud is the Grangerford-Shepherdson trouble in chrysalis, a desultory tale told by a passenger as the *Gold Dust* passes through the chute of Island Number 8. On the upstream voyage as yet anonymous strollers forecast David Garrick the younger and Edmund Keen the elder. John A. Murrell's inheritors hint at revenge in the staterooms of a wrecked steamboat and other creatures of midnight presage the turmoil of search and escape through underbrush. Nor are these volumes the only ones in which pupal stages of incidents in "Huckleberry Finn" may be observed: most of the books that precede have passages of premonition. Why not? It was a book he was foreordained to write: it brought harmoniously to a focus everything that had a basic reality in his mind.

The opening is just "Tom Sawyer" and pretty poor "Tom Sawyer" at that. Huck's report of his emotions while ghosts are talking to him in the wind is a promise of what is to come, but Tom Sawyer's gang commenting on "Don Quixote" lacks the fineness of its predecessor. Discussions of ransom and Tom's exposition of Aladdin's lamp are feeble; such finish as they have comes from Huck's tolerant but obstinate common sense, here making its first experiments. But no flavor of the real Odyssey appears until Miss Watson forbids him to avert by magic the bad luck made inevitable by spilled salt, thus precipitating his trouble, and he immediately finds in the snow the impression of a boot heel in which nails make a cross to keep off the devil. . . . It is expedient to list here the book's obvious faults. After a first half in which, following the appearance of old man Finn,

---

[5] Critics who enjoy dealing with the unconscious mind as the womb of art are offered such passages for amusement. I reluctantly confess, however, my fear that they will not indicate a father fixation, Mark's incestuous love of his sister, a forgotten reading of Nathaniel Wanley, or zoöphily.

no touch is unsure, Mark's intuition begins to falter occasionally. When the Duke has Louis XVII learn a Shakespearian speech compounded out of Sol Smith and George Ealer, high and poetic reality lapses into farce. (Predictably. The humorist's necessity to write burlesque had frequently ruined fine things in the earlier books.) The King's conversion is weakened by his use of pirates instead of the neighborhood church which his predecessor Simon Suggs had more persuasively employed. (Predictably. The necessity to carry a joke into cosmic reaches had betrayed him often enough before.) Huck's discourse on the domestic manners of royalty is a blemish. (Extravaganza had diluted satire in many earlier contexts.) Huck's confusion when he tries to lie to the harelipped girl is perfunctory. (Improvisation had substituted for structure sufficiently often in Mark's previous fiction.) The concluding episodes of the attempted fraud on the Wilks family are weak in their technical devices — the manipulation required to postpone the detection of imposture, for instance, is annoying. Thereafter the narrative runs downhill through a steadily growing incredibility. The use of ghosts, the deceptions practiced on Aunt Sally and Uncle Silas, the whole episode built around the delivery of Jim from prison — all these are far below the accomplishment of what has gone before. Mark was once more betrayed. He intended a further chapter in his tireless attack on romanticism, especially Southern romanticism, and nothing in his mind or training enabled him to understand that this extemporized burlesque was a defacement of his purer work. His boundless gusto expended itself equally on the true and the false. . . . Predictably. It has been observed that he was incapable of sustained and disciplined imagination. One could expect it no more reasonably here than in "The Innocents Abroad."

So, though I regard comparisons as worthless in æsthetics, the obligation of a critic of Mark Twain rests on me to point out these selfsame faults in the only American novel which even enthusiasm can offer to dispute the preëminence of "The Adventures of Huckleberry Finn." Much more identity than has ever been noticed in print exists in the careers of Mark Twain and Herman Melville, whose minds were as antipathetic as religion

THE ARTIST AS AMERICAN

and reality or the subjective and the objective worlds can be. Similarly, Jonathan Edwards's successor, when he came to write his masterpiece, plentifully anticipated the errors of Mark Twain and went beyond them. "Moby Dick" has, as fiction, no structure whatever. Its lines of force mercilessly intercept one another. Its improvisations are commoner and falser than those in Huck Finn. It does not suffer from burlesque (exuberant vitality had no place in Melville's nature) but its verbal humor is sometimes more vicariously humiliating than such passages as Huck's discussion of kings — a miracle, no doubt, withheld Mark Twain from the mere jokes habitual to him. And, though Melville could write great prose, his book frequently escapes into a passionately swooning rhetoric that is unconscious burlesque. He was no surer than Mark, he was in fact less sure, of the true object of his book, and much less sure of the technical instruments necessary to achieve it. That much of weakness the two novels have in common. It is convenient to point out, this much having been said, that they are otherwise antipathies. "Moby Dick" opposes metaphysics to the objective reality of "Huckleberry Finn." It is a study in demonology, bound to the world of experience by no more durable threads than a few passages in the lives of mates, harpooners and sailors who are otherwise mostly symbol or mist. They were the book's disregarded possibility of great realism. Melville preferred to sigh through eternity after the infinite. It is a search which has an eternal value for some minds. Other minds, if they look to fiction for values of time instead of eternity and of the finite instead of the infinite, are likely to relinquish the *Pequod's* voyage toward fulfillment of man's destiny and prefer a lumber raft's voyage down inland waters after no more ambitious purpose than to see what the world is like.

The title announces the structure: a picaresque novel concerned with the adventures of Huckleberry Finn. The form is the one most native to Mark Twain and so best adapted to his use. No more than Huck and the river's motion gives continuity to a series of episodes which are in essence only developed anecdotes. They originate in the tradition of newspaper humor, but the once uncomplicated form becomes here the instrument of great fiction. The lineage goes back to a native art; the novel derives from the folk and embodies their mode of thought more purely and more completely than any other ever written. Toward the beginning of this preface it was asserted that the life of the southwestern frontier was umbilical to the mind of Mark Twain. The blood and tissue of "Huckleberry Finn" have been formed in no other way. That life here finds issue more memorably than it has anywhere else, and since the frontier is a phase through which most of the nation has passed, the book comes nearer than any other to identity with the national life. The gigantic amorphousness of our past makes impossible, or merely idle, any attempt to fix in the form of idea the meaning of nationality. But more truly with "Huckleberry Finn" than with any other book, inquiry may satisfy itself: here is America.

The book has the fecundity, the multiplicity, of genius. It is the story of a wandering — so provocative a symbol that it moved Rudyard Kipling to discover another sagacious boy beneath a cannon and conduct him down an endless road, an enterprise that enormously fell short of its model. It is a passage through the structure of the nation. It is an exploration of the human race, whose adjective needs no explicit recording. It is an adventure of pageantry, horror, loveliness, and the tropisms of the mind. It is a faring-forth with inexhaustible delight through the variety of America. It is the restlessness of the young democracy borne southward on the river — the energy, the lawlessness, the groping ardor of the flux perfectly comprehended in a fragment of lumber raft drifting on the June flood. In a worn phrase — it is God's plenty.

The arrival of Huck's father lifts the narrative from the occupations of boyhood to as mature intelligence as fiction has anywhere. The new interest begins on a major chord, for old man Finn is the perfect portrait of the squatter. Behind him are the observations of hundreds of anonymous or forgotten realists who essayed to present the clay-eaters or piney-woods people, as well as a lifelong interest of Mark Twain's. It is amazing how few pages of type he occupies; the effect is as of a prolonged, minute analysis. There is no analysis; a clear light is focused on him and the dispassionate, final knowledge of his creator permits him to reveal himself. We learn of him only that he had heard about Huck's money "away down the river", but a complete biography shines through his speech. This rises to the drunken monologue about a government that can't take a-hold of a prowling, thieving, white-shirted free nigger. The old man subsides to an attack of snakes, is heard rowing his skiff in darkness, and then is just a frowsy corpse, shot in the back, which drifts downstream with the flood.

Something exquisite and delicate went into that creation — as into the casuals of the riverside. Mrs. Judith Loftus is employed to start Huck and Jim upon their voyage. She is just a device, but she outtops a hundred-odd patient attempts of fiction to sketch the pioneer wife. In her shrewdness, curiosity, initiative and brusque humanity one reads an entire history. Mere allusions — the ferryboat owner, the oarsmen who flee from smallpox, even raftsmen heard joking in the dark — have an incomparable authenticity. There is also the crowd. The loafers of Brickville whittle under the store fronts. They set a dog upon a sow that has "wholloped" herself right down in the way and "laugh and look grateful for the noise." Presently a bubble rises through this human mire: the drunken Boggs, the best-naturedest old fool in Arkansaw, comes riding into Brickville, on the wawpath. Colonel Sherburn finds it necessary to shoot him; and then, in one of the most blinding flashlights in all fiction, a "long, lanky man, with long hair and a big white fur stovepipe hat on the back of his head" rehearses the murder. "The people that had seen the thing said he done it perfect." So Buck Harkness leads a mob to Sherburn's house for a lynching but the Colonel breaks up the mob with a speech in which contempt effervesces like red nitric.

But in such passages as this, the clearly seen individuals merge into something greater, a social whole, a civilization, seen just as clearly. Pokeville, where the King is converted at the camp-meeting, Brickville, and the town below the P'int where a tanner has died are one with Dawson's Landing and Napoleon — but more concentrated and thereby more final. It seems unnecessary to linger in consideration of this society. At the time of its appearance in 1885 a number of other novelists, perhaps fecundated by "The Gilded Age", were considering similar themes. The name of any one of them — Charles Egbert Craddock or Mary E. Wilkins or Edward Eggleston will do — is enough to distinguish honest talent from genius. The impulse weakened under the æstheticism of the Nineties, and it was not till after the World War that the countryside again received consideration in these terms. To set Brickville against Gopher Prairie or Winesburg is to perceive at once the finality of Mark Twain. The long lanky man in a white stovepipe hat who rehearses the death of Boggs has recorded this society with an unemotional certainty beside which either Mr. Lewis's anger or Mr. Anderson's misery seems a transitory hysterics.

The completeness of the society must be insisted upon. One should scrutinize the family of the dead tanner and their friends and neighbors, and orient them by reference to the family of Colonel Grangerford. The Wilkses belong to the industrious respectability of the towns. Their speech and thinking, the objects of their desire, the circumstances of their relationships are the totality of their kind. The funeral of Peter Wilks is, as fiction, many themes blended together; it is, among them, a supreme exhibition of the midcontinental culture of its time — almost an archæological display. When the undertaker tiptoes among the mourners to silence a howling dog and returns to whisper "He had a rat", something final has been said about this life. But Colonel Grangerford is a gentleman. Incidentally to the feud, which is the principal occupation of this episode, Southern gentility is examined. James's Basil Ransom was an embraced tradition; Colonel Grangerford is a reality. His daughter's elopement, a device for the precipitation of the plot, is out of fiction; the feud itself, with all the lovingly studied details of the scene, are from life. Gentility decorates the parlor with Emmaline Grangerford's verse and sketches. Its neurons show in the management of more than a hundred niggers quite as positively as in the parlor, or in the ceremonies of family intercourse and the simple code of honor, so indistinguishable from that of the Iroquois, which results in mass murder.

The portraiture which begins among the dregs with old man Finn ends with the Grangerfords. Between these strata has come every level of the South. What is the integrity of an artist? It would seem to consist in an intelligence which holds itself to the statement of a perceived truth, refusing to color it with an emotion of the artist's consequent to the truth. . . . These scenes are warm with an originality and a gusto that exist nowhere else in American fiction, and yet they are most notable for Mark Twain's detachment. There is no coloration, no resentment, no comment of any kind. The thing itself is rendered. If repudiation is complete, it exists implicitly in the thing.[6]

The differentiation of the speech these people use is so subtly done that Mark had to defend himself against an accusation of carelessness. He did not want readers to "suppose that all these characters were trying to talk alike and not succeeding." Superlatives are accurate once more: no equal sensitiveness to American speech has ever been brought to fiction. But a triumph in dialect is after all one of the smaller triumphs of novel-writing, and the important thing to be observed about Huckleberry's speech is its achievement in making the vernacular a perfect instrument for all the necessities of fiction. Like Melville, Mark Twain could write empty rhetoric enough when the mood was on him, and the set pieces of description in the travel books are as trying as the McGuffey selections which may have influenced them, while a willingness to let tears flow menaces a good many effects elsewhere. Yet his writing is never mediocre and is mostly, even in the least pretentious efforts, a formidable strength. Beginning with "Life on the Mississippi" it becomes, as Mr. Ford has remarked, one of the great styles of English literature. No analysis

---

[6] Criticism has spent some pain on Mark Twain's deletion from "Life on the Mississippi" of a passage which, he was persuaded, might affect sales in the South. Apparently those who were outraged by this pandering to prejudice did not bother to read the suppressed passage. It is considerably less offensive to Southern sensibilities than several passages which remain in "Life on the Mississippi" and beside a good half of "Huckleberry Finn" it is innocuous.

need be made here: its basis is simplicity, adaptability, an intimate liaison with the senses, and fidelity to the idioms of speech. Against the assertions of criticism, it should be remembered that such a style is not developed inattentively, nor are infants born with one by God's providence. Mark's lifelong pleasure in the peculiarities of language, which has distressed commentators, was the interest of any artist in his tools. . . . The successful use of an American vernacular as the sole prose medium of a masterpiece is a triumph in technique. Such attempts have been common in two and a half centuries of English fiction, but no other attempt on the highest level has succeeded. In this respect, too, "Huckleberry Finn" is unique. Patently, American literature has nothing to compare with it. Huck's language is a sensitive, subtle, and versatile instrument — capable of every effect it is called upon to manage. Whether it be the purely descriptive necessity of recording the river's mystery, or the notation of psychological states so minute and transitory as the effect on a boy of ghosts crying in the wind, or the fixation of individuality in dialogue, or the charged finality that may be typified by the King's "Hain't we got all the fools in town on our side? And ain't that a big enough majority in any town?" — the prose fulfills its obligation with the casual competence of genius. The fiction of Mark Twain had brought many innovations to the national literature — themes, lives, and interests of the greatest originality. This superb adaptation of vernacular to the purposes of art is another innovation, one which has only in the last few years begun to have a dim and crude but still perceptible fruition.

A tradition almost as old as prose narrative joins to the novel another tributary of world literature when a purely American wandering brings two further creatures of twilight to the raft. The Duke of Bilgewater and the Lost Dauphin were born of Mark's inexhaustible delight in worthlessness, but are many-sided. Pretension of nobility is one of his commonest themes, here wrought into pure comedy. The Duke is akin to characters in the other books; the King embodies a legend widespread and unimaginably glorious on the frontier. The ambiguity surrounding the death of Louis XVII gave to history riots, dynasties and social comedies that still absorb much reverence in Florence and Paris. It gave mythology a superb legend, which at once accommodated itself to American belief. Up the river from New Orleans, one of the most pious repositories of allegiance, stories of the dethroned Bourbon gratified believers during three generations. The legend must have entertained Mark's boyhood but the circumstances of his Dauphin suggest that he more enjoyed the appearance of Eleazar Williams, who became an international celebrity in 1853. The whole course of his life probably gave him no more satisfying exhibition of the race's folly than the discovery of a Bourbon king in the person of this Mohawk half-breed turned Christian and missionary, who had systematically defrauded his church and his people. The story is one of the occasional ecstasies with which history rewards the patient mind.

The two rogues are formed from the nation's scum. They are products of chance and opportunity, drifters down rivers and across the countryside in the service of themselves. The Duke has sold medicines, among them a preparation to remove tartar from the teeth; he has acted tragedy and can sling a lecture sometimes; he can teach singing-geography school or take a turn to mesmerism or phrenology when there's a chance. The King can tell fortunes and can cure cancer or paralysis by the laying on of hands; but preaching, missionarying, and the temperance revival are his best lines. American universals meet here; once more, this is a whole history, and into these drifters is poured an enormous store of the nation's experience. They have begotten hordes of successors since 1885 but none that joins their immortality. They belong with Colonel Sellers: they are the pure stuff of comedy. Their destiny is guile: to collect the tax which freedom and wit levy on respectability. Their voyage is down a river deep in the American continent; they are born of a purely American scene. Yet the river becomes one of the world's roads and these disreputables join, of right, a select fellowship. They are Diana's foresters: the brotherhood that receives them, approving their passage, is immortal in the assenting dreams of literature. Such freed spirits as Panurge, Falstaff, Gil Blas and the Abbé Coignard are of that fellowship; no Americans except the Duke and the Dauphin have joined it. None seems likely to.

Yet the fabric on which all this richness is embroidered is the journey of Huck and Jim down the Mississippi on the June rise. There, finally, the book's glamour resides. To discuss that glamour would be futile. In a sense, Huck speaks to the national shrewdness, facing adequately what he meets, succeeding by means of native intelligence whose roots are ours — and ours only. In a sense, he exists for a delight or wonder inseparable from the American race. This passage down the flooded river, through pageantry and spectacle, amidst an infinite variety of life, something of surprise or gratification surely to be met with each new incident — it is the heritage of a nation not unjustly symbolized by the river's flow. Huck sleeping under the stars or wakefully drifting through an immensity dotted only by far lights or scurrying to a cave while the forest bends under a cloudburst satisfies blind gropings of the mind. The margin widens to obscurity. Beyond awareness, a need for freedom, an insatiable hunger for its use, finds in him a kind of satisfaction. At the margin, too, the endless flow speaks for something quite as immediate. It is movement, not quiet. By day or darkness the current is unceasing; its rhythm, at the obscure margin, speaks affirmatively. For life is movement — a down-river voyage amidst strangeness.

Go warily in that obscurity. One does not care to leave Huck in the twilight at such a threshold, among the dim shapes about which no one can speak with authority. Unquestionably something of him is resident there — with something of Tom, the disreputables, Colonel Sellers and some others. But first he is a shrewd boy who takes a raft down the Mississippi, through a world incomparably alive. With him goes a fullness made and shaped wholly of America. It is only because the world he passes through is real and only because it is American that his journey escapes into universals and is immortal. His book is American life formed into great fiction.

Somewhere in the person of Mark Twain, who wrote it, must have been an artist — as American.

The artist's career is worth a summary. More widely and deeply than any one else who ever wrote books, he shared the life of America. Printer, pilot, soldier, silver miner, gold-washer, the child of two emigrations, a pilgrim in another, a sharer in the flush times, a shaper of the gilded age — he, more completely than any other writer, took part in the American experience. There is, remember, such an entity. It seems necessary to explain that America has existed, has had a past — that life has been turbulent here as elsewhere, and has dealt with its conditions and received a shape. There is more of America in Mark Twain's books than in any others. "Roughing It" and "Life on the Mississippi" record their part of that experience: nothing will ever take their place. "The Gilded Age" and "Pudd'nhead Wilson" have the same authority in their own fields. "The Adventures of Tom Sawyer" and "The Adventures of Huckleberry Finn" are born of America — it is their immortality. . . . Whatever else this frontier humorist did, whatever he failed to do, this much he did. He wrote books that have in them something eternally true to the core of his nation's life. They are at the center; all other books whatsoever are farther away.

He wrote them with splendor. All his life his imagination delighted in the superhuman. He had gigantic ideas about the heavenly bodies — they also occupied a position from which the human race looked infinitely little. There was, in interstellar space, room for him and time for him as there was not always in the cramped world. He liked the flight of comets. They were messengers of brilliance — their flaming tails were gorgeous across the sky; and his warmth and delight found them kindred. So, in 1910, he was fascinated by the return of Halley's comet. He had been born with it and, he felt sure, he would die with it. He did. The traveler of space diminished in the western sky. It may have brought with it some one to take his place. If so, the American claimant has not yet spoken. The night has been empty of that fiery dust; the nation's literature has been empty of greatness.

BIBLIOGRAPHY

THIS bibliography is presented merely as a check list in support of statements in the book offered as assertions of fact and here brought for the first time into relationship with Mark Twain, or here presented in contradiction to what has been previously written about him. To print a list of all the sources consulted in the preparation of this book would constitute an insufferable display and would waste paper. The preparation of a critical bibliography would be a species of the same waste, since only students of Mark Twain would have any use for it and since abundant criticism of the material used is contained in the text. The effort here is merely to show responsibility for assertions and to protect me from idle controversy.

For matters of description and opinion no bibliography is offered. The reader is invited to assume that a long study of the history of the frontier has familiarized me with what has been written about it and that I do not herein express opinions about writers whose books I have not read. It would be silly to list in this bibliography classics of American literature and equally silly to list here such commonplaces of American humor as the works of Artemus Ward and similar writers. A bibliography of the humor most important to my text appears in Appendix A; in the list that follows appear only humorists upon whom rest important implications of the book.

References to books of Mark Twain are invariably by chapter, so that any edition will suffice. When the reference includes a page number, that number refers to the Household Edition.

I have consulted a great mass of unpublished material relating both to Mark Twain and to the principal topics which are discussed. No mention of this is made in the bibliography. Such of it as has proved important is referred to in the notes.

Many people have told me anecdotes about Mark Twain. I have used none of them.

Aldrich, Mrs. Thomas Bailey. "Crowding Memories." Boston: Houghton Mifflin Co. 1920.

Alter, J. Cecil. "James Bridger." Salt Lake City: Shepard Book Co. 1925.

"An Old Tale for the New Year, or Mike Fink." Excerpts from Casseday's "History of Louisville, 1852." New York: James A. Andersen, Printer. 1928.

Arvin, Newton. "Hawthorne." Boston: Little, Brown and Co. 1929.

Avery, S. P. "The Harp of a Thousand Strings." New York: Dick and Fitzgerald. 1858.

Baird, Robert. "View of the Valley of the Mississippi: or the Emigrant's and Traveller's Guide to the West." Philadelphia: H. S. Tanner. 1832.
The same. Another edition. 1834.

Baldwin, Joseph G. "The Flush Times of Alabama and Mississippi: a Series of Sketches." New York: D. Appleton and Co. 1853.

"Banvard or the Adventures of an Artist." London: Printed by Reed and Pardon. n. d.

"Banvard's Geographical Panorama of the Mississippi River, with the Adventures of the Artist." Boston: John Putnam, Printer. 1847.
The same. Another edition. 1847.

"Banvard's Geographical Panorama of the Mississippi, with the Story of Mike Fink, the Last of the Boatmen, a Tale of River Life." Boston: John Putnam, Printer. 1847.
The same. Another edition. 1847.

"Banvard ou les Aventures d'un Artiste." Paris: Typographie Dondey-Dupré. 1850.

"Banvard's Royal Geographical Panorama of Mississippi, Missouri and Ohio Rivers." London: Printed by Reed and Pardon. 1852.

Beard, George M. "A Practical Treatise on Nervous Exhaustion." New York: William Wood and Co. 1880.

Beer, Thomas. "The Mauve Decade." New York: Alfred A. Knopf. 1926.

Bennett, Emerson. "Wild Scenes on the Frontier: or Heroes of the West." Philadelphia: Hamelin and Co. 1859.

Benton, Thomas H. "Thirty Years' View." 2 vols. New York: D. Appleton and Co. 1854.

Bonney, Edward. "The Banditti of the Prairies." Chicago: E. Bonney. 1850.

Brinley, Francis. "Life of William T. Porter." New York: D. Appleton and Co. 1860.

Brooks, Van Wyck. "The Ordeal of Mark Twain." New York: E. P. Dutton and Co. 1920.

—"The Pilgrimage of Henry James." New York: E. P. Dutton and Co. 1925.

Browne, John Ross. "Crusoe's Island." New York: Harper and Brothers. 1867.

Burleigh, H. T. "Negro Minstrel Melodies." With a preface by W. J. Henderson. New York: G. Schirmer. 1910.

Burlin, Natalie Curtis. "Hampton Series: Negro Folk Songs." New York and Boston: G. Schirmer. 1918.

Burton, William E. (Ed.) "Burton's Comic Songster." Philadelphia: James Kay, Jun. and Brother. 1838.

Campbell, Alexander. "Delusions." With Prefatory Notes by Joshua V. Himes. Boston: Benjamin H. Greene. 1832.

Carr, Lucien. "Missouri: a Bone of Contention." Boston and New York: Houghton, Mifflin and Co. 1888.

Chaff, Gumbo (Elias Howe, Jr.). "The Ethiopian Glee Book: A Collection of Popular Negro Melodies." Boston: Elias Howe. 1848. The same. No. 2. 1848. The same. No. 3. 1849.

Christensen, A. M. H. "Afro-American Folk Lore." Boston: J. G. Cupples Co. 1892.

"Christy's Negro Serenaders." New York: T: W. Strong. n. d.

Clemens, Samuel L. "Sketches." Toronto: Belfords, Clarke and Co. 1879.

—"Mark Twain's Library of Humor." New York: Charles L. Webster and Co. 1888.

—"The Curious Republic of Gondour." New York: Boni and Liveright. 1919.

Clemens, Will M. "Mark Twain: His Life and Work." Chicago: F. Tennyson Neely. 1894.

Coates, Robert M. "The Outlaw Years." New York: The Macaulay Co. 1930.

Cobb, Joseph B. "Mississippi Scenes; or, Sketches of Southern and Western Life and Adventure." Philadelphia: A. Hart. 1851.

Cole, Harry Ellsworth. "Stagecoach and Tavern Tales of the Old Northwest." Cleveland: The Arthur H. Clark Co. 1930.

Cohen, Lily Young. "Lost Spirituals." New York: Walter Neale. 1928.

Combs, Josiah H. "Folk-Songs du Midi des États-Unis." Paris: Les Presses Universitaires de France. 1925.

Cox, John Harrington. "Folk Songs of the South." Cambridge: Harvard University Press. 1925.

Crockett, Col. David. "Col. Crockett's Exploits and Adventures in Texas." London: R. Kennett. 1837.

—"Life of Col. David Crockett." Philadelphia: G. G. Evans. 1859.

Dakin, Edwin Franden. "Mrs. Eddy: the Biography of a Virginal Mind." New York: Charles Scribner's Sons. 1929.

D'Arusmont, Fanny W. "Views of Society and Manners in America." New York: E. Bliss and E. White. 1821.

Davis, Sam P. (Ed.) "History of Nevada." 2 vols. Reno — Los Angeles: The Elms Publishing Co. 1913.

Dean, M. C. (Ed.) "The Flying Cloud and 150 Other Old Time Poems and Ballads." Virginia, Minnesota: M. C. Dean. 1922.

Derby, Capt. George Horatio (John Phoenix). "Phoenixiana." 2 vols. Chicago: The Caxton Club. 1897. [Important for the identification of a drawing mentioned in my text.]

Devol, George H. "Forty Years a Gambler on the Mississippi." Second edition. New York: George H. Devol. 1892. [Copyright, 1887.] The same. Reprinted as a new book. New York: Henry Holt and Co. 1926.

Dixon, William Hepworth. "New America." Fifth edition, revised. 2 vols. London: Hurst and Blackett. 1867.

—"Spiritual Wives." Fourth edition. 2 vols. London: Hurst and Blackett. 1868.

Dorr, Rheta Childe. "Susan B. Anthony." New York: Frederick A. Stokes Co. 1928.

Dow, Lorenzo Jr. "Short Patent Sermons." New York: L. Long and Brothers. 1850.

Dureau, B. "Les États-Unis en 1850." Paris. 1891. [Reprint. Original edition, 1851.]

Elliott, Maud Howe. "Three Generations." Boston: Little, Brown and Co. 1923.

Eskew, Garnett Laidlaw. "The Pageant of the Packets." New York: Henry Holt and Co. 1929.

Fenner, Thomas P., Rathbun, Frederick G., and Cleaveland, Bessie. "Cabin and Plantation Songs." Third edition. New York: G. P. Putnam's Sons. 1901.

Fish, Carl Russell. "The Rise of the Common Man, 1830–1850." (Vol. VI. In a History of American Life.) New York: Macmillan Co. 1927.

Fiske, Rev. Samuel. "Mr. Dunn Browne's Experiences in Foreign Parts." Boston: John P. Jewett and Co. 1857.

Flint, Timothy. "Recollections of the Last Ten Years." Boston: Cummings, Hilliard and Co. 1826.

—(Ed.) *The Western Monthly Review.* Vol. III, July 1829–June 1830. Cincinnati: E. H. Flint.

Ford, Thomas. "A History of Illinois." Chicago: S. C. Griggs and Co. New York: Ivison and Phinney. 1854.

Ford, Worthington Chauncey. (Ed.) "Letters of Henry Adams (1858–1891." Boston: Houghton Mifflin Co. 1930.

France, Anatole. "Vie de Jeanne D'Arc." 2 vols. Paris: Calmann-Lévy. 1908.

Frank, Waldo. "Our America." New York: Boni and Liveright. 1919.

Freeman, John. "Herman Melville." London: Macmillan and Co., Ltd. 1926.

Gerstäcker, Frederick. "Western Lands and Western Waters." London: S. O. Beeton. 1864.

Gilder, Rosamond. (Ed.) "Letters of Richard Watson Gilder." Boston and New York: Houghton Mifflin Co. 1916.

Gillis, William R. "Memories of Mark Twain and Steve Gillis." Sonora, California: The Banner. 1924.

—"Gold Rush Days with Mark Twain." New York: Albert and Charles Boni. 1930.

Goodwin, C. C. "As I Remember Them." Salt Lake City. 1913.

Gould, E. W. "Fifty Years on the Mississippi." St. Louis: Nixon-Jones Printing Co. 1889.

Greene, Asa (Elnathan Elmwood, Esq.). "A Yankee among the Nullifiers." New York: Wm. Stodart. 1833.

Hall, James. "Letters from the West." London: Henry Colburn. 1828.

—(Ed.) "The Western Souvenir: a Christmas and New Year's Gift for 1829." Cincinnati: N. and G. Guilford.

—"Tales of the Border." Philadelphia: Harrison Hall. 1835.

—"Statistics of the West." Cincinnati: J. A. James and Co. 1836.

—"Notes on the Western States." Philadelphia: Harrison Hall. 1838.

—"The Wilderness and the War Path." New York: Wiley and Putnam. 1846.

—"The West: Its Commerce and Navigation." Cincinnati: H. W. Derby and Co. 1848.

—"The Romance of Western History, or Sketches of History, Life, and Manners in the West." Cincinnati: Applegate and Co. 1857.

Hamon, Louis ("Cheiro"). "Cheiro's Memoirs." Philadelphia: J. B. Lippincott Co. 1912.

Harris, George W. "Sut Lovingood." New York: Dick and Fitzgerald. 1867.

Hart, Fred H. "Sazerac Lying Club." San Francisco: Henry Keller and Co. 1878.

Harte, Geoffrey Bret. "The Letters of Bret Harte." Boston: Houghton Mifflin Co. 1926.

Henderson, Archibald. "Mark Twain." London: Duckworth and Co. 1911.

Hibben, Paxton. "Henry Ward Beecher." New York: George H. Doran Co. 1927.

Higginson, Mary Thacher. (Ed.) "Letters and Journals of Thomas Wentworth Higginson, 1846–1906." Boston: Houghton Mifflin Co. 1921.

Higginson, Thomas Wentworth. "Cheerful Yesterdays." Boston: Houghton, Mifflin and Co. 1898.

Hildebrand, Samuel S. "Autobiography: the Renowned Missouri 'Bushwhacker'." Jefferson City: State Times Book and Job Printing House. 1870.

Hingston, Edward P. "The Genial Showman." New York: Harper and Brothers. 1870.

Holt, Henry. "Garrulities of an Octogenarian Editor." Boston and New York: Houghton Mifflin Co. 1923.

Honce, Charles. (Ed.) "The Adventures of Thomas Jefferson Snodgrass, by Mark Twain." Chicago: Pascal Covici, Publisher, Inc. 1928.

Howard, H. R. "Pictorial Life and Adventures of John A. Murrell, the Great Western Land Pirate." Philadelphia: T. B. Peterson and Brothers. n. d.

—"The History of Virgil A. Stewart." New York: Harper and Brothers. 1836.

Howe, M. A. DeWolfe. "Memories of a Hostess. A Chronicle of Eminent Friendships." Boston: The Atlantic Monthly Press. 1922.

—"Barrett Wendell and His Letters." Boston: The Atlantic Monthly Press. 1924.

Howell, John. (Ed.) "Sketches of the Sixties: by Bret Harte and Mark Twain." San Francisco: John Howell. 1926.

The same. "The second edition with new material and illustrations." San Francisco: John Howell. 1927.

Howells, W. D. "Literary Friends and Acquaintances." New York: Harper and Brothers. 1901.

—"My Mark Twain." New York: Harper and Brothers. n. d. Cp. 1910. Pub. September, 1910.

Humfreville, J. Lee. "Twenty Years among Our Hostile Indians." New York: Hunter and Co. 1901.

James, Henry. (Ed.) "The Letters of William James." Second edition. Boston: Little, Brown and Co. 1926.

James, Uriah Pierson. "James' River Guide." Cincinnati: U. P. James. 1860.

Johnson, James Weldon. (Ed.) "The Book of American Negro Spirituals." New York: The Viking Press. 1925.

Johnson, Merle. "A Bibliography of the Work of Mark Twain, Samuel Langhorne Clemens." New York and London: Harper and Brothers. 1910.

Johnson, Robert Underwood. "Remembered Yesterdays." Boston: Little, Brown and Co. 1923.

"Jones, Major" (William T. Thompson). "John's Alive; or, the Bride of a Ghost, and Other Sketches." Philadelphia: David McKay. 1883.

Josephson, Matthew. "Portrait of the Artist as American." New York: Harcourt, Brace and Co. 1930.

Kennedy, R. Emmet. "Mellows: a Chronicle of Unknown Singers." New York: Albert and Charles Boni. 1925.

Landon, Melville D. (Eli Perkins). "Kings of the Platform and Pulpit." Akron, Ohio: The Saalfield Publishing Co. 1908. [Reprint.]

Lang, Andrew. "Maid of France." New edition with a preface by Mrs. Andrew Lang. London: Longmans, Green and Co. 1922. [First edition, 1908.]

Lawton, Mary. "A Lifetime with Mark Twain." New York: Harcourt, Brace and Co. 1925.

Leland, Charles Godfrey. "Memoirs." New York: D. Appleton and Co. 1893.

Leland, Henry P. "The Grey-Bay Mare, and Other Humorous American Sketches." Philadelphia: Claxton, Remsen and Haffelfinger. 1870. [First edition, 1856.]

Leman, Walter M. "Memoirs of an Old Actor." San Francisco: A. Roman Co. 1886.

Lewis, Oscar. "The Origin of the Celebrated Jumping Frog of Calaveras County." San Francisco: The Book Club of California. 1931.

Lieber, Franz. "The Stranger in America." 2 vols. London. 1835.

Linn, William Alexander. "The Story of the Mormons." New York: The Macmillan Co. 1902.

Longstreet, Augustus Baldwin. "Georgia Scenes." New York: Harper and Brothers. 1840.

The same. Another edition. New York: Harper and Brothers. 1846.

The same. Another edition. New York: Harper and Brothers. 1851.

—"Stories with a Moral." Compiled and edited by Fitz R. Longstreet. Philadelphia: The John C. Winston Co. 1912.

Loud, Grover C. "Evangelized America." New York: Lincoln Mac-Veagh. 1928.

McGill, Josephine. "Folk-Songs of the Kentucky Mountains." Introductory Note by H. E. Krehbiel. New York: Boosey and Co. 1917.

McMurtrie, Douglas C. "A History of California Newspapers." New York: Plandome Press. 1927.

Macrae, David. "The Americans at Home." 2 vols. Edinburgh: Edmunston and Douglas. 1870.

Mackay, Charles. "Life and Liberty in America." Second edition. London: Smith, Elder and Co. 1859.

Marjoribanks, Alexander. "Travels in South and North America." London: Simpkin, Marshall and Co. 1853.

Marryat, Capt. "A Diary in America with Remarks on Its Institutions." New York: D. Appleton and Co. 1839.

Marsh, J. B. I. (Ed.) "The Story of the Jubilee Singers." Seventh edition. London: Hodder and Stoughton. 1877.

Martineau, Harriet. "Society in America." 3 vols. London: Saunders and Otley. 1837.

—'Retrospect of Western Travel." 3 vols. London: Saunders and Otley. 1838.

Matthiessen, Francis Otto. "Sarah Orne Jewett." Boston: Houghton Mifflin Co. 1929.

Merwin, Henry Childs. "The Life of Bret Harte." Boston: Houghton Mifflin Co. 1911.

Michaud, Régis. "Mystiques et Réalestes Anglo-Saxons." Paris: Librairie Armand Colin. 1918.

—"Panorama de la Littérature Américaine Contemporaine." Paris: Kra. 1926.

—"Le Roman Américain d'Aujourd'hui." Paris: Boivin et Cie. 1926.

—"Ce Qu'il Faut Connaitre de l'Ame Américaine." Paris: Boivin et Cie. 1929.

Mighels, Henry R. "Sage Brush Leaves." San Francisco: Edward Bosqui and Co. 1879.

Miller, William. "Evidence from Scripture and History of the Second Coming of Christ." Boston: B. B. Mussey. 1840.

Mitchell, Edward P. "Memories of an Editor." New York: Charles Scribner's Sons. 1924.

Morris, Lloyd. "The Rebellious Puritan: Portrait of Mr. Hawthorne." New York: Harcourt, Brace and Co. 1927.

Mulford, Prentice. "Prentice Mulford's Story." New York: F. J. Needham. 1889.

Mumford, Lewis. "The Golden Day. A Study in American Experience and Culture." New York: Boni and Liveright. 1926.

—"Herman Melville." New York: Harcourt, Brace and Co. 1929.

Neal, Joseph C. "Charcoal Sketches: or, Scenes in a Metropolis." Philadelphia: Carey and Hart. 1843.

Nevins, Allan. "The Emergence of Modern America." (Vol. VIII. In a History of American Life.) New York: Macmillan Co. 1927.

Nugent, William Henry. "The Sports Section." In *The American Mercury*, Vol. XVI, No. 63 (March, 1929).

Nye, Frank Wilson. "Bill Nye, His Own Life Story." New York: The Century Co. 1926.

Odum, Howard W., and Johnson, Guy B. "Negro Workaday Songs." Chapel Hill: The University of North Carolina Press. 1926.

Olliffe, Charles. "Scènes Américaines." Deuxième Édition. Paris: Amyot, Libraire. 1853.

Olmsted, Frederick Law. "A Journey in the Back Country." New York: Mason Brothers. 1861.

Paine, Swift. "Eilley Orrum, Queen of the Comstock." Indianapolis: The Bobbs-Merrill Co. 1929.

Parker, Rev. Samuel, A. M. "Journal of an Exploring Tour beyond the Rocky Mountains." Fifth edition. Auburn: J. C. Derby and Co. 1846. [First edition, 1838.]

Parton, James. "Life of Andrew Jackson." 3 vols. New York: Mason Brothers. 1860.

Paskman, Dailey, and Spaeth, Sigmund. "Gentlemen, Be Seated!" New York: Doubleday, Doran and Co. 1928.

Pattee, Fred Lewis. "A History of American Literature Since 1870." New York: The Century Co. 1915.

Peck, Harry Thurston. "Twenty Years of the Republic, 1885–1905." New York: Dodd, Mead and Co. 1906.

Pennell, Elizabeth Robins. "Charles Godfrey Leland: a Biography." 2 vols. Boston: Houghton, Mifflin and Co. 1906.

Perkins, A. E. "Negro Spirituals from the Far South." In *Journal of American Folk Lore*, Vol. XXXV (1922), 223–249.

Phillips, Ulrich Bonnell. "Life and Labor in the Old South." Boston: Little, Brown and Co. 1929.

Pike, Gustavus D. "The Singing Campaign for Ten Thousand Pounds." New York: American Missionary Association. 1875.

Pitts, J. R. S. "Life and Bloody Career of the Executed Criminal James Copeland, the Great Southern Land Pirate." Second edition. Jackson, Mississippi. 1874.

Pond, Major J. B. "Eccentricities of Genius." New York: G. W. Dillingham Co. 1900.

Pound, Louise. "American Ballads and Songs." New York: Charles Scribner's Sons. 1922.

Powell, John J. "Nevada: the Land of Silver." San Francisco: Bacon and Co. 1876.

Puckett, Newbell Niles. "Folk Beliefs of the Southern Negro." Chapel Hill: The University of North Carolina Press. 1926.

Quaife, M. M. (Ed.) "Absalom Grimes: Confederate Mail Runner." New Haven: Yale University Press. 1926.

Quick, Herbert, and Quick, Edward. "Mississippi Steamboatin'." New York: Henry Holt and Co. 1926.

Richepin, Jean. "L'Ame Américaine à Travers Quelques-uns de Ses Interprètes." Paris: Ernest Flammarion. n. d.

Ripley, Eliza. "Social Life in Old New Orleans." New York: D. Appleton and Co. 1912.

Roath, David L. "The Five Love Adventures of Solomon Slug: and Other Sketches." New York: Bunce and Brother. 1852.

Rourke, Constance. "Troupers of the Gold Coast." New York: Harcourt, Brace and Co. 1928.

—"American Humor." New York: Harcourt, Brace and Co. 1931.

Russell, Charles Edward. "A-Rafting on the Mississip'." New York: The Century Co. 1928.

Sachs, Emanie. "The Terrible Siren." New York: Harper Brothers. 1928.

Sandburg, Carl. "The American Songbag." New York: Harcourt, Brace and Co. 1927.

Santayana, George. "Character and Opinion in the United States." New York: Charles Scribner's Sons. 1920.

Saxon, Lyle. "Father Mississippi." New York: The Century Co. 1927.

Sears, Clara Endicott. "Days of Delusion." Boston: Houghton Mifflin Co. 1924.

Seitz, Dan C. "Artemus Ward: a Biography and Bibliography." New York: Harper and Brothers. 1919.

Shillaber, B. P. "Knitting-Work." Boston: Brown, Taggard and Chase. 1859.

—"Partingtonian Patchwork." Boston: Lee and Shepard. 1875.

Sims, J. Marion. "The Story of My Life." New York: D. Appleton and Co. 1884.

"Sketches and Eccentricities of Col. David Crockett." New York: Harper and Brothers. 1833. [Tenth edition, 1837.]

Stedman, Lucy, and Gould, George M. "Life and Letters of Edmund Clarence Stedman." 2 vols. New York: Moffat, Yard and Co. 1910.

Stenhouse, T. B. H. "The Rocky Mountain Saints." London: Ward, Lock, and Tyler. n. d.

Stewart, William M. "Reminiscences." Edited by George Rothwell Brown. New York: The Neale Publishing Co. 1908.

Stoddard, Charles Warren. "Exits and Entrances." Boston: Lothrop Publishing Co. 1903.

Stoddard, Richard Henry. "Recollections: Personal and Literary." New York: A. S. Barnes and Co. 1903.

Summers, Montague. (Ed. and trans.) "Sinistrari: Demoniality." London: The Fortune Press. 1927.

—(Ed.) "Guazzo: Compendium Maleficarum." London: John Rodker. 1929.

Talley, Thomas W. "Negro Folk Rhymes." New York: The Macmillan Co. 1922.

Tandy, Jennette. "Crackerbox Philosophers in American Humor and Satire." New York: Columbia University Press. 1925.

Taylor, Marshall W., D.D. "A Collection of Revival Hymns and Plantation Melodies." Cincinnati: Marshall W. Taylor and W. C. Echols. 1882.

"The American Joe Miller." New York: H. Long and Brother. 1849. The same. Illustrated edition. New York: H. Long and Brother. 1849.

The Christian Science Journal. Vol XIII (April, 1895). Boston: Christian Science Publishing Society. [On flyleaf: "S. L. Clemens, 1903."]

Trowbridge, John Townsend. "My Own Story." Boston: Houghton, Mifflin and Co. 1903.

Vaughan, Victor C. "A Doctor's Memories." Indianapolis: The Bobbs-Merrill Co. 1926.

Von Horn, W. O. "Auf dem Mississippi." Wiesbaden. 1859 (?).

Wade, John Donald. "Augustus Baldwin Longstreet." New York: The Macmillan Co. 1924.

Walton, Augustus Q. "A History of the Detection, Conviction, Life and Designs of John A. Murel, the Great Western Land Pirate." Cincinnati. n. d.

The same. Another edition. Athens, Tennessee: Republished by George White. Printed at the *Journal* Office. 1835.

Watterson, Henry. (Ed.) "Oddities in Southern Life and Character." Boston: Houghton, Mifflin and Co. 1887. Cp. 1882.

Wendell, Barrett. "A Literary History of America." New York: Charles Scribner's Sons. 1900.

Wickwar, J. W. "Witchcraft and the Black Art." New York: Robert M. McBride and Co. 1926.

Wright, William (Dan DeQuille). "History of the Big Bonanza." Hartford, Conn.: American Publishing Co. San Francisco, Cal.: A. L. Bancroft and Co. 1876.

Young, John P. "Journalism in California." San Francisco: Chronicle Publishing Co. 1915.

NEWSPAPER HUMOR OF THE SOUTHWESTERN FRONTIER

THE humor of frontier newspapers has had no adequate treatment. A rich field which is almost untouched is here called to the attention of scholars — with the warning that a single lifetime will not suffice for a comprehensive study of it. It is to be hoped that Franklin J. Meine will publish his bibliographies and will commit to print as much as possible of his information and opinion, and that the researches of Professor Fred W. Lorch and Professor Walter Blair will be continued. To students of American life and literature the work of such men is tremendously valuable.

The purpose of this appendix is to account to the critical reader for the basis of criticism in my text and to save students who are interested in the subject the unfruitful part of my own search. A fairly complete understanding of the field is unobtainable except by labor in the newspapers themselves, especially the *Spirit of the Times,* among which much of my own study was pursued. Much material has been brought together in books, however, and it seems desirable to mention a number of them.

I. A volume in the "Americana Deserta" series (Knopf), of which I am the general editor, was prepared by Franklin J. Meine for the specific purpose of making this humor available to students. Mr. Meine is the outstanding authority on this field — in fact, the only authority. His collection, "Tall Tales of the Southwest" (New York: 1930), documents my discussion of this humor and Mark Twain's relation to it. His Introduction is the best treatment of the field in print and his notes and bibliographies are invaluable.

II. T. C. Haliburton, the creator of Sam Slick, made two contemporary collections of this humor, apparently from the newspaper sources themselves. I have an affection for these books, since they were the clue that led me to the literature itself — the first evidence I had that a literature which I by then knew must exist and whose specifications I could almost write, did in fact exist. They are, however, all but useless to a student, since Haliburton did not identify either the authors of his selections or the sources from which he took them. (All of them can be identified from the literature itself.) They helpfully support my opinion that verbal prudery became fashionable in England earlier than in the United States. They are:

Haliburton, T. C. "Traits of American Humor." London: Hurst and Blackett. n. d. (Probably published in the early Sixties. There was an earlier, three-volume edition.)
—"The Americans at Home, or Byways, Backwoods, and Prairies." 3 vols. London: Hurst and Blackett. 1854.

III. "The Library of Humorous American Works." This is a series of paper-backed volumes variously published in New York and Philadelphia during the Forties and Fifties. Because of the fragility of its bindings and because its illustrations by Felix O. C. Darley have been eagerly sought by collectors, it has become extremely rare. Of the thirty-three volumes usually listed on the back cover, I have been able, employing all the resources of the old-book market, to buy just eight. Mr. Meine, I believe, has succeeded in collecting the whole list, and I have used them all in libraries and collections. The series includes a number of books not relevant to this discussion, such as reprints of Joseph C. Neal's "Charcoal Sketches", "Peter Faber's Misfortunes", and "Peter Ploddy", of Frank Forrester's "Deer Stalkers", "The Quorndon Hounds", "My Shooting Box" and "Warwick Woodlands", and of Brackenridge's "Major O'Regan's Adventures" and "Adventures of Captain Farrago" — as well as a number of collections of newspaper humor from the East. But also it contains the richest selection of southwestern frontier humor available outside the files of newspapers.

I cannot attempt an accurate bibliography of these books. Some of them were originally published in this series; others are reprints. Some were copyrighted by T. B. Peterson and Brothers of Philadelphia, who were apparently the initiators of the series — which was also pirated in New York from time to time. Some were copyrighted by T. B. Peterson, some by Carey and Hart, some by Hart. I cannot say — and am not interested in saying — which were piracies, which originals, which reprints. Nor do I guarantee the dates which follow — I have seen too many variants. These notes are based exclusively on the volumes which I have in my own library or which I have had access to elsewhere. It is to be hoped that Mr. Meine will soon untangle this snarl. An accurate bibliography of the series would be very useful.

At any rate, the titles that follow contain, in varying degrees, material reprinted from frontier newspapers or from newspapers which took it from the source, or reprinted from such papers as the *Spirit of the Times*, for which frontier correspondents wrote. They have all been very useful in the formation of my ideas, and the student who has not time for the newspapers themselves will find these books his best material.

Known variants and partial reprints are not listed. It should be noted, however, that a considerable number exist.

Burke, T. A. (Ed.) "Polly Peablossom's Wedding." Philadelphia. Copyright, 1853.

Burton, William E. "The Yankee among the Mermaids, and other Waggeries and Vagaries." Philadelphia: T. B. Peterson and Brothers. 1843.

Corcoran, D. "Pickings from the Portfolio of the Reporter of the New Orleans 'Picayune'." Philadelphia: Carey and Hart. 1846.

Durivage, Francis A., and Burnham, George P. "Stray Subjects, Arrested and Bound Over: Being the Fugitive Offspring of the 'Old 'Un' and the 'Young 'Un'." Philadelphia: T. B. Peterson and Brothers. n. d.

Field, Joseph M. ("Everpoint" of the St. Louis *Reveille*.) "The Drama in Pokerville; the Bench and Bar of Jurytown and Other Stories." Philadelphia: T. B. Peterson and Brothers. 1847.

Hooper, Johnson J. "Adventures of Captain Simon Suggs." Philadelphia. 1845.

—"Widow Rugby's Husband." 1851.

"Madison Tensas, M.D." "Odd Leaves from The Life of a Louisiana 'Swamp Doctor'." Philadelphia. 1850 (?).

Porter, William T. (Ed.) "A Quarter Race in Kentucky." Philadelphia. 1846.

—"The Big Bear of Arkansas." Philadelphia. 1845.

Robb, John S. "Streaks of Squatter Life and Far Western Scenes." Philadelphia. 1847.

Smith, Sol. "The Theatrical Apprenticeship and Anecdotal Recollections of Sol Smith." Philadelphia: Carey and Hart. 1847. [Copyright notice and dedication dated 1845.]

—"The Theatrical Journey-Work and Anecdotal Recollections." Philadelphia: T. B. Peterson and Brothers. 1854.

Stahl (George M. Wharton). "The New Orleans Sketch Book." Philadelphia: T. B. Peterson and Brothers. 1843.

Thompson, William Tappan. "Major Jones's Courtship." Philadelphia. 1844.

—"Major Jones's Chronicles of Pineville." Philadelphia. 1845.

—"Major Jones's Sketches of Travel." Philadelphia. 1847.

Thorpe, T. B. "The Mysteries of the Backwoods, or Sketches of the Southwest." Philadelphia: Carey and Hart. 1846.

The works of Hooper, Thompson, and Thorpe had regular trade editions, of various dates, and some of those of Thompson were reissued after the Civil War. Attention should also be called to Sol Smith's "Theatrical Management in the West and South for Thirty Years", published by Harper and Brothers in 1868. This brings together the two books listed above and completes Smith's autobiography.

IV. "Peterson's Illustrated Uniform Edition of Humorous American Works." This is a series of books issued later than the foregoing — usually in the late Fifties — by T. B. Peterson or T. B. Peterson and Brothers of Philadelphia. It contains one of the innumerable paper editions of "The American Joe Miller", three series of Dow Jr.'s "Short Patent Sermons" in paper and cloth, a two-volume cloth edition of Frank Forrester's "Sporting Scenes and Characters", an edition of "Sam Slick the Clockmaker" in paper and cloth, and a similar edition of "The Humors of Falconbridge." These are of no importance for the present subject.

But also it contains "Piney Woods Tavern, or Sam Slick in Texas" (1858) by "Philip Paxton" (S. A. Hammett), which is of considerable importance to this study, and several volumes which consist each of two numbers of the "Library of Humorous American Works" bound together in cloth. Of these I have not been able to find "Major Jones's Courtship and Travels": I conclude that this number consists of Thompson's "Major Jones's Courtship" and "Major Jones's Sketches of Travel." The remaining numbers are much more accessible than their paper-backed originals. The dates given here are those of the series: the copyright dates of its components sometimes differ from those of the earlier series.

"Big Bear's Adventures and Travels." 1858. Containing "The Big Bear of Arkansas", 1846; "Stray Subjects", 1846.

"Major Jones's Scenes in Georgia." n. d. Containing: "Chronicles of Pineville", 1848; "Polly Peablossom's Wedding", 1851.

"Major Thorpe's Scenes in Arkansaw." 1858. Containing: "A Quarter Race in Kentucky", 1846; "The Drama in Pokerville", 1846. Also published as "Colonel Thorpe's Scenes in Arkansaw" — identical except for frontispiece and one plate.

"Simon Suggs' Adventures and Travels." n. d. Containing: "Adventures of Captain Simon Suggs", 1848; "The Widow Rugby's Husband", 1851.

"The Swamp Doctor's Adventures in the South-West." 1858. Containing: "Odd Leaves from the Life of a Louisiana 'Swamp Doctor'," 1843; "Streaks of Squatter Life", 1846.

V.   Paxton, Philip (S. A. Hammett). "A Stray Yankee in Texas." New York: Redfield. 1853.

Longstreet, Augustus Baldwin. "Georgia Scenes." New York: Harper and Brothers. 1840. (See the Bibliography.)

Cobb, Joseph B. "Mississippi Scenes; or, Sketches of Southern and Western Life and Adventure." Philadelphia: A. Hart. 1851.

Harris, George W. "Sut Lovingood." New York: Dick and Fitzgerald. 1867.

Montesano, B. R. "Redstick or Scenes in the South." Cincinnati: U. P. James. 1856.

APPENDIX B

From the *Spirit of the Times*, May 26, 1855, p. 170.

FROGS SHOT WITHOUT POWDER

Written for the New York "Spirit of the Times", by Henry P. Leland.

IN such a low stage as the Mississippi undertook to travel down to the Gulf in, during the past winter, even a fast steamboat is a "slow coach", especially if she draws more water, by several inches, than you can find on the bars; and so I found that, spite of rifle practice at wild fowl, going ashore when we wooded or tied up all night, overhauling a bound-down boat, passing a sunken steamer, and all the other little outside diversions, time hung heavily on hand. "Social Hall" was the real Exchange where most of the passengers managed to work off any uncurrent hours they might have on hand for current drinks; here, too, was the favorite spot for hearing good stories, and smoking cigars, the flavor of both being often rather too strong for the saloon.

One evening, an unusually cold one, we rounded to at a wood wharf in Arkansas, where we were to wood and tie up for the night; as usual, the passengers came out "to prospect." The red light from the pitch pine, as it blazed up, showed a steep bluff, and a very large wood pile. The planks of our boat were run out; the deck-hands, in a long line, at a very quick step, "put" over them, returning on board with the cotton-wood piled upon their shoulders; the mate stood on shore, by the light, as usual, "cussing" away at the hands; the clerk having measured the wood and struck a bargain, came off, and with him the owner of the wood. As for the latter, figure a man about as long as a clothes-pole, with a white blanket coat hung on him reaching to his heels; a broad brimmed felt hat on, a large-size cane in his hand, and a thin, sallow face, showing traces of determination and whiskey admirably blended. Entering the cabin, he sauntered up to the bar-keeper, and in a few minutes the latter was seen bringing out bottle after bottle of Old Bourbon whiskey, which were duly put down at the foot of the "Arkansaw traveller"; there he stood like a blasted old cypress, with a good-size crop of "knees" below him.

"Two dozen bottles. Is that enough?" asked the bar-keeper, as he took down the last bottle of the count.

"It'll last, with the few barr'ls on hand, tell you work up stream again. I don't use up so much now as I used to do. And that 'ar little wood-pile o' mine keeps me in licker better nor it ever did afore. I've got six niggers chopping, and run three teams, so I shan't run dry if old Mississip does!"

The "Arkansas Traveller" herewith straightened out for shore, followed by a "nigger" bottle-holder. His speech, delivered within hearing of a crowd in "Social Hall", was the cause of some hearty laughter. "The little wood pile" he spoke of extending along shore as far as the eye could reach, at least at night, by torchlight, gave one the idea that the "Traveller" must be owner of a pretty good sized thirst, to enable him to drink up a wood pile, the continued drain on which was meanwhile filled up by the aforesaid six niggers and three teams. All hoped he wouldn't run dry, and he got full credit for his abstemiousness from water which, like the Western editor, he wouldn't waste by drinking, when every drop was required for purposes of navigation! One remark brought out another, one story another, 'til at last the pilot of our boat — everybody calls him John — commenced giving in his sporting experience. From buffalo hunting down to frog killing was something of a jump, but John made it with

"After all, buffalo hunt is a very fair thing, but a frog's hind legs are just about as good. They cook 'em right in New Orleans, and I don't know anything suits me much better. When I was a boy, thar was nothing I liked so well. The d———l of it was, I hadn't always money to buy powder with to shoot the creeturs, and so I tried spearing 'em, hooking 'em with red flannel bait, setting traps for 'em, teaching a little spaniel dog of mine to catch em; but somehow I never could get enough at a time.

"One day I was travellin' round the pond, tryin' to invent some way of laying hold of a lot for supper, when an idea jumped through my head, and afore it could get out I grabbed it. Cutting a long elder stick, as straight a one as I could find, I split it in two, lengthwise, dug out the pith, and so made a long narrow trough. Going up to the house, I filled my pockets with No. 7 shot, and coming back to the pond, snaked round 'til I saw a thundering big 'Bull-paddy' sunning himself right under a clump of weeds; he was rolling his eyes round like a stage-actor, and opening his mouth as if he were going to swallow the pond. There he sat! Slowly and gradually I crept up behind him, 'til I got near enough to run the elder trough out, so that its eend was about two feet 'bove his nose. Taking a handfull of shot, I put one into the eend of the trough and let it run down; it fell in the water — plunk! About an inch front of him; he jumped at it, missed it, and then squatted quietly down again, with his mouth wide open. I let another lot of lead slide, and he caught it, and another, and another, 'til he had swallowed 'em all, and I hadn't a shot left in my pocket. There he sot, and when I stepped out from the grass, may be he didn't try to jump: his legs flew up and down like drum sticks, but the rest of him wouldn't work — he had too big a load on! So I picked him up, held my hat under him, gave him a squeeze, and the shot run out in a stream, like they would from a pouch. Fact! And I tell you what, after that I always *shot frogs without powder!*

INDEX